THE GUINNESS HISTORY OF
THE
BRITISH
ARMY

John Pimlott

GUINNESS PUBLISHING

Published in Great Britain by
Guinness Publishing Ltd.
33 London Road, Enfield, Middlesex EN2 6DJ

"Guinness" is a registered trademark of
Guinness Publishing Ltd.

First published 1993

ISBN 0-85112-711-8

A catalogue record for this book is available from the
British Library

Designed by Stonecastle Graphics Ltd.

Picture Research by Image Select

Maps by Lovell Johns

Typeset by Ace Filmsetting Ltd, Frome, Somerset

Printed and bound in Great Britain by
The Bath Press, Bath

Picture acknowledgements
The publishers wish to thank the following for
permission to reproduce pictures in this book:

Ancient Art and Architecture Collection
Archiv für Kunst und Geschichte
Image Select
Mansell Collection
Mary Evans Picture Library
Peter Newark's Historical/Military Pictures
Popperfoto
Ronald Sheridan

CONTENTS

FEATURE BATTLES

LIST OF MAPS

INTRODUCTION

······························

'WE CALL up to seven men "thieves"; from seven to thirty-five a "band"; above that is an army.' This definition, taken from the Laws of Ine, compiled between AD 688 and 694, may be restrictive by modern standards, but it does suggest that an army is something more than just a group of mindless brigands. It is an organized human mass, prepared to threaten or use physical force to achieve particular objectives laid down by a central authority. Today we would expect that authority to be a government or recognized political body; in 7th-century Britain it would have been a local chieftain or regional ruler. In both cases, however, the roles of the army are the same – to protect territory or resources and project power and influence. In this sense, armies have not changed through the centuries – it is just that they have become more acceptable as institutions of state, carrying out duties that are generally recognized as contributing to the common good.

The British Army enjoys such acceptability in our modern society. Despite debates about its size and composition, the Army is seen by the majority of the population as an integral part of the state, protecting the people against internal and external enemies and acting as a symbol of Britain's influence in the wider world. Its chief strength lies in its continuity, for the Army has served both monarch and state without a break since 1661. During that time it has kept aloof from politics, owing its allegiance to the Crown rather than political parties, and despite a habit of losing early battles in major conflicts, it has not actually lost a war since 1783. It has not always been popular – for much of its 332-year history, the Army has been distrusted as an instrument of state repression and despised as a repository of men who were the dregs of society – but it has built up traditions of service and sacrifice that have helped to preserve its reputation even when it was not in the public eye. All these factors have combined to make the British Army a unique institution, the history of which is the subject of this book.

But it would be wrong to assume that the Army suddenly appeared in 1661 as if conjured out of the air. Before moving on to examine the last 332 years, it is necessary to look back at the Army's antecedents, searching for the themes and precedents that lend the force its special character.

John Pimlott
RMAS 1993

······························

CHAPTER ONE

THE ORIGINS
(to 1660)

·······························

THE ANGLO-SAXON ARMY

A foot-soldier of the 9th century, armed with a long-handled axe. He appears to be wearing a protective undergarment and a crude helmet to minimize injury in battle.

THE period from the withdrawal of the Roman garrison in about AD 410 to the coming of the Normans in 1066 saw massive changes in English society. A plethora of small Anglo-Saxon kingdoms gradually developed into a single monarchy, the Vikings were opposed and eventually absorbed, and Christianity acted as a powerful unifying force. The extent of the fighting that took place between rival factions is difficult to gauge, but there is no doubt that armies existed and that their actions helped to create change.

Early Anglo-Saxon armies were small, probably comprising no more than 300 men, but they were organized for battle. At the centre was the king's body-guard or war band, a group of semi-professional warriors armed with swords, spears and axes. In return for the king's protection and a share in any loot, they tended to be intensely loyal, often fighting to the death to defend their master. They were supported, as the need arose, by free landholders who, as part of their right to own land in the king's domain, had an obligation to serve in a local militia known as the *fyrd*. Although there is some controversy about the extent to which the *fyrd* was actually used, there is plenty of evidence as to its theoretical composition, particularly in 9th-century Wessex, where King Alfred defined its precise nature as part of his response to the Viking invasion. According to surviving documents, Wessex was divided into military districts. Within these, every five 'hides' of land (about 600 acres) had to provide an armed man at the king's summons, available to serve for two months or the duration of a campaign. Such men would have been no more than light infantry, capable of using rudimentary weapons such as spears or converted agricultural implements. At the same time, however, any owner of more than five 'hides' of land was required to serve as a *thegn* (or thane), appearing in the field fully equipped with heavier weapons such as sword or axe and, if he was wealthy enough, with a horse as well. In battle, everyone tended to fight on foot, the

THE BATTLE OF HASTINGS

When Edward the Confessor died without heir on 5 January 1066, England was plunged into crisis. Although it was widely believed that Edward had pledged the succession to William of Normandy, this was disputed by Harold Godwinsson of Wessex, who had himself crowned King of England, and by Harold Hardrada, King of Norway. In September Hardrada, in alliance with Harold's brother Tostig, advanced up the River Humber to threaten York. Harold marched quickly with his *housecarls* and elements of the southern *fyrd* to catch the Vikings by surprise at Stamford Bridge, eight miles east of the city. Despite his crushing victory on 25 September, he was too far away to prevent a Norman landing at Pevensey in Sussex two days later.

William's army, estimated to comprise about 7000 men, captured Hastings and began to lay waste to the surrounding countryside, in hopes of forcing Harold to react before he had recovered from his northern campaign. The ploy worked, for Harold, after an epic march to London (which he reached with his *housecarls* on 6 October), set out for the south coast with very few archers or infantry. By the morning of 14 October he had reached Senlac Hill, to the northwest of Hastings; a mile away, on Telham Hill, the Normans were waiting. Harold drew his army, comprising about 7500 men (2000 *housecarls* and the remainder ill-prepared members of the *fyrd*) into a defensive position to await attack.

The ensuing battle was hard-fought. William initially sent his light troops forward to probe Harold's position, but they were easily repulsed. He then mounted a full-scale infantry attack that caused some casualties among Harold's men, although in the end the Normans withdrew in some disorder. Norman horsemen were committed next. They failed to breach the enemy defences, but as they pulled back, a substantial part of Harold's force broke ranks and followed them, thinking that the battle had been won. The withdrawal of the cavalry has often been described as a deliberate ruse by William, but modern historians have raised doubts, arguing that such a decision would have been extremely dangerous. Whatever the truth, however, the pursuing English troops were destroyed, leaving Harold's army significantly weakened. Even so, it took an all-arms attack by William late in the day finally to overwhelm the English, who had stood firm for nearly eight hours. Harold and most of his *housecarls* were killed and, as the survivors of the *fyrd* fled, William marched on London. On Christmas Day 1066 he was crowned King of England.

The final Norman assault on the Saxon positions on Senlac Hill (Hastings), 14 October 1066, as depicted by R. Caton Woodville. An arrow seems poised to enter Harold's eye – something that almost certainly never happened.

thegns occupying the front ranks of a wedge formation that broadened out to contain the mass of more lightly armed men.

Alfred took the process further, reorganizing the Wessex *fyrd* so that half of it was mobilized at any one time while the other half remained on the land to produce the annual harvest. He even went so far as to rotate the two at regular intervals and to build special fortresses, known as *burghs*, to house his embodied men. Alfred had, in effect, created a standing army, available for action at a moment's notice, but the arrangements do not appear to have survived his reign. By the time Cnut ascended the throne of England in the early 11th century, the previous system had been restored. Cnut and his immediate successors had a royal bodyguard of heavily armed warriors, known as *housecarls*, but if the king needed a larger force he had to call out the *fyrd*. Such a combination of professional cadre and amateur 'horde' had the advan-tage of being relatively cheap to maintain, but in the event of war it had its limitations. The *fyrd* was poorly trained and unused to the discipline needed in battle. It could hold its own in the unsophisticated context of the *mêlée*, and some historians have argued that elements of the *fyrd* were more effective than traditionally assumed, but it stood little chance of success if it encountered a better-organized enemy force, such as the Normans at Hastings in 1066 (*see box*). In such circumstances, the *housecarls* were left to bear the brunt of the fighting. But however well they fought, they were few in number and vulnerable to being overwhelmed. This pattern – of a small, deter-mined, but ultimately poorly prepared British force over-come by better-trained European opposition – is one that was to be only too recognizable to the British Army in later centuries, being repeated at the beginning of the war against Revolutionary France in the 1790s and the two World Wars of the 20th century.

THE IMPACT OF THE NORMANS

When William of Normandy gained the English throne in 1066, he did so by force of arms, imposing his rule on a population that felt little immediate loyalty to the new monarch. He ensured control of the kingdom by distrib-uting land to his supporters as part of a feudal system. By the time of William's death in 1087 the whole of England, except for land held directly by the king or Church, had been granted to chosen lords as *fiefs*; in return they were obliged to render military service to the monarch on demand. Each lord in turn granted land tenancy to knights and vassals on his estate, helping to produce an infrastructure geared to the provision of fighting men. It has been estimated that William could, in theory, call on the services of 5000 mounted knights, each armed at his own expense with lance, sword and kite-shaped shield. In addition, as part of the process of imposing Norman rule, William initiated the construction of castles. By 1100 there were at least 84 major castles, mainly of a motte-and-bailey design, dotted around the country to protect border areas, ports and communication routes as well as to intimidate the Anglo-Saxon population and so prevent rebellion. The possibility of popular revolt meant that although the *fyrd* still existed (as the 'feudal host'), it could no longer be trusted because it was Anglo-Saxon, and was rarely called out. Inevitably, it fell into decline.

The feudal system, like its Anglo-Saxon predeces-sor, had its limitations. As William's successors attempted to extend their authority into Scotland and Wales, while simultaneously fighting the French, they needed access to larger numbers of trusted men than the system was capable of providing. At the same time, individual tenants often held land from more than one lord, an anomaly that raised the possibility of conflicting loyalties at times of crisis. In an effort to cope with the latter problem, the tenant was expected to acknowledge his obligation to his principal lord (usually the king), while commuting his lesser loyalties into money payments known as *scutage*. Under Henry I (1100–35) *scutage* was paid to lesser lords only, the king retaining the services of knights for up to 40 days a year in peace and two months in war. As the 12th century progressed, however, this commitment became unpopular among landholders intent on asserting their independence, and it was common for *scutage* to be paid even to the monarch, who then used it to hire mercenaries to create an army according to need. The *fyrd* was not ignored – in 1181 Henry II reorganized it into a national militia by the Assize of Arms, laying down the precise obligations of all freemen to defend the state in an emergency – but it was not available to fight in foreign wars, principally because its members were needed on the land.

A tradition was growing that a standing army in England was unnecessary. If the country was directly threatened, all freemen would rush to its defence; if foreign conflict was unavoidable, mercenaries could be hired for the duration and then dismissed. Individual English knights continued to serve their monarch – a number of them accompanied Richard I on the Third Crusade in 1189 – but they usually found themselves commanding foreign soldiers. It was a cheap way of waging war and one that caused minimum disruption to English society.

During this period the mounted knight developed as a symbol of military capability, combining the personal protection of armour with the power of a cavalry charge. Although in retrospect this capability may seem to have been exaggerated, there is no doubt that infantry soldiers armed with nothing more lethal than spears or axes were vulnerable to defeat. During the 12th and 13th centuries, however, developments in both weapons technology and tactics began to redress the balance. As early as the Battle of Beaumont (1125) against the French, English horsemen were disrupted by archers using crossbows. At the Battle of Stirling Bridge (1297) the Scots deployed their infantry, equipped with pikes, into defensive formations that proved difficult for the knights to penetrate – a tactic not dissimilar to the 'squares' formed by musket-armed infantry at Waterloo over five centuries later (*see* p.68). In the event, at Stirling Bridge Edward I broke up the Scots' deployment by sending his archers forward in advance of the knights to fire a hail of arrows that fell on the enemy from above: an early example of the value of all-arms co-operation on the battlefield. The fact that the archers were equipped with the longbow was significant: this weapon represented a dramatic new development that was to give the English a tactical advantage until it was countered by the general use of firearms nearly 200 years later.

The English first encountered the longbow in Wales during the 13th century, where it proved to be ideal in rough country unsuited to the deployment of cavalry. Welsh bowmen were hired as mercenaries and gradually their expertise was absorbed by the English, who fully exploited the fact that the longbow gave twice the range and six times the firing rate of the crossbow. Traditionally made of yew, the longbow was over six feet in length and, in the hands of an experienced soldier, up to ten arrows a minute could be fired to a range of more than 250 yards, producing a shower of missiles that quickly demoralized an enemy force. At shorter range an arrow, fitted with a barb and fletched with goose or peacock feathers, could penetrate an inch of solid timber or, more significantly,

A drawing from a late 13th-century manuscript depicting a knight preparing for battle. In the top right-hand corner a servant is handing down the knight's helmet or 'great helm'.

most types of armour then in use. Constant practice at the butts, set up in villages and towns throughout England during the 14th century, ensured that English bowmen attained a high degree of accuracy. Their skills were to be refined in battles against the French in the 14th and 15th centuries.

THE HUNDRED YEARS WAR

Between 1337 and 1453 England and France were more or less constantly at war, fighting for control of the English Duchy of Gascony and, at various times, even for the French throne. Ever since 1066 the Norman kings of England and their successors had continued to hold vast territories in France. By the 1330s, however, only Gas-

English longbowmen at the Battle of Crécy, 1346. This detail from the Chronicles of Froissart *gives some idea of the equipment used, although it is unlikely that soldiers on campaign would have been so uniformly dressed.*

cony in the south-west was retained by the English king. But even these reduced dominions provided cause for conflict, since as Duke of Gascony the English king owed allegiance to the French crown. When the French Capetian dynasty died out in the direct male line in 1328, Edward III of England laid claim to the French throne through his maternal grandfather, Philip the Fair. But the crown went to his cousin, Philip of Valois, who became Philip VI. Soon the two kings were fighting a border war in Scotland and Flanders, the Scots having made common cause with France in the 'Auld Alliance', the Flemish cloth towns being drawn by economic self-interest to the English side. In 1339–40 Edward led a small army to Flanders that achieved little; the only battle of note was at sea, off Sluys in 1340, where English archers completely overwhelmed the French in a pattern of events that was soon to become familiar.

On land, the English conducted a strategy of

Personality Profile:
KING EDWARD III (1312–77)

The son of King Edward II and Isabella of France, Edward III came to the throne in 1327. Initially his position was weak, chiefly because of the influence enjoyed by his mother's lover Roger Mortimer, but when Mortimer was killed in 1330 Edward was able to assert his power. He led an army against the Scots, winning a decisive battle at Halidon Hill (1333), after which he turned his attention to France, where Philip VI's declaration that Edward no longer had any rights to Gascony triggered what would become known as the Hundred Years War (1337–1453). During the early campaigns of that conflict Edward won a sea battle off Sluys (1340) and, in company with his son, the Black Prince, crushed the land forces of France at Crécy (1346), where the advantage enjoyed by English longbowmen over mounted men-at-arms was fully exploited. Edward went on to capture Calais (1347) and, by the Treaty of Brétigny (1360), forced the French to accept his rights in Gascony. However, at home he encountered the growing power of Parliament, particularly over its right to vote funds to pay for the war, and his reign was not marked by any great domestic reforms. A great believer in chivalry, his most lasting memorial was the Order of the Garter, founded in 1348.

First-Hand Account:
THE BATTLE OF CRÉCY

'. . . As the sun began to set, the first line of battle of the [French] army advanced, trumpets and cornets sounding, drums and kettledrums rolling; and the noise of the French troops seemed like thunder to the English. The French crossbowmen began the attack; their crossbow bolts did not reach the English, however, but fell a long way off. Much to the terror of the crossbowmen, the English archers began to pick off their closely-packed enemies with arrows . . .
Realising that the crossbowmen were not harming the English, the French men at arms, mounted on young warhorses and agile chargers, rode down . . . the crossbowmen who were between them and the English, charging headlong into the English ranks in order to display their prowess . . . The English . . . quickly dug a large number of pits in the ground near their front line, each a foot deep and a foot wide, so that if the French cavalry approached, their horses would stumble in the pits . . . When [the French] attacked the well armed English, they were cut down with swords and spears, and many were crushed to death, without a mark on them, in the middle of the French army, because the press was so great . . . So the fearful face of war was displayed, from the setting of the sun until the third quarter of the night, during which time the French raised a general war-cry three times and charged fifteen times, but nonetheless fled defeated.'

The Chronicle of Geoffrey le Baker, written in 1357–60

chevauchée, sending forces deep into enemy territory to burn and plunder in the hope of undermining French control. This was Edward's intention in July 1346, when he landed near Cherbourg with 10,000 men and marched to cross the Rivers Seine and Somme. But Philip responded swiftly, marching to block Edward's progress with an army estimated to contain over 40,000 soldiers, including up to 6000 Genoese crossbowmen. Edward deployed his men along a 2000-yard ridge between the villages of Crécy and Wadicourt, about nine miles north of Abbeville, and waited for the French to attack. His men-at-arms, successors to the feudal knights, occupied positions on the left and right, with the archers drawn up in wedge formation in between and on the flanks. The French did not appear until late in the day, by which time they had to attack into the setting sun. As the Genoese archers moved forward to skirmish they came under a hail of longbow fire and, demoralized by the sound of cannon, began to retreat. In doing so they ran straight into the path of the French men-at-arms, who rode over them to begin a series of suicidal charges against the English line that went on until after dark (*see box*). The French lost 'eleven great lords, eighty-three bannerets, over twelve hundred knights and some thousands of common sol-

War broke out again in 1369, although in the meantime the Black Prince had fought in Spain, where England and France were supporting rivals for the throne of Castile. His victory at Najéra (3 April 1367) was based on the familiar pattern of enemy men-at-arms falling victim to the English longbow, but the French were learning how to cope. As early as the Battle of Cocherel in 1364 Bertrand du Guesclin, the future Constable of France, defeated English archers by attacking them in the flank. As the century progressed, the French men-at-arms began to encase themselves in thicker armour, sacrificing mobility but enhancing their chances of survival on the battlefield. At the same time, the quality of English leadership declined – the Black Prince died in 1376 and his father a year later, initiating a power struggle that was not to be fully resolved until 1403, when Henry IV defeated Sir Henry Percy ('Hotspur') at the Battle of Shrewsbury. By then, the French had captured nearly all the English territory on the continent and were even mounting naval raids along the coast of Wales.

King Edward III of England, best remembered for his impressive victories against the Scots at Halidon Hill (1333) and the French at Crécy (1346). He ruled from 1327 until his death in 1377.

diers', almost all to the English archers. It was a remarkable victory.

Ten years later, it was repeated in similar circumstances at Poitiers. Edward III's son, Edward the Black Prince, led a *chevauchée* north from Bordeaux towards the River Loire, aiming to repeat the success he had enjoyed the previous year in a raid that had taken him as far as Narbonne on the Mediterranean coast. The French were determined to stop him and, as he pulled back towards Bordeaux in September 1356, they brought him to battle. The Black Prince, heavily outnumbered, occupied a defensive position which the French, despite the lessons of Crécy, attacked in waves. The first assault was broken up by the English archers, upon which the French men-at-arms attacked on foot to engage in hand-to-hand combat. The battle went badly for the English until, in a sudden lull, the Black Prince ordered his men-at-arms to mount their horses and charge the enemy line. It was a gamble that paid off; by the end of the day the recently crowned King John II of France, together with nearly 1500 members of his nobility, had been captured. Four years later, the Treaty of Brétigny not only confirmed English rights over Gascony, but handed over no less than a third of the land of France in full sovereignty to the English king.

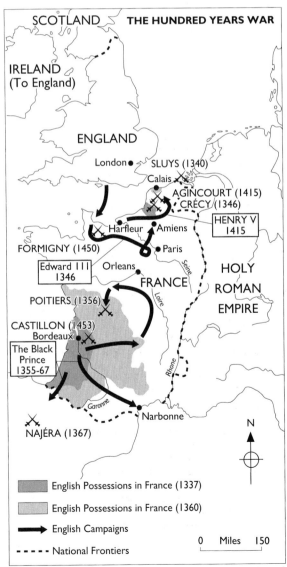

THE HUNDRED YEARS WAR

SCOTLAND

IRELAND
(To England)

ENGLAND

London • SLUYS (1340)
Calais

AGINCOURT (1415)
CRÉCY (1346)

HENRY V
1415

Harfleur Amiens

FORMIGNY (1450)

Paris

Edward III
1346 Orleans

HOLY
ROMAN
EMPIRE

FRANCE

POITIERS (1356)

CASTILLON (1453)
Bordeaux

The Black
Prince
1355-67

Narbonne

NAJÉRA (1367)

N

English Possessions in France (1337)

English Possessions in France (1360)

English Campaigns

National Frontiers

0   Miles   150

THE BATTLE OF AGINCOURT

In August 1415 Henry V of England, with an army of about 10,000 men (2000 men-at-arms and 8000 archers), landed in northern France and laid siege to Harfleur, which finally fell on 22 September. Henry then decided to march the remains of his force – he had lost probably a third of his men by this stage – from Harfleur to the English enclave at Calais, to impress the enemy with his freedom of movement and to ensure the survival of his soldiers during the winter. The march began on 8 October. At first, all went well, but as the English approached the River Somme on 13 October they received news that a large French army, estimated to comprise about 25,000 men, was moving to block their path. Despite marches of 18–20 miles a day, it proved impossible to outmanoeuvre the French, who eventually positioned themselves astride the road to Calais, close to the village of Agincourt. Late on 24 October Henry halted, aware that a battle was unavoidable. He had no more than 1000 men-at-arms and 5000 archers under his command.

Early on 25 October, the two armies deployed. The English soldiers, tired, wet and suffering from dysentery, took up positions between two woods. They could only manage a single line of battle, with archers on the flanks and in two wedge formations connected by dismounted men-at-arms. Little more than 1000 yards to their north were three lines of Frenchmen, the vast majority of them men-at-arms – the first two lines dismounted, but with cavalry to their rear and flanks. For four hours the armies waited, until Henry ordered his archers to advance to within 300 yards (extreme longbow range) of the enemy. The archers loosed off a volley of arrows, hoping to provoke the French into an attack.

It worked. As the arrows rained down, the French responded by sending their flank cavalry into the attack, followed by their first and second lines of dismounted men-at-arms, many of whom were wearing full armour. The English archers, protected by lines of sharpened stakes, forced the cavalry to turn away, straight into the path of the men-at-arms. Despite some disruption, the French pressed forward to engage the English men-at-arms, and found themselves crowded into a narrowing channel of advance. At first, the English line buckled, but as the French had no space in which to use their weapons, the breach could not be widened. Meanwhile, the French second line, unaware of the problem of space, pushed forward, jamming the first line up against the English. Archers, armed with mallets, axes and daggers, moved in to kill the men-at-arms, adding to the general *mêlée*. Some Frenchmen were sent sprawling in the mud, where they were crushed underfoot; others were knifed through slits in their armour and remained standing upright in the crush. When the survivors finally extricated themselves, it was said that the English were surrounded by piles of bodies 'taller than a man's height'. The French third line of mounted men did not intervene.

The battle was not quite over. Henry, worried that the French cavalry might still attack, and aware of an assault on his baggage train by armed peasants, estimated to number over 2000, to be killed. Before the order could be fully carried out, however, the French withdrew. Although exact casualty figures are not known – most sources cite up to 10,000 French dead, including three dukes, 90 lords and 1560 knights, with only 'a few hundred' English dead or wounded – no-one can dispute that it was a decisive English victory.

First-Hand Account

'[The French cavalry] threw themselves on the English archers, who had their sharp stakes fixed before them; but the ground was so soft that the said stakes fell. And the French all retreated excepting three men, of whom Sir William [de Savense] was one; to whom it unluckily happened that by their horses falling on the stakes they were thrown to the ground, among the archers and were immediately killed. The remainder, or the greater part of them, with all their horses, from fear of the arrows

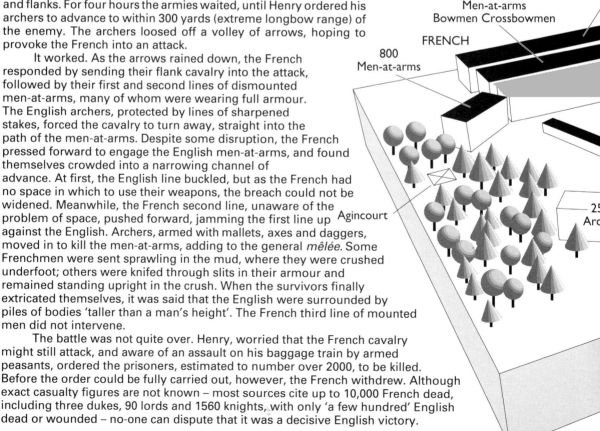

25 OCTOBER 1415

retreated into the French advanced-guard in which they caused great confusion, breaking and exposing it in many places . . . The English archers, perceiving this disorder of the advanced-guard, quitted their stakes, threw their bows and arrows on the ground and seizing their swords, axes and other weapons, sallied out upon them, and hastening to the places where the fugitives had made breaches, killed and disabled the French . . . and met with little or no resistance. And the English, cutting right and left, pushed on to the second line, and then pushed within it, with the King of England in person.'

Chronique de Jean Le Fèvre de St Remy, 1408–35

Personality Profile:

Henry V (1387-1422)

Henry V came to the throne of England in 1413 on the death of his father, Henry IV. He had already experienced battle, having commanded the left wing of the Royal army at Shrewsbury in 1403, where he was wounded in the face by an arrow, but stories of his wild youth abounded. These were probably exaggerated, for when he was crowned he appears to have been transformed overnight into an able administrator and devout monarch. His main foreign policy aim was to revive the claim of his great-grandfather, Edward III (*see box*, p.12), to the throne of France, to which end he led an army to Harfleur in August 1415. His victory at Agincourt two months later was one of the most dramatic in English history. In 1420 he concluded the Treaty of Troyes with the French, whereby he married Catherine of Valois, King Charles VI's daughter, and was made Regent. Two years later, he died while conducting the siege of Vincennes, leaving the throne to his infant son. Although the popular image of Henry V is drawn primarily from William Shakespeare, writing nearly 200 years later, there is no doubt that Henry was, in reality, an inspiring leader and an astute commander.

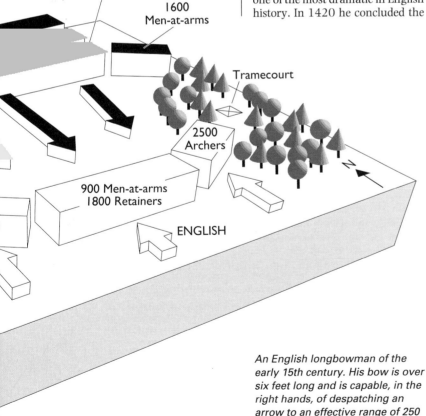

8000 Men-at-arms

1600 Men-at-arms

Tramecourt

2500 Archers

900 Men-at-arms 1800 Retainers

ENGLISH

An English longbowman of the early 15th century. His bow is over six feet long and is capable, in the right hands, of despatching an arrow to an effective range of 250 yards.

The balance was restored in 1415, when Henry V achieved a crushing (and largely unexpected) victory at Agincourt (*see* p.14), in the aftermath of which he assumed the regency of France and conquered Normandy. But his death in 1422 left England virtually leaderless, and although the war dragged on for another 31 years, the French slowly gained the upper hand. The final battle of the Hundred Years War, fought at Castillon on 17 June 1453, was symbolic of a new age of warfare: the English advanced against enemy positions defended by artillery and were routed. The longbow had found its match.

THE WARS OF THE ROSES

By then, however, England was already affected by the dynastic quarrel between the Houses of York and Lancaster, known as the Wars of the Roses, that was to last from 1452 until Henry Tudor's victory over Richard III at Bosworth Field in 1485. The conflict was not continuous – one historian has estimated that the 33 years of war involved only 15 months of campaigning and a mere 12 weeks of actual fighting – but it did cut England off from the main stream of technological and tactical change in Europe. At a time when continental armies were experimenting with early forms of handgun – principally the *arquebus*, a crude type of matchlock that required the application of fire to an open pan of gunpowder to create a detonation – the English were still dependent on archers and lightly armed infantry. Denied the experience of battle in Europe, English military skills developed no further than those apparent at Agincourt.

This was a result not just of isolation and domestic introspection, for much of the experience of the Hundred Years War had been lost as soon as that conflict ended.

The armies that fought at Crécy, Poitiers and Agincourt were raised for limited foreign service only and were disbanded as soon as a particular campaign was over. Because of the protracted nature of the war against France, the system of creating armies had been regularized – by the end of the 14th century it was usual for the king to issue indentures (contracts) to selected officers to provide soldiers in exchange for money – but this was not applicable to forces in England, where there appeared to be no need for a professional army. If the country was threatened, the freemen could be called to arms just as they had been in Alfred's time. Although the *fyrd* as such no longer existed, having been replaced in 1181 by the Assize of Arms and then, in 1282, by the Commission of Array, the latter enabling the king to summon forces from individual counties, the tradition of dependence on locally raised amateurs was still strong. During the Wars of the Roses, the situation was even less satisfactory, for the rival factions could raise men only through appeals for volunteers or by mustering the militia in their own particular areas of control. These arrangements were unlikely to produce anything more sophisticated than an ill-trained horde, capable of little beyond brute force. It is no coincidence that the largest and bloodiest battle ever fought on English soil – at Towton on 29 March 1461 (*see box*) – occurred during this period.

The rival armies in the Wars of the Roses were therefore quite archaic. They were normally divided into three separate formations, known collectively as 'battles' and individually as the vanguard, main battle and rearguard. The vanguard was often given an independent role, probing forward to seize river crossings or warning of an enemy approach. Once engaged, the attacking army would send its archers in first to disrupt the enemy and spread panic, although with both sides able to recruit longbowmen who were familiar with this tactic, it rarely had the desired effect. There was some experimentation with artillery and, as the wars progressed, even with the

---

THE BATTLE OF TOWTON

On 4 March 1461 Edward, Earl of March, son of the recently killed Duke of York and the main Yorkist contender for the throne, was acclaimed King of England as Edward IV. The Lancastrians, led by Queen Margaret, wife of the deposed Henry VI, retired north to recover from a defeat at St Albans on 17 February. Edward followed, reaching Nottingham by 22 March and fighting his way across the River Aire at Ferrybridge in Yorkshire six days later. A few miles to the north, he encountered a Lancastrian army of over 30,000 men deployed along a ridge between the villages of Saxton and Towton. Edward's army was of approximately equal strength.

The battle began in conditions of snow and high wind at 11 a.m. on 29 March. Both sides were drawn up with their archers in front of the infantry, and the fighting commenced with a Yorkist ruse. Lord Fauconberg, commanding Edward's archers, ordered them to loose off a single volley at extreme range, then to withdraw a few paces. With the wind behind them, the missiles reached the Lancastrians, who responded with a rain of arrows that fell short of the enemy line. Fauconberg directed his archers to move forward to rearm by picking up the enemy arrows, just in time to deal with a Lancastrian advance. The ensuing infantry battle was

intense, with Lancastrian soldiers pressing forward to engage on a restricted frontage. Yorkist victory was ensured when the Duke of Norfolk suddenly appeared on the Lancastrian left flank with reinforcements, upon which the Lancastrians broke and fled. Many were caught by Yorkist cavalry as they tried to cross the River Cock and were slaughtered. By the end of the day it was estimated that over 28,000 men had been killed, of which over 20,000 were Lancastrian. Edward marched into York but did not pursue the remains of his enemy much further, preferring to return to London, where he was officially crowned.

---

arquebus, but there was little emphasis on such innovations. Indeed, at the Battle of Northampton (July 1460), the Lancastrians discovered a disadvantage of gunpowder when a rainstorm rendered their guns inoperable. Cavalry appears to have been little used.

THE TUDOR ARMY

An English army did not participate in another European conflict until 1513, when Henry VIII intervened in the Habsburg–Valois Wars on the side of Spain, the Pope and the Holy Roman Empire against the French. Although his father, Henry Tudor (Henry VII), had created the Yeomen of the Guard in 1486 as the first permanent English military force, there was no army available for foreign service and the militia, raised for local service only, could not be used outside England. Instead, Henry VIII had to raise a force from scratch by calling for volunteers. More than 24,000 men came forward, but they inevitably reflected the outdated nature of English tactics; they included no heavy cavalrymen, pikemen or *arquebusiers* and Henry was forced to hire German mercenaries to create a better balance. In the event, the army did not disgrace itself – the town of Thérouanne in northern France was taken after a short siege, and a light-cavalry skirmish at Guinegatte (the 'Battle of the Spurs') ended in victory for Henry's men. It should be pointed out, however, that the army did not encounter the main French forces, which were fighting in Italy, and never posed much of a threat to the French state. A second intervention in 1523 under the Earl of Surrey fared much worse, disintegrating under the pressure of winter weather, while a campaign fought under Henry's leadership in 1542–5 achieved nothing beyond the capture of Boulogne.

Such minor achievements hardly amounted to an impressive record, although this was not recognized at the time. As far as Henry was concerned, his interventions, although financially ruinous, had the desired effect of projecting English influence into Europe; his armies had not been defeated in battle and there had been no direct threat to his throne. Henry saw no reason to raise a standing army or to revise existing tactics; forces could be created as they were needed and supplemented by the hiring of mercenaries fully conversant with new methods of waging war. Even if domestic dangers emerged, the local militia could cope. In 1513, for example, a Commission of Array had called out the forces in Yorkshire, Northumberland, Cumberland, Westmorland and Lancashire to deal with an invasion by James IV of Scotland, and they had won an overwhelming victory at Flodden. Henry did introduce some changes – in the early 1540s he initiated the building of forts along the south coast and founded the Ordnance Department to ensure the provision of cannon and gunpowder – but he did not alter what had already become a traditional English approach to the creation of armies. A combination of extemporized forces for European commitment and locally raised militia for internal duties seemed quite adequate.

These arrangements were not tested further until the end of the 16th century. In 1585, Queen Elizabeth I was drawn into a war with Spain that was to last until her death 18 years later. Although the emphasis throughout was on naval exploits such as Sir Francis Drake's expedition to Cadiz in 1587 and the defeat of the Armada a year later, an English army did fight in the United Provinces of the Netherlands, supporting the Protestant Dutch in their struggle for independence from Catholic Spain. Initially the army was improvised, although the fact that it remained on campaign until taken over by the Dutch in 1594 meant that a more permanent organizational structure had to be imposed on it.

Elizabeth turned to the local militia as a source of recruits. In 1558, the year before her accession to the throne, the Commission of Array had been replaced by a system, based on the obligation of all men between the ages of 16 and 60 to serve in the militia, that was under the control of the Lords-Lieutenant of counties, appointed by the monarch. They were responsible for mustering the men once a year and for ensuring that they received a modicum of training. This system had two distinct advantages: it placed the militia under a more centralized control and provided a reservoir of semi-trained soldiers. Legally, militiamen could only be called upon to defend the state, but the Crown did have the right to order Lords-Lieutenant to provide stipulated numbers of 'volunteers' for foreign service should the need arise. In the absence of genuine volunteers, local justices of the peace could compel 'masterless men' (vagabonds) to make up the numbers, although the extent to which such action was taken is not clear. What is known is that between 1585 and 1603 over 80,000 soldiers were sent to the Netherlands, the majority from the militia.

Such numbers required proper command and administration if they were to make any meaningful contribution during their 18-year involvement in the Dutch Revolt. As the war progressed, certain innovations were introduced. In 1585 the Earl of Leicester was appointed 'Lieutenant and Captain-General' in the Netherlands. Although his successor, Sir Francis Vere, appointed four years later, only merited the title of 'Sergeant-Major General', it was clear that a command hierarchy was emerging. Vere had 'colonel-generals' under him, together with a Master-General of the Ordnance, Master-Gunner and Forage-Master, while the troops themselves were organized into regiments of about 900 men apiece (later reduced to 750), each under a colonel and composed of a number of captain's companies. The government took over responsibility for providing rations, the Ordnance Department issued armour, weapons and gunpowder, and there was even a rudimentary medical service. The army may not have achieved a great deal – it tended to be wasted on peripheral campaigns such as that in Brittany (1590–5), where Spanish forces were aiding the French Catholics against Protestant Huguenots, and was constantly drained to provide forces for naval expeditions – but it gradually began to assume a quite 'modern' appearance. When the Dutch took it over in 1594 – they paid for its upkeep but still received recruits from England – they inherited a force with some potential. This was shown particularly at the Battles of Turnhout (24 January 1597) and Nieuport (2 July 1600), where

English troops under Dutch command gained notable victories.

At much the same time (1600–3), an English army commanded by Lord Mountjoy successfully countered a Catholic revolt in Ireland, led by the Earl of Tyrone, that had been going on since 1593. Mountjoy used techniques that would become familiar to the British Army in its colonial policing campaigns of the 19th century, burning crops and destroying villages in areas that harboured the rebels, while organizing his forces into 'flying columns' capable of matching the guerrilla tactics of his enemy. He even dealt with a Spanish army sent to aid Tyrone, forcing its surrender at Kinsale in January 1602.

Within two years, however, a familiar pattern had

Soldiers of the 16th century. The contrast between the armoured knight on the right and the arquebusier in the centre is striking, indicating the changing nature of weapons and of war.

been reasserted. The transfer of soldiers to the Dutch implied a lack of English interest in the war in Europe, and when James VI of Scotland came to the English throne in 1603 as James I, he not only made peace with Spain but also dismantled the Elizabethan military system. As there was no longer an obvious threat to Protestant ascendancy in Ireland, Mountjoy's army was disbanded, and now that England and Scotland were one kingdom, removing the danger to the northern counties, the militia was allowed to decline – the only exception was in London, where the

English Match Lock, 1615.

An English matchlock of the early 17th century. Although shorter and more manageable than an arquebus, the weapon still required the application of fire to an open pan of powder, forward of the butt.

'trained bands', a total of 6000 men, continued to take their duties seriously. There seemed to be no requirement for a standing army, particularly when both James and his successor, Charles I, tended to remain aloof from the affairs of Europe, where dynastic and religious tensions erupted into the complex series of struggles known as the Thirty Years War (1618–48). Expeditionary forces were raised occasionally – 6000 men were sent to the Netherlands in 1624, and a year later 12,000 were committed to Germany – but they bore no resemblance to their Elizabethan predecessors and made little impact. Although English troops continued to serve as mercenaries in Europe, and four Scottish regiments fought in the Swedish Army under Gustavus Adolphus in the early 1630s, they did so on a private basis. It was not until the 1640s, when England dissolved into civil war, that their experiences, and those of their commanders such as the Earl of Essex, Prince Rupert and George Monck, became significant.

THE FIRST CIVIL WAR

The Civil War that began in 1642 was essentially a constitutional quarrel between king and Parliament over who ruled the country. As early as 1629, when Charles I dissolved Parliament because of its opposition to his demands for increased taxation, it was apparent that a crisis existed, and this was made worse during the succeeding 11 years of incompetent royal government. Attempts by the king to raise funds by other means, notably the extension of 'ship money' from seaports to inland towns in 1635 as a form of taxation to pay for the construction of warships, further alienated the people, but it was his ill-considered policy of trying to impose a new version of the English Prayer Book on the Scots in 1637–8 that brought the crisis to a head. The Scots' response was to sign a National Covenant opposing such a move and, in 1639, to raise an army under Alexander Leslie (later Earl of Leven), that threatened the northern counties of England. In the absence of a standing army, Charles had to resort to calling out the militia in the north, only to find that a generation of neglect had rendered it useless. Although more than 20,000 men were assembled at Newcastle, they were poorly disciplined and badly equipped; as soon as they encountered a Scots force near the border, most of the militiamen fled. A year later, after Leslie had

dispersed another militia army at Newburn, Charles had no choice but to negotiate humiliating terms. By the Treaty of Ripon he abandoned his policy over the Prayer Book and agreed to grant an indemnity of more than £40,000 to the Scots, who remained in possession of parts of northern England until the money had been paid.

Parliament had to be reconvened to provide the necessary funds, but any confidence that Charles may have had about the loyalty of his people in the face of a Scottish invasion was misplaced. A Catholic massacre of Protestant settlers in Ulster in October 1641 fuelled fears of 'popish plots' – fears that were further exacerbated by the influence of Charles' French Catholic queen, Henrietta Maria, and the 'catholicizing' Archbishop of Canterbury, William Laud. When Charles demanded money to pay for a military augmentation in Ireland, some MPs suspected that he would use the soldiers to impose absolute power in England, destroying the rights of Parliament. In November the Commons issued a Grand Remonstrance that gave expression to all the grievances that had built up since 1629 and demanded deep-rooted reforms designed to weaken the influence of the king and his court. Amid rumours that the queen was about to be impeached (put on trial by Parliament for 'high crimes and misdemeanours'), Charles reacted with a petulant display of force. In January 1642, he led a small group of soldiers to Parliament in an attempt to arrest recalcitrant MPs, only

Regimental Tradition:

PONTIUS PILOT'S BODYGUARD

The Royal Scots, raised originally as independent Scottish companies in the service of the French king, have for long been known as 'Pontius Pilot's Bodyguard'. The nickname is said to have originated in 1637 when men of what was then the *Régiment de Douglas* (or *Douglas Écossais*) were arguing with the French *Régiment de Picardie* about which unit had the longer history of service. The French soldiers boasted that they had been on duty the night after the Crucifixion, upon which the Scots were reputed to have replied that, as Pontius Pilot's Bodyguard, 'had we been on duty, we should not have slept at our post'. The nickname accompanied the regiment onto the English establishment in 1670 and is still in use today.

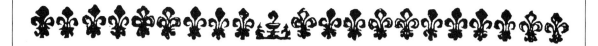

THE
Exercife of the English, in the
Militia of the Kingdome of
ENGLAND.

The title-page to a tract on the militia, written during the period of the First Civil War, shows the uniforms and equipment of a musketeer (left) and pikeman (right).

to find the Commons protected by men of the London Trained Bands. He was forced to abandon the capital and withdraw to York, where he immediately issued Commissions of Array to call out the militia. The Commons responded with their own Militia Ordinance and ordered the Earl of Essex to raise and command an army of 10,000 men. Civil war was now unavoidable.

But armies were difficult to raise. With the exception of the London Trained Bands – the only disciplined body of infantry in the country – no military forces as such existed. The militia was already known to be poor in quality and was further weakened by the rival claims to its allegiance. Both sides had to resort to volunteers drawn from their particular areas of control – Charles enjoyed support in Wales and western England, while Parliament

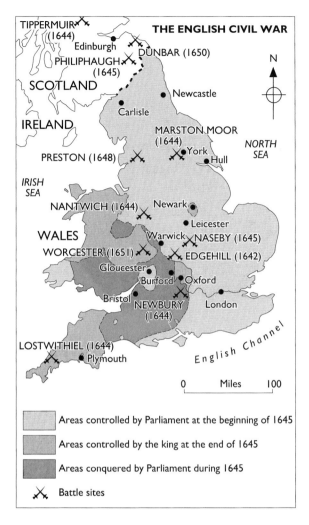

THE ENGLISH CIVIL WAR

N

TIPPERMUIR (1644)
Edinburgh
DUNBAR (1650)
PHILIPHAUGH (1645)
SCOTLAND
IRELAND
Newcastle
Carlisle
MARSTON MOOR (1644)
York
Hull
PRESTON (1648)
NORTH SEA
IRISH SEA
NANTWICH (1644)
Newark
WALES
Leicester
Warwick NASEBY (1645)
WORCESTER (1651)
EDGEHILL (1642)
Gloucester
Burford Oxford
Bristol
NEWBURY (1644)
London
LOSTWITHIEL (1644)
Plymouth
English Channel

0   Miles   100

Areas controlled by Parliament at the beginning of 1645

Areas controlled by the king at the end of 1645

Areas conquered by Parliament during 1645

X Battle sites

centre to engage in close-quarter fighting that eventually petered out with neither side gaining an advantage. The next day, Essex withdrew to Warwick, allowing Charles to occupy Oxford and march towards Reading. From this position the king should have been able to take London, but as he approached Turnham Green on 13 November he encountered a new Parliamentary army that included the London Trained Bands, and pulled back to Oxford. A similar lack of decisiveness in 1643, when the Royalists wasted time laying siege to Hull and Plymouth, gave Parliament a vital breathing space, during which a Solemn League and Covenant was signed with the Scots. Charles now faced enemies on two fronts.

The Scots moved south in 1644 to join the Yorkshire Parliamentary Army under Lord Fairfax and his son, Sir Thomas. They were joined by men of the Eastern Association, drawn from East Anglia; included in their number was a cavalry force under Oliver Cromwell, an MP-turned-soldier who had already displayed his fighting prowess at Edgehill. Lord Fairfax and Cromwell decided to besiege York, leaving the way open for Prince Rupert to advance through Lancashire and across the Pennines. The armies met at Marston Moor on 2 July 1644 and, as at Edgehill, it was the cavalry that dominated the day, with Cromwell's 'Ironsides' attacking on one flank, then recovering to advance round the back of the enemy infantry to destroy the opposite wing. The Royalist infantry were left to be cut down in the centre. It was the largest battle of the war and one of the most decisive – the Royalists lost an entire army as well as control of northern England – but the Parliamentary victory was not fully exploited. Instead of staying together to march south to take the king's headquarters at Oxford, the various contingents split up and went their separate ways. The Scots moved north to besiege Newcastle, the Fairfaxes took their army to besiege isolated enemy strongholds in Yorkshire, and Cromwell marched back to Lincolnshire.

THE NEW MODEL ARMY

Such a wasted opportunity persuaded Parliament to reform its military system with the aim of producing a single army that could be commanded and administered centrally. This would replace the existing profusion of regionally organized regiments, many of which owed their allegiance to local commanders rather than to Parliament, and would ensure that a full concentration of force could be achieved (and maintained) when and where it mattered. But a 'New Model Army' could not be created overnight. By late 1644, recruits were in short supply – both sides in the Civil War were already resorting to impressment (conscription) to keep up their numbers – and Parliament would have to find the money to pay and equip the soldiers to keep them in the field. Thus, although the plan for reform was announced in January 1645, it took time for the Army to become effective.

The plan called for a force of 22,000 men, organized into 11 regiments of cavalry, each of 600 soldiers, plus a regiment of dragoons (mounted infantry) of 1000, and 12

dominated the east and south-east, including London, leaving the Midlands and North to be fought over – but the lack of military experience was quickly apparent. Although commanders who had fought in Europe, such as Prince Rupert for the Royalists and Essex for the Parliamentarians, could be found, their officers were often appointed for their social position rather than their expertise and the men were initially ill-disciplined. The early battles tended to be badly co-ordinated and indecisive.

This was shown to good effect in the opening campaign. Charles raised his standard at Nottingham on 22 August 1642 and marched west towards Shrewsbury to attract support. By October he had about 14,000 soldiers under his command. His strategy was to reoccupy London, by-passing the Parliamentarian army under Essex that had advanced to Worcester with an equal number of men to oppose him. On 23 October, however, the two armies clashed at Edgehill, to the north of Oxford. The battle opened with Royalist cavalry charges led by Prince Rupert and Lord Wilmot that shattered both wings of the Parliamentary force, but a lack of control allowed the horsemen to squander their advantage in a useless pursuit. Meanwhile, Royalist infantry advanced in the

THE BATTLE OF NASEBY

On 30 May 1645 Royalist forces captured Leicester in an attempt to force the Parliamentary army under Sir Thomas Fairfax to abandon the siege of Oxford. The ploy worked. As Charles I led his troops south as far as Daventry, Fairfax moved north to meet him. The king ordered a withdrawal towards Market Harborough, but the Parliamentarians pursued him with vigour. Late on 13 June Parliamentary patrols entered the village of Naseby, about two miles south of Market Harborough, and Charles made the decision to stand and fight.

The Royalist army was outnumbered, with about 9000 men ranged against nearly 13,500 under Fairfax; it also had no clear picture of Parliamentary intentions. Prince Rupert, effectively commanding the Royalist army despite the presence of the king, moved forward to reconnoitre early on 14 June. He was surprised to see both Fairfax and Oliver Cromwell carrying out a similar mission to the north-east of Naseby. Rupert ordered his troops to move west, with the intention of outflanking the enemy, only to find that Fairfax was doing the same. By 9 a.m. both armies were marching in parallel. As they came out onto an open area of ground known as Broad Moor, they turned to face one another. Fairfax deployed his army with infantry in the centre under Philip Skippon and cavalry on both flanks, on the left under Henry Ireton and on the right under Cromwell. Opposite them, the Royalists adopted a similar deployment: infantry in the centre under Sir Jacob Astley, with cavalry under Prince Rupert facing Ireton and under Sir Marmaduke Langdale facing Cromwell.

Just after 10 a.m. the Royalists began a steady advance towards the enemy line. As Astley's infantry made contact with Skippon's men, firing muskets and pushing hard with their pikes, Rupert led a cavalry charge against the Parliamentary left flank. It was a success, sweeping the bulk of Ireton's men from the field, but Rupert's squadrons did not reform – in fact, they did not stop until they reached the Parliamentary baggage train about a mile to the rear. Meanwhile, on the opposite flank, Cromwell watched Langdale's cavalry advance towards him. He waited until they were negotiating rising ground and then led a charge. Not only did this disperse the enemy but Cromwell also kept his men together in its aftermath. The king's infantry were now exposed – Rupert had disappeared on one flank and Langdale had been defeated on the other – and when Cromwell and Colonel John Okey led simultaneous cavalry charges from east and west, there was little the infantry could do. As Charles was led away by his bodyguard Rupert reappeared, but it was too late. Over 4500 Royalists laid down their arms; a further 1000 were killed, compared to perhaps 200 Parliamentarians. The king no longer had an army.

The Battle of Naseby, 14 June 1645. The fight turned on the effectiveness of cavalry, with Cromwell's 'Ironsides' maintaining their discipline and cohesion much better than Prince Rupert's horsemen.

regiments of infantry, each of 1200 personnel. It proved to be too ambitious. Despite a Parliamentary vote of £585,000 to ensure that the soldiers were regularly paid, by May 1645 the Army was under strength and still dependent on impressment. By then, Sir Thomas Fairfax had been given overall command, but it was the influence of Cromwell that proved crucial. Appointed Lieutenant-General of the Horse because of his proven cavalry expertise, he brought with him the virtues and ethos of the Eastern Association, with its emphasis on discipline and religious zeal. The Association was dominated by Cromwell's own Ironsides, prominent among whom was a strongly Puritan element whose members were known as 'Saints'. The latter advocated the 'purification' of those aspects of the Anglican Church they considered too 'Catholic', and the abolition of the monarchy. Their tactical strength lay in their ability to reform after a charge, as they had shown at Marston Moor, but it was the inspiration of their religious beliefs (plus a promise of regular pay) that made them difficult to defeat. As these beliefs spread throughout the New Model Army, it became a formidable instrument

First-Hand Account:
NASEBY

'About ten of the Clock the Battel began, the first Charge being given by Prince Rupert with his own and Prince Maurice's Troops; who did so well, and were so well seconded, as that they bore all down before them, and were (as 'tis said) Masters of six Pieces of the Rebels Cannon. Presently our Forces advanced up the Hill, the Rebels only discharging five Pieces at them, but over shot them, and so did their Musquetiers. The Foot on either side hardly saw each other until they were within Carabine Shot, and so made only one Volley; ours falling in with Sword and butt end of the Musquet did notable Execution; so much as I saw their Colours fall, and their Foot in great Disorder. And had our left Wing but at this time done half so well as either the Foot or right Wing, we had got in a few Minutes a glorious Victory. Our Foot and Right Wing being thus engaged, our left Wing advanced, consisting of five Bodies of the Northern and Newark Horse; who were opposed by seven great Bodies drawn to their right Wing by Cromwell who commanded there, and who besides the Advantage of Number had that of the Ground, ours marching up the Hill to encounter them. Yet I must needs say ours did as well as the Place and their Number would admit; but being flanked and pressed back, they at last gave Ground and fled: Four of the Rebels Bodies close and in good Order followed them, the rest charged our Foot . . .'

Brief Memorials of the Unfortunate Success of His Majesty's Army and Affairs in the Year 1645

that, regardless of problems of recruitment and pay, effectively decided the outcome of the war. On 14 June 1645 the Parliamentarians won the Battle of Naseby (*see box*); in the following year they captured Oxford. Meanwhile a Scottish army defeated Royalists under the Marquis of Montrose at Philiphaugh. Charles surrendered to the Scots who, at the beginning of 1647, handed him over to Parliament. The First Civil War was over.

THE SECOND CIVIL WAR AND COMMONWEALTH

What happened next was to affect English attitudes towards the Army for generations. By 1647 the New

The statue of Oliver Cromwell overlooking Parliament Square, London. As Lord Protector of the Commonwealth (1653–8), Cromwell effectively ruled as a dictator, but his record as a cavalry commander and military reformer during the Civil War was an impressive one.

Personality Profile:

OLIVER CROMWELL
(1599–1658)

Born in Huntingdon of yeoman stock, Oliver Cromwell did not make his mark on English history until the beginning of the First Civil War in 1642. Before then, he had sat as Member of Parliament for Huntingdon (1628–9) and for Cambridge (1640), but had been more involved in local than national politics and had assumed Puritan religious beliefs associated with stern morality. When the war began, he sided firmly with Parliament against the king, raising two regiments of cavalry (known as 'Ironsides' because of their armour and self-discipline), which he led in battle despite his lack of military experience. His first major engagement was at Edgehill (October 1642), but it was at Marston Moor (July 1644) that he showed his true skill, using his troopers to deliver controlled cavalry charges that broke the Royalists. Thereafter, his influence in Parliamentary circles was assured and his grip on the New Model Army, formed on the pattern of the Ironsides' discipline and religious fervour, gradually tightened, particularly after the decisive victory at Naseby (June 1645). When the split occurred between army and Parliament over the post-war constitutional settlement, Cromwell emerged as a key political figure. After defeating the Scots at Preston (August 1648) in the Second Civil War, he supported the dissolution of Parliament, the imposition of army rule and the execution of Charles I. His ruthless campaign against the Catholics in Ireland (1649–50) led to his appointment as commander-in-chief, from which position he gradually assumed dictatorial powers. Cromwell was appointed Lord Protector of the Commonwealth in 1653; despite his record of political reform and an active foreign policy that enhanced English trade, he was forced to depend more and more on military authority, epitomized in the 'rule of the major-generals' (1655–9; *see box*, p.26). When he died in September 1658, Cromwell was buried in Westminster Abbey, but after the Restoration two years later his body was exhumed and hanged.

reconciliation and the establishment of a constitutional monarchy, tried to control the Army by ordering it to dismiss its Puritan preachers, who were demanding radical political change. The Army eventually purged itself of more extremist Puritans, known as 'Levellers', whose activities led to mutiny in a number of regiments, but it was unwilling to bow to Parliamentary interference. Its response was a 'Solemn Engagement of the Army', issued on 5 June 1647, that set up a General Council to represent the views of both officers and soldiers and to act as an alternative to the House of Commons.

Events came to a head when Parliament formally proposed a return to the constitutional balance of August 1641. The Army put forward its own 'Heads of Proposals', advocating limits to the power of Parliament. The king took advantage of the split to negotiate with the Scots, while encouraging Royalist revolts in Wales, Kent and Essex. The latter were swiftly dealt with by elements of the New Model Army in May and June 1648, but it was not until Cromwell had defeated the Scots at Preston on 17 August that the Second Civil War came to an end. Victory inevitably enhanced the power of the Army and this drove the wedge between it and Parliament still deeper. When negotiations between Parliament and the king resumed, based on a search for compromise that would allow Charles to keep his throne, the Army grew increasingly restive.

The result was a military seizure of political power – the only time in modern history that it has happened in England. On 1 December 1648 Charles was arrested and, 24 hours later, regiments of the New Model Army marched into London, demanding a dissolution of Parliament and the creation of a provisional government that would satisfy their demands. In the event, the Commons survived after a purge by Colonel Thomas Pride, who forcibly excluded those MPs who wished to reach an agreement with Charles I, to create an amenable 'Rump'. But the outcome was the same as it would have been had Parliament been dissolved. Following a trial before the High Court of Justice, Charles I was executed on 30 January 1649, the House of Lords was abolished and a 'Commonwealth or Free State' established. England became a republic, dependent for its survival on military force and, increasingly, on one man.

Cromwell was appointed commander-in-chief in 1650, partly in recognition of his ruthless campaign against the Catholics in Ireland (1649–50), and a year later the army was used to defeat yet another Scots invasion. However, like most military governments, that of the Commonwealth rapidly lost the support of the people. Its legitimacy was further undermined in 1653 when Cromwell, growing tired of opposition, dissolved the 'Rump Parliament' and introduced a new constitution under which he became Lord Protector, advised by a council of trusted officers. This led to more widespread opposition and an inevitable trend towards dictatorship; in 1655 Cromwell dismissed his advisory council, divided the country into districts and placed each of them under the control of a major-general (*see box*). The subsequent repression was to be long remembered, reflected in a deep public hatred of a standing army.

When Cromwell died on 3 September 1658, he was succeeded by his son, Richard, who soon proved to have

Model Army was the most powerful organization in the country – disciplined, strongly motivated and clearly capable of defeating its enemies in battle. It was also deeply involved in the politics of the state and, for that reason, should have been disbanded once victory was assured. But it was needed to deal with any Royalist resurgence and to control the Catholics in Ireland. Parliament, intent on

RULE OF THE MAJOR-GENERALS

Cromwell's assumption of absolute power in 1655, when he dismissed his advisory council and imposed his own rule on the Commonwealth, led to signs of opposition within the country. Royalist and Leveller plots were uncovered and there was even a minor uprising in Wiltshire. All of this persuaded Cromwell that the existing system of local government, based on traditional county boundaries and the influence of the landed gentry, many of whom held latent Royalist loyalties, was at fault. In response he divided the country into 11 new districts and placed each under the control of a trusted major-general, supported by mounted militiamen. The aim was to create a force that could monitor events in local areas and suppress any signs of unrest, but the experiment proved to be intensely unpopular. The apparent destruction of county loyalties upset the gentry, whose power inevitably declined; the association of the major-generals with the imposition of Puritan ideals alienated the ordinary people. Within a year, the system was causing more opposition than it had been created to counter, and although it did not survive beyond the recall of the Rump Parliament in May 1659, its memory remained firmly fixed in the popular imagination. More than anything else, it established a hatred of military rule that would be translated into a deep distrust of a standing army in England throughout the 18th and 19th centuries.

little of his father's strength of will. Although he recalled the Rump Parliament in May 1659 in an attempt to regain popular support, he was persuaded by the commander-in-chief, Charles Fleetwood, to send soldiers to dissolve it as soon as Army policies were opposed. Such a blatant use of military force alienated more moderate officers, who used their positions on the republican Council of State to engineer the dismissal of Fleetwood. General George Monck, appointed in his place, marched south from Coldstream at the head of a force of soldiers fresh from duty in Scotland, recalled Parliament and invited Charles I's son to take the throne. On 29 May 1660 Charles II entered London. Although there was no doubt that he would need an army to ensure his survival, its power and influence would have to be curbed. The British Army that traces its continuous history back to the Restoration therefore began life under a cloud of suspicion and distrust. It was to take years to disperse that cloud.

. . . .

CHAPTER TWO

THE STANDING ARMY (1661–1792)

. . . .

THE RESTORATION SETTLEMENT

ON 14 February 1661 two regiments – the last survivors of the Commonwealth Army – laid down their arms in the presence of King Charles II. Known as the Lord General's Regiment of Foot and the Lord General's Lifeguard of Horse, they immediately took up their arms again, this time in the service of the king, as the Lord General's Regiment of Footguards (later the Coldstream Guards) and the Lord General's Troop of Guards (later part of the Life Guards). It was a symbolic moment, forging a continuity between the Parliamentary Army of the Civil War and the new 'Standing Army' of the recently restored English monarch.

They joined units which had guarded the king during his exile: two regiments of Foot Guards (merged in 1665 to form the First, later Grenadier, Guards) and two troops of Horse Guards (later part of the Life Guards). Together with a number of independent companies of old soldiers distributed around the country, principally to defend dockyards and naval stores, they constituted 'His Majesty's Guards and Garrisons' – a total of about 5000 men. Parliament, wary of the potential for retribution from a monarch acutely aware of the fate of his father, was extremely reluctant to accept even this small force. Indeed, most Members of Parliament expressed a belief that permanent military forces were unnecessary; England was protected from external attack by the Navy and from internal trouble by the 'part-time' militia, the latter under the control of county magnates (Lords-Lieutenant) that Parliament could trust. In 1661, 1662 and 1663, Militia Acts were passed by the House of Commons specifically designed to provide such a locally raised force as an alternative to a standing army.

But to Charles II, some sort of personal protection was essential, not just because of what had happened in the 1640s but also because his hold on power was, initially, quite tenuous. As early as 1661 a plan by extreme Puritan 'Fifth Monarchists' seemed to threaten the Restoration, and although this soon fizzled out, it gave the king ample reason to insist on some sort of permanent military force at his disposal. Thus the two Lord's General regiments, together with another Commonwealth unit, the Earl of Oxford's Horse (later the Royal Horse Guards) were maintained. Nor did the process end there, for 1661 also saw the appearance of an infantry unit, the Tangier Regiment of Foot (later the Queen's Royal West Surrey Regiment). This was raised specifically for service in Tangier, which had been brought under English control as part of the dowry of Catherine of Braganza when she married Charles II. By 1663, the standing army had grown to 3574 'Guards' and 4878 'Garrisons', with further forces in Scotland (a separate state until the Act of Union of 1707) and ever-troublesome Ireland.

These developments worried Parliament, with its memories of the Civil War and Rule of the Major-Generals. To MPs, a standing army raised the spectre of martial law, a suspension of liberties and an over-powerful king, especially when Charles II began to use it as an instrument of his own particular policies. Between 1678 and 1681, for example, as the Earl of Shaftesbury and his Whig Party tried to force the king to exclude his Roman Catholic brother James from the succession (Charles having no legitimate offspring), Parliament was removed to Oxford, where guardsmen lined the streets in what was widely seen as blatant intimidation. In addition, there was the fear that Charles would merely ignore Parliamentary worries by diverting money to his army from that voted for the upkeep of the militia. Clearly, if a standing army was necessary to defend overseas possessions and to guard against internal trouble (to say nothing of the external threat from the Dutch, with whom England was at war for most of the 1660s and early 1670s), then from

Parliament's point of view, it needed to be more firmly controlled.

THE GLORIOUS REVOLUTION

Events came to a head when Charles died in 1685, to be succeeded, despite Parliamentary reservations, by his brother, James II. Almost immediately, Charles' illegitimate son, the Duke of Monmouth, tried to usurp the throne, landing in the West Country with a small group of followers and rapidly gaining local support. James dispatched military forces under John Churchill (later the Duke of Marlborough) to deal with the revolt, which came to a bloody end at Sedgemoor on 6 July 1685, but the incident did nothing to undermine royal arguments in favour of a standing army. Indeed, James quickly moved to politicize his military forces, dismissing Protestant officers and replacing them with Catholics he could trust, and wasted no time in raising extra units. Between 1685 and 1688, five new regiments of Horse, two of Dragoons (essentially mounted infantry) and nine of Foot were created and encamped on Hounslow Heath, across which many MPs travelled on their way to the House of Commons. By 1688 the standing army was nearly 40,000 strong and was apparently being prepared as an instrument of religious imposition.

In some desperation, a number of MPs approached William of Orange, leader of the United Provinces (the modern Netherlands) and married to Mary, the staunchly Protestant daughter of James II, to request his intervention. On 15 November 1688, William landed at Torbay at the head of 15,000 Dutch, Danish and German soldiers, hoping that sufficient English leaders would defect to enable him to overthrow his father-in-law. At first, as James concentrated his army in the West Country, it looked as if William was doomed, but when the king ordered his forces to withdraw towards London rather than risk battle, the defections began. Churchill led the way and, as confusion reigned in the English camp, James' army disintegrated. By the end of the year, William was in control.

This was the opportunity Parliament had been waiting for. William, interested primarily in using English power to boost the defence of the United Provinces against the French, showed little regard for the constitutional niceties of his new realm and, quite frankly, distrusted the English Army he had inherited. He made this clear when he ordered the 'purging' of all Catholics from existing regiments – a policy which all but destroyed them – and gave command to non-military men he felt he could trust. He even banished the Guards from London for a time, transferring their duties to Dutch soldiers he had brought with him. Although this did little to maintain military effectiveness, it did imply that William was unlikely to oppose Parliamentary attempts to control the

The Battle of Sedgemoor, 6 July 1685. English soldiers loyal to King James II fought the Duke of Monmouth's rebels near the village of Westonzoyland in Somerset.

standing army. MPs could not insist on disbandment – William was already transferring English regiments to the continent to fight the French and, in 1689, forces loyal to the deposed James were active in both Scotland and Ireland – but they could begin to impose restraints on royal power.

CONTROLLING THE ARMY

The first of these restraints was enshrined in the Declaration of Rights in 1689, for not only did this state categorically that a standing army was illegal without the permission of Parliament, but it also laid down that Parliament would vote money for the Army's upkeep on a regular basis. Thus, if MPs felt that the Army was growing too large for public safety or was about to be used as a political or religious instrument by the monarch, they could refuse to provide the money or cut it down sufficiently to ensure a reduction in the size of the force. The first 'Estimates for His Majesty's Guards and Garrisons' were presented in October 1689, voting money sufficient for 49,238 men in 1690, and thereafter similar bills were presented to the House of Commons each year. The tradition continues today in the Defence Estimates.

A second measure of control had more immediate causes. On 14 March 1689, elements of the Royal Regiment of Foot, about to embark for the continent, mutinied in Ipswich and marched north towards Scotland. In itself, the incident was relatively minor – Dutch troops caught up with the mutineers in Lincolnshire and quickly disarmed them – but it highlighted a potentially significant legal problem. The soldiers were ostensibly subject to the Articles of War: these were issued whenever regiments went on campaign and gave military courts-martial the right to impose punishments that could threaten the 'life or limb' of the men (in other words, execution or flogging), without recourse to Common Law. In 1689 it was pointed out that, as the Royal Regiment was not actually on active service at the time of the mutiny, any court-martial which dealt with the mutineers and imposed violent punishments would be illegal. In the event, most of the men were merely shipped to the continent without any disciplinary measures being taken, but Parliament hastily introduced a Mutiny Act to avoid any future problems, effectively permitting courts-martial to use Common Law to impose military punishments. The first such Act was only temporary, but it soon became obvious that if Parliament refused to sanction military law, discipline would be impossible to impose, leading to disbandment. If the Army was ever seen as dangerous, MPs could delay or even refuse to pass the Mutiny Act, leaving the monarch with little choice but to disband the force. By the early 1690s, the renewal of the Mutiny Act was an annual event; it still has to be renewed today, although it now happens every five years as part of the Armed Forces Act.

These measures clearly suited Parliament and helped to establish the Army as a permanent, albeit distrusted, institution of state, but they did nothing to allay any fears the monarch might have about military forces being used against the throne, as they had in the 1640s. All soldiers owed their allegiance to the monarch, but it was the officers who were the key. From the beginning it was accepted by Parliament that the monarch had the right to appoint and promote all army officers, and this was never queried. However, it was apparent from the purges carried out by both James and William in the 1680s that it was possible for this right to be abused. Parliament therefore supported the purchase of commissions, at least up to the rank of colonel, and William III and his immediate successors were happy to maintain such a system. After all, if a man invested his money in an army career, he was less likely to give his backing to political moves that might overthrow the existing system and lose him his fortune. This did not mean that only the very rich could enter the army; in many cases it was the lesser gentry, raising money through the sale or mortgage of land, who engaged in military service. To Parliament, they were the backbone of England, with a wary distrust of royal power; to the monarch, they were conservative men who would be loath to organize rebellion for fear of losing their money.

All this took place against a backcloth of active service and expansion, for William wasted no time in using his new army to fight in Europe, while also dealing with the troubles in Ireland. William's defeat of forces loyal to the deposed James at the Battle of the Boyne in July 1690 was followed by mopping-up operations which culminated in the surrender of Limerick in October 1691. Despite such successes, however, by 1694 the Army had been increased to nearly 94,000 men, the bulk of whom were in Flanders defending the United Provinces. They did their job well, although few decisive battles were fought, but their continued existence worried Parliament. When the Nine Years War ended at the Treaty of Ryswick in 1697, Parliamentary pressure for disbandment was revived. William, having effectively lost control of military finance, had no choice but to comply. By 1700, the Army had been reduced to only 7000 men in England, plus 12,000 in Ireland. It was a pattern that was soon to become familiar: during times of war or national emergency, Parliament was prepared to fund relatively large forces, but as soon as peace was restored, the instrument of financial control enabled MPs to insist on quite drastic reductions. The only advantage to emerge was that, almost unrecognized, the principle of maintaining a standing army, however small, had been established.

THE WAR OF THE SPANISH SUCCESSION

The importance of that principle became apparent in 1702, when Britain again became involved in a European conflict – the War of the Spanish Succession. The threat of French power being extended to Spain (and the Spanish Empire in the New World) led Austria, the United Provinces, England (Britain from 1707) and a number of German states to ally together against Louis XIV. Fortu-

THE BATTLE OF BLENHEIM

Early on the morning of 13 August 1704, sheltered by mist, an Allied army of 52,000 men under the command of the Duke of Marlborough, with Prince Eugène of Savoy in support, advanced towards the River Danube. In its path lay a Franco-Bavarian army of 56,000 troops under Marshal Tallard. Although caught by surprise, Tallard's position was strong: his flanks were anchored by hills and the Danube, with the Nebel stream protecting his front. Tallard packed most of his infantry into two villages – Oberglau on his left and Blenheim on his right – out of which he hoped to mount counter-thrusts against any Allied attack across the Nebel; he kept his cavalry in reserve on a low ridge to the rear.

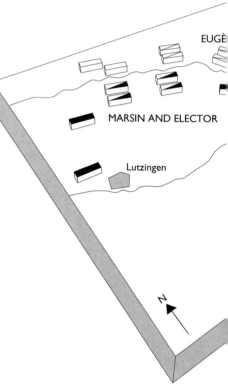

Marlborough, recognizing the potential weakness of Tallard's deployment, decided to concentrate his initial attacks on the villages, containing and neutralizing them before any crossing of the Nebel. Prince Eugène was ordered to march on Oberglau, while Brigadier Rowe, commanding a force of predominantly British troops, attacked Blenheim. The redcoats got to within about 30 paces of the enemy defences before being repulsed, but their actions had the desired effect: in panic, the commander of Tallard's right wing, the Marquis de Clérambault, pushed 27 battalions into the village. Here they found it difficult to deploy and were contained by further Allied attacks.

Meanwhile, on the Franco-Bavarian left, Eugéne's assault on Oberglau had been fought off; and it began to look as if Marlborough's flank would be turned. However, under the Duke's personal supervision, cannon were brought up and the enemy attack stalled, leaving Oberglau, like Blenheim, neutralized. Marlborough then ordered his centre to cross the Nebel, and although a French cavalry charge almost checked progress, Brigadier Lord Orkney brought up Allied cavalry to bolster the advance. By 6 p.m., after five hours of fighting, the French and Bavarians were in retreat, leaving the garrison at Blenheim to surrender at 9 p.m. The battle had cost the Allies 12,000 casualties, but they captured 14,000 enemy troops, while many more drowned in the Danube. It was, in Orkney's words, 'the greatest and completest victory that has been gained these many ages'.

First-Hand Account

'About 3 a clock in the afternoon our English on the left was ordered by My Lord Duke to attaque a village on the left full of French called Blenheim wch. village they had fortified and made soe vastly strong and barackaded so fast wth. trees, planks, coffers, chests, wagons, carts and palisades that it was almost an impossibility to think wch way to gett into it . . . Yett we according to command fought our way into the village wch. was all of a fire, and our men fought in and through the fire and persued others through it, untill many on both sides were burnt to death.

'Att length the enemy making all the force they could upon us forced us to retreat and to quitt the village having lost a great many of our men, but we rallyed againe, having received some fresh ammunition, resolving to give the enemy another salute . . . The village was sett on fire before we came to it by the enemy whereby they thought to have blinded our gunners, but great and greivous were the cryes of the maimed, and those suffering in the flames after we entered this village and none is able to express it but those that heard it.'

John Marshall Deane, Private Sentinel in Queen Anne's First Regiment of Foot Guards

From John Marshall Deane, *A Journal of Marlborough's Campaigns during the War of the Spanish Succession 1704–1711*, edited by D. G. Chandler, Society for Army Historical Research, Special Publication No. 12 (1984), pp.11–12

13 AUGUST 1704

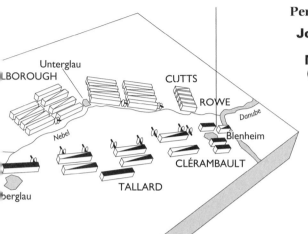

Unterglau
LBOROUGH
CUTTS
ROWE
Danube
Nebel
Blenheim
CLÉRAMBAULT
TALLARD
berglau

British, Austrians, Danes,
Hanoverians, Brandenburgers

▱ Cavalry
▭ Infantry

French and Bavarians

◪ Cavalry
▰ Infantry

Personality Profile:

**John Churchill,
1st Duke of
Marlborough
(1650–1722)**

Son of Sir Winston Churchill, a Royalist who had lost his property during the Civil War, John Churchill obtained his first commission, in the Guards, through connections at the Court of Charles II.

After service in Tangier (1668–70) and in the Third Dutch War (1672–3), he married Sarah Jennings, whose ambition and influence at Court were to play a key role in his rise to high command. Under James II, Churchill played a leading part in the suppression of the Monmouth Rebellion (for which he was created Earl of Marlborough), but in 1688 he deserted the king and transferred his allegiance to William of Orange. In 1702 he was given a dukedom and command of the Anglo-Dutch army in Flanders; between then and 1711 he fought a series of memorable campaigns against the French (*see box*, p.33). With the money voted to him by a grateful Parliament he built Blenheim Palace in Oxfordshire, named after his most notable victory.

Allied cavalry drive their Franco-Bavarian opponents into the Danube at Blenheim, 13 August 1704, where Marlborough and Eugène of Savoy inflicted the first major defeat on a French army in over 50 years.

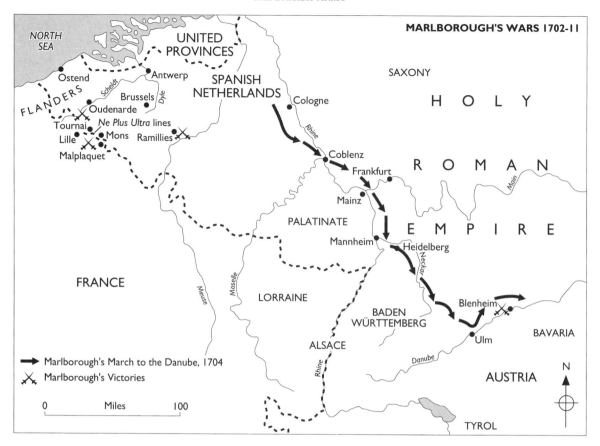

NORTH SEA

UNITED PROVINCES

Ostend

Antwerp

FLANDERS

Scheldt

Brussels

Dyle

SPANISH NETHERLANDS

Cologne

SAXONY

H O L Y

Oudenarde

Ne Plus Ultra lines

Tournai

Lille

Mons

Ramillies

Coblenz

Rhine

R O M A N

Malplaquet

Frankfurt

Main

Mainz

E M P I R E

FRANCE

PALATINATE

Mannheim

Heidelberg

Neckar

Moselle

LORRAINE

Meuse

BADEN WÜRTTEMBERG

Blenheim

Ulm

BAVARIA

ALSACE

Rhine

Danube

AUSTRIA

N

TYROL

➤ Marlborough's March to the Danube, 1704

✗ Marlborough's Victories

0   Miles   100

The Battle of Malplaquet, 11 September 1709. The battle was a 'Pyrrhic victory' for Marlborough: about a quarter of the Allied army was killed or wounded. The French lost 12,000 men.

MARLBOROUGH'S WAR

The Duke of Marlborough, despite his appointment to command an Anglo-Dutch army in the Low Countries during the War of the Spanish Succession, was always subordinate to Dutch civilian 'field deputies'. Their timidity in both 1702 and 1703 denied him any advantage from effective manoeuvres. It also allowed the French to concentrate and defeat the Austrians on the Danube, opening the way to Vienna. Faced with the imminent break-up of the Grand Alliance, Marlborough decided to march part of his army from Flanders to the Danube in 1704, with the aim of taking the enemy by surprise. To avoid clashes with the Dutch deputies, he conducted the operation in great secrecy. Marlborough was to reap the reward for his strategic boldness at Blenheim on 13 August (*see feature battle*, p.30).

In 1705, Marlborough's army was back in the Low Countries, where once again the interference of Dutch deputies prevented the exploitation of moves to outflank the enemy. It was not until the French Marshal Villeroi left the safety of defensive lines on the Dyle River in 1706 that Marlborough could force a battle. On 23 May, at Ramillies, he masked his real intentions by launching an attack on the enemy left wing, then shifted his reserves to the right, and routed the enemy in less than four hours. The victory allowed the Allies to capture Brussels, Antwerp and Ostend.

Marlborough was hampered by poor weather during the campaigning season in 1707, and it was not until the following year that he resumed his offensive. On 11 July 1708, near the village of Oudenarde, his regiments caught up with and engaged the main French force close by the River Scheldt, enveloping its right flank and forcing it to retreat.

Marlborough's plan to march immediately on Paris was vetoed, and the campaign bogged down in a siege of Lille, allowing the French to recover. In 1709 Marlborough attacked again, taking Tournai and forcing the French to accept battle at Malplaquet, near Mons. On 11 September a hard-fought and costly engagement, in which the British lost 14,000 casualties, led to French defeat but left the Allies exhausted.

Marlborough was to fight one more campaign, in 1711, during which he brilliantly outflanked the *Ne Plus Ultra* ('thus far and no further') lines in Flanders, but support for the war was waning in London. After lengthy negotiations, the Treaty of Utrecht was signed in 1713. Britain gained territory in North America and the Mediterranean, together with enhanced influence in Europe based in no small measure on the growing reputation of the British Army.

nately, the English Army could be expanded fairly rapidly by recruiting officers and soldiers disbanded in 1697, and an expeditionary force was dispatched to Flanders without much delay. Of equal significance was the fact that command of the combined Anglo-Dutch force was given to the Duke of Marlborough as Captain-General. Between 1702 and 1712, he conducted a series of campaigns that were to establish the fighting prowess of British troops (*see box*). His victories at Blenheim (1704), Ramillies (1706), Oudenarde (1708), Malplaquet (1709) and against the *Ne Plus Ultra* entrenchments (1711) – although achieved by Allied rather than purely British forces – showed that British regiments, ably commanded, were the equal of any in Europe. Although the Allies fared less well in Spain, where British forces contributed to an ultimately abortive attempt to prevent Louis XIV's grandson from assuming the throne, the war produced substantial gains. By the Treaty of Utrecht in 1713, Britain received Nova Scotia and Newfoundland from the French and Gibraltar and Minorca from the Spanish. Such an increase in overseas territory inevitably required the maintenance of a standing army.

Marlborough's victories depended on more than fighting skill, however, for he was the first British general to recognize the importance of administration. In a strictly military sense, this meant logistics – ensuring that sufficient supplies of food, equipment, weapons and ammunition were available for the various campaigns. Marlborough's brilliant march from Flanders to the Lower Danube in 1704, catching the French by surprise and culminating in the Battle of Blenheim, could not have

been contemplated without logistic back-up, and Marlborough's nickname among his soldiers, 'Corporal John', reflected the impact of his emphasis upon supply. But there was more to it than this; success depended on the willingness of politicians in London to release money for the purchase of supplies, as well as on the capabilities of the civilian-dominated administrative system to deliver them to the campaign area. To a significant extent, Marlborough was lucky; in addition to his rank as Captain-General (effectively Commander-in-Chief of the Army), he was also Master-General of the Ordnance, responsible for the provision of equipment and weapons. Furthermore, he enjoyed influence at Court, at least until 1710, and had a close ally in the Lord Treasurer, Lord Godolphin, enabling him to ensure the release of funds. Such a unique combination of responsibilities and political support needed to be exploited, and part of Marlborough's genius undoubtedly lay in his ability to do so. However, none of his successors was ever to enjoy so much power.

ARMY ADMINISTRATION

The reason for this was that, as the Army had emerged from the conflict between Crown and Parliament in the late 17th century, it had been subject to a series of 'checks and balances' designed to prevent its exclusive use by one side or the other. Thus, although the Crown retained the

THE JACOBITE REBELLIONS, 1689–1746

Between 1689 and 1746 a number of attempts were made by Scottish Jacobites to restore the House of Stuart to the throne of England. The first of these, led by James Graham, was defeated by a regiment of Cameronians at Dunkeld in 1689. In 1715 another Highland army, marching south from Perth, was checked by the Duke of Argyle outside Stirling, and the rebellion collapsed when the remainder of the rebels were defeated at Sheriffmuir and Preston. James Stuart (the 'Old Pretender'), son of the deposed James II, landed in Scotland when the fighting was virtually over, and returned to France a few weeks later.

French support was vital to the Jacobite cause, and in 1745, in an attempt to divert British forces from Europe, a French frigate landed Prince Charles ('Bonnie Prince Charlie' or the 'Young Pretender'), the son of James Stuart (now styled James III), in the Hebrides. The Highland clans rallied to the Prince, creating an army which seized Edinburgh in September 1745 before defeating a British force, mostly of local militia, at Prestonpans. In October, the Prince crossed into England, hoping to link up with French units poised to invade from Dunkirk. The Duke of Cumberland was hastily recalled from the continent, although this did not prevent the

Jacobites from reaching Derby. However, the Highlanders were tired and the French invasion force, blockaded by the Royal Navy, was unable to move; in desperation the Jacobites retreated. A brief recovery led to another British defeat at Falkirk, but Cumberland's experienced redcoats soon retook Edinburgh (January 1746). The Highlanders fell back to Inverness, taking up positions at Culloden. There, on 16 April, Cumberland routed the Jacobites in a one-sided engagement, heralding a period of ruthless suppression of the Highland way of life. It was the last battle fought on British soil and one of the most decisive.

right to appoint all officers, it was Parliament that decided on the size of the force and on its equipment by virtue of its control of the purse strings. If the monarch was not particularly interested in military affairs – as was the case between 1702 and 1714, when Queen Mary and then Queen Anne were on the throne – it was possible for a C-in-C like Marlborough to gain considerable influence. However, once the Hanoverians took over, they insisted on a full execution of their military responsibilities. For most of the 18th century, therefore, the monarch was an active participant in the running of the Army; indeed, under the first three Georges, between 1714 and 1820, the king tended to assume the role of C-in-C during periods of peace, taking an active interest in all officer appointments and promotions and only delegating responsibility to a military man when the size of the Army precluded such close control. It has been argued that the constant shift between royal and military command, especially in the late 18th century, was one of the main reasons for administrative chaos at the beginning of major wars.

But the monarch could never act alone. From as early as the Civil War, much of the mundane work of officer promotion was done by a Secretary at War, acting, as his title suggests, as the monarch's personal secretary. He handled all correspondence and, as the 18th century progressed, acted as a link between the Army and the king, enjoying virtually unlimited access to the Royal Closet. The system worked both ways, for the king could also use the Secretary at War as a channel through which new regulations, based on ideas which came from the king himself or from his military advisers, could be passed to the Army. A Board of General Officers was set up as early as 1705–6, tasked with duties that ranged from the need for new drill regulations to overseeing the patterns of clothing worn by the various regiments. In addition there was an Adjutant-General, responsible for the discipline of the Army, and a Quartermaster-General, responsible for bil-

leting, and they too could advise the king. From about 1760, all such military officials, together with the C-in-C if one was appointed, occupied offices in the Horse Guards. Their influence varied: under a C-in-C such as the king's younger son, the Duke of Cumberland, who held the post

William Augustus, Duke of Cumberland (1721–65), son of King George II. He fought at Dettingen (1743) and Fontenoy (1745) and commanded at Culloden (1746), earning the nickname 'Butcher' for his brutal suppression of the Scots.

from 1745 until 1757, the military voice was strong, but in the absence of a C-in-C, it tended to be muted. In 1789, for example, during a period when no C-in-C existed, the Adjutant-General, Sir William Fawcett, pointed out to an officer interested in gaining royal attention, that 'as I am usually the last person who has the honour of going into the Closet, it is then generally too dark for His Majesty to be able to read any paper'.

This system was complicated by a number of factors. Chief among these was the role of Parliament, for the use of the Army as an instrument of policy, as well as its size and cost, was controlled by politicians. At the highest level, the Secretaries of State for the North and South, responsible for relations with northern and southern Europe respectively, dealt with the deployment of the Army and its commitment to campaigns. This was unaltered by the reorganization of duties and change of titles to Secretaries of State for Foreign and Home Affairs in 1782. But they rarely corresponded directly with the Army, leaving that to the War Office, headed by the Secretary at War who, despite his close association with the monarch, was invariably a serving MP. As such, he tended to be the government's spokesman in the Commons on military affairs and usually moved on when the government changed. His responsibilities included preparing the annual Estimates, seeing the latter (along with the renewal of the Mutiny Act) safely through the House, and answering queries about the Army and justifying policy. This meant, of course, that the Secretary at War was associated with both Crown and Parliament, a situation that sometimes placed him in a difficult position between two bodies with differing views. Moreover, after the Pay Office Act of 1783, which tightened control over the Paymaster-General (who was responsible for administering the cost of the Army), the Secretary at War was answerable to Parliament for the actual disbursement of the money voted in the annual Estimates.

But these arrangements did not apply to the Army as a whole. Neither the Royal Regiment of Artillery, created in 1716, nor the Military Artificers (later the Royal Engineers), created in 1787, came under the War Office, being administered by an Ordnance Board under the Master-General of the Ordnance. Military transport was not even part of the Army, being provided by civilian contractors administered by the Treasury. Of greater significance, a considerable part of the Army – 12,000 men per annum between 1699 and 1769, 15,000 per annum between 1769 and 1801 – was paid for and administered by the Irish rather than the British Parliament. This had the advantage of ensuring that a relatively strong strategic reserve existed, regardless of policies adopted in London, and it also helped to preserve the peace in Ireland, but in administrative terms it further complicated an already complex system. The Irish Establishment was subject to the orders of a Lord Lieutenant in Dublin, acting as the monarch's representative, and he had his own military staff to help him. New regulations could only be passed from the War Office in London via the Secretary of State, and even then there was no guarantee that they would be adopted. In addition, the appointment or promotion of officers in Ireland, although still subject to royal approval, was always more corrupt than in Britain, reflecting the Lord Lieutenant's need to maintain a

'friendly' ministry in Dublin by offering rewards to politicians who supported him. For much of the 18th century, the Irish Establishment was in effect a separate army, with regiments kept small so that more of them could be maintained in Ireland, outside the control of the British Parliament. This led inevitably to problems of co-ordination when regiments needed to be transferred to the British Establishment for campaigns or overseas service. When British regiments served in India, a similar problem arose, for they were paid for and administered by the East India Company, a commercial organization beyond the remit of the War Office.

OFFICERS AND REGIMENTS

Such a lack of centralized control was reflected in the organization of the units that made up the standing army. For much of the 18th century, each regiment of cavalry and infantry was seen as the personal property of the colonel who commanded it. He was responsible for providing its clothing and, until the 1730s, its weapons, from which he was expected to make a financial profit to compensate for very meagre pay provided by central funds. Although it would be wrong to presume that every colonel neglected his unit in pursuit of money, the system was wide open to abuse. Every soldier received his pay from the government, but out of this certain deductions were made which were supposed to be used for the purchase of clothing and the provision of 'necessaries' (personal equipment). Each colonel employed a civilian agent who was responsible for receiving and disbursing the money raised. If clothing could be provided for less money than was available, the profit stayed in the colonel's hands. The emphasis was therefore always on economizing, and although the Clothing Board (part of the Board of General Officers) insisted on inspecting the patterns of clothing to ensure uniformity, there was no guarantee of quality. Some units ended up being dressed in rags and, before the Ordnance Board took over the provision of arms, were equipped with non-standard muskets. Further profit to the colonels came from the pay of non-existent soldiers. Some of these were officially sanctioned before the reforms of 1783 swept them away, but others were merely unofficial gaps in the ranks maintained for personal gain. During the first half of the century, captains of companies enjoyed similar privileges, further undermining military effectiveness.

Arrangements such as these have contributed to a widely held image of 18th-century Army officers as corrupt and uncaring amateurs, but this is an injustice. Clearly, such men did exist, taking advantage of the purchase system to progress rapidly through the commissioned ranks with little thought for their profession or their soldiers. It was not unknown, for example, for an officer to receive his first commission (as a cornet in the cavalry or ensign in the Foot Guards or Foot) at a very young age and then to purchase forward to the rank of colonel without gaining any real experience: Lord George Lennox, the second son of the Duke of Richmond, for

THE WAR OF THE AUSTRIAN SUCCESSION (1740–8)

In December 1740, Frederick II of Prussia invaded the Austrian province of Silesia, hoping to exploit the weakness of the new Empress, Maria Theresa. France, Bavaria and Saxony soon joined in the attack, triggering the formation of an alliance between Austria, Britain and the United Provinces. The British government, fearful of French control of the Austrian Netherlands and aware of the threat to Hanover, despatched a force of 16,000 troops under Lord Stair to join an Allied army in Flanders.

In the spring of 1743, after lengthy preparations (during which Prussia and Austria made peace), the Allies moved east into the valley of the Main. Stair found himself heavily outnumbered, and was forced to retreat along the north bank of the river under constant French attack. On 27 June, as French columns cut the Allies off at front and rear, defeat seemed inevitable, but a rash attack by one of the French detachments close to the village of Dettingen gave Stair his chance. King George II, who had joined Stair's army, took part in the ensuing battle – the last British monarch actually to accompany his troops into action – and witnessed some hard fighting. French cavalry was repulsed by steadfast British infantry, after which the 4th, 6th and 7th Dragoons mounted a counter-attack. Under sustained, if occasionally ill-directed, fire from the infantry, the French broke and ran. It was enough to enable the Allies to escape, having lost over 2000 men killed or wounded.

In 1744, the French managed to overrun most of West Flanders without encountering a coherent Allied challenge, but in the following year a new British commander, the Duke of Cumberland, concentrated a fresh army around Brussels, with which he set out to relieve the siege of Tournai. On 11 May, the rival armies clashed near the village of Fontenoy; Austrian and Dutch assaults on the French flanks failed, but a methodical advance in the centre by British infantry managed to break through, creating a solid phalanx of soldiers which quickly attracted counter-attacks. After three hours, Cumberland was forced to order a withdrawal, conducted without panic but in the knowledge that the Allies had lost the battle. It is estimated that each army suffered about 7000 casualties.

British forces were withdrawn soon afterwards to deal with the Jacobite rebellion, and it was not until 1747 that a new campaign against the French could be mounted. It was not a success, ending in Allied defeat at Lauffeldt in the Austrian Netherlands on 2 July. In October 1748 the fighting was brought to an end by the Treaty of Aix-la-Chapelle, but it was little more than a temporary truce in the long-running conflict between Britain and France. Nevertheless, the Army had gained invaluable experience of fighting European enemies.

example, was commissioned at the age of 13 and by 1758, still only 20, was commanding the 33rd Foot as a lieutenant-colonel. Equally, officers were renowned for taking as much leave as possible, especially in peacetime and particularly if their units were in an unhealthy location such as the West Indies. But these were the exceptions rather than the rule. It has been estimated that only about a quarter of regimental officers came from families rich enough to afford accelerated promotion, leaving the rest, drawn from 'private Gentlemen without the advantage of Birth and friends', from families with a tradition of military service and even from those promoted from the ranks, to live on their pay and await opportunities. They tended to stay with their regiments, helping to establish a tradition of quiet professionalism which is often overlooked. Without them, the regimental system would never have emerged.

This does not alter the fact that the majority of officers had to purchase their commissions, and the system does require explanation, not least because, like the proprietary colonelcies, it was open to abuse. The Hanoverian monarchs disliked purchase, but were unable to end it, having inherited an already well established process; instead, they tried to control and regulate its worst excesses. By Royal Warrants in 1720 and 1722, the price of commissions was fixed and strict rules laid down that they could only be sold to officers holding the next rank down, or, in the case of a first commission, to 'Gentlemen' approved by the regimental colonel and the king. Once accepted for a first commission, the officer deposited the regulated amount with the government and, if he then wanted promotion, he paid the 'difference' between the value of his existing commission and the new one, building up an investment that would be realized when he finally retired. This was all very well, but some commissions were more desirable than others, and it was usual for officers to pay more than the regulated price to their predecessors. As no-one actually lost money, and the process as a whole avoided the need for government to pay officers' pensions, such private arrangements were usually ignored. Of more pressing concern was the abusive practice of infant purchase and, associated with it, the problem of inexperienced officers moving up the ladder. By the 1780s precise rules had been introduced, restricting the age of first commission to 16 and insisting that officers served for set times in each rank before being allowed to 'purchase forward'. Undoubtedly abuses still existed, but for most of the officer corps such regulations were welcome.

There were other ways of gaining promotion, which did not involve money. Some officers raised men for rank, recruiting a set number of soldiers during times of emergency in exchange for a commission. Arthur Wellesley

A satirical print of the mid-18th century depicting a youthful officer being restrained by an experienced sergeant. Cases of premature purchase and promotion may be found at this period, but the abuse was not widespread.

(the future Duke of Wellington), for example, gained his captaincy in this way in 1790, raising 100 men for an independent company of foot when war with Spain seemed imminent. Normally, such commissions could not then be sold, although this did not prevent the officer from purchasing the next rank up in the normal way. Other non-purchase commissions became available when an officer died in service, his purchase money then being forfeit; such commissions were offered, without payment of the 'difference', to the next senior officer in the regiment. This created a 'chain-reaction', as all promotions did, until a first commission became vacant; this was often reserved for 'deserving sergeants', who could also be promoted as quartermasters or adjutants. They rarely progressed further but did provide a leavening of experience within the regiments.

If an officer decided to retire (or had no choice because his regiment was about to be disbanded), he could either sell out – in which case he received the value of his existing commission, plus anything beyond if it was purchased by someone else – or he could go onto the 'half-pay', receiving that amount from government on the understanding that he would be available for future service if needed. During peacetime, half-pay officers were constantly searching for vacancies, pushing the non-regulated price up but ensuring that there was always a choice, often of highly experienced men. Despite its drawbacks, the system seemed to work.

THE SOLDIERS

It would be difficult to reach such an optimistic conclusion in terms of the ordinary soldiers. No-one could doubt their bravery in battle, but for much of the 18th century the Army was desperate for recruits and was forced to make do with men of limited potential. Recruiting parties, normally consisting of an officer, a couple of non-

British soldiers (left) and Hanoverian troops (right) at the time of the American War of Independence, 1775–83; a light dragoon is in the background. British use of German regiments was a feature of the 18th century.

commissioned officers (NCOs) and a drummer, scoured the countryside for men. Their job was not easy. Neither Catholics nor Non-Conformists were allowed to enlist, which excluded a substantial proportion of the population of Ireland, later such an important source of recruits. The offer of a military career was hardly attractive to any except the most desperate members of society. Harsh discipline, poor pay and living conditions and the prospect of an early death either through disease or in battle, could only be counteracted by promises of glory, foreign travel and loot, which appealed to few beyond the most gullible. Some men undoubtedly joined because they wanted to be soldiers, and the existence of good NCOs in many regiments clearly indicates that a worthwhile career was possible, but they tended to be the exception. As Lieutenant-Colonel John Blackadder of the 26th Foot pointed out in the early part of the century, the Army was composed principally of 'a parcel of mercenary, fawning, lewd dissipated creatures, the dregs and scum of mankind'. It is a picture of the 18th-century British soldier that has endured to the present day.

It has been estimated that, between about 1750 and 1795, regiments needed to recruit 1.5 per cent of their strength every month in peacetime and 2.1 per cent in wartime, just to replace men lost through death, desertion or drafting. Sometimes the problem became so acute that special Press Acts were passed by Parliament to allow Justices of the Peace and local Constables to 'press' (force

into service) 'all such able-bodied, idle, and disorderly persons who cannot upon examination prove themselves able to exercise and industriously follow some lawful trade or employment'. Such Acts were in force in 1704–12, 1745–6, 1755–7 and 1778–9, coinciding with periods of major war, and it was not unknown for these to be supported by offers of short-term enlistment (usually for three years or the duration of the conflict) in an effort to attract men who would otherwise be unlikely to serve. The latter ploy could backfire, as in 1783–4 at the end of the American War of Independence, when soldiers enlisted for 'the duration' mutinied because they thought that the government was reneging on its promise. At other times, convicted criminals such as insolvent debtors could be released from gaol if they agreed to enter the Army, and on very rare occasions capital sentences could be commuted to life-time military service. Criminals were not welcomed by many regiments. Indeed, in 1787 two new battalions of the 60th Foot were raised specifically as penal units, to be stationed permanently in the Leeward Islands in the Caribbean. Most of the men sent out to these battalions were soldiers sentenced by military courts-martial, but a small number came from civilian gaols.

Recruits from sources such as these were never enough to fill the ranks. The bulk of the men had to be raised by voluntary enlistment, accepting a cash bounty offered by the recruiting parties and agreeing to serve for life (in effect, about 20 years). Men with a trade or settled

THE SEVEN YEARS WAR IN EUROPE (1756–63)

Between 1748 and 1756 a 'diplomatic revolution' took place in Europe, which saw France and Austria, with some support from Russia, Sweden and Saxony, align themselves against Frederick II of Prussia. Under threat of being surrounded, he made a pre-emptive strike into Saxony in 1756, following it up in 1757 with an advance into Bohemia. As Prussia's enemies recovered and closed in, Frederick turned to Britain for help. An 'Army of Observation' of Hessian, Prussian and Hanoverian troops commanded by the Duke of Cumberland was deployed to western Germany where, on 26 July 1757, they encountered a French invading force at Hastenbeck. Cumberland was defeated and forced to sign the Convention of Kloster Zeven on 8 September, by which he agreed to disband his force.

The London government, under William Pitt the Elder, refused to accept the terms of the Convention and sent British troops to reinforce the remains of Cumberland's army,

now under the command of Ferdinand of Brunswick. They arrived at Emden in August 1758, but it was nearly a year before they did any fighting. In April 1759 Ferdinand was defeated at Bergen, near Frankfurt, after which he fell back northwards, leaving the French under the Marquis of Contades to seize a supply base at Minden on the banks of the River Weser. Ferdinand refused to assault what appeared to be an impregnable French position; instead, he manoeuvred his Anglo-German army to tempt Contades out. On 1 August 1759, he succeeded, but the battle did not go according to plan. A brigade of British and Hanoverian infantry, misinterpreting its orders, launched a frontal assault on French cavalry in the centre and, against all odds, held firm when counter-attacked. Despite bitter hand-to-hand fighting, the infantry, supported by light artillery, then pressed forward; in Contades' own words, 'eight or ten battalions on an open heath [had] defeated sixty-one French squad-

rons'. It was a remarkable achievement, but it was not exploited, the Allied cavalry under Lord George Sackville failing to move forward to deliver the *coup de grâce*. In the aftermath of the battle, British infantry picked roses to wear in their caps (*see box*, p.40), while the cavalry appeared 'in mournful silence, as if covered in shame'. Sackville was recalled to Britain. As Lord George Germain he later became Secretary of State for the Americas.

The cavalry restored their reputation at Emsdorf and Warburg in 1760 – it was in the latter action that the Marquis of Granby, leading the charge, lost his wig and went at the enemy 'bald-headed' – but the French advance into Brunswick and Hanover could not be halted. Ferdinand managed to mount counter-attacks in 1761 and 1762, during which British regiments fought at Kloster Kamp, Vellinghausen and Wilhelmstahl, but exhaustion was setting in on both sides. The war ended in February 1763 with the Peace of Paris.

Regimental Tradition:

MINDEN DAY

Six British battalions took part in the epic battle against French cavalry at Minden: the 12th, 20th, 23rd, 25th, 37th and 51st Foot (later the Suffolk Regiment, Lancashire Fusiliers, Royal Welch Fusiliers, King's Own Scottish Borderers, 1st Battalion Royal Hampshire Regiment and 1st Battalion King's Own Yorkshire Light Infantry respectively). With the exception of the Royal Welch Fusiliers, all continued to celebrate the anniversary of the battle by wearing roses in their hats on 1 August every year. In the Lancashire Fusiliers, for example, the tradition was for every man to wear red and yellow roses, while in the Officers' Mess any officer who had not yet done so was expected to eat a rose, handed to him in a silver finger bowl filled with champagne.

home life were unlikely to be attracted and, as recruits had to appear before a magistrate within 48 hours to swear that they were true volunteers, the chances of trickery by recruiters were limited. This did not prevent recruiting sergeants from occasionally pressing the 'King's Shilling' into the hands of men deliberately made drunk, and then persuading them when sober that they had to serve. But in most cases recruits were men who were desperate to escape civilian life, usually because of a lack of employment. The promise of a uniform, food and shelter could be enough to sway the balance.

Once enlisted, the soldier was usually sent straight to his regiment, if it was stationed in Britain, or to a depot to await transport abroad. There he was inspected to see that he was of the stipulated height (usually 5ft 4in or more) and was not suffering from physical defects that might limit his capabilities. If accepted, he would then begin his training; if rejected, he would be given money to carry him back to his place of enlistment. The latter arrangement could be abused – some men made a career of enlisting in different regiments for the bounty in the full knowledge that they were unfit – and during wartime the standards were allowed to slip. In most cases, if the recruit could stand and carry a musket, he was retained.

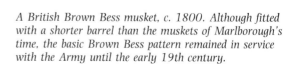

A British Brown Bess musket, c. 1800. Although fitted with a shorter barrel than the muskets of Marlborough's time, the basic Brown Bess pattern remained in service with the Army until the early 19th century.

British infantry, wearing roses in their tricorn hats, stand firm against a French cavalry attack at the Battle of Minden, 1 August 1759 (above). The painting by A. Caton Woodville gives a good impression of the confusion of battle.

But retention was a major problem in its own right. Despite the cash bounty given on enlistment, soldiers invariably found themselves in debt from the very beginning of their service, since deductions were made from their meagre pay (eightpence a day to a private in the infantry) to provide them with clothing, 'necessaries' and food. As the initial deductions were insufficient for these purposes, the difference had to be 'lent' to the soldiers by the regiment, creating a debt that was never fully repaid. In addition, the soldiers soon found that they were subject

to military discipline, often for seemingly minor offences, and that they were part of a force that was universally unpopular. In desperation, many men deserted at the first opportunity, further exacerbating the manpower problem. The regiments then had to replace the soldier and accept that the money spent on him so far had been wasted. Even if regiments did manage to fill their ranks, they rarely retained the recruits, losing some to disease and others to the official policy of drafting – that is, taking men from one regiment to complete another that was about to go abroad, where recruiting would be more difficult. In 1755, for example, when the 44th and 48th Foot were about to embark in Ireland for active service, they received 256 drafts from other units remaining behind, leaving those units decimated and temporarily unfit for duty.

THE ROLES OF THE ARMY

Having joined a regiment, the recruit could find himself stationed in a variety of locations, reflecting the diversity of roles that the Army was expected to perform. For much of the 18th century, units were retained in Britain to defend the country against external threat and to provide

Personality Profile:

JAMES WOLFE (1727–59)

Born at Westerham in Kent, James Wolfe followed his father into the Army, fighting at the Battle of Dettingen as Adjutant to the 12th Foot when only 17 years old. He went on to see further action against the Jacobites in 1746 and was present at Culloden. During the early stages of the Seven Years War he commanded a brigade in Amherst's expedition to seize Louisburg (1758) and was then given command of the force tasked to take Quebec. His surprise attack against the fortress on 12–13 September 1759 paved the way for a British takeover of Canada, but Wolfe did not live to see the results. Badly wounded in the battle on 13 September, he died soon afterwards. He was only 32 years old.

THE CAPTURE OF QUEBEC

Once Lord Amherst had captured the French fortress at Louisburg, on Cape Breton Island, in 1758, the British were able to push up the River St Lawrence into Canada. Their way was blocked at Quebec, where a garrison of about 5000 French troops under the Marquis of Montcalm occupied seemingly impregnable positions. In 1759 a British force of some 3000 men under Major-General James Wolfe entered the St Lawrence on board Royal Navy ships, aiming to take Quebec.

After consultations with his officers, Wolfe decided on a surprise attack, not on Quebec itself but further upstream, with the intention of taking the fortress from the landward side. On the night of 12–13 September, with oars muffled, the British troops rowed past French sentries and guard-boats at Quebec and then scrambled up a little-known path onto the Plains of Abraham. When dawn broke, Montcalm found himself at a disadvantage, with his troops poorly de-ployed. Although the ensuing battle was hard-fought, it lasted no more than 15 minutes. In the process Montcalm was killed and Wolfe was mortally wounded. With Quebec secure, the British were able to take Montreal and later the whole of Canada for the Crown.

The death of General James Wolfe at Quebec, 13 September 1759, at the moment of his greatest achievement.

a back-up to civilian authorities involved in policing or collecting revenue – duties that were much the same in Ireland. In both cases, the regiments could also be used as a strategic reserve, available to reinforce colonial garrisons such as those in Gibraltar, Minorca, the West Indies and North America, or to create an expeditionary force for service on the continent of Europe, should war break out. It was not unknown for a regiment to be sent to the colonies and left to rot – the 38th Foot, for example, served in the West Indies from 1706 until 1765 – but from 1749, during peacetime at least, attempts were made to rotate units on a set pattern. Each year, a number of regiments would move from Britain to Ireland, replacing others sent out to colonial garrisons to relieve units which would then return to Britain. The aim was to avoid regiments spending too long in unhealthy climates – the West Indies, for instance, were renowned for wiping out large numbers of men through disease. However, the constant battle to ensure that all three roles – domestic policing, colonial protection and possible European commitment – were satisfied, suggested that the Army was often being asked to do too much. In peacetime it was kept deliberately small by politicians fearful of its power and aware of its cost; in wartime, particularly if campaigns took place in Europe as well as the colonies, it was overstretched – a situation exacerbated by the need to expand its size rapidly.

The anti-Catholic riots in London, June 1780, in a painting by Seymour Lucas. The disturbances, which lasted a fortnight, are usually known as the Gordon Riots after their main instigator, Lord George Gordon. Anti-riot duty was a frequent Army task in the 18th century.

DOMESTIC DUTIES

Britain was clearly the most attractive station, but this does not mean that the regiments there had nothing to do. In 1715 and 1745–6, they had to fight against Jacobites intent on restoring the Stuarts to the throne (*see box*, p.34) and, once the Highland clans had been defeated at Culloden in April 1746, their job was to ensure that Scotland remained quiet – a policy involving a variety of measures from road-building to outright repression. Similarly, during the wars against France and Spain, regiments were needed to defend the coasts in case of invasion, something which the militia, despite being preferred by Parliament to a standing army, proved incapable of doing. But these were exceptional tasks that had the advantage of a modicum of popular support; for most of the time the Army in Britain was deployed in ways that did little to endear it to the public.

Soldiers rarely lived in barracks, being quartered among the people in public houses, where reputations for hard drinking and licentiousness were quickly and unavoidably made. This alienated them from the more respectable elements of society, while their duties in aid of the civil power made them unpopular among their own class. If, for example, a riot occurred and the local magistrates could not cope, they usually called in military forces to restore law and order. The process was complex

– the magistrates had to petition the Secretary of State who, if he agreed to the request, authorized the Secretary at War to order the troops to the affected area – but in the absence of a civilian police force there was no real alternative. Rioting was almost a way of life among some sectors of 18th-century society, and the incidence of trouble was high, ranging from the Glasgow Riots of 1725 to the anti-Catholic Gordon Riots of 1780. According to one estimate, between 1740 and 1775 alone there were 159 major disturbances in England, many of which required military intervention. A squadron of Dragoons or a company of Foot could disperse a crowd by charging at it with swords drawn or by firing a musket volley in its direction, but such actions ensured that in the eyes of the people the Army was little more than an instrument of state repression. When it is added that regiments, usually of cavalry, were constantly patrolling the coasts on the look-out for smugglers, it may be appreciated why the Army was not a popular organization.

Similar duties were carried out by units in Ireland (although until Wolfe Tone's rebellion of 1798 the country was relatively quiet), and in both the West Indies and North America when the need arose. Slave revolts in the Caribbean had to be put down and, in America, it was the actions of British regiments at Concord in 1775, searching for illegal arms, that helped to trigger the Revolution. But regiments in the colonies were there primarily to provide protection against external attack, fighting campaigns to preserve or extend British influence and, in the process, gaining experience in a wide variety of climates and terrain.

COLONIAL WARS

With the sudden expansion of British overseas territory by the Treaty of Utrecht in 1713, it was inevitable that clashes would occur with the French and Spanish in areas as diverse as North America, India, the West Indies and the Mediterranean. During periods of peace, such locations did not always require permanent garrisons. However, as the 18th century progressed, crises in the colonies tended to occur despite the best efforts of European diplomacy, and required the presence of troops. In North America before 1763, French settlers to the north and west of New England conducted spasmodic campaigns to prevent British expansion. The fighting, carried out by locally raised militia and Indian units, backed by only a few regular regiments, took place in forested and hilly terrain around the Great Lakes, where control of isolated forts was seen as vital. Such operations were beset by problems of logistics and movement, while the fighting often degenerated into guerrilla-style ambushes. Nor did the British always prevail: in July 1755 a mixed force of regulars and militia under Major-General Edward Braddock, advancing to take Fort Duquesne to the south of Lake Erie, was ambushed by French and Indian troops on the Monongahela River. Over 900 British soldiers, including Braddock, were killed; among the survivors was Colonel George Washington of the Virginia Militia.

Probing attacks such as this continued into the Seven Years War (1756–63; *see box*, p.39), persuading the British to concentrate on destroying French influence in North America once and for all. The seizure of Louisburg on Cape Breton Island in 1758, carried out by 12,000 troops under Lord Amherst, opened the route down the St Lawrence River to the French strongholds at Quebec and Montreal. A year later, James Wolfe took Quebec (*see box*, p.42), rendering the French position untenable, and at the Treaty of Paris in 1763 New France (Canada) was ceded to the British. But this was not the end of the Army's involvement. Once North America was secure, local settlers began to resent a continued military presence and attempts by the London Parliament to impose taxes to pay for it. Between 1775 and 1783, British troops had to fight a bitter war against the American rebels, fighting not only conventional set-piece battles such as Bunker Hill (17 June 1775) and Princeton (3 January 1777), but also small-scale engagements against rebel forces prepared to use their knowledge of terrain to conduct hit-and-run attacks (*see box*, p.46).

The fact that the British lost the American War, accepting the independence of the United States in 1783 after being outmanoeuvred and forced to surrender at both Saratoga (17 October 1777) and Yorktown (19 October 1781), highlighted the problems of fighting colonial wars in the 18th century. As long as the enemy

The British attack on American rebel positions at Bunker Hill (Breed's Hill) on the Charlestown Peninsula, 17 June 1775, depicted in a contemporary print. A British battery in Boston has set fire to Charlestown.

THE BRITISH IN INDIA, 1740–61

By the middle of the 18th century, France and Britain were vying for commercial and strategic influence in India, particularly in the Carnatic in the south and Bengal in the north-east. British interests, represented by the Honourable East India Company with trading stations at Bombay, Madras and Calcutta, had been steadily undermined since the 1670s, when a French company had built rival stations at Pondicherry, 150 miles south of Madras, and Chandernagore, close to Calcutta. In the 1740s, under Governor Dupleix, it was the French who seemed to have gained the upper hand. During the War of the Austrian Succession, Dupleix seized Madras, and although it was handed back in 1748 in the Treaty of Aix-la-Chapelle, British weakness was apparent.

Despite peace in Europe between 1748 and 1756, fighting continued in India. In the process, the East India Company's armed forces were reorganized by John Stringer Lawrence and the first British regular unit, the 39th Foot, was committed; these improvements allowed Lawrence to secure the Carnatic by the mid-1750s, but the French soon shifted their emphasis to Bengal, capturing Fort William, Calcutta, in 1756. A small British-Indian force under Robert Clive sailed from Madras in October, recapturing the fort three months later.

Clive advanced to seize Chandernagore before pushing on against the local Indian ruler, Surajah Dowla. By 22 June 1757, Clive's force of 750 European and 2500 Indian troops were facing Surajah's army of 50,000 men just north of Plassey on the River Cossimbazar. Deploying his men in and around an orchard, Clive brought up his artillery to engage the enemy guns and see off a cavalry charge. A massed infantry attack was held by the steady musketry of the British-Indian troops, who then put in a charge of their own. The enemy broke and ran. At a cost of 60 casualties, Clive had cleared Bengal of all opposition. Four years later, after operations initially led by Lawrence and then by Eyre Coote, the Carnatic was similarly cleared. When Pondicherry surrendered on 16 January 1761, French power in India came to an end.

Robert, Lord Clive (1725–74). After his victories at Arcot (1751) and Plassey (1757), he was appointed Governor of Bengal (1757–60 and 1764–7), ensuring a firm imposition of British rule by the East India Company.

THE AMERICAN WAR OF INDEPENDENCE (1775–83)

Resentment among American colonists at British policies of taxation and trade broke into open rebellion on 19 April 1775, with an engagement between local militia and British regulars at Lexington, 20 miles from Boston. The Americans tried to exploit the surprise they had achieved by laying siege to Boston. The British won a costly victory at Bunker Hill (more accurately Breed's Hill) on the Charlestown Peninsula on 17 June, but their commander, Major-General William Howe, was in an untenable position. On 13 April 1776, he evacuated the city, moving north to regroup.

In July Howe arrived off New York, already held by American forces under George Washington, and on 22 August he landed on Long Island, forcing the rebels to pull back across Manhattan Island. Washington tried to make a stand at Harlem Heights and at White

THE AMERICAN WAR OF INDEPENDENCE 1775-83

Quebec

QUEBEC

St Lawrence

Montreal

Lake Champlain

MAINE (Part of MASS.)

Lake Ontario

Lake Huron

Fort Ticonderoga

SARATOGA (1777)

BEMIS HEIGHTS (1777)

NEW HAMPSHIRE

Hudson

Niagara

Buffalo

FREEMAN'S FARM (1777)

MASS.

BUNKER HILL (1775)

Boston

LEXINGTON (1775)

Detroit

Lake Erie

PRINCETON (1777)

CONN.

R.I.

NEW YORK

PENNSYLVANIA

VALLEY FORGE (1777-8)

NEW YORK (1776)

NEW JERSEY

TRENTON (1776)

BRANDYWINE CREEK (1777)

Philadelphia

Ohio

MARYLAND

DELAWARE

Appalachians

VIRGINIA

YORKTOWN (1781)

GUILFORD COURT HOUSE (1781)

NORTH CAROLINA

COWPENS (1781)

CAMDEN (1780)

SOUTH CAROLINA

Savannah

CHARLESTON (1780)

Augusta

GEORGIA

SAVANNAH (1779)

- - - - State Borders

✕ Battle sites

0   Miles   200

N

Plains, but Howe outmanoeuvred him on both occasions before taking up winter quarters in New York. Washington had better luck later in the year when he crossed the River Delaware to face Lord Cornwallis in New Jersey, defeating a Hessian force at Trenton (26 December 1776) and a British detachment at Princeton (3 January 1777). Cornwallis retired to Brunswick (New Jersey) for the winter.

The British campaign in 1777 was ambitious. While Howe advanced to threaten Philadelphia, General Sir John Burgoyne moved south from Montreal towards Albany (New York State), aiming to split New England from the other colonies. Howe succeeded, defeating an American force at Brandywine Creek in September and forcing Washington to with-

draw to winter quarters at Valley Forge; but Burgoyne's advance turned into disaster, with defeats at Freeman's Farm (19 September) and then at Bemis Heights (7 October). Ten days later, at Saratoga, Burgoyne surrendered his remaining 5700 men to an overwhelming American force. This defeat helped to persuade the French to enter the war on the side of the Americans, widening the conflict considerably.

The British changed their strategy in 1778. General Sir Henry Clinton, Howe's successor, evacuated Philadelphia and concentrated his forces around New York, while Cornwallis led an invasion of the southern colonies. By April 1780 the British had taken Savannah and Charleston; they went on to defeat an American force at Camden (16 August 1780) and advanced

north into Virginia. Unfortunately for Cornwallis, he then encountered two fresh American armies, commanded by Baron Steuben and the Marquis de Lafayette respectively. He withdrew to the port of Yorktown, hoping to be supported by the Royal Navy, but the arrival of a French fleet in Chesapeake Bay left him no choice but to surrender on 19 October 1781. Although a state of war was to exist until September 1783, the fighting was effectively over.

Lord Cornwallis offers his sword in surrender to George Washington at Yorktown, 19 October 1781. The arrival of a French fleet in Chesapeake Bay, shown in the background, was a crucial factor in the British defeat.

was relatively unsophisticated and capable of little beyond guerrilla warfare, existing garrisons, backed by local militias, could just about cope. But when more conventional operations became necessary, the provision of extra regiments and supplies proved extremely difficult. In 1775, the British Army was not large, having been reduced at the end of the Seven Years War 12 years earlier, and an immediate reserve, capable of commitment to North America, did not exist. Even when reinforcements had been raised – not least by recruiting German mercenaries – the theatre of war remained more than 3000 miles away, leading to problems of communication and, especially, resupply. Throughout the conflict, British efforts were characterized by a lack of command co-ordination, a shortage of troops and a failure of logistics. The soldiers themselves fought well, but could do little in the face of such weaknesses. Their problems were exacerbated in 1778, when France joined the war on the side of the Americans. This marked the beginning of an escalation of military commitment that was eventually to see Britain fighting the Spanish and Dutch as well, necessitating more widespread campaigns.

Some of these were fought in the West Indies, where British regiments had helped to carve out a valuable empire earlier in the century, principally by seizing small islands while French, Dutch or Spanish attention was diverted by events in Europe. Security in the Caribbean depended on seapower – all military operations involved amphibious attacks or the defence of isolated garrisons that the Navy kept supplied. Given the high incidence of disease, notably yellow fever, in the region, the British always faced a dilemma over manpower. This was highlighted in 1783 when General Henry Seymour Conway, C-in-C of the Army, engaged in long arguments with his political masters over peacetime deployment. If large numbers of units were maintained permanently in the West Indies, they would soon be decimated by disease; if only small garrisons were maintained, they might well be destroyed in the event of future war before reinforcements could be shipped out. By the early 1790s it had been decided that the permanent garrisons should be large enough to withstand attack; a sensible policy in strategic terms, but one that condemned British soldiers to an unhealthy and unpopular posting.

Equally unpopular was India, where a combination of disease and constant fighting led many soldiers to imagine that, once committed, they would never return. Although most of the campaigns on the sub-continent, fought for the control of areas around Bombay, Madras and Bengal, were conducted by troops raised and paid for by the East India Company, regular British units did have to be used occasionally. The first was the 39th Foot, which fought under Robert Clive at the Battle of Plassey in 1757 (see box, p.45), and by the 1780s permanent deployments were taking place. Indeed, it was the prospect of being sent to India that led the 77th Highlanders to mutiny in Portsmouth in 1783.

Finally, after the Treaty of Utrecht in 1713 British regiments had to be stationed in the Mediterranean, where garrison duty at Gibraltar and Minorca proved to be comparatively healthy but tedious. Lack of space meant that soldiers had little opportunity for training (and even less for desertion). The effects of this on morale may help

to explain the relative ease with which the French were able to capture Minorca in 1756 and again, with Spanish aid, in 1782, after which it was returned to Spain. Similar attacks on Gibraltar were fought off, most notably during the 'Great Siege' of 1779–83 (see box, p.49), but it was yet another location that needed to be constantly defended. Throughout the 18th century, colonial protection alone was enough to keep the Army busy, but it was not the only overseas duty that had to be carried out.

EUROPEAN COMMITMENT

British involvement in the affairs of Europe was unavoidable. When William III was on the throne, his interests lay primarily in his home country of the United Provinces and, as has been noted already, he regarded the English Army as little more than a welcome reinforcement to Dutch units fighting the French. Admittedly, it was always in British interests to ensure that the Dutch coast was not controlled by an enemy, particularly if that enemy had naval power, but it could be argued (as indeed it was by some British politicians) that conflicts such as the Nine Years War were fought in pursuit of Dutch rather than British policies. A similar situation arose after 1714, when the Elector of Hanover, great-grandson of James I through the Protestant line, assumed the British throne as George I, for his interests, and those of his immediate successors George II and George III, lay as much in northern Germany as in Britain. Thus, whenever enemy states threatened Hanover, British troops tended to be deployed to defend it. During both the War of the Austrian Succession (1740–8; see p.36) and the Seven Years War (1756–63; see p.39), substantial British forces were committed to the continent, principally to protect Hanover against the French.

It was during these campaigns that the reputation of the British Army, already established under Marlborough,

BRITISH BATTLES IN EUROPE 1743-60

THE SIEGE OF GIBRALTAR (1779–83)

On 12 April 1779 an anti-British alliance was signed between France and Spain; by 21 June Spanish forces had laid siege to Gibraltar, hoping to take advantage of British weakness to regain the territory. The Gibraltar garrison, commanded by General George Augustus Eliott (later Lord Heathfield), comprised five British and three Hanoverian battalions of Foot, plus artillery and engineers – a total of 5382 men. They occupied an area of about three miles by three-quarters of a mile, manning gun positions which contained 452 cannon, 70 mortars and 28 howitzers, with 100 guns in reserve. Although four more British battalions were landed in 1780 and 1782 by blockade-breaking naval convoys, the garrison never exceeded 7200 men. Against them, by 1782 the French and Spanish had mustered nearly 40,000 troops.

Yet the garrison did not surrender. As early as 12 September 1779 Eliott showed his resolve by ordering a heavy bombardment of enemy lines, and on 26–27 November 1781 he went further by despatching about a third of his force to raid Franco-Spanish gun positions. Ten months later, a sustained British artillery barrage using red-hot shot managed to disrupt an enemy attempt to attack Gibraltar from floating gun-batteries. When hostilities ended in early 1783, the survival of Gibraltar was one of the few victories that Britain could claim in the generally disastrous war of 1775–83.

was confirmed in the eyes of other European powers. It was not a process that always ran smoothly. At the Battle of Dettingen (27 June 1743), for example, it was generally held that, although the French were routed, British infantry had displayed signs of poor fire discipline, and the cavalry had been ill-coordinated. But the ability of British troops to withstand the shock of battle (their first in Europe since Marlborough's time) was apparent. This was reinforced at the Battle of Fontenoy (11 May 1745), when British regiments shattered the centre of the French line and then stood firm for nearly three hours under sustained counter-attack, before withdrawing in good order. A similar feat at the Battle of Minden (1 August 1759; *see* pp.40–1), although spoilt by a failure of the British cavalry under Lord George Sackville to pursue the broken enemy, led many to believe that British infantry were among the best in the world. Despite the harshness of military life, and the poor quality of many recruits, the British soldier, displaying characteristics of bravery and resolution, fought in some memorable engagements.

But the fact remains that European commitment was expensive in terms of men and money, and this led to a reluctance among British politicians to lay permanent emphasis on the role. During periods of peace, the Army was reduced, often quite drastically – in 1763, at the end of the Seven Years War, an army of nearly 200,000 men was cut to 45,000 virtually overnight – and no garrisons were maintained on the continent. This meant that training for European war was never continuous, and regiments were forced to relearn tactical lessons every time a new conflict began – a process made infinitely more difficult as it coincided with the disruption caused by sudden expansion to the size of the Army. Furthermore, British politicians preferred to support garrisons and campaigns in the colonies, where profits could be gained for relatively small investment. As the 18th century progressed, there emerged what became known as a 'Blue-Water Strategy', involving tying enemy forces down in Europe using allied armies while seizing islands in the West Indies or trading stations in India. This was one possible answer to the problem of overstretch, but as long as Britain had interests in Europe, whether political or strategic, it was not one that could be exclusively pursued. By the 1790s, as Britain faced the threat of an ideological conflict with Revolutionary France, the Army was still expected to satisfy all three of its roles – domestic defence, colonial protection and European commitment – during periods of war. It would take time and harsh experience to acquire this capability.

. . . .

CHAPTER THREE

THE REVOLUTIONARY AND NAPOLEONIC WARS (1793–1815)

·····························

THE ARMY IN 1793

IT HAS for long been argued that the British Army in 1793 was in a parlous state, short of recruits, badly officered and appallingly administered by time-serving politicians. In more recent years, however, this view has been challenged. The Army may have been small – just over 50,000 effective soldiers – but it was up to strength; its internal management, especially in terms of finance, had been steadily improved; and its officers were, on the whole, eager to serve. Moreover, in line with the accepted British policies of the time, the Army was deployed to reflect a balance between home defence, colonial protection and possible European commitment, with a discernible emphasis on the overseas garrisons. In the event of a future war, it was to be expected that the strategy would be one of colonial expansion and limited European involvement, following a trend that had developed throughout the 18th century. Finally, despite continued problems of training consistency in an age when the regimental colonels were still seen as the proprietors of their units and allowed a certain degree of freedom, there was evidence that new training doctrines were being considered. The adoption in the early 1790s of Colonel David Dundas' *Principles of Military Movements* as a source of infantry

— RAISING A REGIMENT – THE 92ND (GORDON) HIGHLANDERS —

On 10 February 1794 the Duke of Gordon was authorized to raise a regiment of Highlanders from his extensive estates in Scotland. His son, the Marquis of Huntly – then serving in the 3rd (Scots) Guards – was given command and officer commissions were granted to a variety of gentlemen, many with previous military experience, in exchange for raising stipulated numbers of recruits. The Duke of Gordon, after whom the regiment would be named, used his influence as clan chief to ensure that men were provided, although he was competing with the newly raised 79th (Cameron) Highlanders and his own Gordon (or North) Fencibles, the latter created in 1793 for home service only. In an effort to persuade men to enlist, the Duchess of Gordon, a renowned beauty, dressed in Highland garb and rode round the country fairs, principally in Inverness-shire, offering a kiss and a guinea to those who agreed. One story told of a 'young blacksmith, remarkable for his strength and good looks' who accepted the kiss and the guinea, 'but to show it was not the gold that tempted him, tossed the guinea among the crowd'.

The regiment was embodied on 24 June 1794 at Aberdeen, taking its place in the Army as the 100th Foot. In July it was transported to Southampton and then, in September, to Gibraltar, by which time it comprised 29 officers, 29 sergeants and 748 rank and file, the vast majority of whom were Highlanders in both language and dress. After service in Corsica and Ireland, the regiment was renumbered the 92nd (Highland) Foot in October 1798, but was already widely known as the Gordon Highlanders.

training common to all battalions represented a significant shift towards centralized control.

But it would be naive to presume that the Army was ready to face a major war in 1793. The 18th-century pattern of peace-time parsimony had not altered in the aftermath of the American War of Independence, meaning that a fairly rapid expansion would be necessary once a new war began, while the similar pattern of political control, epitomized by the failure to appoint a Commander-in-Chief during periods of peace, condemned the Army to a degree of confusion and chaos as that expansion took place. In addition, the Army's confidence had taken a hard knock during the American War, and if it proved necessary to commit British troops to conventional operations in Europe, their experience of such operations was poor – their last battle against a European army had been more than 30 years ago. A balanced assessment of the Army's state in 1793 would therefore seem to be that it was by no means as weak as historians have made out, but that it was geared to peace-time duties and would have to go through a traumatic period of expansion and change if it was to face its enemies on the continent of Europe.

THE NEW WAR

This became apparent as the threat from Revolutionary France emerged in 1792–3. Although Britain's Prime Minister, William Pitt, remained aloof from the European coalition that attacked France in 1792, he was aware of the dangers inherent in a revolution that preached liberty, equality and fraternity as well as 'hatred against kings', particularly when the latter sentiment was manifested in the trial of Louis XVI. Indeed, when the French king was publicly executed in January 1793, it sent a shiver through the royal courts of Europe and ensured renewed opposition to the spread of revolutionary ideology. But the real threat was a more traditional one, for when French forces started massing against the Austrian Netherlands with the intention of seizing the coastline directly opposite England, Pitt had little choice but to prepare for war. The fact that he was pre-empted by a French declaration of hostilities against both Britain and the Netherlands on 1 February 1793 merely confirmed the danger.

The effects of this on the Army were predictable. Even before the war began, preliminary moves in the shift from a peacetime to a wartime administration had been made, with the appointment of Lord Amherst as C-in-C on 30 January 1793. Unfortunately, he was 76 years old at the time and, having been out of touch with military affairs since 1782, was ill-suited to the task of preparing the Army for war. He was not to be replaced until February 1795, by which time a series of disasters had beset the Army, both in Europe and the West Indies. Amherst cannot be held solely to blame, however, for Pitt continued to exercise control over strategy, aided by his Secretaries of State for Home and Foreign Affairs, Henry Dundas and William Grenville respectively. This triumvirate of advisers to the king proved to be incapable of

'The French Invasion; or John Bull, bombarding the Bum-Boats'. A James Gillray cartoon of November 1793 sums up the prevailing attitude to war with France. The invasion threat was minimal at the time.

reacting to the new style of warfare that emerged in France to defend the Revolution. Thus, although Pitt's plans for the commitment of a relatively small force to aid the Dutch merely followed accepted British strategy, the Army came up against ideologically inspired French troops who were raised by conscription (the *levée en masse*) and prepared to absorb enormous casualties in unsophisticated but overwhelming advances. By comparison, the British Army was still dependent on volunteers (*see box*, p.50), and although an expansion was ordered in 1793, it could never hope to match the numbers being raised by its enemy. In common with other 18th-century European armies, that of Britain was about to be overwhelmed by the sheer size and force of a fully mobilized France.

THE CAMPAIGN IN FLANDERS 1793–5

The decision to send a detachment of Foot Guards to Holland was made on 16 February 1793, in response to a French attack from the direction of Antwerp. The Duke of York, George III's second son, was appointed to command the expeditionary force, and a total of just over 6500 men embarked at Greenwich nine days later. By then, the Dutch had been forced back beyond Breda and were desperate for help. York could do little, for although his British troops landed at Helvoetsluys in reasonable order, his instructions were vague and a promised reinforcement of 13,000 Hanoverian and 8000 Hessian troops had not yet materialized. Moreover, the Allied command chain was chaotic and it was not until 1 March, when an Austrian force suddenly attacked the French from across the River Meuse, that a coalition army began to emerge under the overall command of Prince Josias of Coburg-Saalfeld. The French pulled back, abandoning Antwerp and Brussels.

This opened up the possibility of an Allied assault into France itself, but the opportunity was wasted. Instead of initiating a swift attack, Coburg insisted on conducting a ponderous advance, laying siege to border fortresses according to the traditions of 18th-century warfare. York, reinforced by a brigade comprising the 14th, 37th and 53rd Foot, was directed to concentrate his army in support of Coburg, preparatory to an attack on Valenciennes. This began in May and, by all accounts, the British contingent did well, capturing Famars Camp and contributing in no small measure to the seizure of Valenciennes on 28 July. But York was under orders from London to proceed to Dunkirk, regarded as an important objective in terms of maintaining free passage through the Straits of Dover. The British, with Austrian and Hanoverian units in support, reached Dunkirk on 24 August, pushing the French back behind inadequate defences. Unfortunately, York lacked the heavy artillery required to conduct a siege and, after an Austrian setback at Hondschoote on 8 September, he had to retreat. A month later, the main Austrian army was defeated at Wattignies, forcing York back through Ypres and Nieuport to winter quarters in Ostend.

The 1793 campaign was therefore less than successful, for although individual British units did well, a number of problems had emerged, indicating the unsuit-

First-Hand Account:
THE RETREAT INTO GERMANY, 1794–5

'On the common, about half a mile off the high road, we discovered a baggage cart, with a team of five horses, apparently in great distress; I galloped towards the spot, and found the poor animals were stiff, but not dead; the hoar frost on their manes plainly shewing they had been there the whole night. Not perceiving any driver, I struck my sword repeatedly upon the canvas tilt, inquiring at the same time if there was any person in the cart. At length a very feeble voice answered me, and some one underneath the cart appeared to be making an effort to arise. A pair of naked frost-nipt legs were then advanced, and the most miserable object I ever beheld sunk heavily upon the ground; the whole of his cloathing so ragged and worn, that I can scarcely say that he was covered. So stiff and frozen was this miserable wretch, that he was by no means capable of moving; he informed me, that his regiment (the fifty-fourth) which he was following the preceding night, had lost its road, and in turning into another he found his horses incapable of clearing the cart from the ruts, and that himself and his two comrades were left behind to proceed in the best manner they could; the two men he spoke of were then lying dead in the cart, having all three endeavoured to communicate to one another a degree of warmth, by creeping close together.

'We placed the miserable survivor upon one of the horses of his team, and led him forwards until he joined the battalion, by that means his life was prolonged, yet, I fear, but for a season, for when placed in the hospital, his toes dropped off, frost-bitten, and his mass of blood appeared in a corrupted state . . .'

Extract from a letter 'from an officer of the Guards', January 1795

From Captain L. T. Jones, 14th Foot, *An Historical Journal of the British Campaign on the Continent in the Year 1794; with the Retreat Through Holland, in the Year 1795*, Swinney and Hawkins, Birmingham, 1797

FLANDERS and the NETHERLANDS, 1793-1809

Helder
Zype
Hoorne
Egmont
UNITED NETHERLANDS
Walcheren
Flushing
Ostend
Dunkirk
Nieuport
Hondschoote
Tourcoing
Wattignies
Valenciennes
Beaumont
Landrecies
FRANCE
AUSTRIAN NETHERLANDS
N
0   Miles   50

ability of the Army for sustained war. York's ability to co-operate with his allies was undermined by the insistence that he split away from the main force to lay siege to Dunkirk, implying a lack of strategic wisdom in London, while the failure to provide him with siege artillery suggested poor pre-planning. In addition, York had problems with his Hanoverian troops – as early as 26 April two of the regiments mutinied over their conditions of service – and the British reinforcements he received were often of poor quality, requiring extra training before being committed to battle. Indeed, as the need to raise an expeditionary force for the West Indies arose in late 1793, York even found that the troops he had were being withdrawn; by October he had fewer than 4000 British soldiers under his command.

By April 1794, however, reinforcements had been received. The Allied army, now under the command of the Emperor of Austria, opened the new campaigning season by moving against Landrecies. British troops performed well at Vaux (17 April), Beaumont (26 April) and Willems (10 May), but an Austrian defeat at Tourcoing (17–18 May) forced York to pull back, spreading his army thinly to defend the area around Tournai. A month later, the Austrians suffered another defeat at Fleurus and the coalition began to collapse. French attacks along the Dutch coast threatened to cut York off from his supply bases in England; his army began a retreat that was to prove impossible to reverse. As the winter weather closed in, British morale showed signs of cracking, manifested in cases of indiscipline and looting, and the subsequent withdrawal into Germany saw the virtual destruction of York's command (see box, p.52). Fewer than 6000 British soldiers were eventually evacuated from Bremen in March 1795, leaving the French in possession of the whole of the Netherlands. It was not an auspicious start to the war.

CAMPAIGNS IN THE WEST INDIES, 1793–7

The situation was little better in the West Indies. As soon as war was declared in February 1793, local British forces succeeded in seizing the island of Tobago, occupied by the French since 1781, and landed on Saint-Domingue, but attempts to exploit the royalist-republican split among French colonists on Martinique failed. This meant that if the traditional strategy of colonial campaigning was to be followed, an expeditionary force would have to be despatched from England, ideally to arrive in the Caribbean in November, before the onset of the 'sickly season'. Henry Dundas, as Secretary of State for Home and Colonies, was responsible for organizing such a force, but he was overworked and the relevant orders were delayed. In addition, it proved difficult to put the force together quickly, partly because of a shortage of troops in Britain and partly because of the demand for units to fight in Flanders, at Toulon (see box) and on board the fleet as marines. As a result, when the force, commanded by Lieutenant-General Sir Charles Grey, finally set sail on 26 November it was eight weeks behind schedule and comprised only 7000 men, about half the number originally envisaged. The transports carrying the troops did not arrive in Barbados until early January 1794, leaving little time in which to mount a campaign.

In the event, Grey did achieve results. By 25 March he had seized Martinique at a cost of fewer than 100 men killed; on 4 April he accepted the surrender of St Lucia and on the 22nd of the same month he defeated a French garrison on Guadeloupe, the capitulation of which also included the smaller islands of Marie-Galante and Desiderada. But he was incapable of going further. No more reinforcements were available from Britain and the troops he already had were suffering badly from yellow fever. Thus, when the French attacked Grande Terre (the eastern half of Guadeloupe) in June 1794, the British garrison was down to 13 officers and 174 men fit for service, incapable of doing a great deal to prevent defeat. Even when Grey managed to reinforce his remaining foothold on Basse Terre (the western half of the island), mounting a counter-attack on Grande Terre on 1 July, it was obvious that his soldiers had lost their edge. Repulsed by the French, the British suffered 543 casualties for no appreciable gain; the men were, in Grey's own words, 'quite exhausted by the unparalleled services of fatigue and fire they had gone through, for such a length of time, in the worst climate'.

TOULON, 1793

On 28 August 1793 a mixed force of British, Spanish and émigré French troops under the command of Admiral Lord Hood occupied the port of Toulon, where the population was in revolt against the revolutionary government in Paris. The port was surrounded by a string of forts, designed to protect both the town and the anchorage, but Hood had insufficient troops available to hold them all. Initially, his British contingent comprised no more than 1200 men from the 11th, 25th, 30th and 69th Regiments of Foot, all of whom had been embarked on the fleet as marines when the war began, and although they were supported by nearly 3000 Spaniards, the latter soon proved to be unreliable. Despite the arrival of Sardinian, Neapolitan and some additional British troops (the latter drawn from the 2nd and 18th Regiments of Foot), the land commander, Lord Mulgrave, could do little to strengthen the defences against a French force that quickly grew to over 20,000 men, including the young Napoleon Bonaparte as captain of artillery. An ill-directed attack on a French redoubt at Aresnes, to the west of the port, on 29 November led to heavy British losses, after which the defences began to crack. On 17 December Bonaparte led an assault on Point l'Eguilette, overlooking the inner harbour, upon which the Spanish and Neapolitan contingents withdrew from Toulon without consulting their allies. On the 19th, Hood evacuated the remains of his force, leaving most of the heavy equipment behind. It was, in common with many of the expeditions at the beginning of the Revolutionary War, a badly managed affair.

As the sickly season progressed, the combination of torrential rain and oppressive heat took its toll. By 1 September, for example, the garrison at Basse Terre had only 470 men fit for duty out of a nominal roll of 2249, while by the end of the year, of the 4000 men who had landed on Saint-Domingue, fewer than 1800 were still alive. Nor were reinforcements easy to find, for although Henry Dundas (by now Secretary of State for War) did gather about 4400 extra troops in England, chiefly by robbing York in Flanders, they did not set sail for the West Indies until 22 October 1794. By then, the remnants of the British garrison on Guadeloupe were close to surrender, and Saint-Domingue was under threat. To make matters worse, the troop reinforcements were delayed by gales. Lieutenant-General Sir John Vaughan, who replaced Grey when the latter returned to England in late 1794, had no choice but to assume the defensive.

The campaign, therefore, had gone from success to stalemate in a very short time, chiefly because the Army was being asked to do too much, not merely in the Caribbean but world-wide. Nor did the pressures decline, for in early 1795 a number of British possessions in the West Indies, taken from the French during the Seven Years War and still containing substantial French-speaking populations, rose in revolt. By March Vaughan was having to deal with insurrections in Grenada and St Vincent; in June the island of St Lucia had to be abandoned and two months later a separate revolt, this time involving freed slaves known as 'Maroons', broke out in Jamaica. Each required an extra commitment of troops, making any renewed Caribbean offensive unthinkable, particularly as reinforcements from England were being delayed and disease was still rampant.

Dundas' response was to organize the largest expedition mounted to date from the shores of Britain – a total of more than 30,000 men under the command of Major-General Sir Ralph Abercromby – with the aim of recovering St Lucia and Guadeloupe and seizing the whole of St Domingo (comprising French Saint-Domingue and Spanish Santo Domingo, recently ceded to France). His main problem was one of manpower, but with the Flanders expedition over and a poor harvest in 1794 producing distress throughout the country, recruits were being raised. In addition, German and Swiss mercenaries could be hired to make up the numbers. By September 1795 23 battalions of British infantry had been assembled at Southampton and Cork, but difficulties in providing the necessary shipping caused delays; although some of the transports set sail in October, others were still being prepared in January 1796. Even so, it was an impressive achievement and one that promised success.

This was not to be realized easily. Severe gales disrupted the first troop convoys in November 1795 and again in January/February 1796, with some of the ships returning to port and others battling through to the Caribbean; Abercromby himself did not reach Barbados until 21 April. By then, the garrisons on St Vincent and Grenada urgently needed reinforcement and the Dutch possessions of Demerara and Essequibo were demanding protection now that the French were occupying Holland. Abercromby had therefore to divert part of his force, although this did not prevent him from mounting an attack on St Lucia, taken after heavy fighting on 26 May.

St Vincent and Grenada were secured in June; in Jamaica the Maroon revolt was gradually countered and, although the operations were not carried out particularly efficiently, most of St Domingo was in British hands by the end of the year. But the costs were high, with sickness taking a dreadful toll: in 1796 nearly 14,000 men died, the vast majority of yellow fever, malaria and other tropical diseases.

In 1797, one more Caribbean expedition was mounted. In February Abercromby took the Spanish colony of Trinidad, but three months later he was forced to abandon an attack on Puerto Rico. By then, disease and enemy action had added another 6000 to the death list and Britain had no more soldiers to give. Despite the relative success in consolidating Britain's strategic position in the West Indies, denying her enemies the wealth and trade of the region, the campaign as a whole had been poorly managed and exceptionally costly. More to the point, it had done nothing to prevent French advances in Europe, for although small incursions had been made onto the continent, notably at Quiberon in September/October 1795, they had achieved little, leaving Pitt to face the fact that however effective colonial campaigns might be, it was in Europe that the fight against Revolutionary France had to be conducted. If the Army was ever to contribute to that fight, it would have to be virtually rebuilt and, on the evidence of the expeditions to Flanders and the Caribbean, made significantly more efficient. The British pattern of fighting the first battles of a war with an outmoded and obsolete army, requiring reform after inevitable early defeats, was being repeated.

REBUILDING THE ARMY

The instrument of reform was already at hand. On 10 February 1795 the Duke of York, recently recalled from Flanders, was appointed 'Field Marshal on the Staff', replacing Amherst as effective Commander-in-Chief of the Army. From his office at the Horse Guards, a steady stream of orders emerged, designed to rectify the obvious deficiencies which had been noted during the campaigns in Flanders and the West Indies. York was to remain as C-in-C until 1827, except for two years between 1809 and 1811 when he was forced out of office because of a scandal involving his mistress, Mary Anne Clarke. By the end of his term of office, the Army had been improved beyond recognition; as Sir Herbert Taylor, York's Military Secretary for much of the period, noted in 1827, 'the merit of rescuing the army from its impaired condition, of inspiring, establishing and maintaining its system; of introducing that administration in every principle and every detail, which has raised the British Service and promoted its efficiency, belongs exclusively to His Royal Highness'.

York's first task was to wrest control of the Army from the civilian politicians, particularly the Secretary at War, who represented the peacetime system of administration. Clearly, the C-in-C could not dictate strategy – that remained a prerogative of the Cabinet, advising the king – but he could ensure that such things as officer

Frederick, Duke of York (1763–1827). As Commander-in-Chief of the British Army from 1795, he was responsible for much-needed reforms, although as a commander in the field he had his weaknesses.

promotion, soldiers' conditions of service and military training were placed in the hands of professional staff officers under his command. To this end, he appointed a Military Secretary, through whom officers could correspond with the C-in-C, and enhanced the positions of subordinates such as the Adjutant-General and Quartermaster-General in the Horse Guards. What he was doing was to create a rudimentary General Staff, the role of which would be to ensure that reform was carried out efficiently and quickly.

The next stage was to improve the professionalism of regimental officers. Many of the abuses associated with the purchase system, especially the ability to buy rapid promotion regardless of previous experience, had re-emerged during the rapid expansion of the Army that had occurred since 1793. In order to attract officers, who in turn would raise soldiers as part of their duty, the government had allowed existing regulations to lapse, with the result that, in the words of York's biographer, John Watkins, writing in 1827, 'boys on the lower forms at school, and even infants in the nursery were gazetted as lieutenant-colonels of regiments to the detriment of veterans grown grey in the service of their king and country'. York moved quickly to impose reform, reasserting the rule that no-one should be able to purchase a first commission before the age of 16, and insisting that no officer should be promoted captain without at least two years' service or field officer (major or lieutenant-colonel) with less than six. In 1802 he went one stage further, giving his support to the establishment of a military school at Great Marlow for cadets aged 13 to 16, who would attend a four-year course before purchasing their commissions in the usual way. Ten years later this became the Royal Military College Sandhurst, and although there was no requirement for all potential officers to attend, it was designed to offer professional training equivalent to that

THE IRISH REBELLION, 1798

By the late 1790s Britain's position in Ireland was under threat. Radicals belonging to Wolfe Tone's United Irishmen were actively engaged in military preparations to oppose British rule, and this tempted the French to send troops to their support. In February 1797 a French fleet on the way to Ireland was forced to seek shelter in the Welsh port of Fishguard. The Pembrokeshire Militia captured all the French soldiers put ashore, but the incident did nothing to ease government fears of enemy interference in Irish affairs. One result was a policy of ruthless repression, carried out by locally raised militia and Yeomanry units, that crippled the United Irishmen. In desperation, the remaining radicals rose in

revolt, capturing Wexford by the end of May 1798.

In the event, the rebellion was easily put down. Despite a shortage of regular troops and a dismal record of ill discipline among the Irish militia, the British closed in on the rebels, defeating them at Vinegar Hill on 21 June. By then, however, the French had hastily prepared a force of 900 veteran troops under General Joseph Humbert, who landed at Killala, County Mayo, on 22 August. The French, gathering support as they went, advanced to Castlebar and, after defeating a British force under Major-General Gerard Lake, crossed the River Shannon. But they could do no more. Lake, reinforced by British regulars, outmanoeuvred Humbert

and forced him to surrender at Ballinamuck on 8 September. The threat to British security was over, although the subsequent repression of the Irish people was to be long remembered.

The rebellion was to have an equally long memorial in the British Army. On 12 January 1799 King George III ordered that the 5th (Royal Irish) Regiment of Dragoons, among whom a conspiracy had been discovered during the rebellion, was to be disbanded. It was not re-raised until February 1858, by which time it was regarded as a junior regiment. Thus, when it was amalgamated with the 16th The Queen's Lancers in 1922, the latter took precedence, producing the seemingly illogical title of 16th/5th.

provided to the Royal Artillery at Woolwich since 1741. Staff training was also available at Sandhurst for older officers, many of whom were later to serve with the Duke of Wellington in the Peninsular campaign (*see* p.63).

Moving on to the soldiers, York made a number of improvements to their terms and conditions of service. Chief among these was an increase in pay, introduced in 1795. This coincided with the provision of proper rations and the building of barracks, the latter to improve discipline by doing away with the invidious system of quartering soldiers in public houses. The elaborate dress of the 18th century was also changed, with soldiers no longer having to pull their hair back in powdered queues or to wear impractical long-skirted coats that lessened their fighting efficiency; indeed, York even issued greatcoats to soldiers at government expense, probably in response to the heavy losses from cold during the retreat into Germany in 1794–5. Finally, he addressed the question of soldiers' health, insisting on the appointment of properly qualified medical officers, the provision of hospitals and the introduction of vaccinations against disease. Small wonder that he became known as the 'soldier's friend'.

Such reforms allowed the Army to attract a better class of recruits, but they would be of little value unless they were properly trained. During the poorly administered expansion of 1793–5, when enormous numbers of regiments were raised with no regard to their efficiency, the earlier attempts to centralize training procedures had lapsed, leading in part to the disasters in Flanders and the West Indies as inadequately trained soldiers had been committed to battle. York rectified this, partly by reiterating the need for infantry units to follow David Dundas' *Military Movements* and partly by introducing new training manuals. In July 1795, the Adjutant-General ordered all cavalry regiments to adhere to a system of drill and manoeuvre recently compiled by Dundas, and two years later Major John Gaspard Le Marchant's *Rules and Regulations for the Sword Exercises of Cavalry* were also imposed. Nor did York confine his efforts to horsemen alone: in 1797 he began to reform the light troops of the Army, ordering commanding officers to pay special attention to their training as skirmishers, and six years later he directed Major-General Sir John Moore to conduct experiments with a 'Corps of Light Infantry' at Shorncliffe Camp (*see box*, p.60). He also called for the formation of a 'Corps of Riflemen', regimented as the 95th Foot in 1802 and redesignated The Rifle Brigade in 1816 after sterling service in the Peninsula and at Waterloo. Other new units were raised – as early as 1793 the Master-General of the Ordnance instituted the Royal Horse Artillery and six years later the Treasury was persuaded to allow a Royal Waggon Train to be created – but it was undoubtedly York's efforts that helped to form and regulate the army that Wellington later led to victory.

A recruiting poster for the 1st or King's Dragoon Guards, c. 1800. The glowing description of Army life is somewhat undermined by the need to offer a bounty to any 'Bringer of a good Recruit'.

THE HELDER CAMPAIGN

Before that could happen, however, the Army as a whole had to gain experience and learn how to win its battles. It proved to be a painful process, in which many of the problems noted between 1793 and 1797 were repeated. Nowhere was this more apparent than in the Helder campaign of August–October 1799 when, despite early success, British and Russian troops under the overall command of the Duke of York were forced to conduct a humiliating withdrawal back to England. It was a familiar pattern of events.

The Helder, situated on the tip of a peninsula which divided the Zuyder Zee from the North Sea in Holland, was chosen as an objective partly because of its importance as a naval base and partly because it was thought that the Dutch, under French occupation since 1794, were ready to rise in revolt. York first mooted the idea of an expedition to the king in November 1798, but it was not until the following January that it was taken seriously by Pitt and his advisers. They managed to gather a force of nearly 30,000 British soldiers and persuaded the Russian Tsar to contribute a further 18,000, all of whom would be carried to the Helder by the Royal Navy. The aim was to seize the area as a base for future operations in conjunction with Dutch rebels, threatening the French hold on the whole of the Netherlands.

It did not go according to plan. Co-operation between the army and navy was poor – after the landings on 27 August, the fleet sailed past the Helder to receive the surrender of Dutch warships but then took little active part in the campaign – and, as in Flanders six years earlier, inter-allied command links were weak. When York arrived on 7 September – the same day on which the Russian force came ashore – he found that the commander of the British contingent, Lieutenant-General Sir Ralph Abercromby (last seen in the West Indies), had made no attempt to advance beyond the shoreline or to conduct a reconnaissance of enemy positions. Instead, his troops were strung out along the so-called Zype Line, just to the south of their landing site, facing a Franco-Dutch army that was rapidly increasing in size. There was no sign of any Dutch revolt.

But the situation did offer room for optimism. The enemy right flank, to the south-east of the Zype Line at Hoorne, was not well defended. York therefore ordered a thrust under Abercromby in that direction while the rest of the Anglo-Russian force conducted a frontal assault on Bergen in the centre. The attack was scheduled to begin at daybreak on 19 September, but it soon went wrong. The Russians advanced two hours too early, giving the game away, while Abercromby, although in possession of Hoorne, did nothing to turn the enemy flank. After only a few hours of fighting, York ordered his troops to return to the Zype Line. Another attack on 2 October, this time towards Egmont on the coast, fared better, forcing the enemy back to a line further south, but again the advantage was not exploited. Indeed, when York ordered an advance on Kastrikum four days later, the enemy had recovered and was in the process of mounting its own counter-attack. The resulting battle was confused and appeared to be indecisive, particularly as the Russians were proving less than effective. York seemed to lose his nerve, convinced by his own half-hearted generals that the campaign could not be sustained, and on 7 October he ordered his army to pull back yet again to the Zype Line. Three weeks later hostilities ceased and, under the terms of a local agreement, the Allies reboarded their transports. The campaign had achieved nothing of value.

It was apparent that the British had learnt little from nearly seven years of war. Inter-service and inter-allied co-operation were weak, British generals were indecisive and the troops, despite displays of fighting ability once battle was joined, were seemingly incapable of grasping or exploiting tactical advantages. The real fault lay at the top, for although York may have been an impressive C-in-C in terms of implementing reforms, he was clearly not an effective commander, lacking the intuition needed to seize and maintain the initiative. At the same time, he was badly served by his subordinates, implying a lack of natural talent among available generals. What was needed, as so often in British Army history, was the emergence of officers who, having experienced and survived the recent disasters, were capable of responding to the new pressures of war. One of these was Sir John Moore, who was in fact badly wounded while serving as a brigade commander in the Helder campaign;

another was Arthur Wellesley (later the Duke of Wellington), who had experienced the defeat of 1794–5 in Flanders and was currently learning his art the hard way in India (*see box*, p.58). The talents of men such as these were sorely needed, but it would take time for them to be realized. Until then, the Army had to make do with what it had got. Sometimes this was enough to ensure success, but it was a hit-and-miss affair, fitting the recurring pattern of British military amateurism that always seemed to be present during the early stages of a major conflict.

THE CAMPAIGN IN EGYPT

One of the rare success stories of the war against Revolutionary France occurred in Egypt in 1801, when an expeditionary force of 16,000 British soldiers wrested the country from a French army that had originally occupied it under Napoleon Bonaparte three years earlier. Napoleon had abandoned his troops in 1799 to further his political career in Paris, leaving them isolated but apparently secure. They posed a threat to British domination in the eastern Mediterranean and there was a fear in London that they might be used to forge a link with pro-French native forces in India. The decision to mount the British operation was taken in late 1800, by which time Pitt, rather belatedly, had agreed to a substantial increase in the size of the Army, providing funds that would boost it to the unprecedented heights of 300,000 men (220,000 regulars and home-based 'Fencibles', plus 80,000 militia). It was a sign that the war, at last, was being taken seriously.

But the shortage of talented generals was still apparent. Despite his less than glorious record in the Helder campaign, Abercromby was chosen to command the Egyptian expedition, chiefly because there was no-one of comparable stature available. Among his subordinates was Moore, recovered from his latest wounds, and it was he who led the British spearhead ashore at Aboukir Bay on 8 March 1801. His brigade, comprising the 23rd, 28th, 42nd and 58th Foot as well as four companies of the 40th, landed within range of French guns in Aboukir Castle but wasted no time in confronting the enemy. A rapid advance up a steep sand-hill caught defending troops by surprise, forcing their withdrawal, and this enabled the rest of Abercromby's men to land safely. Four days later, the British began their advance on Alexandria, 12 miles away.

They encountered the main enemy force on 21 March, close to Alexandria. The French commander, General Menou, opened the battle with a feint on his left and a major attack on Moore's brigade on the right. The 42nd Highlanders (Black Watch) fought exceptionally well, maintaining coherence even after being attacked by cavalry, but it was the 28th Foot (1st Battalion, Gloucestershire Regiment) who achieved lasting fame. Engaged by infantry to their front, they suddenly came under pressure from cavalry behind them, upon which the rear rank turned round and faced the new threat. Their coolness under fire earned them the right to wear

CAMPAIGNS IN INDIA, 1799–1806

The French occupation of Egypt in 1798 opened up the strategic possibility of an overland advance on India, where Tippoo Sahib of Mysore, intent on vengeance against the British for their attacks on his state six years earlier, was openly courting French support. Troops of the East India Company, reinforced by British regulars that included the 33rd Foot under Colonel Arthur Wellesley, invaded Mysore from both east and west in 1799. On 4 May, after a short siege, the capital, Seringapatam, was taken and Tippoo's army destroyed. Among the 10,000 dead was Tippoo himself.

This left the East India Company in complete control of southern India, but brought it into direct confrontation with the Mahratta Confederacy further north. Two of the Mahratta leaders, Daulat Rao of Scindia and Ragoji Bhonsla of Berar,

combined forces in 1803 to create an army of nearly 100,000 men. In response the British C-in-C, Lord Lake (last seen in Ireland in 1798, *see box*, p.55), ordered a two-pronged assault on Scindia to protect Company possessions at Bombay in the west and Calcutta in the northeast. Taking personal command in the north, Lake assembled an army of 10,000 men at Cawnpore and, in July 1803, set out up the River Ganges to seize the fortress at Aligarh. From there he advanced to take Delhi before moving south to Agra. On 1 November he defeated the remains of the northern Mahratta army at Laswari and a month later entered Gwalior, the capital of Scindia. Meanwhile, further south, Wellesley (now a major-general) had advanced from Poona in August 1803 to capture Ahmednagar. The Mahrattas fell back to Assaye where, on 23 Sep-

tember, Wellesley's army of about 6000 men, including the 19th Light Dragoons and 74th and 78th Highlanders, achieved a costly but crushing victory. After a pause to recover, Wellesley resumed his advance, sweeping the enemy aside at Argaum on 29 November. A month later, Daulat Rao and Ragoji Bhonsla sued for peace.

But the war was not yet over. In early 1804 Jeswunt Rao Holkar, a Mahratta leader who had hitherto remained aloof, suddenly entered the fray, pushing Lake's forces back towards Agra before advancing on Delhi. A series of forced marches allowed Lake to recover the initiative and Holkar fled, closely pursued by British cavalry. In January 1805, Lake laid siege to Bhurtpore – an operation that ended in failure in April – but Holkar was no longer a major threat, eventually retreating into the Punjab. Peace was

British troops (probably the 42nd Highlanders) attack French positions at Alexandria, 21 March 1801, capturing an enemy colour. The battle brought a welcome British victory in the long war with Revolutionary France.

regimental badges on both the front and back of their headdress, an honour maintained by the Gloucestershire Regiment throughout its subsequent history. It was the sort of incident that helped to build the fighting spirit of the Army.

Despite casualties of nearly 1500 men, the British secured victory at Alexandria, pushing the French back into the city, where they were besieged. Abercromby, wounded in the battle, died a week later with his record significantly enhanced, but it was Moore who showed the importance of inspired leadership, for without his efforts at both Aboukir and Alexandria the French defeat would have been much more difficult to effect. As it was, Alexandria fell in April, allowing the British to reconquer the whole of Egypt by September.

By then, Pitt had been replaced as Prime Minister by Henry Addington, who actively pursued the possibility of peace with France. The result was the Treaty of Amiens, signed on 27 March 1802. Britain kept Trinidad (taken from Spain) and Ceylon (taken from Holland in 1796), but agreed to hand back all other captured territories, including the French islands in the West Indies. In a move that was by now familiar, Addington celebrated by ordering a reduction to the size of the Army, taking it down to a strength of only 113,000 men. It was to be supported at home by 48,000 members of the militia, but they were a poor substitute for the laboriously created regular units,

many of which faced disbandment. In the event, war with France was renewed in May 1803, before the reduction could be fully implemented, but the speed with which the government had moved to effect financial savings came perilously close to destroying all the benefits so painfully accrued since 1793.

THE WAR AGAINST NAPOLEON

Addington, who was to remain in power until replaced by Pitt in May 1804, reacted to the new conflict by adopting a defensive strategy, concentrating on the protection of Britain against possible invasion. The militia was called out as early as March 1803 (it was to remain embodied until the end of the war 11 years later) and locally recruited volunteer units were raised, dedicated to home defence. By comparison, the regular Army was increased by only 37,000 men (to a total strength of just over 150,000), and no significant overseas operations were planned. Such a lack of aggression may have contributed to Napoleon's decision to prepare an invasion of England in 1804, although by the same token it could be argued that Addington's emphasis on domestic defence helped to prevent the invasion from taking place. But whatever the judgement, the fact remains that the regular Army was starved of manpower and equipment during the early years of the conflict against Napoleon.

This situation was exacerbated by the poor man-

negotiated in January 1806, although it would take another war (1817–19) before the Mahratta Confederacy was finally crushed.

British and Indian troops storm the fortress of Seringapatam, 4 May 1799, defeating the forces of Tippoo Sahib of Mysore. The victory gave the East India Company complete control of southern India.

SHORNCLIFFE CAMP, 1803–4

The Experimental Rifle Corps, created in 1799 on the orders of the Duke of York, represented an attempt to match the French *tirailleurs* or skirmishers who preceded the main body of an army to disrupt enemy formations. Under the supervision of Colonel Coote Manningham and Lieutenant-Colonel William Stewart, the new unit (soon to be known as the 95th Foot) concentrated on training its soldiers in tactics, fieldcraft and accurate shooting, in the latter case using the Baker rifle instead of the Brown Bess musket. In 1803 it was decided to extend the experiment by creating a 'Corps of Light Infantry' at Shorncliffe in Kent, commanded by Major-General John Moore.

Moore was aware of what was needed: 'The service of Light Infantry does not so much require men of stature as it requires them to be intelligent, hardy and active.' Taking up his appointment in June 1803, he stressed the need for soldiers who would be prepared to use their initiative on the battlefield, acting in small groups that would advance ahead of the main body or warn of an enemy approach. This would require an ability to use the ground for cover, to shoot effectively and to make tactical decisions without reference to higher command – characteristics that could be developed only when the individual soldier had confidence in himself and his comrades as well as pride in his profession. By 1804 Moore's brigade, then comprising the 14th Light Dragoons, 43rd, 52nd and 95th Foot, had gained a reputation for physical fitness and efficiency, based in no small measure on realistic training carried out by officers who were encouraged to treat their soldiers as men rather than machines. The benefits were to be felt in both the Peninsular campaign and at Waterloo during the next 11 years.

BUENOS AIRES, 1806–7

On 27 June 1806 a British force of 1500 men under the command of Colonel William Carr Beresford landed near Buenos Aires as part of an ambitious strategy to seize the Spanish colonies in Latin America. Despite an occupation of both Buenos Aires and Montevideo, the force was far too small to carry out its task. A Spanish counter-attack in early 1807 left Beresford with no choice but to surrender.

By then, however, the British government had decided to reinforce the expedition and, unaware of Beresford's fate, 10,000 men under Lieutenant-General John Whitelocke were on their way across the Atlantic. They landed close to Montevideo before marching towards Buenos Aires, only to find that the region was now well defended. After an abortive attack on Buenos Aires on 5 July 1807, in which small parties of British troops were cut off and annihilated in the streets of the city, Whitelocke withdrew, abandoning all operations in exchange for a ceasefire. The remains of his army were lucky to be allowed to leave Latin America, but Whitelocke himself was less fortunate. When he returned to Britain, he was court-martialled and cashiered, taking the blame for what had been a poor strategic plan.

agement of recruitment and the plethora of different military organizations that existed. It was all very well for the government to call out militia units, but they absorbed over 70,000 men – about 20 per cent of available military manpower – at any one time and were, by the nature of militia service, confined to home duties only. The same was true of the new volunteer companies, which attracted over 414,000 men by December 1803, and although this figure declined to about 300,000 by 1804–6, it was a substantial number of eligible men to divert from possible regular enlistment. As the war progressed, various attempts were made to rationalize the system. These ranged from the creation of an Army of the Reserve, raised by ballot for service in the British Isles, to a reorganization of the militia that was designed to transform it into a source of partially trained recruits for the regular Army, but they

A British rifleman, c. 1808. Trained for skirmishing, the soldier is lightly equipped. He is using a Baker rifle and, in accordance with his training, is taking an aimed shot, holding the rifle steady.

took time to implement. It did not help that regular service was still unattractive, particularly in terms of pay. In 1806 a regular soldier received about 30s 4d (£1.52) a month, compared to an artisan's average wage of 112s (£5.55) for the same period, with the added risk to the soldier of death, disease or injury. Recruitment picked up once the government introduced new terms of enlistment after 1806, allowing men to volunteer for limited rather than indefinite regular service – something that led to substantial numbers of militiamen transferring to the regulars – but the Army did not rise significantly above 230,000 men at any time before 1815. If it was to have any impact at all on the war against Napoleon, it would have to substitute quality for quantity. Judging from its past record, achieving that quality would be a long and laborious process.

BATTLES LOST AND WON

The need for improvement became apparent as Addington's successors shifted from a defensive to an offensive strategy in 1806. Despite a rare victory over the French at Maida in Lower Calabria on 4 July 1806, when 4800 men under General Sir John Stuart intervened to support the Queen of Naples against Joseph Bonaparte, the previous pattern of overseas campaigning soon reasserted itself. The failure of a British force under Lieutenant-General John Whitelocke at Buenos Aires in 1807 (*see box*, p.60) did little to

enhance the prestige of the Army, and the heavy losses from disease suffered on the island of Walcheren two years later (*see box*, p.63) seemed to indicate a return to the disasters of 1793-7 in the West Indies. Even in the Iberian Peninsula, soon to be the scene of dramatic British victories, the campaign began badly. Although a force of 10,000 men under Lieutenant-General Sir Arthur Wellesley landed in Portugal and defeated the French at Rolica and Vimeiro in August 1808, any advantage was lost when the overall British commander, General Sir Hew Dalrymple, negotiated the Convention of Cintra. It allowed the enemy army to withdraw unmolested.

Worse was to come. On 8 October 1808 Sir John Moore, left in command of British troops in Portugal after both Dalrymple and Wellesley had been recalled, was ordered to take the bulk of his force into northern Spain to support Spanish armies opposing French occupation. It turned out to be a foolish move. Although the Spanish appeared to be enjoying success, having retaken Madrid and forced the French to pull back to Vitoria, they were badly organized and poorly commanded. In addition, once news of French setbacks reached Napoleon, he travelled to Spain with a substantial part of his highly experienced *Grande Armée*. Thus when Moore set off from Lisbon with 20,000 soldiers on 16 October, marching towards Salamanca to link up with 17,000 men under General Sir David Baird, advancing out of Castile, he entered a

French troops advance into Vimeiro village, 21 August 1808. The fighting in the narrow streets was confused and bloody, although it constituted only a small part of the battle, which was won by Sir Arthur Wellesley.

potential trap. By 15 November, when Moore entered Salamanca, Napoleon had already defeated the main Spanish army and was preparing to reoccupy Madrid before advancing into Portugal at the head of 80,000 men. Moore was in danger of being cut off from his supply bases and, despite a further move beyond Salamanca to take Sahagun on 21 December, it was soon apparent that retreat was his only option. His orders, issued on Christmas Eve, were greeted with anger and dismay by his soldiers.

The 230-mile retreat across the mountains north of Astorga to Corunna, where the Royal Navy was waiting to evacuate Moore's army, took nearly three weeks to complete. It was conducted in appalling winter conditions through desolate countryside. Some units, notably the brigade of light infantry under Major-General Robert Crauford and the cavalry under Lord Henry Paget, maintained their discipline throughout, protecting the rear of the British column, but others cracked under the strain, abandoning their equipment and succumbing to the winter cold. On 31 December Moore sent Crauford west towards Vigo in a vain attempt to split the pursuing enemy, but the nightmare continued. It was not until 11 January 1809 that the main body under Moore reached Corunna, by which time more than 5000 men had been lost. Five days later the French attacked, hoping to disrupt the evacuation already taking place. In the ensuing battle Moore was killed, although not before the enemy advance

Lieutenant-General Sir John Moore, killed at Corunna, 16 January 1809. Remembered as much for his training of light troops at Shorncliffe in 1803–4 as for his fighting skills, his loss was keenly felt by the Army.

THE PENINSULAR WAR 1808-14

Personality Profile:

LIEUTENANT-GENERAL SIR JOHN MOORE (1761–1809)

It is a widely held belief that, if he had survived, John Moore would have rivalled the Duke of Wellington in terms of military reputation. Born in Glasgow, Moore received a commission in the 51st Foot (1st Battalion, King's Own Yorkshire Light Infantry) in 1776, seeing service in the American War of Independence before entering Parliament as MP for Linlithgow Burghs in 1784. By 1790, when he left Parliament, he was a lieutenant-colonel; eight years later he had been promoted to major-general after taking part in campaigns in Corsica (1794) and the West Indies (1796-7). Wounded at the Battle of Egmont during the Helder expedition in 1799 and again while leading his troops at Alexandria two years later, he was chosen in 1803 to command the nascent 'Corps of Light Infantry' at Shorncliffe (*see* p.60), where he introduced radical new training methods. Knighted in 1804 and promoted to lieutenant-general a year later, he assumed command of British troops in Portugal after the humiliating Convention of Cintra in 1808. His subsequent advance into northern Spain was well conducted, but French counter-moves forced him to retreat to Corunna where, in January 1809, he was killed. The Army lost a brave fighting general and a superb trainer of men.

had been stalled. Over the next few days nearly 24,000 men were successfully evacuated from Corunna and Vigo, but when they disembarked in England, lice-ridden and in rags, there was no disguising that yet another 'shameful disaster' had occurred.

WELLINGTON IN THE PENINSULA

It was at this point that the government turned to Sir Arthur Wellesley for advice, recognizing that he had not been to blame for the humiliation of the Convention of Cintra and had, in fact, conducted the short campaign of August 1808 with remarkable success. On 7 March 1809 he submitted a memorandum to Viscount Castlereagh, the Secretary of State for War, in which he argued that Portugal could be defended regardless of events in Spain, as long as an adequate army under strong command was despatched to Lisbon to reinforce the 10,000 men left there by Moore five months earlier. Castlereagh was clearly convinced by this argument, and on 22 April Wellesley landed at Lisbon to command a force of 20,000 British troops, 3000 members of the King's German Legion (*see box*, p.64) and an estimated 16,000 Portuguese. He faced a daunting task. Ranged against him were three French armies – at Oporto to the north, Ciudad Rodrigo to the north-east and Badajoz to the east – each of which was capable of matching the numbers under his command. Altogether, the French had nearly 200,000 troops in the Iberian Peninsula, and although many of these were tied down by Spanish guerrillas (who also cut communications between the French commanders, making co-ordination difficult), Wellesley could only aim to defeat each enemy army in turn, retreating into Portugal whenever he felt threatened by overwhelming numbers. It was this factor that made the Peninsular campaign, conducted between 1809 and 1814, such a see-saw affair of advance and withdrawal, but it was a measure of the brilliance of Wellesley that he was prepared to fight in

WALCHEREN, 1809

Despite the growing professionalism of the British Army, indicated by events in the Peninsula in 1809, it could still be involved in disastrous operations. The most dramatic of these occurred in the summer of 1809, when the government ordered an attack on the island of Walcheren, at the south-western tip of the archipelago protecting the Scheldt estuary in Holland. A force of 44,000 men, commanded by General Sir John Pitt, second Earl of Chatham (William Pitt's elder brother), was

assembled and, supported by an immense fleet under Admiral Sir Richard Strachan, was put ashore on 30 July. At first all went well – the town of Flushing was taken on 15 August – but Chatham refused to exploit his advantage by advancing on Antwerp. The French and Dutch effectively sealed off Walcheren, leaving the British to suffer the ravages of 'Walcheren fever' (a form of malaria) as they struggled to survive in the low-lying polder-land. In September Chatham was ordered to return to Britain with the bulk of

his force, although nearly 17,000 soldiers remained behind as a garrison until they too were evacuated in December. By then, over 4000 men had died of disease. The *Morning Chronicle* summed up the expedition on 26 February 1810:

> Lord Chatham with his sword undrawn,
> Kept waiting for Sir Richard Strachan;
> Sir Richard, eager to be at 'em,
> Kept waiting too – for whom?
> Lord Chatham!

THE KING'S GERMAN LEGION

In December 1803 George III, Elector of Hanover as well as King of Great Britain and Ireland, authorized the creation of the King's German Legion (KGL). Made up principally of officers and men who had fled from Hanover after the French seizure of the electorate in July, it was effectively an army-in-exile administered by the British. By January 1805 the KGL comprised two cavalry regiments, two Light and four Line infantry battalions and five batteries of artillery, the bulk of which were committed to Portugal in 1808. The 3rd Hussars and the 1st and 2nd Light battalions took part in the retreat to Corunna, leaving the 1st, 2nd, 5th and 7th Line battalions at Lisbon to become part of Wellesley's army. They were joined in early 1809 by the 1st Hussars, widely regarded as the most effective light cavalry unit in the Peninsula; by 1812 the KGL was contributing four cavalry regiments and five infantry battalions to the campaign. Although a shortage of Hanoverian soldiers forced the KGL to widen its recruitment, taking men from throughout Germany, the reputation of the regiments remained high. After the peace in 1814 most of the non-Hanoverians were discharged as a new Royal Army of Hanover was created, but a total of five cavalry regiments and eight infantry battalions fought at Waterloo a year later under the KGL designation. They were among the most effective of Wellington's troops.

such a way. In the process, his army gained the experience and expertise needed to achieve some memorable victories.

Wellesley's first objective was Oporto, defended by 20,000 French soldiers under Marshal Soult. The main British force of 18,000 men advanced from Coimbra on 7 May, with the Portuguese providing flank protection; four days later Wellesley crossed the River Douro to catch Soult by surprise. The French withdrew with cavalry at their heels, retiring north to Galicia across mountainous terrain. By early June Portugal had been cleared of enemy troops, enabling Wellesley to turn his attention to Spain. His aim was to make contact with a Spanish army of 30,000 men under General Cuesta before marching against Marshal Victor at Talavera. Despite problems caused by the indiscipline of Cuesta's men, who raced towards Madrid only to encounter an enemy army of 46,000 well-trained soldiers, the British force of 20,000 took up strong positions at Talavera, where they were attacked by the French on 27 and 28 July. The battle, which earned Wellesley his more familiar title of Viscount (later Duke of) Wellington, was won primarily by the discipline of the British infantry, who lay behind the crest of a ridge to escape French fire, then stood up, poured volleys into the enemy and charged with the bayonet. The French faltered and, under pressure from Allied cavalry, withdrew, having suffered 7000 casualties. By comparison, the British lost 5000 men and gained the field.

But the advantage could not be exploited. On 2 August Wellington received reports that a new French army of 20,000 men had advanced across his rear to take Plasencia, threatening his links with Portugal. He therefore moved his army back to Almaraz on the River Tagus before withdrawing towards Badajoz in the south-west. The French followed, although when it was apparent to them that Wellington had no intention of giving battle, they marched north again to deal with yet another Spanish uprising. Wellington took the opportunity to travel to Lisbon to supervise the construction of defences around the city (the 'Lines of the Torres Vedras'), while his army occupied winter quarters around Abrantes and along the River Mondego. A French attack was unlikely once the weather worsened.

Both sides prepared for a fresh campaign in 1810. Wellington, having vowed never to attempt another operation in conjunction with the ill-disciplined Spanish, concentrated on the defence of Portugal. The Portuguese militia, about 45,000 strong, was called out and arrangements made for the evacuation of the entire area through which the French, dependent for supplies on what they captured, might advance. In addition, the Lines of the Torres Vedras, comprising fixed defences to the north of Lisbon, were completed, giving the Anglo-Portuguese forces a secure base to which they might withdraw. Meanwhile, Wellington's main army of 60,000 men, half of whom were British, guarded the likely French approach routes in the Mondego and Tagus valleys. They did not have long to wait. By June 1810 Marshal Masséna, one of Napoleon's more experienced generals, had gathered 86,000 men to form the Army of Portugal, and was ready to advance.

Masséna began his campaign by laying siege to, and capturing, Ciudad Rodrigo and Almeida, although in the process he gave clear warning that his main line of advance would be along the River Mondego. Wellington reacted by concentrating his army on top of a 10-mile ridge at Busaco, on the road from Almeida to Coimbra. When the French attacked the ridge on 27 September 1810, they suffered a costly defeat, but this was no more than a delaying action. As soon as it was over, Wellington pulled back towards his prepared defences outside Lisbon. The French were left to march across land deliberately laid bare of supplies, before encountering the elaborate earthworks and trenches which made up the Lines of the Torres Vedras. Although Masséna held on throughout the winter, his army rapidly lost cohesion, and in March 1811 he had no choice but to order a retreat into Spain. As his soldiers struggled over the mountains of central Portugal, they were harried mercilessly by guerrillas and kept on the move by the advance guard of Wellington's army. The French fell back to Almeida and Ciudad Rodrigo. They left 25,000 of their comrades behind.

Wellington's next task was to capture the frontier forts at Almeida and, further south, at Badajoz, preparatory to an invasion of Spain. It proved to be a difficult task. On 11 May 1811, as British troops laid siege to Almeida,

British troops belonging to Colborne's brigade under attack by Polish lancers at the Battle of Albuera, 16 May 1811. These infantrymen were practically annihilated in one of the fiercest battles of the Peninsular campaign.

THE SIEGES OF CIUDAD RODRIGO AND BADAJOZ

On 8 January 1812, Wellington advanced to lay siege to the Spanish border town of Ciudad Rodrigo, situated on a hill about 100 feet above and to the north of the River Agueda. His move caught the French garrison by surprise and, by the end of the day, men of the Light Division had seized outlying defences known as the Greater and Lesser Tesons, to the north-west of the town. Trenches were dug to protect the British artillery, which began its bombardment on 13 January. Two breaches were made in the enemy defences and, six days later, these were assaulted by the 3rd and Light Divisions, spearheaded by groups of volunteers known graphically as the 'forlorn hope'. They suffered grievous losses, made worse by the sudden explosion of a buried mine, but as diversionary attacks elsewhere confused the French, the town was taken. The siege as a whole cost Wellington over 1000 casualties but opened the route into Castile.

Before he could take that route, however, Wellington had to move south to protect his flank, laying siege to Badajoz on the River Guadiana. By 17 March British and Portuguese troops had surrounded the town, concentrating their attention on Fort Picurina in the south-east. Under atrocious weather conditions, trenches were dug towards the fort and the artillery opened up on 25 March. That night men of the 3rd Division stormed Picurina, exposing the main defences around Badajoz. By 6 April three breaches had been made, enabling Wellington to order an assault by the 4th and Light Divisions, with subsidiary attacks against Badajoz Castle and the north-western defences by the 3rd and 5th Divisions respectively. The 'forlorn hope' approached the main breaches at 10 p.m. on 6 April but made little progress; if the 3rd Division had not managed to take the castle and come up behind the defenders, the assault would have failed. As it was, the siege cost nearly 5000 Allied casualties. The survivors, intent on revenge, looted Badajoz in 48 hours of deliberate destruction.

Regimental Tradition:

BADAJOZ DAY

Every year, the Worcestershire and Sherwood Foresters Regiment celebrates Badajoz Day. It commemorates the part played in the storming of the town by men of the 45th Foot (1st Battalion, Sherwood Foresters), and particularly the exploits of Lieutenant Macpherson. Part of the 'forlorn hope' in the assault on Badajoz Castle on 6 April 1812 (*see box*, p.65), Macpherson was badly wounded but determined to capture a French flag flying from one of the towers. When he succeeded in doing so he replaced it with his scarlet coatee (jacket) to signal his triumph. Every 6 April thereafter, the 45th flew a scarlet coatee from their flagstaff. This tradition has continued to the present day, despite amalgamations with the 95th Foot in 1881 and the Worcestershire Regiment in 1970. Also on 6 April, the Regimental Colours are handed over for safe-keeping to the sergeants of the regiment in memory of the fact that, once the siege of Badajoz was over, few officers of the 45th remained fit for duty.

The French assault on the defences of Ciudad Rodrigo, 10 July 1810. Wellington's troops retook the town with Spanish assistance 18 months later.

a reorganized French army under Masséna suddenly attacked them at Fuentes d'Oñoro. The fighting was desperate – Wellington was later to admit that this was the closest he came to defeat in the Peninsula – but the stubborn resolve of the redcoats forced the enemy back. Five days later the Anglo-Portuguese army besieging Badajoz was attacked by Soult at Albuera. In the aftermath of a brutal and bloody engagement, characterized by orders to the 57th Foot (1st Battalion, Middlesex Regiment) to 'die hard' in the battle, neither side claimed victory, although it soon became apparent that the French had withdrawn. Even so, Wellington's plans for an offensive into Spain had to be postponed until his shattered battalions could be reinforced. Almeida was taken, but as the winter weather closed in, the siege of Badajoz had to be abandoned. The French, now under the command of Marshal Marmont, were content to suspend operations until the spring.

This proved to be a mistake. On 1 January 1812 Wellington resumed the offensive despite the intense cold, aiming to lay siege to Ciudad Rodrigo and Badajoz before marching into central Spain. By early April both forts had been taken (*see box*, p.65); two months later Wellington's Anglo-Portuguese army crossed the River Agueda and advanced towards Salamanca, capturing the town on 17 June. Marmont deliberately drew Wellington deeper into Spain along stretched supply lines, refusing to give battle, and on 16 July threatened to outflank his opponent on the River Douro. Wellington pulled back towards Salamanca, tempting Marmont to over-extend his advance. On 22 July, on a plain beneath the Arapiles Heights to the southeast of Salamanca, the French spearhead was suddenly attacked in the flank by the British 3rd and 5th Divisions, hidden from Marmont's view by folds in the ground. As the French infantry reeled from the shock, they were hit by a stunning cavalry charge carried out by the British Heavy Brigade, commanded by General Le

WAR IN AMERICA (1812–15)

The British policy of trying to interdict neutral trade with France by stopping merchant ships on the high seas inevitably alienated the United States of America. On 18 June 1812, the US Congress declared war on Britain and ordered a three-pronged offensive into Canada. It did not go well. In the west the Americans were defeated by a mixed force of Canadian militiamen and British regulars, losing Forts Mackinac and Dearborn (at either end of Lake Michigan) as well as Detroit. In the centre, along the Niagara frontier, nearly 1000 American troops were forced to surrender at Queenston (Canada), while the attack in the east, towards Montreal, soon petered out. A renewed offensive in 1813 fared little better in the area to the east of Niagara, where the British counter-attacked and burned Buffalo, although in the west, after a US naval victory on Lake Erie, American troops did force a British withdrawal.

In 1814 the Americans tried to exploit their slight advantage by committing a 3500-man army to the Niagara frontier. Despite a victory over British regulars at Chippewa River (5 July), the Americans were stopped at the Battle of Lundy's Lane (25 July) and forced to pull back. A month later, a British amphibious force entered Chesapeake Bay, sailed up the River Potomac and attacked Washington, burning the Capitol and other government buildings. A similar attack on Baltimore was met with more effective defence in September, upon which the British sailed back to the West Indies. But they soon returned, this time to attack New Orleans with over 8000 veteran troops newly arrived from Europe. On 23 December, they landed at Bayou Bienvenu and marched towards New Orleans along a narrow route between the River Mississippi and an area of swampland. They soon encountered defences manned by 5700 American troops under Major-General (and future President) Andrew Jackson. A frontal attack by the British on 8 January 1815 was disastrous – they suffered over 2000 casualties before withdrawing – but the battle was, in fact, unnecessary. Two weeks earlier, peace terms had been negotiated at Ghent, although it took time for the news to cross the Atlantic. The Battle of New Orleans was a pointless end to a pointless war.

Marchant (who was killed in the process). By nightfall, Marmont's Army of Portugal had collapsed, losing an estimated 14,000 men and 20 guns; Marmont himself, wounded in the early stages of the engagement, was on his way back to France. It was Wellington's most impressive victory to date.

An immediate consequence was the liberation of Madrid, effected by Wellington's troops on 12 August, but the French were by no means finished. As the British and Portuguese marched north to lay siege to Burgos, General Clausel (Marmont's successor) rallied his forces and moved against Wellington, while further south an army of 60,000 Frenchmen advanced towards the Spanish capital. Faced with possible encirclement, Wellington pulled back to Salamanca and then to Ciudad Rodrigo, abandoning all his territorial gains of the year, including Madrid. By October, his troops were dispersed in winter quarters in central Portugal.

THE ROAD TO VICTORY

Despite the apparently indecisive nature of operations in 1812, the French hold on Spain had been weakened. The defeat at Salamanca undermined French morale and gave renewed hope to the people of Spain, a significant proportion of whom engaged in, or actively supported, guerrilla attacks that diverted substantial numbers of French soldiers from the front line. Thus when Wellington began his next campaign in May 1813, his chances of success were higher than ever before. He now had over 80,000 Allied troops under his command, half of whom he sent towards Salamanca and half along the River Esla with the intention of encircling the enemy army in Castile. The French withdrew through Valladolid, Palencia and Burgos, but on 21 June were forced to make a stand at Vitoria to protect their retreating columns. The ensuing battle, although a victory for Wellington, was marred by a failure to pursue the broken enemy – British soldiers seemed far more interested in looting the French baggage train – but the results were impressive. By the end of the month northern and central Spain had been cleared except for small garrisons in San Sebastian and Pamplona (which Wellington proceeded to besiege) and the French had withdrawn into the Pyrenees. Operations in eastern Spain, carried out by a British force of 8000 men that had landed at Alicante in 1812, were less successful, but to all intents and purposes the Iberian Peninsula was now in Allied hands.

After 20 years of war the British Army was at last achieving decisive results. This trend continued during the final months of the Peninsular War. Despite French counter-attacks in July 1813, delivered around Roncesvalles and the Maya Pass, Wellington succeeded in taking both Pamplona and San Sebastian by October. He then moved against enemy positions along the River Bidassoa with the intention of invading France, winning the Battle of the Nivelle in November and approaching the city of Bayonne on either side of the River Nive a month later. At the same time, British forces in eastern Spain advanced as far as Gerona, putting additional pressure on the French, who were also having to contend with Austrian, Russian and Prussian attacks from the east. Thus when Wellington resumed his offensive in January 1814, he did so against weakened opposition. On 27 February he won the Battle

THE BATTLE OF WATERLOO

Early on Sunday 18 June 1815 the 68,000 men of Wellington's Anglo-Dutch army took up positions, after a wet and miserable night, along a crescent-shaped ridge to the south of Mont St Jean. Wellington had chosen the ground with care to ensure that he had the advantage of shelter from French artillery fire, although his line was by no means impregnable. The bulk of his forces were deployed to cover his centre, marked by a crossroads just to the north of the farm of La Haye Sainte, and right, where the ridge curved south towards the château and farm of Hougoumont. His left, towards Papelotte and La Haye, was less strongly defended, although Wellington hoped that the gap would be filled by Prussian troops, marching from the east under Marshal Blücher, as the day went on. Both La Haye Sainte and Hougoumont contained Allied garrisons, partly to attract enemy attention but also to force the French to concentrate their main assault on the fairly narrow corridor between the two farms.

Facing the Allies were about 72,000 Frenchmen under the overall command of Napoleon – the first time that he and Wellington had met on the field of battle. The Emperor's plan was to begin with a massive artillery barrage and an attack on Hougoumont, intended to force Wellington to commit his reserves to the defence of the chateau. This would weaken the Allied centre preparatory to a major French infantry assault. Hougoumont was attacked at 11.30 a.m. and, defended by British Foot Guards, was to be the scene of desperate fighting throughout the day, although the fact that it never fell to the French meant that Wellington's right flank was secure.

First-Hand Account

'As the enemy's artillery was taking off a great many of our men, we were ordered to lie down, to avoid the shots as much as possible; and I took advantage of this circumstance to obtain an hour's sleep, as comfortably as ever I did in my life, though there were at that time upwards of three hundred cannon in full play. But our services were now soon to be required. A considerable number of the French cuirassiers made their appearance, on the rising ground just in our front, took the artillery we had placed there, and came at a gallop down upon us. Their appearance, as an enemy, was certainly enough to inspire a feeling of dread – none of them under six feet; defended by steel helmets and breastplates, made pigeon-breasted to throw off the balls. Their appearance was of

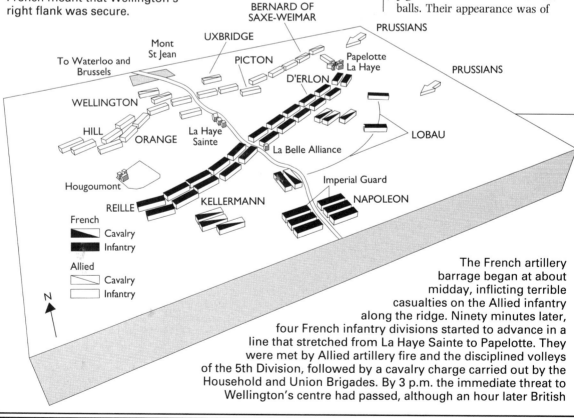

The French artillery barrage began at about midday, inflicting terrible casualties on the Allied infantry along the ridge. Ninety minutes later, four French infantry divisions started to advance in a line that stretched from La Haye Sainte to Papelotte. They were met by Allied artillery fire and the disciplined volleys of the 5th Division, followed by a cavalry charge carried out by the Household and Union Brigades. By 3 p.m. the immediate threat to Wellington's centre had passed, although an hour later British

18 JUNE 1815

such a formidable nature, that I thought we could not have the slightest chance with them. They came up rapidly, until within about ten or twelve paces of the square, when our rear ranks poured into them a well-directed fire, which put them into confusion, and they retired; the two front ranks, kneeling, then discharged their pieces at them. Some of the cuirassiers fell wounded, and several were killed; those of them that were dismounted by the death of their horses, immediately unclasped their armour to facilitate their escape . . . My comrade . . . was on my right hand, in the front face of the square in the front rank, kneeling; he had a trifling defect in his speech; at every charge the cavalry made, he would say, "Tom, Tom, here comes the *calvary*" . . .'

Sergeant Thomas Morris,
2nd Battalion, 73rd Regiment

Sergeant Thomas Morris, *Recollections of Military Service in 1813, 1814, and 1815,* James Madden and Co., London, 1845

Personality Profile:

Arthur Wellesley, 1st Duke of Wellington (1769–1852)

Arthur Wesley – the family name was changed to Wellesley in 1798 – was the fifth son of the 1st Earl of Mornington. He joined the Army in 1787 as an ensign in the 73rd Foot, but saw little regimental service, acting as aide-de-camp to the Lord-Lieutenant of Ireland until 1793. By then, he had gained rapid promotion, chiefly by means of purchase, and was a lieutenant-colonel in the 33rd Foot. He took the regiment to Flanders in 1794 and participated in the dismal retreat to Germany in 1794–5 (*see* p. 52). In 1797, as a full colonel, he accompanied the 33rd to India, where he achieved a reputation as an effective commander (*see* box, p. 58), initially at Seringapatam (1799) and, as a major-general, at Assaye and Argaum (1803). Knighted in 1804, he was promoted to lieutenant-general four years later and given command of British forces committed to the defence of Portugal. His victories at Rolica and Vimeiro were impressive, but his

association with the Convention of Cintra (*see* p. 61) threatened to end his career. However, after Sir John Moore's death at Corunna in January 1809, the government turned to Wellesley for advice, and in April he was sent back to Portugal. His subsequent campaigns in Portugal, Spain and France (1809–14) confirmed his reputation as an astute, often brilliant, general. He was prepared to give ground when necessary, drawing the French into untenable positions, yet at the same time was capable of seizing any opportunity to attack. His victories at Talavera in 1809 (for which he was created Viscount Wellington) and Salamanca three years later are often cited as his most impressive. By 1814 he was a duke and a field marshal, but it was at Waterloo on 18 June 1815 that he reached the height of his fame, commanding Allied forces that, aided by the Prussians, inflicted a crushing defeat on Napoleon. Wellington served as C-in-C in France until 1818, when he returned to Britain to pursue a political career which included terms as prime minister in 1828–30 and 1834, but it is as a military commander – the best produced by Britain since Marlborough – that he is remembered.

infantry were presented with the amazing sight of nearly 4000 French horsemen coming towards them. The infantry immediately 'formed square' to create solid fortresses out of which musket fire could be poured to disrupt any cavalry charge (*see cover picture*). Protected by artillery, none of the squares was broken and, as French casualties mounted, the cavalry withdrew. Elsewhere, however, the French did enjoy success, taking La Haye Sainte when the defenders ran out of ammunition. This persuaded Napoleon that the Allies were cracking. At 6 p.m. he ordered his remaining reserve – seven battalions of the Imperial Guard – to advance across ground to the right of Hougoumont. They did so with superb discipline, despite coming under intense artillery fire, but as they approached the ridge they encountered British infantry that had been sheltering on the reverse slope. As volley after volley poured into the French ranks, the Imperial Guard faltered and broke. Wellington, aware by now that the Prussians had arrived to cover his left flank, signalled his forces to advance. They proceeded to sweep the enemy from the field.

The battle, in Wellington's own words, was 'the nearest run thing you ever saw in your life', but it was decisive. At a cost to the Allies of about 22,000 casualties, Napoleon's dream of a restored empire lay shattered.

of Orthez, to the east of Bayonne; within weeks he had captured Bordeaux and pushed forward as far as Toulouse, where the final battle of the war took place on 10 April. By then, Paris had fallen to the eastern allies, Napoleon had abdicated and French resistance had crumbled.

The Peninsular campaign had cost the British Army about 40,000 dead since 1808, but in the process its reputation as a fighting force had been enhanced immeasurably. This owed much to the genius of Wellington, but there can be no doubt that the Army itself had improved significantly since 1793. It had learnt a variety of lessons from its earlier defeats, not least the need for professional skill. During the Peninsular campaign, for example, light cavalry concentrated on the roles for which they had been raised originally – reconnaissance, outpost duty and skirmishing – and although Wellington never laid great emphasis on his horsemen, units such as the 14th and 16th Light Dragoons, as well as their counterparts in the King's German Legion, gradually gained experience and expertise. Similarly, the artillery played a vital role, providing flexible and integrated firepower on the battlefield, while the engineers proved their worth during siege operations. In the build-up to battle, the 95th Foot (Rifles) acted as skirmishers to absorb the initial enemy thrusts and give warning of an impending attack; once battle was joined, the key to success was good fire discipline in the infantry, who often waited until the French were close before rising from hidden positions to pour volleys of musket fire into their ranks, followed by a bayonet charge. In certain circumstances, as at Salamanca, a charge by heavy cavalry could have tremendous additional impact.

If all these elements operated together, the army in the Peninsula was extremely difficult to defeat, although its true strength lay in its internal discipline. This was achieved partly by flogging and, on occasion, executing recalcitrant soldiers, but there was more to it than that. New recruiting methods, especially the offer of short-service engagements, attracted more intelligent and self-motivated men (as indicated by the plethora of soldiers' memoirs that appeared after 1815), while the growth of regimental identity provided a focus for loyalty and pride. In addition, there was an inevitable development of professional expertise among the officers and men who survived the various battles, enhanced by a deepening trust in Wellington as their commander – 'the long-nosed bugger who defeats the French'. The Peninsular army had its problems – it was never large, its supply system did not always work and many of its soldiers were undoubtedly

the 'scum of the earth' – but by 1814 Wellington had forged it into a formidable instrument.

THE WATERLOO CAMPAIGN

But the war against Napoleon was not over. Exiled to the island of Elba by the victorious Allies in 1814, he escaped and returned to France in March 1815, determined to resume his imperial role. The Allies immediately raised forces to oppose him, although in the case of Britain this was by no means easy. Many of the Peninsular veterans had been sent to America, where a war had been going on since 1812 (see box, p.67), or were being transported to colonial garrisons in the post-war distribution of units; some were even in the process of being disbanded. Thus, when Wellington assumed command of about 68,000 British, Dutch, Hanoverian and Brunswicker soldiers, only about half of the British contingent of 24,000 had served under him in the Peninsula. Those units that were experienced were undoubtedly of high quality, including the 52nd Foot (Light Infantry) and 95th Foot (Rifles), but others, such as the 3rd battalion of the 14th Foot, comprised little more than half-trained recruits, recently drawn from the militia. However, Wellington could call on the support of 113,000 Prussians under Marshal Blücher. Together, they defended the Low Countries.

The campaign began on 15 June when Napoleon crossed the River Sambre in an attempt to drive a wedge between Wellington and Blücher. On 16 June he attacked the Prussians at Ligny, forcing them back towards Wavre, away from Wellington's army. Meanwhile, another French force under Marshal Ney advanced towards Wellington at the important cross-roads at Quatre Bras, where a bloody yet indecisive battle occurred, also on 16 June. It was during this engagement that the 69th Foot, ordered not to go into a 'square' by the inexperienced Prince of Orange, was virtually wiped out by French cavalry. On 17 June Wellington secretly withdrew from Quatre Bras; by the following morning his entire army was in position astride the main road to Brussels, occupying the Mont St Jean ridge just to the south of the village of Waterloo. It was there on 18 June that one of the most decisive battles in history took place (see p.68). Napoleon was finally defeated and the reputation of the British Army firmly established. It was to live on that reputation for the next 40 years.

CONGREVE'S ROCKETS

In 1808 Sir William Congreve, working at the Royal Laboratory at Woolwich, invented a rocket for use on the battlefield. Mounted on a triangle and with a range of about 3500 yards, it could be fired towards the enemy, making up for its lack of accuracy by spreading panic and confusion. In June 1813 various rocket detachments of the Royal Artillery were sent to Germany, where they took part in the Battle of Leipzig (16–19 October 1813). A Rocket Troop, commanded by Captain E. C. Whinyates, was present at Waterloo in June 1815, although Wellington was not an enthusiast, insisting that the troop should also deploy cannon. The rockets were used, however, most notably during the retreat from Quatre Bras.

CHAPTER FOUR

WATERLOO TO MONS (1815–1914)

....

CONTINUITY AND CHANGE

BETWEEN the close of the Napoleonic Wars and the beginning of the First World War, the British Army faced rapidly expanding commitments in both domestic and imperial defence. This growth took place in the familiar context of voluntary enlistment and a society which, if not actively hostile, was decidedly indifferent to soldiers. Not only did it seem that public opinion could only be aroused by disasters such as befell the Army during the Crimean War (1853–6) and again during the early stages of the South African War (1899–1902), but also that reforms were then instituted as a result of temporary agitation, only to be overtaken by succeeding crises. Certainly, there are continuities in the Army's development between 1815 and 1914; there are, for example, apparent similarities between the reforms attempted by Edward Cardwell as Secretary of State for War between 1868 and 1872 and those of Richard Burdon Haldane, who held the office between 1906 and 1912. However, traditional images of complacency during this period do not convey the full story.

MILITARY STAGNATION AFTER WATERLOO

Between 1815 and 1854, there was much about the Army that would have been entirely familiar to British soldiers of the second half of the 18th century, if not before. Indeed, it has often been maintained that the Army was frozen at the moment of its victory at Waterloo. It was an image supported by the vivid war reports from the Crimea by William Howard Russell, correspondent for *The Times*, and by the report of the radically driven Select Committee on the Army before Sebastopol, the parliamentary motion for the establishment of which in January 1855 led to the fall of the Earl of Aberdeen's government.

Other evidence also suggests the same conclusion. The Duke of York, who had commanded the Army in its first campaign of the Revolutionary Wars in Holland in the 1790s (*see* p.55), remained Commander-in-Chief until his death in 1827. His successor was the Duke of Wellington, although he resigned when appointed prime minister a year later. Even so, Wellington continued to exert a powerful influence through his successor as C-in-C, Lord Hill, who had been one of his divisional commanders in the Peninsular campaign. When Hill died in 1842, Wellington resumed the office of C-in-C, occupying the position until his death in 1852. Moreover, throughout the period 1827–52 the Military Secretary at the Horse Guards (the location of the C-in-C's offices) was Lord Fitzroy Somerset, formerly Wellington's secretary in the Peninsula. As Lord Raglan, Somerset was to command the Army in the Crimea (*see box*, p.81). Lord Hardinge, who succeeded Wellington as C-in-C, had also fought in the Peninsula and, of the five divisional generals chosen for command in the Crimea, four were also Peninsular veterans. The fifth, the Duke of Cambridge, was only 35 years old, but had been chosen primarily through royal pressure since he was the Queen's cousin.

Yet there is also evidence that people at the time were not aware of any major problems. Even Russell, though he was admittedly making the comparison for effect, wrote of the Crimean expeditionary force that 'it was the noblest army ever sent from these shores'. The traditional view of the Army's stagnation during the first half of the 19th century therefore needs to be re-examined.

THE CONQUEST OF INDIA, 1819–49

By 1819 about two-thirds of the Indian sub-continent was controlled by the British East India Company from its bases in Bombay, Madras and Calcutta. Since the defeat of Tippoo Sahib at Seringapatam in 1799 (*see* p.58), campaigns had been fought against the Pindaris (1812–17), the Gurkhas (1814–16) and the Mahrattas (1817–19) to secure most of central India up to the River Sutlej in the north-west and Nepal in the north-east.

But the Company's territorial holdings were still not secure, so further campaigns were necessary. In 1824 an expeditionary force entered Burma to take Rangoon and in 1839 a similar move was made into Afghanistan, the main aim of which was to forestall Russian expansionism by putting the pro-British ruler Shah Shujah on the throne. A mixed British-Indian force took Kabul, only to trigger resistance from Afghan tribesmen used to the bitter cold and mountainous terrain. In January 1842 the British forces tried to withdraw into India through high, snow-choked passes. Near Gandamak, at the end of a disastrous retreat, the last remnants of the 44th Foot were wiped out, with only one man surviving. A replacement army took its revenge later in the year, but all ideas of permanently occupying Afghanistan had to be abandoned.

This was a rare defeat, however. In 1843 Sir Charles Napier occupied Scinde after the Battle of Miani (announcing the fact with a single-word despatch, *Peccavi* – Latin for 'I have sinned'). This left the British free to concentrate their efforts against their major remaining enemy, the Sikhs. A Sikh army crossed the River Sutlej in autumn 1845, laying siege to Ferozepore and Ludhiana while building a huge fortified camp at Ferozeshah. British-Indian troops under General Sir Hugh Gough immediately moved forward, inflicting an initial defeat on the Sikhs at Mudki before advancing towards Ferozeshah. Poor communications led to a delay before the attack could begin on 21 December, and the battle soon degenerated into a confused, noisy affair in which neither side was prepared to give ground. Indeed, it continued into the night and, after a pause to regroup, into the next day as well, when victory for Gough was assured only after further heavy fighting. The British-Indian force suffered over 2400 casualties, with both the 9th and 62nd Foot losing more than 300 men. In January 1846 Sikh troops threatening Ludhiana were defeated at Aliwal, where the 16th Lancers conducted an epic charge against Sikh infantry squares; in February Gough destroyed an enemy camp at Sobraon on the Sutlej to end the First Sikh War.

The Second Sikh War was more decisive. In January 1849 Gough advanced from Lahore to Chillianwala, where he engaged the Sikh army in a scrappy night battle that neither side could rightly claim as a victory. The ensuing engagement at Gujerat was a more skilfully fought affair. Here, British success was assured, principally by effective use of artillery, and on 10 March the Sikhs surrendered.

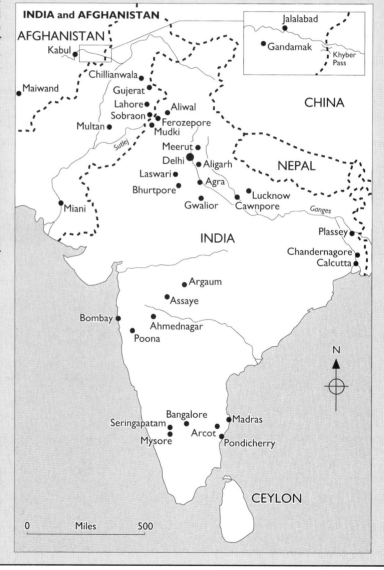

THE ARMY AND THE PEOPLE

Public attitudes towards the Army in Britain had certainly not changed much since the 18th century. It is interesting to note that while there were, between 1830 and 1850, some 58 parliamentary bills or select committee reports concerning prisons, 51 on health matters, 44 on education and 32 on factories, there were only 23 on the Army, the great majority of which were of purely minor significance. Civilian reformers had little to say about the Army beyond demands for economy. With the exception of a periodic interest in the effect of flogging, there was no real concern about the conditions under which soldiers served.

There were a number of reasons for this continuing marginalization of the Army from society. For one thing, it remained scattered across the globe, and out of sight tended to mean out of mind. The Empire had expanded from 26 colonies in 1793 to 43 in 1815, and then continued to expand at a steady rate between 1815 and 1865. Such growth was of immense significance to the Army's development, but public awareness of the implications of imperial commitment was minimal. As Sir John Seeley was to remark in his celebrated series of lectures, *The Expansion of England*, in 1883, Britain had 'conquered and peopled half the world in a fit of absence of mind'. The public cared only that such expansion should be financed on a shoestring. The Army remained small and its resources could never meet its increasing commitments. Rarely exceeding two per cent of the male population of the United Kingdom, the Army's establishment was cut to 149,000 men in 1816 and was down to 109,000 by 1837 before recovering to 152,000 by 1848. In 1854, when the Army was again 152,000 strong, some 27,000 men were stationed in India, 50,000 in the settled colonies of Canada, Australia, New Zealand and South Africa, and another 23,000 in other colonies.

In addition, there were the 315,000 men of the army of the East India Company. This had the advantage of being paid for by the Indian government, and it made Britain's overall manpower roughly equal to that of the main continental European states. However, it was not readily available much beyond India's frontiers. Thus, after deducting garrisons for the United Kingdom, the Army was hard put indeed to find the 27,000 men sent to the Crimea. The British or Indian Armies fought some 17 major campaigns throughout the Empire between Queen Victoria's accession in 1837 and the outbreak of the Crimean War, but – with the possible exception of the loss of the army sent to Afghanistan in 1842 and the popular enthusiasm for the anti-Russian crusade in 1854 – such campaigns had little impact on the British public.

A cartoon pillories the Army for its actions at Peterloo, 16 August 1819. Although the 'massacre' of demonstrators was caused by Yeomanry rather than regular cavalry, the role of the Army was widely condemned.

DOMESTIC DUTIES

Of more pressing concern was the possibility of a renewed threat of invasion from France. Despite the Crimean alliance, deep suspicions of the French remained and it was believed by some that steam-power had 'bridged the Channel', to quote Lord Palmerston in 1845. Invasion scares occurred in Britain in both 1846–7 and 1851–2, and again in 1858–9. While soldiers such as Wellington and Hardinge urged the rapid expansion of the Army to meet such threats, this was not a solution likely to commend itself to politicians or public. Thus the debate revolved around the capacity of the Royal Navy as the first line of defence and the possibility of reform of the militia or a revival of the volunteer movement of the Revolutionary and Napoleonic Wars – or both – as a means of securing the second line of defence. Indeed, the militia was to be reformed in 1852 and the volunteers revived in 1859.

In many respects, therefore, the Army was not regarded as having a decisive role in home defence. It was unfortunate that the one role in which its services were still required – that of maintaining domestic order – naturally brought it into conflict with society. The amateur members of the mounted Yeomanry had survived the demobilization of other auxiliary forces in 1815 and performed an active role in lending aid to the civil power. But in view of the Yeomanry's alleged Tory

political leanings, magistrates much preferred to have regular troops available. Moreover, there were plenty of disturbances in Britain between 1815 and 1848 – the Pentrich Rising in 1817 in Derbyshire, the 'Peterloo Massacre' in Manchester in 1819, a near insurrection at Merthyr Tydfil in June 1831, and the various manifestations of Chartism in the late 1830s and into the 1840s, which included an attempted uprising at Newport in Monmouthshire in November 1839.

In fact, few troops were required to disperse the handful of disturbances that did seem to have more than rudimentary purpose or organization. A single volley by a detachment of the 45th Foot, for example, was sufficient to suppress between 4000 and 5000 Chartists at Newport in 1839. In reality, deaths at the hands of the forces of law and order were comparatively rare in Britain between 1815 and 1848. South Wales saw arguably the worst violence, but troops still opened fire on only three occasions, killing one person in 1816, between 16 and 25 at Merthyr Tydfil in 1831 and between 12 and 20 at Newport in 1839. The 'Peterloo Massacre', which principally involved the Yeomanry, accounted for 11 deaths. Britain was not actually unpoliced, but it was not until 1856 that the County and Borough Police Act made the establishment of constabularies mandatory. For the Army, its role in aid of the civil power was still an important domestic duty and one always likely to increase its isolation from society.

SOCIAL COMPOSITION OF THE ARMY

The Army also continued to be distanced from society by its social composition. The Royal Commission on Purchase in 1857 was to remark that the middle classes seemed to have 'no place in the army under the present system' and, of course, purchase was not to be abolished until 1871. Non-purchase commissions accounted for only an average of 19.3 per cent of those granted between 1830 and 1859, and it was still possible for commissions to change hands at prices well above the regulation tariff. In 1826, for example, Lord Lucan purchased command of the 17th Lancers for an estimated £25,000 and his brother-in-law, Lord Cardigan, who had been dismissed from command of the 15th Hussars in 1834 for quarrelling with his officers, reputedly paid £40,000 for command of the 11th Hussars in 1836: in both cases the regulation price was only £6175. Officers therefore remained largely drawn from the traditional landed elite. Figures are subject to some variance in terms of interpretation, but in 1830 it is generally assumed that 53 per cent of officers were from landed or gentry families. The majority of the remainder are sometimes termed middle class, but it is clear that they were drawn from small landed proprietors or military

Potential recruits are treated to stories of Army life by sergeants of a Lancer and a Dragoon Guard regiment, c. 1855. The exploits of the cavalry in the Crimea are doubtless being used to advantage.

families hardly representative of the commercial groups which might normally be regarded as middle class. Certainly, the Army's leadership remained predominantly drawn from the land-owning classes in an increasingly urban and industrialized society.

While wealth from any source could buy commissions and officers increasingly held their social position because they were officers and not because they were necessarily gentlemen, there was little likelihood that the Army's rank and file would become any more representative of society as a whole. Army life remained distinctly unattractive, with enlistment remaining for life, which was interpreted as being between 21 and 24 years depending on the branch of service, until 1847. Indeed, a parallel provision for a limited term of enlistment of

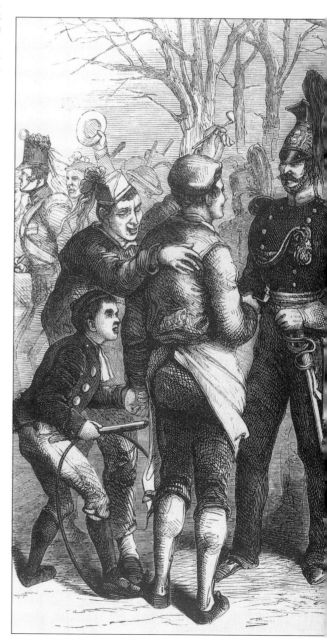

seven years, introduced in 1806, had been discontinued in 1829. Throughout the first half of the 19th century, pay remained at the rate of 1s 1d (5½p) per day fixed in 1800, although stoppages varied from period to period. Diet was poor, salted meat in particular contributing to disease, as did alcohol and insanitary barracks: indeed, in 1856 it was calculated that while inmates of British prisons enjoyed an average of 1000 cubic feet of space each, a soldier had but 400 cubic feet in barracks. Urine tubs were left in the rooms all night and simply rinsed out in the morning before being used to carry rations. One report during the Crimean War stated that 'the air was offensive both from the men's breath and from the urine tubs in the room, and, of course, some soldiers do not keep their feet very clean, especially in summer time'.

CONDITIONS OF SERVICE

With upwards of two-thirds of a man's service likely to be abroad, the resulting death-rate was appallingly high. A detailed survey of the Army's health, carried out between 1835 and 1842, revealed that since 1817 the death-rate of males of military age – taken to be between 18 and 45 – in Britain had varied between an annual rate of 11.5 per 1000 and 16 per 1000, depending on location. Among soldiers garrisoned in Britain, the death-rate averaged 15.3 per 1000 per annum between 1817 and 1836, with deaths from tuberculosis five times higher than in the British population as a whole. Overseas, it averaged 69 per 1000 in India, 85 per 1000 in the West Indies, 483 per 1000 in Sierra Leone and a staggering 668 per 1000 in the Gold Coast. Small wonder that the Army continued, as in the past, to rely upon the social misfits, the unemployed, the criminal classes and the rural poor (especially the Irish) for its recruits. About 42 per cent of the Army's rank and file was recruited in Ireland in 1830, but this declined to some 37.2 per cent in 1840 and to 28.4 per cent by 1861, reflecting large-scale emigration to the United States and elsewhere. Irish emigration, together with rural depopulation and an increasingly buoyant domestic labour market in Britain as a whole, meant that the Army found it increasingly difficult to attract the 11,000 to 12,000 recruits it needed each year in peacetime.

ATTEMPTS AT REFORM, 1815–55

The Army's system of administration remained that of the late 18th century, with the same division of authority between multiple departments and the same conflicting and often ill-defined responsibilities. Parliament, concerned only with restricting the military budget, played a limited role, while paradoxically the role of the Crown increased significantly through the close interest in the Army displayed by William IV and then by Prince Albert.

Nevertheless, the Army did not go unreformed between 1815 and 1854, primarily because there were some politicians who took an interest in the Army and also an increasing number of younger officers who began to assert that they belonged to a distinct profession. Indeed, most reforms were internally generated by officers at regimental level, supported by some influential individuals in higher ranks, such as G. R. Gleig, Chaplain-General from 1844 to 1875, and Lord Frederick Fitzclarance, who unfortunately died at the age of only 55 while serving as C-in-C at Bombay in 1854. These men and others like them publicized their ideas through a growing number of professional military bodies such as the United Service Institution, founded in 1829, and the Royal Artillery Institution, founded in 1840. Professional military journals such as the *United Service Journal*,

THE LOSS OF THE *BIRKENHEAD*

On 17 January 1852 the *Birkenhead*, a paddle-steamer frigate converted to carry troops, left Cork with over 500 British soldiers from a variety of regiments on board, bound for South Africa. She arrived at Simon's Bay near Cape Town on 23 February after a rough passage, but put to sea again two days later, her captain under orders to land the troops at Port Elizabeth, round the Cape of Good Hope on the south-east coast. Next morning she ran aground off Danger Point, about 50 miles from Simonstown. As the sea rushed in to swamp the bow of the ship, the troops were called on deck by their officers and told to await instructions. There was no panic as the soldiers were ordered off in parties to help the sailors and to ensure that all women and children on board were saved. Twenty-five minutes later, the *Birkenhead* began to break up and the men were given permission to abandon ship; less than half survived. When news of the disaster reached London in early April, it was reported as a superb example of military discipline and self-sacrifice. The Duke of Wellington, by now in his 83rd year, commented favourably on the conduct of the soldiers, many of whom were barely trained recruits, and in Prussia the story was read out at the head of every regiment in the army. It did much to enhance the reputation of the British soldier.

founded in 1827, and the *United Service Gazette* and *Naval and Military Gazette*, both founded in 1833, provided them with further channels through which to disseminate their views. In 1837 the last two journals sold over 125,000 copies between them.

Reforming officers demanded an extension of, and higher standards in, military training and professional education. They supported more practical education for artillery and engineer officers at the Royal Military Academy Woolwich in 1846, the introduction of commissioning examinations for cavalry and infantry officers at the Royal Military College Sandhurst in 1849, promotion examinations to the rank of captain in 1850, and the eventual creation of the Staff College at Camberley in 1858 from the former Senior Department of the RMC. The growing threat from France encouraged further reform after Hardinge's appointment as C-in-C in 1852. A proper engineering school of instruction was established at Chatham in 1852, an artillery school at Shoeburyness in the same year and a musketry school at Hythe in 1853. Hardinge had been involved in a number of these initiatives and he was responsible for the establishment of a 'camp of exercise' at Chobham in 1853, Fitzclarance also holding one at Poona in the same year. Land at Aldershot was purchased in 1853 and 1854 to provide a more permanent site for manoeuvres. Hardinge also oversaw a six-fold increase in the number of field artillery pieces in the Army and the introduction of the rifled musket.

The position of the private soldier also underwent a steady transformation through the efforts of the military press and of military reformers. The latter included G. R. Gleig and the key figure of Henry Grey, Viscount Howick (later 3rd Earl Grey), who was Secretary at War from 1835 to 1839 and Secretary of State for War and the Colonies from 1846 to 1852. One important development was increased control over, and reduction of, corporal punishment. In 1836 a Royal Commission recommended a range of penalties, such as an increased use of imprisonment, as alternatives to flogging. Howick reduced the maximum number of lashes permitted to 50 in 1846. More military cells were provided as the debate then moved on to the appropriate level of severity of a military prison regime. At the same time, Howick and others urged

a conscious attempt to ameliorate the condition of the soldier's life-style in a way that provided some alternative to drink as a recreation. Good-conduct rewards were introduced in 1836, garrison libraries in 1840, garrison cricket pitches in 1841, savings banks in 1842 and compulsory education in 1850. The last was especially desirable since about 20 per cent of the Army's recruits could neither read nor write and a further 18 per cent could read but not write.

It was Howick, too, who ordered the survey of Army health mentioned earlier. As a result, a system of 10-year rotation was introduced in the western hemisphere in 1837, whereby a regiment would first serve three to four years in the Mediterranean, three to four years in the Caribbean and then the remaining years in North America, before returning to the United Kingdom. The regiment would thus become acclimatized to hotter regions before going to the West Indies, and end in the healthiest area of all, which was Canada. A more informal system of rotation was also introduced in the eastern hemisphere by 1848 and, by 1853, the Army's health was much improved. Partly because of a shortfall in recruits, Howick also advocated shorter service as a means of attracting more men by equalizing military service with other working-class occupations; in 1847 terms of between 10 and 12 years, depending on the arm of service, were substituted for life enlistment. However, the precise effect of this change would not be clear for at least 10 years and it had the disadvantage of failing to provide for an adequate trained reserve. Moreover, all this did not necessarily improve the Army's image, although it was being increasingly less seen as a corruptor of public morals. The reported courage of soldiers during the sinking of the troop-transport *Birkenhead* in February 1852 (*see box*) marked perhaps the beginning of the shift towards the ideal of the 'Christian soldier'.

However, Howick was not able to carry into effect the additional barrack building he would have liked, and it proved impossible to raise soldiers' pay. Consequently,

The troopship Birkenhead *breaks up off the coast of South Africa, 26 February 1852. The brave conduct of the troops on board, many of them recruits, significantly enhanced the reputation of the Army.*

desertion remained high at times of prosperity in Britain or whenever regiments were on service in North America or Australasia. Nor did Howick have much support as yet for the idea of persuading the colonies to do more for their own defence, or implanting military colonies of former servicemen, as in Austria or Russia: one of the first experiments in establishing a military colony in the eastern Cape ended with the massacre of almost the entire contingent by 'Kaffirs' (members of the Xhosa tribe) in 1850. In general, those reforms that were effected met entrenched opposition from Wellington, and it was only when Hardinge became C-in-C that any real progress was made.

ARMY ADMINISTRATION AND REFORM

Above all, Wellington's opposition was felt in the area of administration, since he declined to accept any diminution of the powers of the C-in-C which might arise from consolidation of the departments responsible for the Army. Primarily, he feared that yet further reductions in the size of the Army might be effected if the budget was no longer obscured by division between several departments. Thus, when in 1837 a Royal Commission dominated by Howick recommended that the Secretary at War be brought into the Cabinet, Wellington insisted that this would make the post too powerful in relation to the C-in-C. Nonetheless, when any campaign began, the local commander of British forces reported directly to the Secretary of State for War and the Colonies. Indeed, in 1851 Wellington had to rely on the newspapers for his information on the latest fighting in South Africa. Hardinge was to find himself in exactly the same position at the outbreak of the Crimean War.

In June 1854, however, some three months after the despatch of the expeditionary force to the Crimea but before any actual military disasters, the Secretary of State for War and the Colonies was divested of his responsibility for the Colonies. With further administrative changes resulting from the shortcomings revealed in the war itself, administration became divided effectively between the Secretary of State for War and the C-in-C in February 1855, with the office of Secretary at War being merged with that of Secretary of State for War. The post of Master-General of the Ordnance was also abolished and the Treasury and Home Office relieved of their share of military administration.

The degree of reform in the Army between 1815 and 1854 should not be exaggerated: it was piecemeal and haphazard, with skirmishing over particular issues at different times rather than advances over a broad front. Nor did the reforms have a significant impact in terms of the Army's likely performance in major wars, since colonial expeditions had ensured that there would be few opportunities to undertake large-scale exercises. Indeed, of the five divisional commanders appointed in 1854 only two had commanded more than a battalion in the field.

THE CRIMEAN WAR (1853–6)

In July 1853 a Russian army occupied the Turkish provinces of Moldavia and Wallachia (in modern Romania) in response to a dispute over control of the Holy Places in Turkish-controlled Jerusalem. Britain and France, in an alliance designed to control Russian expansionism in Europe, agreed to support the Turks, and sent naval forces to Constantinople. They were drawn into the Black Sea after the Turkish navy had been destroyed at Sinope. The Russians – thwarted in Romania – then invaded Bulgaria, prompting Britain and France to declare war on the Tsar on 27 March 1854.

An Anglo-French expeditionary force moved to Varna, on Turkey's Black Sea coast. When the Russians refused to accept proffered peace terms, the decision was taken to destroy Russian naval power in the Black Sea by attacking Sevastopol – a port and naval base in the Crimea. Between 13 and 18 September 1854 the expeditionary force, comprising about 51,000 infantry and 1000 cavalry, landed on a deserted beach some 30 miles north of their objective. But already, with heavy losses through sickness and evidence of poor planning, the war was not going well for the Allies.

A Russian force of 36,400 men waited for the Anglo-French units on heights above the River Alma, on the route to Sevastopol, and it was here on 20 September that the first battle of the Crimean War took place. It was a hard-fought affair, in which British troops attacked up-hill into the face of well-placed Russian guns, losing nearly 3000 casualties. As the Russians withdrew, the Allies closed in on Sevastopol, marching round the port to the south to set up bases at Kamish and Balaklava. A bombardment of Russian defences began on 17 October, but did little appreciable damage, and eight days later the Russians almost broke the siege at the Battle of Balaklava (see p.80).

On 5 November the Russians tried again, attacking at a point between the besieging troops and their field support at Inkerman. In a confused, all-day engagement British infantry refused to give ground, and eventually forced the attackers to withdraw in what was called a 'soldiers' battle'. But the war's main focus was the 11-month siege of Sevastopol, which proved a nightmare, especially in the winter months when supply chains broke and disease set in. By February 1855 the British force had been reduced to 12,000 men, and although the Russian defences were gradually destroyed, it was not until 8 September that the port was finally taken after a Russian evacuation. Peace was signed in Paris in March 1856, by which time the Allies had lost over 250,000 men, most of them to disease.

By gathering over 17,000 men together in peacetime, the exercises at Chobham allowed the largest concentration of military men in England since 1815 and attracted considerable public attention. Arguably, they came too late. Moreover, reform had failed to increase manpower or to address problems within the Army's service departments such as ordnance, commissariat and transport and medical organization. Though Hardinge's reforms in 1852–4 were driven by the increased threat of French invasion, the Army remained organized and trained for limited war against non-European opponents. By the time war broke out in 1854, the reforms of the period since 1852 had not yet begun to yield benefits; nor was it the kind of war for which the Army had been prepared. Not only, therefore, were there many lapses in staff work in the Crimea, a major breakdown in medical and supply services and appalling tactical blunders, but Britain's resources were so strained that militia regiments had to be sent to garrison Mediterranean bases.

THE QUESTION OF A RESERVE

Three years later, the Indian Mutiny (*see box*) also stretched manpower to such an extent that only 14 battalions of infantry were left in England by August 1857. The revived militia and volunteers were cheap but hardly an adequate substitute for a trained reserve. The rapid victories of Prussian conscript armies against the Danes in 1864 and the Austrians in 1866 added to a growing recognition that a more extensive reform was

Regimental Tradition:

THE 32ND FOOT AT LUCKNOW

During the siege of Lucknow in 1857, the Residency was held by, among others, the 32nd Foot (later the 1st Battalion, Duke of Cornwall's Light Infantry, now part of The Light Infantry). In recognition of its gallantry, the unit was given the designation 'Light Infantry', itself a singular honour, but it also absorbed a unique tradition. Because of a shortage of wine during the siege, Queen Victoria's health could not be toasted after every evening meal and was, in fact, drunk only on the Queen's birthday. Thereafter, officers of the battalion were permitted to dispense with the loyal toast except on the sovereign's birthday.

required. Such a stimulus was needed, since the pressure for change generated immediately after the Crimean War had not been sustained. In 1859, as Secretary of State for War, Sidney Herbert established a reserve for men taking an early discharge from the Army, but fewer than 3000 had done so by 1866. Herbert, who suffered from increasing ill-health prior to his death in 1861, also failed to achieve the relatively modest reform of the purchase

THE INDIAN MUTINY (1857–8)

In 1857, Indian troops were issued with a new Enfield rifle, the cartridges for which were greased with a mixture of pig and cow fat to facilitate loading. As the cartridges had to be bitten before being used, both Muslim and Hindu soldiers, forbidden by their religions to touch either pork or beef respectively, were appalled; they were convinced that the British were intent on making them 'outcaste' as a preliminary to imposing Christianity. Other sentiments, ranging from latent Indian nationalism to dissatisfaction with East India Company rule, undoubtedly had their part to play in the uprising that ensued, but the problem with the cartridges acted as a catalyst.

The Mutiny began at Meerut in March 1857, when the 19th Native Infantry refused to obey their officers. Although that particular unit was quickly disbanded, its actions triggered a chain of similar events throughout northern and central India. On 10 May the 3rd Light Cavalry mutinied in Meerut, and the next day, despite a gallant defence of the arsenal by men of the British Commissariat Ordnance Corps, Delhi fell to the mutineers. A British-Indian force was hastily raised in Calcutta which succeeded in reaching a ridge outside Delhi by 7 June, but it was too weak to retake the city.

Meanwhile, in Cawnpore other native units joined the Mutiny, besieging a small British garrison which, on 27 June, was massacred as it withdrew under terms of a locally arranged truce. Lucknow came under threat, and on 30 June began one of the most celebrated

sieges in British military history, as British and loyal Indian troops under the Governor of Oudh, Henry Lawrence, held out in the Residency. They were not relieved until 25 September. By then, forces had been gathered for the reoccupation of Delhi, the battle for which began on 11 September. After intensely heavy fighting, British and Indian troops cleared the city by the 20th. The Mutiny was effectively over, although it was to take until the summer of 1858 for the last remnants of trouble to be rooted out.

It was obvious from the events of 1857–8 that the East India Company was incapable of ruling India unaided. In November 1858 India came under Crown control and the Company was disbanded, its native military forces becoming the Indian Army.

THE BATTLE OF BALAKLAVA

The British base at Balaklava was defended by two understrength cavalry brigades, a single Highland battalion and a force of about 3000 Turks. The Russian attack on 25 October 1854 was designed to take and hold the heights above Balaklava, severing communications between the base and the main British force at Sebastopol.

Initial Russian moves were successful, overrunning Turkish positions on the heights and capturing some artillery pieces. As the Russians moved down towards Balaklava, however, the 93rd Highlanders, standing two-ranks deep in a 'thin red line', halted the attack. This enabled reinforcements to be brought forward and, as the Russians were recovering, General James Scarlett's Heavy Brigade, comprising Dragoon Guards and Dragoons, thundered into the enemy flank. Despite being outnumbered almost three to one, the Heavy Brigade forced the Russians to withdraw.

There now occurred one of the most famous and wasteful actions of British military history. The British commander, Lord Raglan, aware that the Russians were about to drag away the captured Turkish guns on the heights, ordered the Light Brigade, comprising Hussars, Light Dragoons and Lancers, to intervene. Lord Cardigan, commanding the brigade, misinterpreted the orders and directed his force of 673 men to charge directly towards the main Russian positions in front of them. The 'Charge of the Light Brigade' ended in inevitable disaster, for although the bravery of the Light Brigade could not be doubted, only 370 of the soldiers returned unscathed. The battle petered out, leaving the Russians still in possession of the redoubts above Balaklava but the base itself secure.

First-Hand Account:

The Charge of the Light Brigade

'The trumpets now sounded the advance . . . We moved off, soon breaking into a gallop . . . As we moved off, the Russians opened fire from all their batteries. The round shot passed through us and the shells burst over and amongst us, causing great havoc. The first man of my troop that was struck was Private Young, a cannon ball taking off his right arm. I, being close on his right rear, fancied I felt the wind from it as it passed me. I afterwards found I was bespattered with his flesh. To such a nicety were the enemy's guns elevated for our destruction that, before we had advanced many hundred yards, Private Turner's left arm was also struck off close to the shoulder and Private Ward was struck full in the chest. A shell too burst over us, a piece of which struck

The Charge of the Light Brigade, 25 October 1854. This glorious yet wasteful action led a French commander, General Bosquet, to mutter the immortal words, 'C'est magnifique, mais ce n'est pas la guerre'.

25 OCTOBER 1854

Cornet Houghton in the forehead and mortally wounded him . . .

'We now came under a terrific fire, for the infantry in and about the Redoubts kept up a continual fusilage as we came opposite them, but the men hung well together, keeping their line and closing in as their comrades fell back wounded or killed. Many riderless horses were now galloping along with us, forcing their way into the ranks and keeping their places as well as though their masters had been on their backs . . . At this time we were at a sweeping gallop. In another moment we passed the [Russian] guns, our right flank brushing them . . .'

Sergeant-Major George Loy Smith, 11th Hussars

George Loy Smith (11th Hussars), *A Victorian RSM. From India to the Crimea*, Costello, Tunbridge Wells, 1987/copyright Royal Hussars Museum, Winchester, pp.131–3

Personality Profile:

Lord Raglan (1788–1855)

The eighth son of the 5th Duke of Beaufort, Fitzroy Henry James Somerset served throughout the Peninsular War as secretary to the Duke of Wellington and was present at most of the battles of that campaign. At Waterloo in 1815 he was still at Wellington's side, losing an arm to enemy fire. During the long peace that ensued, he continued to serve the Duke and, in 1852, was created 1st Baron Raglan. Two years later he was chosen to command the British forces committed to the Crimea, but by then he was both old and ill, sometimes confusing his staff by assuming that he was still fighting the French rather than the Russians. Although his forces won the Battles of Alma, Balaklava and Inkerman, Raglan's generalship was questioned, especially over the confused orders given to Lord Cardigan that triggered the ill-fated Charge of the Light Brigade. Raglan died in the Crimea, one of countless victims of the terrible epidemic of disease that destroyed the British contingent.

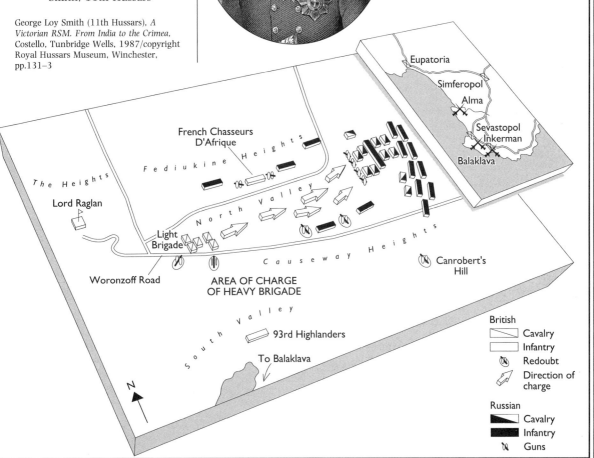

Troops of the British Army and East India Company assault the Kashmir Gate, Delhi, September 1857. The recapture of the city, which had been held by rebels since May, effectively marked the end of the Indian Mutiny.

system he attempted. This followed the virtual collapse of a campaign for abolition mounted by the radical Crimea veteran Sir George de Lacy Evans, whose vociferous advocacy of reform had prompted the Royal Commission on Purchase in 1857. But Herbert did contribute to some improvements in Army education – culminating in the establishment of the Staff College – and in medical organization. The medical reforms certainly fell short of the demands made by Florence Nightingale and her supporters. The latter, who were trying to implement the recommendations of a Commission of Enquiry into the sanitary state of the Army, established in 1857, depicted themselves as ranged against an entrenched inertia and conservatism within the War Office and military establishment.

Not even the concern for national defences, prompted by the continuing threat from France, could shake Treasury opposition to expenditure on barrack or hospital construction and renovation. In March 1867 another Secretary of State for War, General Jonathan Peel, attempted a reform of the reserve, unveiling a scheme to provide 80,000 men for overseas or home service. Characteristically, however, so little inducement was offered for enlistment that barely 40,000 men had done so by 1870, the majority opting firmly for home defence only. One advance came in 1867 when Parliament – albeit by one vote – restricted flogging to men on active service, but this was an exceptional and emotive issue with a potential

impact on the newly expanded electorate of the Second Reform Act. In any case, restriction cost nothing. Flogging was not totally abolished until 1881.

THE CARDWELL REFORMS

Whatever the precise effect of Prussia's continental victories, which was to be further magnified by her success in the Franco-Prussian War (1870–1), it was actually a more traditional concern for retrenchment that was most evident in the comprehensive reform of the Army's organization undertaken by Edward Cardwell, Secretary of State for War in William Gladstone's administration between 1868 and 1872. This reform was to shape the Army for the rest of the century.

Howick had originally suggested withdrawing garrisons of regular troops from the 'white' colonies, and Cardwell now carried this into effect, with Australia, New Zealand and Canada becoming responsible for their own defence. Not only did this save money and manpower, but it also made military service potentially more attractive by reducing the period likely to be spent overseas. It enabled Cardwell to introduce short service on the Prussian model, with infantrymen initially engaging for six years with the Regular Army and six years on the Reserve. The expectation was that a sufficient number of men would extend their service for longer periods to maintain a permanent nucleus of experienced soldiers with the colours. At the

Edward, Viscount Cardwell (1813–86). As Secretary of State for War between 1869 and 1874, he introduced wide-ranging Army reforms that included the reorganization of infantry regiments on a county basis.

same time, the requirement for long-service pensions would be considerably reduced, while Britain would also acquire a trained reserve, readily available in case of emergency.

While the Army as an institution enjoyed increasing popularity for its imperial role through such mediums as the Music Hall, adventure writers such as W. E. Henty, war artists such as Lady Butler and the increasingly extensive coverage of its campaigns by war correspondents such as Archibald Forbes, military service itself was no more attractive than before. Unskilled labourers remained the largest single category of recruits throughout the second half of the 19th century: in 1898, for example, 68 per cent of recruits were so described. Despite the strenuous efforts of Cardwell's successors – not least the Conservative Edward Stanhope, who occupied the War Office from 1887 to 1892 – to improve the lot of the ordinary soldier, military service still implied few opportunities for recreation, discouragement of marriage, a lack of training in trades to fit a soldier for civilian employment after discharge and, indeed, virtually no provision for veterans.

No politician was prepared to implement an increase in pay sufficient to make the Army competitive with civilian wage-rates. Wastage through such causes as desertion remained high and the Army was compelled to reduce its physical standards – between 1861 and 1883 the minimum height requirement dropped by five inches. Given the reluctance to raise basic pay, the only alternative means of acquiring sufficient military manpower

would have been continental-style conscription, and this was recommended by the Wantage Commission in 1892. However, this kind of compulsion, previously applied to the militia for home defence but finally abandoned in 1831, had been so unpopular as to convince politicians that the suggestion of any form of conscription spelled political suicide at the ballot box. Thus the Army remained reliant on what one soldier referred to as the 'compulsion of destitution'.

THE ABOLITION OF PURCHASE

The concern for financial savings also provided the impetus for Cardwell's abolition of purchased commissions, although the process ultimately cost some £8 million in compensation paid to officers who were losing their financial investment in their commissions. Initially, Cardwell had merely wished to modify the system by dispensing with the lowest commissioned ranks of cornet (in the cavalry) and ensign (in the infantry). However, the opposition to this relatively modest proposal from those fearing that they would not be compensated for prices paid over and above the regulation tariff, led to the setting up of a Royal Commission, which demonstrated the impossibility of preventing such over-regulation payments under existing law. Cardwell therefore resolved to abolish the system as a whole, abolition eventually being carried by Royal Warrant in November 1871 when the government's bill failed to pass the House of Lords.

Just as with the changes in military service, the end of the purchase system did not necessarily mean a dramatic reorientation within the officer corps. This was partly because of the persistence of regimental tradition and partly because of the continuing expense of being an officer, since an individual's financial standing was still taken into account when he applied for a commission. It was calculated in the 1870s that an officer would require an annual private income of at least £200 in an infantry battalion and at least £1000 in a cavalry regiment. Thus some poorer officers, such as the young Winston Churchill in the 1890s, chose to serve in India, where living expenses were less. In any case, both the traditional landed elite and those aspiring to that status in what was a remarkably open society for those who acquired wealth, were increasingly attending elitist Public Schools. The Army may not have attracted the ablest products of such schools, nor did the latter teach specifically military subjects, but they did provide the kind of character training invariably equated with leadership.

LOCALIZATION AND LINKED BATTALIONS

The end of purchase facilitated another aspect of Cardwell's scheme by enabling him to bring regular officers and those of the auxiliary forces, who had not been subject to purchase, within a unified command structure. Under what became known as 'localization', two regular battalions of infantry were linked with militia and volunteer battalions in territorial districts served by a single recruit depot. The idea was not only to draw the auxiliary forces into closer union with the regulars but also to forge an association between the regular battalions and a particular locality in the interests of better recruiting. Moreover, while one linked regular battalion served abroad, it would be supplied with reinforcing drafts from its partner battalion serving at home which would be fed, in turn, from the recruit depot.

Localization was bedevilled from the beginning by the impossibility of maintaining equality in the number of battalions at home and abroad. Periodic campaigns such as those against the Ashanti in 1873–4 and against the Zulus in 1879, the latter coinciding with the Second Afghan War of 1878–80, resulted in home battalions being hurried abroad and those remaining at home becoming – in a phrase of Garnet Wolseley – 'squeezed lemons' in supplying constant drafts to battalions overseas. In 1872 there had been 70 battalions at home and 71 abroad, but by 1879 there were only 59 at home. Both the Stanley Committee in 1876 and the Airey Committee in 1878–9 criticized the defects of the system, but they were ignored. Indeed, in 1881 Hugh Childers completed the Cardwell scheme by permanently linking the battalions – the process was known as 'territorialization' – and converting battalions of militia or volunteers into battalions of the new county regiments. Few regulars or auxiliaries appreciated losing traditional titles and neither localization nor territorialization could address the fact that the many regimental depots in the South of England were entirely remote from the majority of potential recruits, who were located primarily in London or the industrial North and Midlands. The 'Pimlico Highlander' thus became a popular image of the unlikely composition of some new county regiments.

RATIONALIZING ARMY ADMINISTRATION

Cardwell's final contribution to the Army's development was to continue the rationalization of its administration by making the C-in-C directly subordinate to the Secretary of State for War and by delegating supply and financial matters respectively to equally subordinate officials, the Surveyor-General of the Ordnance and the Financial Secretary. The symbolic end of the duality in power exercised by the C-in-C and Secretary of State since 1855 was signified by the removal of the office of the former from the Horse Guards to the War Office in Pall Mall. In practice, however, much of the old duality persisted for the remainder of the century since, as politicians, Secretaries of State were subject to the vagaries of the electoral system. Between 1885 and 1887, for example, four individuals held the office during the course of five

administrations. Accordingly, successive transitory holders of the office, who often had little military knowledge, tended to defer not only to virtually permanent officials, but also to the massive authority of the Duke of Cambridge, who had become C-in-C on the death of Hardinge in 1856 and was not forced into retirement until 1895.

If anything, the Cardwell reforms exacerbated the struggle inside the War Office for, under the new system, the soldiers had little effective say in the determination of the military budget, which depended upon political and economic calculations invariably unrelated to military perceptions of need. Thus it became customary for the soldiers to demand too much in order to compensate for the inevitable reductions demanded by the Treasury, a process characterized by the Stephen Commission in 1887 as 'extravagance controlled by stinginess'. However, because of a refusal by its incumbent to accept responsibility for the efficiency of the Army during a war scare with France in 1888, the post of Surveyor-General was abolished and matters of supply returned to military control. But the soldiers were unable to wrest back budgetary control from the Financial Secretary.

WOLSELEY VERSUS ROBERTS

Politicians were also able to exploit the rivalry which emerged between groups within the Army's leadership in the 1870s and 1880s. Ostensibly such divisions were concerned with strategy. What might be termed the 'Home Army' school, associated primarily with the adherents of Garnet Wolseley, maintained that the Army's principal tasks were to prepare for a possible war against Russian ambition in Europe and to defend Britain itself against possible French invasion. By contrast, the 'Indian' school, increasingly represented by associates of Frederick Roberts, believed that the real threat to the Empire was that of a Russian descent on the North-West Frontier of India through Afghanistan.

The struggle was not confined to strategy alone, however, for it ranged over the whole edifice of the Cardwellian system. Wolseley, for example, favoured short-service; Roberts, however, believed that only longer terms of service would adequately meet the needs of Indian defence, arguing that it was essential to maintain a large British garrison in India in addition to native troops (the East India Company's army having come under Crown control after the Mutiny). In practice, the struggle manifested itself primarily in the competition between the rival groups or 'rings' for key staff appointments in the respective British and Indian Armies, and for active service commands on campaign. The process was further confused by the attempts of a conservative military establishment, as represented by the Duke of Cambridge, to prevent the ascendancy of the Wolseley 'ring' in particular. While the Wolseley and Roberts 'rings' were the best known, they were not the only groups seeking influence over military policy. Between 1876 and 1878, for example, when there was a genuine risk of war with Russia over the latter's Balkan ambitions, individual

CAMPAIGNS IN EGYPT AND SUDAN, 1882–98

British interest in Egypt was guaranteed once the Suez Canal was opened in 1869, linking the Mediterranean to the Red Sea and significantly shortening the journey from Europe to the Far East. Shares in the Suez Canal Company, which administered the waterway, were secured by British prime minister Benjamin Disraeli, but events in Egypt soon threatened the security of the Canal. By May 1882 Colonel Ahmed Arabi ('Arabi Pasha') had seized power in Cairo, upon which the British decided to commit an expeditionary force to secure the region. Commanded by Garnet Wolseley (*see* Victorian Military Heroes, p.86), it comprised over 40,000 troops (7000 of them from India) and had as its objective the occupation of Egypt.

The force sailed into the Canal, landing at Ismailia. Arabi's main army, encamped at Tel-el-Kebir, cut off water supplies to Ismailia, forcing Wolseley to advance quickly towards a dam on the Sweet Water Canal at Kassassin, 20 miles inland,

Once in possession of water, he moved on to attack Tel-el-Kebir on 13 September. The battle lasted only 35 minutes, at the end of which the British had inflicted a stunning defeat, losing 480 of their own soldiers but scattering the enemy horde. Arabi was overthrown and Cairo occupied.

Almost immediately, trouble flared up in neighbouring Sudan, where Mohammed Ahmed declared himself Mahdi (or 'Guide', in Arabic) and seized control in the name of Islam. The Egyptian government, which administered Sudan, appealed to Britain for help; in January 1884 General Charles Gordon was appointed Governor-General of Sudan and given command of 4000 Egyptian troops. A month later, he was in Khartoum, but the Mahdi quickly moved to cut him off. After some delay, a relief force was gathered in Cairo under Wolseley's command, aiming to advance along the Nile. Administrative problems proliferated, delaying the advance; by December Wolseley was still nearly

200 miles from his objective and Gordon's situation was desperate. A 'flying column' of 2000 men was detached to race for Khartoum, but despite victories at Abu Klea and Gulat, when it arrived on 28 January 1885 it was too late. Gordon had been killed two days earlier (*see* Victorian Military Heroes, p.86).

Gordon's death was avenged by General Herbert Kitchener, who led an Anglo-Egyptian force along the Nile towards Khartoum. The campaign was very slow-moving – Kitchener paused for long periods to build up supplies along a specially constructed railway – and it was not until 2 September 1898 that the Mahdi's army was engaged at Omdurman. It was a one-sided contest, in which British firepower inflicted a crippling defeat on the Mahdi. Victory allowed Kitchener to occupy the whole of the Sudan, and to see off a belated attempt by the French to intervene at Fashoda in the extreme south, thereby ensuring that the western approaches to the Red Sea were secure.

ministers were taking military advice from a number of soldiers. These included the Inspector-General of Fortifications, Lintorn Simmons, and, especially, Colonel Robert Home of the infant Intelligence Branch in the War Office. Wolseley for one was deeply suspicious of the influence of such technical specialists.

THE NEED FOR A GENERAL STAFF

Many of these problems would have been overcome by the establishment of a proper General Staff along continental lines, to assess policy options and to advise politicians on how objectives might be met with the resources available. Such a General Staff was unacceptable to liberal-minded politicians, who feared that the military would acquire too much influence over policy-making and tie their hands in future diplomatic crises by presenting too rigid a strategic plan as a *fait accompli*. As a consequence, the recommendation of the Hartington Commission in 1891 that the office of C-in-C be abolished and replaced by a Chief of Staff was abandoned, although an Army Board (later the War Office Council) and a Joint Naval and Military Committee were established. Far from being the radical depicted by the Duke of Cambridge, Wolseley equally disliked the

concept of a Chief of Staff and, upon finally succeeding the Duke as C-in-C in 1895, he complained that the War Office Council had made his own post like 'a fifth wheel on a coach'.

THE STANHOPE MEMORANDUM

At least the Intelligence Branch, which became the Intelligence Division in 1886, was able to draw up a number of successive schemes for the mobilization of the Army from 1875 onwards. Moreover, in response to the demands of both Cambridge and Wolseley for a precise statement of the Army's duties during the war scare of 1888, the Secretary of State for War, Edward Stanhope, issued a Memorandum that, for the first time, listed the Army's priorities. These were support for the civil power in the United Kingdom, the defence of India, the maintenance of imperial garrisons, the defence of the United Kingdom and, lastly, an expeditionary force for Europe, although the latter was considered 'sufficiently improbable' as to make any such arrangements unnecessary. It may appear curious that aid to the civil power should still be regarded as a significant military task as late as 1888, but in reality there were continuing occasions upon

VICTORIAN MILITARY HEROES

Charles George Gordon (1833–85): as a captain of Royal Engineers, Gordon achieved fame initially in China, where between 1859 and 1865 he helped to defend the imperial dynasty from revolutionaries during the Taiping rebellion – exploits which won him the nickname 'Chinese Gordon'. In 1874 he moved to Egypt, where he fought the slave-trade in Sudan, and 10 years later he returned under British instruction to oppose the Mahdi. Besieged in Khartoum for 10 months, he was killed by the Mahdi's followers on 26 January 1885.

Herbert Horatio Kitchener (1850–1916): after involvement in the abortive expedition to save Gordon in Khartoum in 1884–5, Kitchener was made C-in-C of the Egyptian Army, in which capacity he led the operations to destroy the Mahdi which culminated at the Battle of Omdurman (1898). After serving in the South African War (1899–1902), initially as Lord Roberts' Chief of Staff and then as C-in-C, he moved to India, also as C-in-C (1902-9), then back to Egypt as British representative there. As Field Marshal and 1st Earl Kitchener of Khartoum, he was appointed Secretary of State for War in 1914 and was responsible for raising a volunteer army of nearly three million men (Kitchener's Army; *see* p.98). He was drowned in June 1916 when the ship carrying him to Russia hit a mine.

Frederick Sleigh Roberts (1832–1914): as a young officer in the Bengal Artillery, Roberts won the

ROBERTS

Victoria Cross during the Indian Mutiny, although he did not catch the public eye until 1880, when he led an expeditionary force into Afghanistan to raise the siege of Kandahar. Appointed C-in-C India in 1885, he was made 1st Earl Roberts in 1893 and a Field Marshal two years later. Sent out to South Africa in late 1899 as C-in-C, he reversed the run of Boer victories and took Pretoria. He returned to Britain to become C-in-C of the British Army, but the post was abolished in 1904.

Garnet Joseph Wolseley (1833–1913): commissioned into the 80th Foot in May 1852, Wolseley saw service in Burma, the Crimea and the Indian Mutiny before moving to China in 1860. His first independent command was in Canada in 1870, where he suppressed the Red River rebellion, but his true fame came with his victory over 'Arabi Pasha' at Tel-el-Kebir (1882). Although forces under his command failed to save Gordon in Khartoum in early 1885, Wolseley was not held to blame; by 1895, as 1st Viscount Wolseley, he was C-in-C of the British Army, having done much to ensure reform.

GORDON

KITCHENER

WOLSELEY

which military support was required. Just a few years later, in 1893, troops opened fire while on duty during an industrial dispute at Featherstone Colliery in Yorkshire.

By this time, there had been a degree of modernization of weaponry and some of the transport problems encountered in colonial campaigning had been addressed by the establishment of an Army Service Corps in 1889, responsible in part for maintaining transport capability at all times. This meant that, in the event of a crisis, units did not have to wait for transport to be provided from local sources and were, as a result, far more flexible. Indeed, whatever its problems of recruitment and administration, the Army excelled in the many 'small wars' it waged between the Crimean War and the South African War of 1899-1902. There were at least 35 campaigns of major significance between 1872 and 1899 alone: some of these were fought to annex territory, others to secure frontiers, to restore order or to punish those who had violated Pax Britannica. Often the Army fought not only the enemy but also the terrain and climate, as was the case in Abyssinia in 1867–8. This was one campaign in which use could be made of Indian troops beyond India's frontiers, others being the Perak campaign in the Malay States in 1875, Egypt in 1882 and the Sudan in 1884.

Much was improvised, not least the staff system. Wolseley gave increasing preference to Staff College graduates in his campaigns despite the fact that the favouritism implied in the 'rings' bred resentment elsewhere in the Army and did not always encourage the initiative of subordinates. Invariably, too, campaigns had to be conducted swiftly because of the risk of disease.

Opponents ranged from Afghans to Maoris and from Dervishes to Zulus, such enemies often being formidable foes in their own element. On occasions, of course, disaster befell the imperial forces, as at Isandhlwana against the Zulus in January 1879, at Maiwand against the Afghans in July 1880 and at Majuba Hill against the Boers in February 1881. The British Army learned few tactical lessons in colonial campaigns, largely because methods that were obsolete in a European context, such as forming 'squares', continued to be effective against poorly armed opponents. But campaigning gave the Army practical experience and also encouraged the adoption of more comfortable service dress. In 1896 an official manual on colonial campaigning appeared in the form of Colonel C. E. Callwell's *Small Wars: Their Principles and Practice*.

However, the largest number of men put in the field between 1854 and 1899 was the 16,000 sent to Egypt in 1882 and none of the Army's opponents since 1856 could be regarded in any way as equivalent to a continental regular army. (The fate of most indigenous opponents in the face of superior British technology and firepower is perhaps best illustrated by the 11,000 Mahdists mown down for the loss of fewer than 400 British casualties in an obliging frontal assault at Omdurman in Sudan in September 1898.) It should also be pointed out that, although Cardwell had revived the idea of large-scale

British troops of Lord Chelmsford's relieving force survey the battlefield at Isandhlwana in Zululand, site of the annihilation of seven companies of the 24th Foot on 22 January 1879.

peacetime manoeuvres for the first time since the camp at Chobham in 1853, these were only held from 1871 to 1873 and not again until 1898.

THE SOUTH AFRICAN WAR AND ITS IMPACT

Thus the Army was hardly prepared in 1899 for the challenge of a war in South Africa against well-armed Europeanized opponents. It was a war which eventually required the use of almost 450,000 men drawn from throughout the Empire, including 238,000 regulars or reservists from the United Kingdom, 18,000 regulars from India, over 90,000 militia, Yeomanry and volunteers from Britain, and 30,000 colonial volunteers. Over 100,000 casualties were suffered from battle or disease against Boer forces estimated at no more than 50,000 at most. In particular, the psychological shock of the triple defeats of Colenso, Magersfontein and Stormberg in the 'Black Week' of 10–15 December 1899 was considerable.

Roberts, who had earned a reputation in India as 'Our Only Other General' (to match that of Wolseley in Africa as 'Our Only General'), became C-in-C in South Africa after Colenso, with the conqueror of the Sudan, Herbert Kitchener, as his Chief of Staff. Adapting to the new conditions apparent in the Boer use of modern firepower from concealed entrenchments, Roberts defeated the main Boer army at Paardeberg in February 1900 and took the capitals of the Boer republics of the Orange Free State and the Transvaal (Bloemfontein and Pretoria) in March and June respectively. He then returned to Britain to succeed an ailing Wolseley as C-in-C. However, it was to take Kitchener another two years to suppress the continuing guerrilla warfare, hence the immense manpower eventually utilized.

Not surprisingly, the performance of the Army led to new demands for reform. Accordingly, while Roberts attempted to address tactical matters, St John Brodrick as Secretary of State for War proposed a large increase in the size of the Army and the creation of six Army Corps, each

Horse-drawn artillery crosses the River Modder in South Africa, 1900. The photograph gives a good indication of terrain and of the difficulties of movement in an area devoid of proper roads.

WARS IN SOUTH AFRICA, 1878–1902

By 1878 the British had consolidated their hold over South Africa, defeating the 'Kaffirs' (Xhosa tribe) and assuming control of Boer settlements in the Transvaal. Pressure from the Zulus in the east, under their warlike chief Cetewayo, led to an ill-considered British attack under Lord Chelmsford. He split his force once he had crossed the River Buffalo into Zululand and, on 22 January 1879, one of his columns, comprising seven companies of the 24th Foot with native support, was overwhelmed and annihilated at Isandhlwana. A gallant defence of the outpost at Rorke's Drift by 139 men under Lieutenants Bromhead of the 24th and Chard of the Royal Engineers, during which 11 VCs were won, did little to disguise the enormity of the disaster, although Chelmsford made amends on 4 July 1879 when, with a better-organized force, he defeated Cetewayo at Ulundi.

The British then had to deal with a revolt in Transvaal, where Boer settlers resented foreign rule. In December 1880, they attacked a British column moving towards Pretoria and in the following month

the main British advance from Natal was halted at Laing's Nek. The British commander, Sir George Colley, tried to take a Boer position at Majuba Hill on 26 February 1881, only to be defeated by superior marksmanship and firepower. This, the First Boer War, ended with a British agreement to allow Transvaal a degree of independence.

Eighteen years later, President Kruger of the Transvaal issued a demand for the complete independence of both his own republic and that of neighbouring Orange Free State, following it up with attacks on Natal and Cape Colony. Mafeking, Kimberley and Ladysmith were all besieged and, as the British tried desperately to ship reinforcements to South Africa, the Boers inflicted a series of stunning defeats, three of which – at Colenso, Magersfontein and Stormberg – occurred in the same 'Black Week' (10–15 December 1899). Shocked, the British government appointed Lord Roberts to take command in South Africa, with Kitchener as his Chief of Staff. Arriving in January 1900, just in time for yet another defeat, this time at Spion Kop on the route to

Ladysmith, Roberts concentrated all the forces he could to relieve Kimberley. Once this had been achieved, Kitchener went on to engage the main Boer army at Paardeberg on 18 February, forcing surrender eight days later. Ladysmith was relieved on 1 March and Bloemfontein, the capital of Orange Free State, taken on the 13th, although Mafeking was not relieved until 17 May. In June, British forces marched into Pretoria, the capital of the Transvaal, and it seemed as if the war was over. Both Boer republics were annexed and Kruger forced into exile.

But the Boers were not finished. Using their local knowledge and local support, they organized themselves into highly mobile 'commandos' and fought an effective guerrilla campaign. Kitchener, left as C-in-C when Roberts returned to Britain in December 1900, took two years to suppress the Boers, using techniques which included the burning of farmhouses and detention of Boer families in 'concentration camps'. The Second Boer War officially ended with the Treaty of Vereeniging on 31 May 1902.

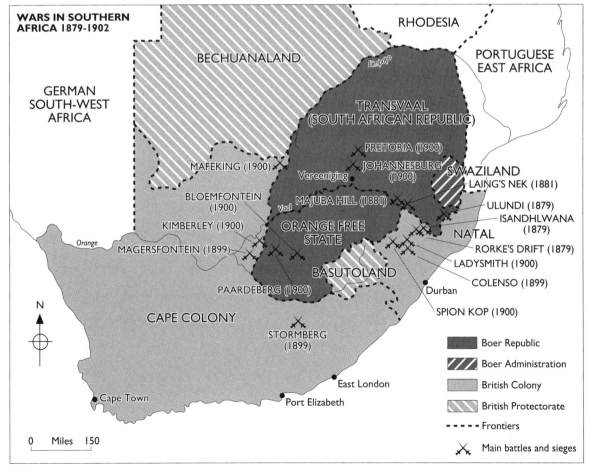

WARS IN SOUTHERN AFRICA 1879-1902

RHODESIA

PORTUGUESE EAST AFRICA

GERMAN SOUTH-WEST AFRICA

BECHUANALAND

Limpopo

TRANSVAAL (SOUTH AFRICAN REPUBLIC)

PRETORIA (1900)

MAFEKING (1900)

Vereeniging

JOHANNESBURG (1900)

SWAZILAND

LAING'S NEK (1881)

BLOEMFONTEIN (1900)

Vaal

MAJUBA HILL (1881)

ULUNDI (1879)

KIMBERLEY (1900)

ORANGE FREE STATE

ISANDHLWANA (1879)

NATAL

Orange

MAGERSFONTEIN (1899)

RORKE'S DRIFT (1879)

LADYSMITH (1900)

BASUTOLAND

COLENSO (1899)

PAARDEBERG (1900)

Durban

SPION KOP (1900)

N

CAPE COLONY

STORMBERG (1899)

East London

Cape Town

Port Elizabeth

0   Miles   150

Boer Republic

Boer Administration

British Colony

British Protectorate

- - - - Frontiers

✕ Main battles and sieges

A Squadron Corporal Major of the Household Cavalry bids farewell to his sweetheart on his departure for South Africa, 1899. Sentimental, posed photographs such as this typify the mawkish Victorian attitude to war.

of which would comprise 40,000 men, with the auxiliary forces contributing to the three Corps among them designated for home defence only. To find the additional regulars, Brodrick proposed to increase pay and to introduce a three-year term of service. Amid general scepticism over the recruiting targets and the perceived failure of Brodrick's proposed reform of the War Office itself to meet criticisms advanced in the report of the Royal Commission on the Conduct of War, chaired by Lord Elgin in July 1903, Brodrick departed to the India Office. His successor, Hugh Arnold-Forster, produced a different reform scheme, based on a substantial reduction to the auxiliary forces and the establishment of both long- and short-service regular armies serving simultaneously. However, Arnold-Forster not only met considerable resistance from representatives of the auxiliaries, but was also undermined by being effectively by-passed by the work of a small War Office (Reconstitution) Committee chaired by Lord Esher.

THE ESHER REFORMS

Working with great speed, Esher's committee produced three reports between January and March 1904, recommending a permanent secretariat for the infant Committee of Imperial Defence, which had been established as a special forum for the discussion of defence issues in February 1903; an Army Council within the War Office; and a General Staff with a Chief of Staff replacing the C-in-C and becoming First Military Member of the Army Council. The committee enjoyed the executive authority not only to suggest these changes but also to appoint the first incumbents of the Army Council. Roberts was informed by letter on a Sunday afternoon that the new Council would begin its work the next day and that he was dismissed. The first Chief of Staff was General Neville Lyttelton, who had been serving as C-in-C in South Africa since the end of hostilities. In fact, while the Army had a Chief of the General Staff whose relationship with Arnold-Forster was to prove less than satisfactory, there was no actual General Staff for another two and a half years. Lyttelton's successor as First Military Member, General Sir William Nicholson, was designated Chief of the Imperial General Staff in 1909 to reflect an attempt to fashion greater military co-operation with the 'white' dominions.

THE HALDANE REFORMS

Little of Arnold-Forster's scheme had been implemented by the time the Unionists lost office in December 1905. Like Cardwell before him, the new Liberal Secretary of State, Richard Burdon Haldane, was required to meet the concern of his party for significant economies in the Army estimates. At the same time, he was also constrained by what he believed to be politically practical, and there were elements of his wider design for reform which he felt it necessary to modify rather than risk opposition. That wider design was no less than the creation of a 'real national army, formed by the people', in which the essential point of contact in welding a unity of Army and nation was depicted as a new Territorial Force (TF) to replace, absorb and expand upon the militia, Yeomanry and volunteers. Originally, it was intended that the TF would both support and expand the Regular Army by being ready for overseas service after six months' training following mobilization. In the event, fear of parliamentary opposition led Haldane to switch the emphasis of the TF to home defence only, thus making a nonsense of the whole justification of a six-months' training period as a necessary preliminary to expanding the Army. The powers initially envisaged for the County Territorial Associations, which would administer the new system, were also substantially reduced in the course of the legislation passing through Parliament. The Territorial and Reserve Forces Act came onto the statute book in August 1907,

A company barrack room in England, c. 1896. Despite the spartan conditions, this is a distinct improvement over previous barrack accommodation and illustrates an important aspect of reform in the late 19th century.

Richard Burdon Haldane (1856–1928), Secretary of State for War from 1905 until 1912. His creation of an Expeditionary Force and reorganization of reserves in 1908 helped to prepare the Army for European commitment.

with a starting-date of 1 April 1908. Existing volunteer Battalions of infantry were to become Territorial Battalions of their county regiments and, together with artillery, engineers and other support services, were to be organized into 14 self-supporting reserve divisions. The Yeomanry, now included as part of the TF, would provide the mounted brigades.

THE CREATION OF AN EXPEDITIONARY FORCE

Another variation from the original scheme was that the militia were transformed into a Special Reserve rather than being divided between the TF and Haldane's proposed Expeditionary Force. The Expeditionary Force itself – eventually one cavalry brigade and six infantry divisions, drawn from regular units in the United Kingdom – owed more to the need to achieve financial savings, and to make the resulting organization of the Army fit all potential military requirements, than to the perception of a growing threat from Germany that Haldane later claimed. Indeed, the continuing need to provide reinforcing drafts for imperial garrisons was what determined the size and composition of the Expeditionary Force even if, in line with the undoubted reorientation of British strategic concerns from India to Europe after 1902, a continental commitment eventually proved to be the purpose for which the Expeditionary Force was deployed overseas in 1914.

Essentially, in seeking to meet imperial needs, Haldane restored the Cardwellian terms of regular service and brought the number of battalions serving at home and abroad back into balance. The six large continental-style infantry divisions thus created were no more than the largest force that could be drawn from the Army at home and, even then, a requirement for approximately 150,000 men on mobilization could only be met by fully utilizing the Army and Special Reserves. Nevertheless, the organization and mobilization preparations for the Expeditionary Force progressed well, the timetabling of the latter being completed when Henry Wilson served as Director of Military Operations at the War Office after 1910.

Certainly, Haldane's reorganization and the steps taken by the Army to rectify the tactical errors of the South African War were to result in Britain fielding in 1914 what the Army's official historian described as 'incomparably the best trained, best organized, and best equipped British Army which ever went forth to war'. However, the trained manpower upon which Britain could rely in the event of mobilization was tiny compared to the numbers available to continental states. Moreover, the TF in particular had experienced major difficulties in reaching establishment between 1908 and 1914, and had been much weakened by the denial of the overseas role. Whereas Haldane had confidently predicted that between a sixth and a quarter of the establishment of some 300,000 would voluntarily offer themselves for overseas service in advance of mobilization, only just over 18,000 had actually done so by 1914. The Territorials had undoubtedly enabled Britain to avoid the spectre of continental-style conscription but, in the process, they had been damaged by the criticisms of their military efficiency in a vigorous pro-conscription campaign waged by the National Service League, to which Roberts lent his name. In fact, conscription had been recommended by the Norfolk Commission in 1904 and by the Army Council itself in April 1913, but it was still generally unpopular.

THE CURRAGH INCIDENT

The Army also shared those prevalent assumptions of professional soldiers across Europe that little had really changed in warfare and that modern firepower could be offset if those taking the offensive showed sufficient willpower and determination in crossing the 'zone of fire'. Unfortunately, too, at the very moment when the diplomatic crisis in Europe was deepening, both civil-military relations and the Army's own unity were put under considerable strain by the Irish Home Rule crisis. Faced with the possibility of being compelled to disarm Ulster loyalists to ensure the imposition of Home Rule for Ireland, in March 1914 Brigadier-General Hubert Gough and fellow officers of the 3rd Cavalry Brigade serving at the Curragh Camp near Dublin indicated that they would resign rather than do so. Supported by a substantial number of officers throughout the Army, Gough won a written guarantee from Haldane's successor at the War Office, Jack Seely, that the Army would not be used to coerce Ulster. When the remainder of the Cabinet repudiated the agreement, Seely resigned, together with the Chief of the Imperial General Staff, Sir John French, and the Adjutant-General, Sir John Spencer Ewart. Yet many officers believed that it was an officer's duty to obey any order lawfully given. The officer corps was deeply split over the incident and considerable antagonism surfaced towards the politicians who had thrust the Army into such a position.

ON THE EVE OF GLOBAL WAR

The consequences of the Curragh Incident were still simmering in the Army in late July 1914, at which point its professional attentions were fortuitously focused on the challenge of a major war, albeit one which would result in heavy casualties among its small professional cadre even before the first campaign was over. Arguably, it was indeed the best army Britain had ever fielded, but it still reflected Britain's long-standing failure to match resources to commitments, which in itself stemmed from British society's traditional marginalization of military matters. Within a short time, however, the demands of modern war would result in the acceptance of the compulsion to serve which had been so long avoided.

CHAPTER FIVE

THE FIRST WORLD WAR AND ITS AFTERMATH (1914–39)

·····························

'OVER BY CHRISTMAS'

ON 4 August 1914 the British government declared war on Germany, one of a flurry of declarations which began the First World War. The ostensible reason was Germany's violation of Belgian neutrality, but the crisis which precipitated the war had begun on the other side of Europe with the assassination on 28 June of Archduke Franz Ferdinand, heir to the throne of Austria–Hungary, by a Serb nationalist in Sarajevo. Thereafter, the interlocking system of European alliances had produced mobilization by all the major powers of Europe and a challenge to the stability of the continent that Britain could not ignore.

For most British people, as they cheered the outbreak of hostilities, the war was fought against Germany in defence of Belgium and to preserve the British Empire, with the French and Russians as allies of convenience. Campaigns against Austria-Hungary or against Ottoman Turkey (which joined Germany and Austria-Hungary on 1 November 1914 to form the Central Powers) were seen as 'sideshows'. This attitude was largely reciprocated, with German hatred being directed particularly against Britain for its unexpected support of France. Not that this mattered to the regular soldiers of the British Army in 1914. According to Tom Bridges, who rose from major to lieutenant-general during the war, the British Expeditionary Force (BEF) would just as willingly have fought the French as the Germans.

The First World War marked a major watershed in the Army's evolution, in the development of warfare and in European and world history. For the first time, the forces of the industrial revolution and of modern developed states were turned to waging war on a scale that had previously been only dimly envisaged. Those who spoke on its outbreak of Armageddon and the end of civilization as they knew it were quite right, for it destroyed the empires of Germany, Russia, Austria-Hungary and Turkey and fatally crippled European domination of the rest of the world.

There were, however, excellent reasons for believing that the war would be short – 'all over by Christmas' – precisely because it would be so violent and terrible. The immense financial cost would bankrupt the belligerents within a few months, while the demands for shells and guns would exhaust the magazines and factories of Europe before the spring. Most importantly, from the South African War (1899–1902) and Russo–Japanese War (1904–5), the generals had grasped the immense psychological strain of modern conflict. Battlefield stress ('shell-shock' or, in Field Marshal Earl Haig's words, 'a state of moral and physical decadence') was expected to cripple the mass conscript armies of Europe with their mere two years of training. The BEF sent home its first shell-shock casualties before the end of 1914, although disputes remained on how shell-shock could be distinguished from cowardice. The war lasted four years, not four months, because these calculations underestimated the resilience of modern states and of peoples fighting for survival. But the main reason why armies before 1914 did not prepare for trench warfare by building tanks and stockpiling barbed wire, was that such a war of stalemate and attrition was the last kind of war that they wished to fight. Instead, all countries planned for a short war of manoeuvre in the hope and expectation of a quick victory.

BEF DEPLOYMENT

In the crisis of August 1914, the British government discovered that Britain had only one war plan, to send the BEF to France in accordance with French expectations.

Volunteers of 1914. Men such as these flocked to the Army in answer to Kitchener's call for recruits; many of them were to be sacrificed on the Somme in 1916 or in subsequent battles.

Like the forces of the other European powers, the BEF had been designed, in the event of war in Europe, to fight and win one campaign lasting at most a few months. Legends of its quality and prowess have clustered around the BEF of 1914. It was not quite the perfect fighting machine that is sometimes portrayed, and a third of its men (two-thirds in some units) were recalled reservists rather than serving soldiers. But it was better prepared than any other British Army before or since, and was probably the best single fighting unit of the war. Its main limitation was its size when compared to the armies of millions being mobilized by the other belligerents. Germany mobilized 82 infantry and 11 cavalry divisions in 1914, Russia 110 infantry and 36 cavalry divisions, and France 63 infantry and 10 cavalry divisions. The BEF, comprising six infantry divisions and a single cavalry brigade, was a perfect army in miniature. It was tactically outstanding, but neither the men nor their leaders were trained for mass warfare. The British Army had in addition only enough troops at home and throughout the Empire to form a further five infantry and two cavalry divisions, giving the great British Empire an army the same size as that of Serbia. The Territorial Force, the Indian Army and the small Dominion contingents were considered suitable for home defence only, an attitude that would change before the end of the year.

Mobilization of the BEF went with remarkable and unexpected smoothness. Anticipating only one campaign, the General Staff, in what turned out to be a major error, transformed itself into the BEF's headquarters under Field Marshal Sir John French, recalled to duty following his temporary disgrace over the Curragh Incident in March/April 1914 (*see* p.92). It landed with its troops in France just 10 days after the declaration of war, the first British Army deployed to Europe since the Crimean War in the 1850s. Nevertheless, Field Marshal Lord Kitchener, recalled in the emergency and appointed Secretary of State for War by Prime Minister H. H. Asquith, withheld two of the BEF's six divisions. This was the first of several problems that were to follow in the higher direction of the British war effort. As a peer, Kitchener did not require election to be appointed to the Cabinet, and he had little practical experience of British politics. Furthermore, like all field marshals, he remained on the active list as a serving soldier, and he outranked French. Kitchener was the first British politician to wear uniform while holding office (not even the Duke of Wellington had done so as prime minister) and he treated his appointment generally as that of the recently abolished post of commander-in-chief. With the other leading lights of the Army all in France, Kitchener's immense military prestige gave him an unprecedented personal domination over the British war effort for the next 18 months, to the increasing irritation and resentment of his Cabinet colleagues and military commanders.

Personality Profile:

FIELD MARSHAL SIR JOHN FRENCH (1852–1925)

Commissioned into the 19th Hussars in 1874, John Denstone Pinkstone French came to prominence during the South African War (1899–1902), when he commanded the British cavalry division with distinction. Widely regarded as one of the ablest commanders in the British Army, he was appointed Chief of the Imperial General Staff in 1912 and promoted field marshal the following year. In 1914, however, he resigned over the Curragh Incident (*see* p.92). Thus it was something of a surprise when he was given command of the BEF at the outbreak of war a few weeks later. Despite heavy losses at Mons and First Ypres, French was credited with keeping the BEF together as a fighting force, but doubts were raised about his ability to command once the trench deadlock had set in. After the disastrous battles of 1915, particularly Loos, he was recalled and replaced by Sir Douglas Haig. He was elevated to the peerage as Viscount French of Ypres in early 1916.

MONS TO FIRST YPRES

The French war plan called for a direct attack across the common frontier with Germany. The BEF was wanted more for the political gesture of British support which it represented than for its military value, and it was tacked onto the extreme left wing of the French advance, nearest to the Channel ports. Entirely fortuitously, the British advance lay directly in the path of the main German effort in its attempt to execute the great enveloping wheel of the Schlieffen Plan through Belgium and behind the main French forces. On 23 August 1914 the British Army fought its first battle in North-West Europe since Waterloo in 1815, as the BEF collided with the advancing German spearheads at the little Belgian town of Mons (*see box*). Despite being outnumbered by almost three to one, the deadly fire of the BEF's infantry and artillery stopped the Germans in their tracks. Next day, conforming to the French withdrawal, the BEF began the epic 'Retreat from Mons', with cavalry patrols holding the Germans at arm's length while the infantry footslogged through the summer heat. Only once did the cavalry screen fail. Half the BEF was forced to stand and fight at Le Cateau on 26 August, another baffling and bloody shock for the Germans, after which their prey once more slipped away.

By 2 September the BEF was exhausted but safe behind the River Marne to the east of Paris, positioned virtually by accident to play a key role in the new French plan for a devastating counter-stroke against the extended outer hook of the Schlieffen Plan. For the British, the Battle of the Marne (5–9 September) was an affair of marching as much as fighting, manoeuvring into the gap between the two outermost German armies and forcing their retreat. The breakdown of the Schlieffen Plan meant that the war would not be over by Christmas with a German victory. The Marne was thus one of the truly decisive battles of the world, in which a small, high-quality British Army had played a role out of all proportion to its size.

The possibility of a short war of manoeuvre was, however, not quite dead. There followed a desperate scramble by both sides for an open flank in the 'race to the sea'. A confused series of engagements known to the BEF as the Battle of the Aisne (13–25 September), took it ever northwards into Flanders and gradually slowed the pace of advance to a crawl. The line of troops was now almost continuous from the Swiss border to the Channel. Still hoping to outflank the enemy with a new offensive, Field Marshal French advanced the BEF (now reinforced to about twice its original size) into the westernmost corner of Belgium at the town of Ypres, only to meet once again a stronger German offensive coming the other way. Officially dated 20 October–22 November, the First Battle of Ypres was largely a French affair, but once more the stubborn fighting power of the BEF in defence broke more than its own numbers of advancing Germans. The First Battle of Ypres, or 'Wipers' to the troops, marked the final end of mobility and the chance of a short war, and the introduction of trench warfare on the Western Front. It also marked the end of the old BEF, which took 50,000

British and Belgian infantrymen trudge south from Mons in late August 1914, retreating before the might of the German First Army. Nevertheless, the Battle of Mons proved crucial in slowing the German advance.

THE BATTLE OF MONS

As the extreme right wing of the German Schlieffen Plan wheeled into Belgium in August 1914, it encountered insubstantial opposition, occupying Brussels on the 20th and pushing the Belgian Army aside. According to German Intelligence, little stood between General von Kluck's First Army and the French border, opening up the possibility of a wide sweeping movement to the west of Paris to catch the main French forces, engaged to the north and east of the capital, in the rear. Information that elements of the British Expeditionary Force had been committed to the Allied left wing, directly in First Army's path, was dismissed; as early as 19 August the Kaiser had ordered von Kluck to 'exterminate the treacherous English and walk over General French's contemptible little army'.

It proved to be a difficult task. By 22 August, French had pushed his lead infantry formations as far as the Mons-Condé Canal, where they tried to dig in amid coal-tips and scattered villages, protected by a cavalry screen. Early the next morning, as the sun broke through mist and drizzle, the Germans advanced towards the British positions, unaware of their existence. According to one of the British soldiers, the enemy were 'in solid square blocks, standing out sharply against the skyline, and you couldn't help hitting them ... We lay in our trenches with not a sound or sign to tell them of what was before them. They crept nearer and nearer, and then our officers gave the word ... They seemed to stagger like a drunk man hit suddenly between the eyes, after which they made a run for us,

shouting some outlandish cry that we couldn't make out'.

Disciplined and accurate rifle fire halted the German attack, although as the day wore on British casualties mounted, chiefly as a result of artillery bombardments on their positions, and news came in that French forces to the east had pulled back. Rather than continue to occupy a salient, the British began to withdraw early on 24 August. Although the tired and confused soldiers were not to know it, their actions at Mons had forced von Kluck to adopt a more cautious approach, slowing the rate of his advance and giving the French time to recover. Of equal importance, the battle had reminded the Germans that the British Army, although small, was an effective fighting force.

First-Hand Account:

THE CHRISTMAS TRUCE, 1914

'. . . The most strange thing happened on Xmas day. As usual an hour before daybreak we stood over arms in case of attack. Presently we could hear the Germans singing their carols and songs . . . We had had our breakfasts and were enjoying a smoke, when the lookout men shouted down, that an officer and two men were approaching from the German lines. They were entirely without firearm and carried a white flag . . . they came just half way and then halted calling out to us, asking if an officer of ours go out and speak to them. Without a moment's hesitation one of our officers, a captain, jumped the trench and advanced to meet them also unarmed . . . then our officer came back and told us that the Germans wished us to keep up Xmas day with them and that we were to meet them halfway between trenches. We agreed like a shot . . . It may seem strange but the very first thing we did was to shake hands all round then followed an exchange of eatables. They gave us lager beer for Bully Beef and biscuits . . . After this we took to talking . . . then we arranged a boxing contest . . . After dinner we sent a cyclist back to find a football and on his return we played them a match winning easily by 4–1. This ended the day . . . No shots were fired all Boxing Day . . . Of course this could not go on forever so the following morning our artillery fired on their trenches and so we started war again . . .'

Extract from the diary of Sergeant H. D. Bryan

casualties in the battle and 89,000 altogether between August and December 1914, reducing many of its battalions to half-strength or less.

KITCHENER'S NEW ARMIES

In defiance of previous General Staff thinking, Lord Kitchener decided within days of coming to office that the war would last for at least three years and that Britain must create a mass army of at least 60 infantry divisions to be ready by that third year if it was to win. At the time, the total British Army strength, including Regulars, Territorial Force and Reserves, was 733,514 men. On 6 August 1914 Kitchener issued the first of a number of proclamations calling for a first draft of 500,000 volun-

teers to serve in the 'New Armies'. Meanwhile, Regular battalions were withdrawn from garrisons abroad and formed into scratch divisions, and Territorial battalions were asked to volunteer for overseas service. An Indian Corps of two infantry divisions arrived for a year on the Western Front in November 1914, together with two Indian cavalry divisions which stayed until 1918. The 'White Dominions' of Canada, Australia, New Zealand and South Africa, largely populated with first- or second-generation immigrants from Britain, also began to recruit volunteers for their own armed forces to serve alongside the British.

As news of Mons and the Marne spread across Britain, the number of volunteers for Kitchener's New Armies increased dramatically. Between 4 August and 12 September 1914, some 478,893 men came forward, and by the end of the year the total had reached 1,186,337. Thereafter, the number of volunteers rarely dropped much below 100,000 a month (the size of the original BEF), and by the end of 1915 2,466,719 men had been accepted to fight for king and country. Inevitably, motives for volunteering were complex, ranging from a search for adventure to the need to avoid unemployment. But patriotism, opposition to Germany and a desire not to be left out of the excitement were uppermost in the majority of minds. The cheering crowds and recruiting bands represented a unique social phenomenon for Britain, a largely innocent and loyal curiosity to see what modern war was like.

The creation of the New Armies also made the First World War a unique event for the British nation. For the first time in its history, Britain adopted the war strategy of transforming itself into a major continental European land power, building a mass army in order to attack the greatest strength of its principal enemy on the main land front. In its direct confrontation with the German Army on the Western Front, the British Army was taking on the strongest and deadliest military force in the world. The British experience of trench warfare, the nature of battle and the casualties suffered, were not generally worse than those of the other main belligerents. France, for example, lost nearly twice as many dead in the war as Britain from a similar population. The big difference for the British was that, with no peacetime conscription, the great majority of people were totally unaware of their country's military culture and of the everyday realities of military existence. The Regular Army, virtually a colonial police force recruited from very narrow bands of society, was equally ignorant of the country which it was employed to defend. The British had to improvise their Army from almost nothing, while simultaneously fighting a singularly bitter war. In the First World War, the British Army and British society were brought face to face for the first time, and neither has ever recovered from the experience.

Within a few days of Kitchener's call to arms, the flood of volunteers had far outstripped the ability of the War Office to cope. Instead, Kitchener took advantage of local organizations that were creating battalions and offering them to the Army. The structure and attitudes of the Regular Army were still largely those of the Cardwell era, reflecting and defending the values of a stable, agrarian society which had virtually ceased to exist since the 1870s (if, indeed, it ever had existed) with the collapse

THE SHEFFIELD PALS

Enrolment into the 'Sheffield University and City Special Battalion' began on 2 September 1914 amid a blaze of patriotic fervour. Within 48 hours 790 men had come forward, and by 7 September the figure stood at 1303. Proper enlistment began on the 10th, by which time the unit had been renamed the Sheffield City Battalion of the York and Lancaster Regiment, better known as the Sheffield Pals. It was organized initially into four companies, each with its own characteristics. A Company was made up primarily of men from the University, B Company of men from districts outside the city (including contingents from Penistone and Chesterfield), C Company comprised teachers, bankers and students, and

D Company included a large contingent from the *Sheffield Daily Telegraph*. At this stage, the city was responsible for financing, feeding and clothing the recruits, preparatory to official acceptance by the War Office. When that occurred, the unit took its place as the 12th (City of Sheffield) Service Battalion, York and Lancaster Regiment.

In common with many other Kitchener Battalions, the Sheffield Pals took time to organize and train, but in December 1915 they were considered fit enough to send to Egypt to guard the Suez Canal against possible Turkish attack. After only two months, however, they were sent on to France, landing at Marseilles on 16 March 1916 and moving into front-line trenches

for the first time at Colincamps, north of Albert, a fortnight later. On 1 July, the battalion attacked Serre as part of the opening of the Somme offensive. It was a disaster: of the 692 men who went over the top, 248 were killed and over 300 wounded, mostly by machine-gun fire.

The battalion was rebuilt with recruits from Lancashire, Norfolk and Staffordshire, fighting on the Western Front until disbandment in early 1918, but the special character of the unit had gone. Like so many of the Pals' Battalions, its enthusiasm and unique comradeship failed to survive the nightmare of the trenches.

of British agriculture and progressive urbanization. The locally raised volunteer battalions were the product of a new urban civic pride, particularly in the provincial towns and cities of the industrialized North and Midlands.

Factories and football teams together with workingmen's institutes and Sunday Schools produced the 'Pals' Battalions', consisting of men who worked and played together and volunteered to fight together. Two battalions of Barnsley Pals were raised, together with Pals from Leeds, Sheffield (*see box*). Birmingham, Manchester, Liverpool, Salford, and a complete battalion of Accrington Pals from that tiny industrial town. Other Pals' Battalions had a different focus for their loyalty. There were the unashamedly elitist Sportsman's Battalions from London, the Stockbrokers' Battalion, the Glasgow Boys' Brigade Battalion, the Public Schools' Battalion, and the North Eastern Railways Battalion. The Ulster Volunteer Force, which only months before had been on the verge of open civil war against the British Army, produced an entire division of volunteers, the formidable 36th (Ulster) Division, in a calculated gesture of loyalty to the Crown. The Welsh Army Corps had a brief existence before transforming itself into the 38th (Welsh) Division. Complete brigades of Tyneside Scottish and Tyneside Irish were also raised. Perhaps the oddest of the volunteers were the Bantam Battalions of men under the official recruiting height of 5ft 3in, most of which were consolidated into the 35th (Bantam) Division.

In total, of the 404 Service Battalions produced for the British Army during the war, some 145 were raised locally, mainly from the North (Lancashire, Yorkshire, Northumberland and Durham between them provided 134 of all the Service Battalions). A further 318 front-line Territorial Battalions were raised by doubling the size of the Territorial Force, splitting each existing battalion in two and recruiting back up to strength. Other volunteers

A recruiting poster of 1915, designed to appeal to the patriotism of British youth. Love of country was clearly a major reason for men volunteering, but peer-group pressure also played a significant role.

found themselves in the 137 Regular Battalions, including the poets Robert Graves and Siegfried Sassoon as officers in the 2nd Battalion, Royal Welsh Fusiliers.

Rather than adjusting to the reality of an urban, industrialized Britain by creating new regiments, the Army coped with the flood of volunteers by imposing its existing structure upon them. Thus, the Hull Commercials (1st Hull Pals) became the 10th Battalion, East Yorkshire Regiment; the Belfast Young Citizens Volunteers became the 14th Battalion, Royal Irish Rifles; the Barnsley Pals became the 13th and 14th Battalions, York and Lancaster Regiment. By the end of the war in 1918, some regiments like the Royal Fusiliers had more than 20 fighting battalions. Most volunteers displayed complete indifference to these changes and towards the sacred Regular Army totem of the regimental cap badge. Some battalions, such as the Leeds Pals (15th and 17th Battalions, West Yorkshire Regiment) and Liverpool Pals (17th, 18th, 19th and 20th Battalions, King's (Liverpool) Regiment), designed and wore their own insignia; others, such as the Grimsby Chums (10th Battalion, Lincolnshire Regiment), rarely referred to themselves by their official regimental title. In the emergency of the expansion, the great advantage of the Pals system was that the raw battalions came with ready-made social and organizational ties, an existing comradeship on which the Army could build. The disadvantage was that a chance shell on the battlefield could take the breadwinner from every house in a small street in a close-knit Northern town. After nearly two years of training, the Accrington Pals (11th Battalion, East Lancashire Regiment) took 594 casualties on their first day in action (1 July 1916, on the Somme), with devastating effects on the community.

Volunteers not recruited into the Pals' Battalions went directly to the old Regular Battalions or the Territorials, producing what was Britain's first true citizen army. Most brought with them the attitudes of the work-place in dealing with authority, with shop stewards and foremen translated into corporals and sergeants. The Army that they joined was at the height of its pride in its own professionalism and elite status, and in its fierce paternalism treated new recruits virtually as children. The demands of the war kept nearly all capable officers on the Western Front, often promoted one or two ranks above their peacetime level, and to help to train the New Armies the War Office recalled to the colours officers with any previous military experience in preference to promoting volunteers with civilian leadership experience. The Official History lists as typical a battalion with an over-age commanding officer who had retired before the South African War, a completely deaf quartermaster, a lieutenant invalided with a badly broken leg, and no other trained officers. To fill the need for junior officers, the War Office relied at first on direct commissioning of boys from recognized public schools who had received some Officer Training Corps (OTC) instruction. Meanwhile, the huts and barracks had yet to be built, the uniforms and weapons manufactured and the troops trained for a war completely different from either imperial policing or the war of manoeuvre envisaged by the Army before 1914. Much of the evil reputation with which British memoir-writers invested the First World War came not from the fighting but from the hardships of soldiering that the

Regular Army took for granted – the endless delays and boredom, the lack of hygiene and privacy, the arcane snobbery and pettiness and the discovery that the sergeant-major was of dubious parentage.

THE BATTLES OF EARLY 1915

For the British Army, 1915 marked a hiatus in the war while the New Armies were equipped and trained. It was also a year in which Britain – its Army now a pygmy in a world of giants – found its strategy largely dictated by its enemies, by its allies, and by outside circumstances. After the failure of the 1914 plans for victory, there was a degree of improvisation on all sides, with new war aims and strategies being decided while the war seemed to drift. Meanwhile, the armies of Europe had indeed run out of ammunition and shells, and until more were produced any attacks would have to be limited. The British in particular, struggling to expand their small peacetime munitions industry, suffered from problems with both quality and quantity of weapons. Not until 1916 would the Army be properly equipped with trench mortars, steel helmets, Lewis machine guns, hand grenades and the other paraphernalia of trench warfare.

On the Western Front Germany held the strategic advantage, ending 1914 in occupation of virtually all of Belgium except for a salient centred on Ypres, and a considerable area of northern France. The Germans concentrated their efforts for 1915 on shoring up their weaker Austro-Hungarian ally with offensives against Russia, but demonstrated their continuing threat to the Western Front with a surprise offensive against the French and British at the Second Battle of Ypres on 22 April, using poison gas on the Western Front for the first time. This use, under the pressures of military necessity, of a weapon previously banned as inhumane was a foretaste of what was to come. The French, meanwhile, were committed to recovering their lost land and to breaking through to resume a war of manoeuvre in the spring. As in 1914, although the BEF was not under direct French command, its offensives on the Western Front in 1915 were all small-scale contributions to larger French attacks. Considerations of supply and transport also determined that if the British were to use their new mass army in one large formation in the future, the Western Front was the only theatre that could sustain it.

In response to Field Marshal French's demands, replacements and reserves were sent out to the BEF in Flanders, raising its strength to two armies, including Indian and Canadian troops. On 10 March the British Army (still officially the BEF, as it was to remain throughout the war) launched its first spring attack at the Battle of Neuve Chapelle, using a surprise short bombardment of only 35 minutes from 66 heavy guns and hoping for a breakthrough. The attack gained a few hundred yards for 13,000 British casualties. On 9 May the British attacked again alongside the French in the Battle of Aubers Ridge, and again failed to achieve any real advance.

French chose to blame the shortage of artillery

shells for both his failed attacks, and the resulting 'shell scandal' brought down the last Liberal government of Britain, forcing Asquith to form a coalition government on 26 May. Across Europe, the governments and high commands of all the main belligerents also fell or were replaced under the strain of war. Meanwhile, the immense financial burden of the war was absorbed by the invention of deficit financing and growing moves to a command economy. In the course of the war, the British government raised only a third of the money to finance its war effort by taxation, the rest coming from overseas loans which left Britain with a massive national debt. By the end of 1915 the belligerents had committed themselves to the war to a point at which compromise was impossible. Only virtual total victory (or total defeat) would solve their differences.

TRENCH DEADLOCK

The demands for total victory were not matched, however, by the ability to achieve even the most limited advances on the battlefield. The blame placed by French on the lack of guns and shells for his attacks in 1915 had

some justification, but the failure to break through the trench lines which bedevilled all armies on the Western Front until 1918 also reflected a much wider change in the nature of war. The opposing alliances were roughly equal in strength, with no obvious superiority in numbers or technology on either side. The ability of industrialized nations to sustain mass armies meant that continuous trench lines could be held throughout the year, condemning the soldiers to fighting in the rain and snow of the bitterest winter. On the Western Front and the Italian Front (Italy declared war on Austria-Hungary on 23 May 1915) each side deployed about three men to every yard of front, compared to only a tenth of that number on the Eastern Front, where breakthroughs and battles of manoeuvre remained possible. Railways had given armies considerable strategic mobility, enabling them to move troops rapidly to a threatened sector. But tactical mobility on the battlefield had been virtually ended by the high-density firepower which artillery and entrenched infantry in such numbers could generate, and by the protection given to the defender by trenches and barbed wire.

Even if attacking infantry could pass through 'no-man's-land', several interconnected factors prevented a breakthrough. The most significant of these was lack of communications beyond the front line, as time and again small groups of men pushed through the first enemy lines only to be isolated and wiped out before anyone knew of

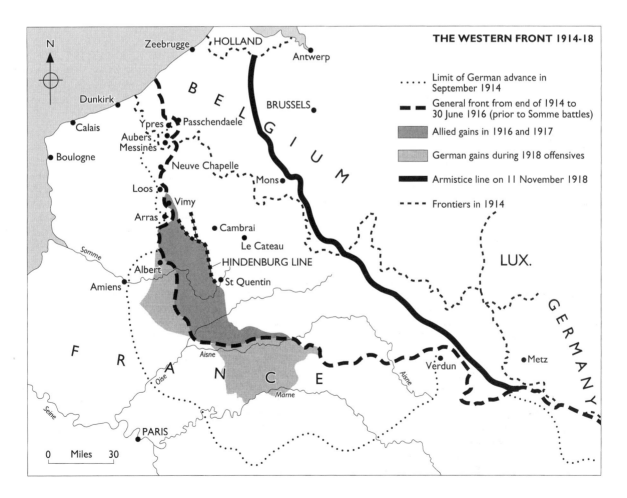

their success. Portable radios did not exist, and communications based on runners, carrier pigeons, signal flags and spotter aircraft were not adequate to control such large armies. The much-criticized 'château generalship' of the Western Front was the only realistic option – at the centre of a telephone network the general could at least control the battle up to his own front line, which again favoured the defender in summoning reserves.

A further limitation on the restoration of mobile warfare was the absence of an effective, fast-moving arm of exploitation for a successful attack. Horsed cavalry proved as vulnerable as infantry to the firepower of the defence, and in most armies was soon relegated to the status of mounted riflemen. The British Army was years ahead of its continental rivals in cavalry tactics, thanks largely to its experience of colonial warfare, and unlike the French and Germans continued to press for the use of cavalry in combination with infantry as an exploitation force. But despite repeated attempts and some limited successes, the British were unable to solve the problem of getting enough cavalry through to exploit an advance until the very end of the war. Also, compared to the size of the New Armies and bearing in mind its intended role, the British cavalry force remained extremely small. At its height on the Western Front it comprised only five divisions, and by the war's end it had shrunk to three small divisions numbering 13,600 men, hardly bigger than the single large BEF cavalry division of 1914. In

contrast, the Machine Gun Corps, formed in 1915 to oversee the tactical use of machine guns, numbered over 52,000 troops by 1918.

Finally, for a British Army that had thought before 1914 of Corps-sized battles lasting at most a few days, the assembly, control and deployment of a mass army required the development of command and staff procedures virtually from scratch. Every British Corps commander on the Western Front commanded more men than Wellington at Waterloo, and the Army commanders above them faced problems of which they had no previous experience. While changes in tactics or development of new weapons might offer hope of a breakthrough, armies needed to disseminate the new ideas and train troops to use them, which took time. In this the German Army, with its 'Great General Staff', had a considerable advantage over its enemies in developing centralized doctrine.

All this meant that major offensives on the Western Front had to be planned as set-piece battles, in the knowledge that control would break down as soon as the attack began. The commitment of reserves, the central means by which commanders could influence a battle in progress, became a matter of guesswork, and battles were

A British soldier emerges from a dug-out into a front-line trench on the Western Front, late 1916. Sandbags for protection and duckboards to counter the mud may be seen to advantage.

more often lost by traffic jams behind the lines than by enemy action. British generals on the Western Front did not fight battles so much as train their armies, draw up their plans and pray to God for success (literally so in the case of Haig), and the great operations over which they presided, stretching across miles of front and months in duration, were totally alien to 'battle' as any previous age had known it. For the generals, the inability of the mighty forces at their command to break through the apparently trivial few hundred yards of no-man's-land was a deeply frustrating experience.

With the block on tactical mobility and exploitation, and the absence of any way to by-pass the continuous lines, the Western Front remained an apparently impenetrable barrier barely 10 miles deep from the rear trenches of one side to those of the other, resolving itself around major towns as railheads. Characteristically, one side held a front-line extending a few miles in front of a town, with enemy forces curling around it to produce a salient. It was this that made the major offensives of the Western Front militarily worthwhile, as an advance of a few miles would bring the enemy railheads within range of long-range artillery, forcing a further withdrawal. The lack of depth on the Western Front was particularly acute at the notorious salient of Ypres, where a British advance of 10 miles would have brought most of the German supply railway system within artillery range, forcing them to give up almost all of the Belgian coast, while an advance by either side of 20 miles would have signalled the end of the war – and did so in 1918. As a result, all armies became increasingly dependent on heavy artillery, previously regarded as little more than garrison troops, to solve the problem of the offensive by sheer weight of firepower directed onto the enemy positions. By 1915 the French dictum that 'artillery conquers, infantry occupies' had become the new orthodoxy.

SIDESHOWS

Already in 1914, again for the first time, the British Army had effectively taken over from the Royal Navy the position and prestige of senior service, dominating British conduct of the war. The explanation for this is to be found partly in the reforms of the Haldane era, in which the Army provided itself with a planning staff, with the result that in 1914 it had a clear plan to offer the government and the Royal Navy had not. But partly it was to be found in the changing nature of war. Developments in submarines and mines had greatly increased the fear in all navies that their surface fleets were excessively vulnerable, particularly close to the shore. German reluctance to commit their fleet to dangerous waters meant that the BEF and all subsequent reinforcements could be moved to France with virtual impunity, but the traditional British option of amphibious landings on the coast of Europe was impracticable. In September 1914 a Royal Navy force was landed to assist in the defence of Antwerp, but had to be withdrawn under German pressure. Thereafter, although the idea of outflanking the Western Front by sea was put forward periodically, it was never seriously considered.

This did not prevent the planning and execution of attacks beyond Europe, however, some of which were necessarily amphibious. On 21 November 1914, for example, an unopposed Indian Army landing at the head of the Persian Gulf captured Basra from the Turks and pressed northwards into Mesopotamia in the hope of reaching Baghdad. This hope came to nothing when the Turks bottled up part of the invading force, under Major-General Charles Townshend, in Kut-el-Amara on 8 December. The ensuing bitter siege, characterized on the British side by muddle and incompetence, ended in Townshend's surrender on 29 April 1916 (*see box*). It took nearly a year for the British to reorganize themselves for another push, with Baghdad finally falling to General Sir

THE SIEGE OF KUT

When Turkey entered the war on the side of Germany and Austria-Hungary in late 1914, the British government grew concerned about the safety of the Persian oil-fields, source of most of Britain's oil supplies. In late November, an Indian division was sent to the head of the Persian Gulf, seizing Basra from the Turks. As the force came under attack, a second division was added, enabling the British commander, General Sir John Nixon, to push deeper into Mesopotamia. One division moved up the River Euphrates to Nasiriya, while the second, under Major-General Charles

Townshend, advanced along the Tigris to Amara. As the Turks fell back, the decision was taken for Townshend to continue as far as Kut-el-Amara, 180 miles closer to Baghdad. Kut was taken on 28 September 1915, after which Townshend pushed on as far as Ctesiphon, where he was checked by Turkish reinforcements on 21 November and forced to retreat.

By then, the British-Indian troops were feeling the effects of the climate and the lack of supplies, so it was a weakened force that finally re-entered Kut in December. The Turks laid siege to the town,

building lines of defences on both sides of the Tigris to prevent British relief efforts and cut off all communications with the outside world. Despite British counter-attacks, some of which got to within hailing distance of the beleaguered garrison, the Turks stood their ground. Meanwhile, as disease and starvation weakened Townshend's men still further, time ran out. On 29 April 1916, the garrison of 13,259 officers, soldiers and non-combatants surrendered, marching into a captivity which few would survive. The Turks were proving to be formidable enemies.

GERMAN EAST AFRICA, 1914–18

When the war in Europe began in August 1914, isolated German colonies seemed easy prey to their more powerful Allied neighbours, and in most cases they did not hold out for long. In German East Africa, however, the local commander, Lieutenant-General Paul von Lettow Vorbeck, determined to tie down British troops in Uganda and Kenya to prevent their transfer to Europe. He succeeded brilliantly, forcing the British to fight a counter-guerrilla war which did not end until 25 November 1918, two weeks after the armistice on the Western Front.

Despite the fact that, at the time, he commanded a force of only 260 Germans and 2472 locally raised askaris, von Lettow Vorbeck's first move was to threaten British positions around Mount Kilimanjaro. In response, the British attempted a landing at Tanga on 2 November 1914, only to meet with disaster as inexperienced Indian troops panicked under fire. Lieutenant-General Jan Christian Smuts, a highly experienced South African soldier, assumed command in 1915, but the Germans, organized into small self-contained companies, merely fell back into the interior, using their local knowledge and local support to mount hit-and-run attacks. By 1918 the Allies had been forced to

devote 130,000 troops to East Africa, at a cost of £72 million. It was an object lesson in the effectiveness of guerrilla warfare, and one that the British were to remember in years to come.

Troops of the King's African Rifles cross the River Ruwi in German East Africa during the long drawn-out campaign against Lieutenant-General Paul von Lettow Vorbeck and his locally raised forces.

Stanley Maude on 11 March 1917. Other 'sideshows' included the defence of the Suez Canal against a possible Turkish threat, the capture of German New Guinea by the Australians and of German South-West Africa by the South Africans, and a protracted guerrilla campaign in German East Africa in the tradition of the 'small wars' of the previous century. Taken altogether, the sideshows and secondary fronts absorbed 3,576,391 British and Imperial troops in the course of the war.

GALLIPOLI

The plans for the largest and most ambitious attempt to outflank the trench deadlock evolved over the winter of 1914, largely as the brainchild of Winston Churchill as First Lord of the Admiralty. It consisted of an attack by

naval forces through the narrows of the Dardanelles, linking the Aegean and Black Seas. The aim was to seize Constantinople, driving Turkey out of the war and opening up warm-water communications with the Russian Empire, which was under severe pressure from German attacks. This imaginative strategic conception foundered on the lack of proper higher political direction of the war as British strategy drifted in early 1915, on the tactical problems of overcoming defensive positions, on the lack of resources for such a venture, and on the same administrative muddle that had led to Townshend's surrender at Kut.

On 15 February 1915 a Royal Navy squadron began the bombardment of the Turkish gun batteries in the Dardanelles in the belief that ships alone might force a passage through without any need to commit troops. This rapidly proved impractical, and with the Turks thoroughly alerted, a joint Anglo-French force under Lieutenant-General Sir Ian Hamilton made an amphibious landing on the Gallipoli peninsula on 25 April (*see*

THE GALLIPOLI LANDINGS

After the failure of the Allied navies to force a passage through the Dardanelles in March 1915, it was decided to commit ground forces to secure the Turkish gun positions at the tip of the Gallipoli peninsula, preparatory to a more effective naval advance. A total of 28,000 British troops, plus 30,000 Australians and New Zealanders and 17,000 French, were made ready, but the recent naval activity had alerted the Turks. Under the able direction of the German General Liman von Sanders, extra divisions were moved into the peninsula and new defences built at likely landing sites.

Despite this, when the landings occurred on 25 April a certain degree of surprise was achieved. The main landings went in at Cape Helles, on the tip of the peninsula, with subsidiary attacks to the north at Ari Burnu (Anzac Cove) and to the south at Kum Kale on the Turkish mainland. In most cases, the troops reached the shore relatively unscathed, but disaster struck on both W and V beaches, on either side of Cape Helles itself. At W beach, the 1st Battalion Lancashire Fusiliers approached a seemingly deserted shore in lighters towed by small tugs, only to be met by a withering fire when they began to disembark. By the end of the day, three Turkish platoons had inflicted over 530 casualties, although positions ashore had been seized. In recognition of the extraordinary bravery shown by the Lancashire battalion, a total of six VCs were awarded for this single day's action.

Similar events occurred on V beach, where lighters carrying the 1st Battalion Royal Dublin Fusiliers were joined by the steamer *River Clyde*, containing men of the 1st Battalion Royal Munster Fusiliers and 2nd Battalion Hampshire Regiment. The Dublins landed first and were badly hit, losing many to Turkish machine-gun fire: one of the survivors described it as 'a perfect inferno', with bodies floating in a sea crimson with blood or piled high on the shoreline. Undaunted, the men in the *River Clyde* prepared to follow, being ordered to leave the steamer through special holes cut in the hull and then along a 'bridge' of lighters hastily lashed together. Very few made it to the shore, and the cries of the wounded added yet another awful dimension to the hellish scene. Those still on board the *River Clyde* had to wait until nightfall to join their shattered comrades huddled beneath the cliffs. It was a traumatic start to the campaign and a sign of things to come, particularly as no attempt had been made to exploit the surprise achieved elsewhere. Gallipoli would quickly degenerate into the sort of stalemate associated with the Western Front.

British troops move towards the landing beaches at Gallipoli, 25 April 1915. The vulnerability of the small lighters, some towed but many depending on the power of oars, is easy to see.

box), only to find itself paralysed by the same conditions of trench deadlock as obtained on the Western Front. The British contribution was the Army's last Regular division together with the Australian and New Zealand Army Corps (ANZAC). After almost a year of stalemate, reinforcements on both sides and failures to break the Turkish line, the last British troops were withdrawn from Gallipoli on 9 January 1916. Hamilton, who was replaced before the end of the campaign, was Kitchener's protégé, and the failure at Gallipoli only served to increase dissatisfaction with Kitchener's direction of the war. His power was progressively reduced and the government was saved any continuing embarrassment over his popularity when he

drowned in the sinking of HMS *Hampshire* on 5 June 1916, on his way to visit Russia.

By its end, the Gallipoli campaign had involved 410,000 British and Imperial troops and 79,000 French, and had cost 25,000 British, 12,000 Australian, New Zealand and Indian, and 10,000 French lives, for little visible result. Nothing daunted, on 5 October 1915 the Allies made an unopposed landing at Salonika in northern Greece (which, like Belgium in 1914, was a neutral country) in a failed attempt to support Serbia. The forces at Salonika, which were largely French but included 400,000 British soldiers, remained penned between the sea and the mountains for the next two years in what the Germans dubbed 'our big prisoner of war camp', before finally contributing to a general advance late in 1918.

CHANGES ON THE WESTERN FRONT

On 25 September 1915, Field Marshal French launched his biggest offensive yet at the Battle of Loos, again as part of a larger French plan, using 12 divisions, including three New Army divisions for the first time. The British were stopped after only a short advance for the loss of 48,000 casualties. French was heavily criticized for his conduct of the battle and, on 19 December, was recalled and replaced by Haig, previously commander of the First Army, as head of the British Army in France and Flanders.

Loos saw the first British attempt to use gas in an attack, released from cylinders to drift across the enemy lines. By this time, artillery tactics had also advanced to the point that guns could fire a sustained box barrage (from the French for 'barrier') of shells on to the rear and flanks of an enemy position. Already in late 1915 some junior commanders on all sides were also experimenting with changes in infantry tactics from the loose skirmish lines of pre-war training to small groups who would advance individually, making the section or platoon an independent tactical unit for the first time in war. These tactics would become general in all armies by 1918.

The key to the artillery tactics which now dominated the Western Front was observation, and this brought the use of aircraft to prominence. In August 1914 the Royal Flying Corps (RFC), an offshoot of the Royal Engineers, had taken four squadrons consisting of 60 assorted aircraft to France with the BEF. At least one of these aircraft provided information on the movement of German troops during the Battle of the Marne, and the first air-to-air combats occurred as pilots and observers fired at each other with rifles and pistols. The first 'kill' of the war was achieved by an RFC machine as early as 25 August 1914.

By spring 1915, machine guns had been fitted to some aircraft, but their principal role remained that of reconnaissance. Before Neuve Chapelle the RFC carried out aerial photography of the German positions marked for attack. These photographs could be turned into trench maps, and by the end of 1915 the RFC had mapped over 12,000 square miles of front. By using a grid-square reference system on these maps, artillery observers in the

GALLIPOLI 1915-16

Suvla

SUVLA FRONT (6/7 August 1915)

Bay

ANZAC FRONT

Z

Anzac Cove

N

Gallipoli Peninsula

Y

X

W

Cape Helles V

S

Dardanelles

Kum Kale

➡ British landings (25 April and 6/7 August 1915)

⇨ ANZAC landings (25 April 1915)

▪▪▪▪▪ Limits of Allied gains (August 1915 to January 1916)

front-line trenches were able to describe a given point to within 50 yards over the telephone; at Aubers Ridge this method was used for the first time in conjunction with aircraft equipped with morse transmitters which reported on their own troops' advance or on enemy guns firing for counter-battery work. The system was used for planning the artillery fire at Loos, and thereafter aerial photography became the RFC's most important role. The procedure became so efficient that during the Battle of the Somme in 1916 one aerial reconnaissance photograph reached the appropriate desk at a Corps headquarters within 30 minutes of being taken over enemy lines. The development of a practical bombsight in time for Loos also allowed the RFC to strike beyond the deadlock of the trenches at enemy railway junctions and supply points.

It was this need for aircraft to assist the artillery that accelerated the development of the 'ace' in his fighter or scout plane. Fighter pilots in single combat over the Western Front may have appeared remote from the war in the trenches, but in fact they were playing a crucial role, dominating the air and allowing unopposed passage for the more vulnerable reconnaissance aircraft over enemy lines. By the second half of the war, loss of air superiority could be catastrophic during an offensive, as with the RFC's 'Bloody April' in 1917 during the Battle of Arras. By 1918 the use of aircraft to support an advance by bombing or machine gunning the enemy ahead of the forward troops had become standard, and specialist ground-attack aircraft had been developed. In September 1918 the British even carried out a resupply of troops on the attack by dropping ammunition to them from aircraft. Meanwhile, the development of longer-range aircraft led to the creation on 1 April 1918 of an independent Royal Air Force (RAF), combining the RFC and Royal Naval Air Service. By the end of the war, the RAF had some 168 squadrons (73 of them in France, including four of longer-range bombers, and 68 in Britain) and over 32,000 personnel.

CONSCRIPTION

As Haig observed in January 1916, he did not possess an Army in France as much as a collection of divisions, as the New Army troops at last began to arrive in large numbers following a year of training. The decision to commit these forces was not taken lightly. By August 1915 the flood of volunteers was drying up, the cost of the war was placing British finances under serious strain, and the failures at Aubers Ridge and Gallipoli gave no hope of victory. Some members of the Cabinet, led by Chancellor of the Exchequer Reginald McKenna, argued that Britain faced financial ruin in attempting to maintain its mass army and war production through the next year, and that British strategy should be based instead on supporting France and Russia with money and weapons while retaining a smaller army.

The unattractive options of risking either bankruptcy or military disaster were debated through the winter of 1915, but McKenna's strategy was not adopted.

Instead, in order to maintain the Army's size, the government introduced conscription for the first time in British history in January 1916 with the Military Service Act. It was extended in May 1916 to include all men between the ages of 18 and 41, and in April 1918 to all men up to the age of 50. Conscription was too politically sensitive, however, to be used in Ireland, particularly after the Dublin 'Easter Rising' of 1916.

Between January 1916 and November 1918 conscription raised a further 2,504,183 men for the Army, giving a total serving during the war of 4,970,902. At any given time after spring 1916 the Army numbered over three million men, of whom one million or more could be found on the Western Front. In the course of the war, the British Army raised 78 infantry divisions for active service. By summer 1916 some 58 of these divisions were on the Western Front, and thereafter the total rarely fell below 50 divisions in four or five Armies, together with five Canadian divisions by the end of the war, five from Australia, one from New Zealand and a South African brigade.

With over a million men, the British Army in France had a military 'population' larger than most cities in Britain, and just as many individual experiences. For many, the Western Front was an unrelieved nightmare, for some it was by no means all bad, and a handful even claimed to enjoy it. For much of the time, most soldiers were involved not in fighting but in the routine and vital support services of industrialized war such as transport, engineering and supply. By the end of the war, the British Army in France needed over 34,000 tons of meat and 45,000 tons of bread just to feed itself each month. The guns and shells for what was after 1915 more often called a 'Big Push' than a battle took months to assemble.

For the infantry, a routine of trench duties developed in which an individual battalion would spend about four days twice a month actually holding the front line. Informal truces often developed between the men on either side of no-man's-land, a less visible form of the famous 'Christmas Truce' of 1914 (*see box*, p.98). Under Haig, the doctrine developed of the 'wearing-out fight' in which constant small aggressions would weaken and demoralize the German defenders for the next Big Push, and trench raids – small, surprise attacks by units up to a battalion to keep the enemy off balance – were encouraged. In what became a standing joke, official pamphlets asked junior officers to consider, 'Have you been sufficiently offensive today?'

THE SOMME

In December 1915, at the Inter-Allied Planning Conference at Chantilly, the governments of Britain, France, Russia and Italy determined to act for the first time as a genuine coalition, by each launching its major offensive in June or July 1916, close enough together to prevent the Germans shifting reserves from one front to the next. This was the only attempt at Allied strategic co-ordination in the war, and it was pre-empted by the Germans. In late

THE FIRST DAY OF THE SOMME

Personality Profile:

Field Marshal Sir Douglas Haig
(1861–1928)

Commissioned from Sandhurst into the 7th Hussars, Douglas Haig saw service in the Sudan (1898) and South Africa (1899–1902) before holding a series of staff posts in India and Britain. In 1914–15 he commanded the British I Corps, later First Army, in the BEF, experiencing the painful transition from mobile to static warfare and from professional to mass army. In December 1915 he replaced French as British C-in-C in France, holding the position for the remainder of the war. As such, he was responsible for the costly attritional battles of the Somme (1916) and Passchendaele (1917), gaining a reputation for unimaginative, uncaring command. This is a little unfair, however, for he also conducted the series of highly effective battles which followed the failure of the German March 1918 offensive, contributing in no small measure to eventual Allied victory. After the war, Haig was raised to the peerage as 1st Earl of Bemersyde, devoting himself to the welfare of ex-servicemen.

As the sun broke through the early morning mist on 1 July 1916, the men of General Rawlinson's Fourth Army, occupying a 20,000-yard line from Serre in the north to Montauban in the south, waited patiently for the signal to attack. A mixture of Regulars, Territorials and New Army troops, they were confident that their advance would herald the 'Big Push' which would end the war. Since 24 June the artillery had been battering the German trenches, and officers had assured the men that no-one could possibly survive the bombardment. It would just be a case of getting up out of the trenches and walking across no-man's-land to occupy shattered enemy positions. In at least one of the waiting battalions, the 8th East Surreys, the troops had been given footballs to kick towards their objectives as they advanced, adding to the carnival air. It was not to last.

At 7.15 a.m. mines were exploded under some of the German positions and the artillery bombardment slackened. Quarter of an hour later, amid shouts and whistles of command, men clambered up trench ladders and began their advance. It was a glorious summer morning, with birds singing in a clear blue sky, but the Germans were by no means unprepared. Although in some areas, particularly where no-man's-land was narrow or mines had been effective, the British managed to reach the enemy trenches before the dazed occupants knew what was happening, in others German machine gunners had time to emerge from their dug-outs and deploy their weapons. The results were devastating, especially in the north where entire battalions of VIII Corps, unable to advance through barbed wire uncut by the artillery, were caught in the open and destroyed. A few small parties penetrated as far as Serre and Beaumont Hamel, only to be cut off or forced to pull back. Further south, elements of the 36th (Ulster) Division, part of X Corps, gained a more dramatic lodgement on the Thiepval-Pozières ridge, but they too had to be withdrawn. Only in the far south was any permanent success achieved, as men of XIII Corps took Mametz and Montauban, but their success was overshadowed by the sheer scale of the disaster elsewhere. By the end of the day, 993 officers and 18,247 soldiers had been killed, 1337 officers and 34,741 men wounded and 2152 listed as missing; more than 30 battalions had suffered over 500 casualties each. It was, and remains, the worst day in the history of the British Army.

First-Hand Accounts:

The Attack on Serre
1 July 1916

'I saw many men fall back into the trench as they attempted to climb out. Those of us who managed had to walk two yards apart, very slowly, then stop, then walk again and so on. We all had to keep in line. Machine-gun bullets were sweeping backwards and forwards and hitting the ground around our feet. Shells were bursting everywhere. I had no special fear except I knew we must all go forward until wounded or killed. There was no going back . . .'

Lance-Corporal W. Marshall,
Accrington Pals

From William Turner, *Pals. The 11th (Service) Battalion (Accrington) East Lancashire Regiment. A History of the Battalion Raised from Accrington, Blackburn, Burnley and Chorley in World War One,* Wharncliffe Publishing, Barnsley, 1987

1 JULY 1916

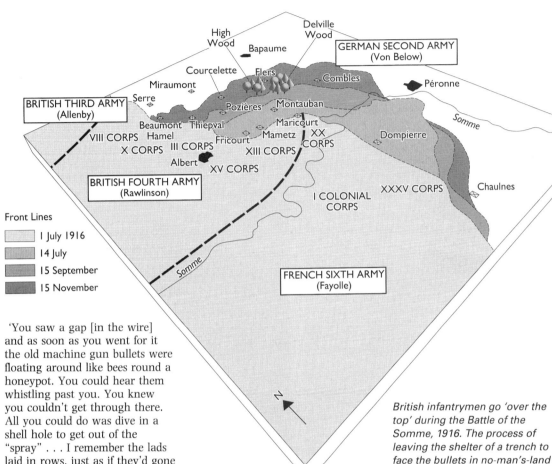

Front Lines

- 1 July 1916
- 14 July
- 15 September
- 15 November

GERMAN SECOND ARMY
(Von Below)

BRITISH THIRD ARMY
(Allenby)

VIII CORPS
X CORPS
III CORPS
XV CORPS
XIII CORPS
XX CORPS
XXXV CORPS
I COLONIAL CORPS

BRITISH FOURTH ARMY
(Rawlinson)

FRENCH SIXTH ARMY
(Fayolle)

High Wood · Delville Wood · Bapaume · Courcelette · Flers · Combles · Péronne · Miraumont · Pozières · Montauban · Serre · Beaumont · Thiepval · Maricourt · Hamel · Fricourt · Mametz · Dompierre · Albert · Chaulnes · Somme

'You saw a gap [in the wire] and as soon as you went for it the old machine gun bullets were floating around like bees round a honeypot. You could hear them whistling past you. You knew you couldn't get through there. All you could do was dive in a shell hole to get out of the "spray" . . . I remember the lads laid in rows, just as if they'd gone to sleep there, and the sun flashing on them bits of tin on their backs all down the lines. Some of the lads I recognised; that's so and so I thought. The machine guns just laid 'em out. They must have stopped one or two bullets and it finished them . . . Them that had made for the gaps in [the German] wire were all piled up. Some were hanging on the wire, hanging like rags. Machine gun bullets were knocking 'em round as if they were washing hung on the line . . .'

Private F. Lindley,
2nd Barnsley Pals

From Jon Cooksey, *Pals. The 13th and 14th Battalions York and Lancaster Regiment. A History of the Two Battalions Raised by Barnsley in World War One*, Wharncliffe Publishing, Barnsley, 1986

British infantrymen go 'over the top' during the Battle of the Somme, 1916. The process of leaving the shelter of a trench to face the bullets in no-man's-land took remarkable physical and mental courage.

1915 the new German Chief of General Staff, General Erich von Falkenhayn, had argued for a change of German strategy. While Britain was now perceived as the main enemy, it still depended for its land forces on the French; if they could be destroyed, the alliance against Germany would collapse.

On 21 February 1916, the Germans launched their major offensive for the year against the French at Verdun. This was planned as a purely attritional battle, not designed to take territory but to destroy the French Army by 'bleeding it white'. The French responded promptly by reinforcing Verdun and the battle was joined, lasting throughout a year of killing to end officially on 18 December. Casualties on either side were not less than 300,000. The provisional plans for a summer offensive had been for a joint Anglo-French attack further south than Flanders, close to the River Somme with Albert as the major railhead. As their casualties rose, the French commitment of troops to this offensive dwindled and their demands for its launch increased.

The plan for the attack, to be launched by 14 divisions of General Sir Henry Rawlinson's Fourth Army with French forces attacking further south, was based on the conviction that the British Army in France was undertrained. Rawlinson's divisions were all New Army, Territorial, or Regular but had been subject to so many replacements that they had lost much of their previous character. All the prejudices of the Regular Army were against the idea that civilians in uniform were capable of mastering, in a few months, the skills and tactical complexities of a real army. Instead, Rawlinson planned to use artillery firepower to substitute for the tactical shortcomings of the infantry. The plan could hardly have been simpler: for five days 2029 British guns, of which 452 were heavy, would fire over 1,500,000 shells at the German front-line positions, with the intention – literally – of killing everyone in them by burying the troops alive in their dug-outs. At the last stage, poor weather led to the bombardment being extended to seven days, and a final total of 1,732,873 shells being fired. In addition, seven British mines had been dug under the German positions and packed with explosives to add to the destruction.

At 7.15 a.m. on the bright sunny morning of 1 July 1916 the British exploded their mines and, as the barrage lifted onto the German second line, the infantry got up out of their trenches and walked forward over no-man's-land. The day was to prove a disaster: by the end of it the British Army had lost 57,470 casualties, including 19,240 dead (*see* p. 108). The German losses on 1 July were reckoned at about 8000. Along much of the front the British had been stopped in no-man's-land without even reaching the German wire.

The first day of the Battle of the Somme, still remembered at ceremonies around the country, has become central to the British view of the First World War as the day on which the British nation lost its innocence about war. It also convinced at least some of the generals that they would have to rely on their troops after all. On 14 July, in the next big push of the Somme offensive at Trones Wood, Rawlinson attacked at night, one of the most difficult manoeuvres in warfare. The same attack also saw the first large-scale use of a 'creeping' barrage, fired to inch forward in front of the advancing infantry.

The combination was so successful that two regiments of cavalry were even pushed through to charge the Germans.

The Somme, unlike Verdun, was never planned as an attritional battle, but it became a similar grinding slog into which divisions would enter for a few days to return at half strength and exhausted. As autumn approached, the most feared enemy became the mud of the waterlogged trenches, which many veterans later believed was the worst of the war, a glutinous quicksand that could drown a man in minutes. Haig kept the offensive going and the Battle of the Somme was not officially declared over until 13 November 1916, when winter and mud made further fighting impossible. The British had advanced about five miles at a cost of about 420,000 casualties; the Germans had suffered approximately the same.

Haig argued that the Somme was a victory in that it fatally weakened the old German Army. He was rewarded by being promoted to field marshal in December 1916. By then, the Asquith coalition government had collapsed under the strain of the war, being replaced by a new coalition under David Lloyd George. Nor were the British the only ones to undergo change: in August 1916, with his strategy a failure, von Falkenhayn was replaced as German Chief of General Staff by Field Marshal Paul von Hindenburg, with Erich Ludendorff as his increasingly dominant deputy. Hindenburg and Ludendorff introduced a new tactical doctrine of defence in depth for the German Army, and construction began on the Western Front of a major defensive system some miles behind the existing German positions, later known to the British as the Hindenburg Line. Haig was right to think that the German Army had been badly damaged, but its leaders were determined not to let it face 'Somme fighting' again. Another by-product of such thinking, and one that was to prove fatal in the long-term, was the German decision to pursue unrestricted submarine warfare against neutral shipping in an attempt to starve the British into submission. In response, on 6 April 1917 the United States of America declared war on Germany, offering immense potential military might to the Allies. It would take some time for this potential to be realized, but once US divisions arrived in Europe, Germany faced an insurmountable problem of numbers.

The British artillery bombardment during the Battle of the Somme, 1916. The heavy losses on the first day (1 July) often disguise the fact that the overall cost of the offensive was horrifically high: 420,000 British casualties by November.

SOMME AFTERMATH

The Somme had also effectively destroyed the volunteer New Armies of 1914. With the addition of conscripts and replacements, most of the Pals' Battalions became indistinguishable from any others by 1917. By the end of the war the British Army was considerably more experienced and professional than it had been in 1916, but it was also distinctly more sullen. By 1918 generals felt that they were scraping the bottom of the barrel for troops and that good fighting divisions were limited to those which had somehow avoided a major battle in the previous six months. Even so, British Army morale and discipline remained remarkably good throughout the war, and large-scale mutinies were rare (*see box*, p.115). In spring 1917 the Russian Empire collapsed in the political chaos and mutiny that led to the 'October Revolution' under Lenin. After its massive losses between 1914 and 1916, the French Army also suffered mutinies in several of its divisions in 1917, and its leaders became reluctant to risk it in further offensives. From the Somme onwards, the British Army would carry the main weight of the war.

Just as the British Army's experience of battle in 1916 was very different from that of 1914, so it would change again by 1918. A soldier who served on the Somme, was wounded and returned to the front in late 1917, would notice that, although the trench-lines had hardly moved, the nature of trench fighting had changed radically. Artillery tactics in particular developed beyond recognition in the course of the war. By 1917 gas shells, instantaneous fuses and sound-ranging equipment were available, and the creeping barrage had become standard. By the end of the war, numbers of guns and shells used in major offensives completely dwarfed those of the Somme and artillery attacks took the form of 'hurricane' bombardments of short duration but unimaginable intensity to shatter the enemy line. By October 1918 the British Army in France had 2200 heavy guns, twice as many as a year before and 20 times as many as in 1915, and Royal Artillery personnel accounted for over a third of Haig's troops.

Infantry tactics also progressed away from the 'wave' formation towards what the British called 'worms' of infantry advancing in single file, equipped by the end of the war with machine guns, grenades and mortars on a lavish scale. Whereas the British infantry division of 1914 had consisted largely of riflemen, the 1918 division contained a range of specialist troops and weapons, including an unofficial scale of up to 30 Lewis guns in each battalion. The British problem, as always, was in disseminating new ideas and training troops to use them. The Germans, with their more centralized system, tended to adopt new tactics a few months ahead of the British and French, often giving them considerable temporary advantages.

British soldiers, usually reckoned to be members of the Royal Irish Rifles but recently described as men of the Sheffield Pals, rest in reserve somewhere on the Somme, 1916. Their faces say it all.

THE TANK

The one idea in which the British led their allies and enemies was the development of the tank (*see box*, p.114). Haig supported the concept of a tracked, armour-plated vehicle carrying guns or machine guns, capable of crossing no-man's-land as well as enemy trenches, and hoped to get 150 of them for the Somme offensive. In the event, 49 'tanks' (so called because they were initially described as 'water tanks' to disguise their true nature) were produced for 1916 as the Heavy Branch of the Machine Gun Corps. Of these, 32 crossed the British front line on 15 September 1916 at the Battle of Flers-Courcelette, although 14 were lost to ditching, breakdowns or German shellfire. The First World War tank was a slow, ponderous vehicle with a cross-country speed of barely half a mile an hour and a range of a few miles, mechanically unreliable and not properly bullet-proof. Even so, immediately after Flers-Courcelette Haig requested production of 1000 tanks for his army.

Despite Haig's enthusiasm, such production rates could not be achieved in the conditions of 1916–17. A year after Flers-Courcelette the new Tank Corps, formed on 27 July 1917, could still field only 136 tanks. Despite repeated demands by Haig for increased production, and even the development of a tank landing craft for amphibious operations, the supply of tanks remained poor. On only two days in the entire war could the British Army field a significant number of tanks: 378 on 20 November 1917 at the Battle of Cambrai and 534 on 8 August 1918

Regimental Tradition:

THE TANK CORPS' BERET

In late 1917 a group of officers of the Tank Corps were discussing what style of dress should be adopted by their unit once the war was over.

At the time they were stationed close to a regiment of French *Tirailleurs Alpins*, who wore a distinctive *béret Breton*, and the idea was mooted that this headdress might be copied in remembrance of Allied co-operation. But the *béret Breton* was seen as too 'sloppy', so letters were sent to a number of English girls' school asking for examples of the berets worn by them. Out of the large selection of designs and colours received, a close-fitting black, beret was chosen and, after something of a fight with the War Office, it was officially adopted by the Royal Tank Corps (now the Royal Tank Regiment) in 1925.

DEVELOPMENT OF THE TANK

The tank was developed in direct response to the tactical problems of trench deadlock on the Western Front. Presented with the combination of mud, barbed wire and enemy machine guns, it was apparent by 1915 that infantry alone could achieve little. They required some means of close support if they were to break through. Artillery lacked the accuracy and airpower was in its infancy, so something new was needed. Lieutenant-Colonel Ernest Swinton, a British Army officer, was in the forefront of those who suggested the development of a machine designed specifically to overcome the physical difficulties of the battle area. Because of the machine guns, any vehicle would have to be protected by armour and capable of suppressing enemy defences, while being designed to move through mud, across shell-holes and trenches and over barbed wire. What resulted was an armoured 'box', armed with either cannon or machine guns, which was mounted on caterpillar tracks to spread the weight. The tank eventually assumed a distinctive 'lozenge' shape to enable it to crawl over trench obstacles. Because it was seen as no more than an infantry-support machine, it was given a top speed of less than five mph. Early models, deployed to France in 1916, were ponderous, mechanically unreliable and extremely uncomfortable for the crews, but they did provide the germ of an answer to the trench stalemate.

Mark V tanks move forward to cross the River Selle, late September 1918, during the offensive against the Hindenburg Line. The tanks are fitted with 'cribs' to facilitate water-crossing.

at the Battle of Amiens. In each case, mechanical problems and German fire reduced the Tank Corps to insignificant numbers within a few days – on the fourth day of Amiens, only six tanks were still available.

To the end of the war artillery and infantry tactics, with tanks as a supporting arm, remained the key to breaking the trench deadlock on the Western Front. Nevertheless, the future potential of the tank was obvious to the British and the French, who had also developed tanks by 1917. The tank remained a blind spot for the Germans, with only 20 of their own giant A7V design being produced by the end of the war, although they also employed captured British tanks. By spring 1918 the British also had the Medium A Whippet, effectively an armoured car on tracks equipped with machine guns only but with a road-speed of nearly 8 mph. The promise of large numbers of the Whippet's successor, the Medium D with a speed of 20 mph, led Lieutenant-Colonel J. F. C. Fuller, the Tank Corps' chief staff officer, to draw up an outline 'Plan 1919' for an all-arms battle based on fast tank exploitation (*see box*, p.120). It is recognized as one of the founding ideas of modern mechanized warfare.

ARRAS

The change in British political leadership in December 1916, with Lloyd George becoming prime minister, coincided with the appointment of a new French commander-in-chief, General Robert Nivelle. Deeply critical of Haig, the losses on the Western Front and the whole conduct of the war, Lloyd George committed the British to support Nivelle's master plan for winning the war in a few weeks. This involved a sudden large-scale assault to break the German front in 24 hours, for which a British preliminary attack at Arras was regarded as essential.

Nivelle's plan was crippled in early 1917 when the Germans withdrew to the now completed Hindenburg Line, giving up a strip of French territory between 10 and 50 miles deep which they had deliberately devastated. Nevertheless, Nivelle insisted on continuing with his plan, and on 9 April Third Army under General Sir Edmund Allenby opened the Battle of Arras, in which the Canadian Corps secured the crucial Vimy Ridge. Allenby's forces and frontage were virtually the same as Rawlinson's on the Somme, but increased use of artillery and more sophisticated tactics held his casualties down to 32,000 over the first three days. By 24 April, the official end of the battle, Allenby had penetrated about four miles, but was still well short of the main Hindenburg Line defences. A brigade of cavalry got through to extend the advance by a mile or so, at great cost to themselves.

Nivelle's main attack started on 16 April and was a limited success, but not the breakthrough that he had promised. Its results included widespread mutinies that crippled the French Army for a year and the rapid dismissal of Nivelle himself. Haig's own plans, meanwhile, had been distorted for several months in advance by the need to fight at Arras. From this time onwards, the British Army's conduct of the war was dominated by the antagonism between Lloyd George and Haig. The latter also managed to find sufficient fault with Allenby to get him removed from the Western Front and sent to Palestine, where he conducted a brilliant campaign of manoeuvre culminating in the seizure of Damascus and the defeat of the Turks (*see box*, p.118).

MESSINES RIDGE

Haig's intention for 1917 had always been to attack at Ypres, where an advance might free the whole of Belgium, but Arras had left him short of time and troops for his offensive. As a preliminary, on 7 June 1917, Second Army under General Sir Herbert Plumer secured Messines Ridge, south of the Ypres salient, in a triumph of engineering and siege-warfare techniques. For nearly two years, British Army tunnelling companies had dug 20 mine galleries underneath the ridge, containing between them 600 tons of explosives. At 3.10 a.m., the British detonated 17 of the mines (two failed to explode and one had been defused by the Germans), blowing the top off the ridge. The noise of the explosion could be heard in London. British and ANZAC troops moved forward to occupy the wreckage within three hours, supported by 2338 guns (828 of them heavy) firing a creeping barrage on a front of nine miles. Plumer's casualties were under 16,000 and German losses were almost certainly greater, possibly for the first time in the war.

PASSCHENDAELE

On 31 July Fifth Army under General Sir Hubert Gough opened Haig's main offensive for the year, the Third Battle of Ypres, after a 10-day artillery bombardment from more than 3000 guns (999 of them heavy). Commonly known as Passchendaele from the small village on top of the ridge eight miles from Ypres, this battle shares the reputation of the Somme for violence, mud and the gap between

MUTINY AT ÉTAPLES

Less than 50 miles from the Ypres salient, the British base camp at Étaples was notorious for its iron discipline, exercised by 'Canaries' (instructors) and 'Redcaps' (military policemen) as they prepared new or returning soldiers for service in the front line. A 10-day course of drill and training in the 'Bull Ring' was widely regarded as worse than being in the trenches, leading to resentment which finally boiled over on 9 September 1917, when a Gordon Highlander was shot and killed by a Redcap who panicked in the face of a crowd demanding the release of a recently arrested New Zealander. The General commanding the camp failed to restore order and a mob of men streamed out into the surrounding villages, searching for drink. The majority soon returned, having looted the local *estaminets* (public houses), but the disturbances continued for about three days, during which Redcaps were beaten up and buildings destroyed. On 13 September elements of the Honourable Artillery Company arrived at Étaples, the ringleaders of the 'mutiny' (an emotive term, ill-suited to describe what was no more than collective indiscipline) were rounded up and courts-martial held. One Regular soldier, who had urged the men to throw an officer into a nearby river, was executed, but the rest of the 'mutineers' were returned to the front line. In retrospect, it is perhaps surprising that more mutinies did not occur.

expectation and achievement. For the first month Gough faced rain and mud, and his tactics of pushing ahead regardless produced heavy casualties with little progress. Haig shifted the main force of the offensive to Plumer's Second Army. The push began on 20 September with a series of limited advances backed by overwhelming artillery concentrations that gave the British possession of the main ridges by 4 October, an advance of more than five miles from Ypres. The later autumn weather was good for this period and in places the ground was so dry that the attacking troops actually suffered problems with dust. Despite the German defensive system, with pillboxes and machine-gun strongpoints replacing continuous trench-lines in most places and defences stretching back in depth for several thousand yards, the British were breaking through and the cavalry was alerted for possible exploitation at the next attack. However, the weather changed once again and heavy rain turned the pock-marked landscape into an expanse of mud every bit as dangerous as that on the Somme.

Although the chances of a major breakthrough were gone, Haig kept the offensive going through the mud for another month in an attempt to find a secure stop-line. Passchendaele village was finally taken by the Canadians on 4 November. On the battlefield, the difference between attacker and defender was obliterated. Estimates of British casualties for Third Ypres came to about 300,000 and were about the same on the German side, although an accurate count was not possible on either side under such conditions. Just as Verdun and the Somme fatally weakened the German Army, so after the experience of Passchendaele the British Army was never the same again.

CAMBRAI

A small boost to morale for both the Army and the increasingly weary Home Front came at the end of 1917, as what had begun as a proposal by Fuller for a 'tank raid' was developed by Third Army under General Sir Julian Byng into a small-scale offensive at Cambrai. Justly celebrated as the first occasion on which a large force of tanks was used in the war, the Battle of Cambrai was launched on 20 November with no preliminary bombardment and no reserves, and tank tactics were allowed to dominate its conduct. The result was a five-mile push into German lines for only 1 500 British casualties. But Cambrai also revealed the severe problems that still existed in British staff-work and administration. Co-ordination broke down between the tanks, the accompanying infantry and the cavalry waiting behind; the latter failed to reach a major gap before the Germans closed it, although two regiments did get behind the enemy lines. After the battle both the Tank Corps and Cavalry Corps headquarters were reduced to planning organizations, and control of their forces in battle was delegated to other commanders. On 30 November the Germans responded with a hurricane bombardment and an infantry attack that retook the lost ground.

THE LUDENDORFF OFFENSIVE

By now Russia was effectively out of the war, freeing considerable German forces for use elsewhere. With barely any US troops yet available, and Britain and France both severely weakened, the Germans had one remaining chance to win the war in 1918 with an offensive on the Western Front, breaking through the British lines. While recognizing the danger, Lloyd George's government was

not prepared to commit yet more troops to the Western Front, even sending a few divisions under Plumer to Italy (*see box*, p. 119) and two Indian cavalry divisions to Allenby in Palestine. In January 1918 Haig was forced to disband a quarter of his infantry battalions in order to keep the others up to strength, reducing his brigades from four to three battalions each. At the same time, after three years of straining for a breakthrough, a British Army which knew almost nothing but attacking tried wearily to train itself in the tactics of defence in depth and to build the defensive systems it would need.

The German blow came on a morning of fog on 21 March 1918 with a hurricane bombardment of unpre-

cedented ferocity against Byng's Third and Gough's Fifth Armies, 10,000 guns firing 1,160,000 shells in five hours followed by 47 divisions in attack. Lacking reserves and proper training, the British line gave way, and within 24 hours the Germans were through the British trench system, achieving in a day the same advance that had taken their enemy the whole duration of the Somme offensive. In the process, the Germans lost 40,000 casu-

Men of a Staffordshire brigade gather to hear from their commander on the banks of the St Quentin Canal, 1918. The fact that, despite their numbers, they constitute only a small formation, indicates the sheer size of the Army at the time.

THE PALESTINE CAMPAIGN, 1917–18

By January 1917, British troops of the Egyptian Expeditionary Force (EEF) had pushed the Turks back from the Suez Canal, through the Sinai Desert, and were poised on the southern borders of Palestine. Two attempts to take the Turkish-held town of Gaza failed (26 March and 17–19 April), alerting the Turks and enabling their German commanders to construct a barrier of fortified positions inland from Gaza to Beersheba. Fortunately for the British, on 28 June General Sir Edmund Allenby, erstwhile commander of the Third Army on the Western Front, took over the EEF, and his arrival gradually transformed the situation.

Gaza was finally taken on 7 November, after a series of cavalry attacks around Beersheba had caught the Turks by surprise and threatened to 'roll up' their line from the east. Once unlocked in this way, the Turkish defences collapsed, allowing the EEF to advance northwards quite rapidly, taking Jaffa on 16 November and the symbolic prize of Jerusalem on 9 December. Further attacks were delayed by the transfer of units from Palestine to France in response to the German March 1918 offensive, but by September 1918 Allenby was ready to move again. His campaign was a masterpiece of surprise and all-arms co-operation. Using his cavalry, and Arab irregulars under Colonel T. E. Lawrence, to tie down Turkish forces in the east before moving the cavalry secretly and swiftly to the west, he sent aircraft to 'blind' the enemy by bombing communications targets. Then, on 19 September, after a short, sharp artillery bombardment, infantry units attacked along the coast towards Tulkarm. This opened the way to a cavalry advance as far as Megiddo, deep in the enemy rear, spreading confusion and cutting off Turkish lines of retreat. Two Turkish armies virtually ceased to exist and a third crumbled as it tried to pull back into Jordan. On 1 October Damascus fell, followed by Aleppo on the 25th. Five days later the Turks, under similar pressure in Mesopotamia, signed an armistice.

General Sir Edmund Allenby (1861–1936), commander of the Egyptian Expeditionary Force 1917–18 and mastermind behind a brilliant campaign to capture Jerusalem and Damascus.

alties and the British 38,000, making this the worst day's fighting of the war.

Fortunately for the British, Ludendorff had launched his offensive in the wrong place, to the south near Albert where Haig could afford to give ground (and had deployed fewer troops as a result) rather than north near the Channel ports. By 5 April the Germans were held east of Amiens, having gouged a salient some 40 miles deep in places out of the British line. Total British losses were about 178,000 men. The French, who became heavily engaged as the battle progressed, lost 77,000 men, and the German losses came to 239,000 men. In the crisis, Gough was dismissed, and Haig agreed on 26 March to the appointment of a French supreme Allied commander on the Western Front, Marshal Ferdinand Foch, in return for French reinforcements.

It is one of the clichés of British Army history that it attacks badly but defends well, and the stopping of the German push was one of the great defensive victories of the war. On 9 April Ludendorff tried again with a smaller

THE ITALIAN FRONT, 1917–18

Between the summer of 1915 and the autumn of 1917 the Italians fought a series of battles against the Austro-Hungarians in the Trentino region and along the River Isonzo. Neither side was able to gain an advantage, but in October 1917, with forces released from the Eastern Front as a result of the Russian Revolution, a German-Austrian offensive south of Caporetto caught the Italians by surprise and forced them to retreat. Faced with the imminent collapse of the Italian Front, the British transferred five divisions – the 5th, 7th, 23rd, 41st and 48th – across the Alps to bolster the defences. By the time they arrived in November and early December, the enemy offensive had petered out, but the Austrians remained in possession of part of the Lombardy plain.

To the British troops involved, Italy was a paradise compared to the Western Front, and it was no surprise to them when, in February 1918, their numbers were reduced, leaving only three divisions in theatre. But these formations did see some fierce fighting. On 15 June 1918 the Austrians attacked in the Asiago sector, held by the 23rd and 48th Divisions, and the situation was only restored after hastily organized counter-attacks in which the CO of the 11th (Service) Battalion Sherwood Foresters won the Victoria Cross. In October British units spearheaded part of the Italian offensive which culminated in the defeat of the Austrians at Vittorio Veneto. An armistice was signed on 3 November.

offensive just south of Ypres, forcing Plumer to give up Messines and most of the Passchendaele salient in a matter of days. The German attacks, based on hurricane bombardments, infantry ('stormtrooper') infiltration tactics and good staff-work, were demonstrations of what the British Army had failed to achieve in the previous year. On 12 April Haig's headquarters made preliminary plans for the evacuation of Calais, and he issued his famous Order of the Day: 'With our backs to the wall and believing in the justice of our cause, each one must fight on to the end'. The German attack slowed and by 29 April the crisis was past. Having failed to break the British, Ludendorff now tested the French with a series of offensives further south between 27 May and 17 July, but all to no avail. After this failure, German Army morale and discipline began to crumble. On 18 July Foch launched a counter-attack on the Marne, over almost the same ground as in 1914, with a predominantly French force that also included British, US and even Italian troops, forcing the Germans back to avoid encirclement.

AMIENS TO THE ARMISTICE

With the Germans overstretched and exhausted, the initiative passed to the Allies. On 8 August Rawlinson's Fourth Army, alongside French forces, launched the Battle of Amiens against the German salient created during the March Offensive. In this battle, for the first time on any scale, British staff-work and communications, helped by the use of wireless sets at all levels from brigade to corps, were equal to controlling their forces. On a front of 11 miles, Rawlinson used 2070 guns (684 of them

Australian troops, bayonets fixed, move along a shallow trench during their assault on Mont St Quentin, September 1918. By this stage in the war, the British were heavily dependent on forces from the Empire.

heavy) in a hurricane bombardment, followed by 13 divisions and the largest deployment of tanks in the war. The newly formed RAF also carried out crucial roles in artillery spotting and ground attack. The German front broke open and the waiting cavalry were pushed through. By the end of the day, Fourth Army was eight miles behind the German front line, having lost 20,000 casualties and taken more than that number of German prisoners.

Amiens began the period known as the 'Hundred Days Battle', a series of offensives from south to north along the British line driving the Germans back. These were, in terms of scale and achievement, the greatest victories in the British Army's history. Even so, it was only possible to break the German front briefly and for a few hours at a time, and only by a massive weight of firepower. Despite Haig's use of his cavalry together with armoured cars and motorized machine-gun battalions, a deep exploitation could not be achieved. Also, it was noticeable that from Amiens onwards the British Army relied increasingly on the still strong Canadian and Australian Corps to help lead its attacks.

On 26 September the British Army demonstrated just how far it had come in a year of learning with an assault on the Hindenburg Line between Bullecourt and St Quentin, retaking in four days the ground already won and lost at the Battle of Cambrai, and breaching the last German defensive position at the St Quentin Canal on 29 September. Unable to hold their ground against these powerful drives, the Germans had already decided to seek peace after Amiens, and diplomatic contacts aimed at an armistice began. Over the next two months the British progressively drove the Germans back from position to position; for the first time since 1914 officers found themselves commanding from horseback to keep up with the advance. On 11 November, the day the Canadians reached Mons, an armistice came into force. Belgium had been liberated and Germany defeated. The British Army stood at the pinnacle of its achievements.

AFTERMATH

This was not, however, the attitude taken by most members of the Army and nation in November 1918. In a war of firepower, the cost of the decision to pursue a strategy of attacking with a mass army had been casualties in proportion to that army's size: 744,702 dead, plus a further 202,321 dead from the Empire. By the end of the war, few of those who had volunteered or been conscripted wanted any part of the Army. At 11 a.m. on 11 November the armistice took effect, and one hour later the order halting conscription was issued in London.

Protests over the government's failure to demobilize the Army started as early as January 1919 in a series of 'soldiers' strikes' conducted very much according to the conventions of civilian industrial relations. At the end of 1918 the Army had numbered 3,779,825 men. Within a year it had been reduced to 888,952 and by 1922 to 217,986 Regular troops, fewer than in 1914. The Army was returned once more to its pre-war status as a long-service imperial police force consisting chiefly of infantry, very much as if the First World War had never happened. In 1919 the government adopted the 'Ten-Year Rule', decreeing that for planning purposes Britain should not expect a major war within 10 years. This reached its final form in 1928 with a rolling 10-year horizon, setting severe limits on the size and finances of the armed forces, before being finally abandoned in 1932.

The difficulty with this sudden reduction in the Army's size was that the war might be over but the fighting was not. With the signing by Germany of the Treaty of Versailles on 28 June 1919 the British Army had to find an occupation force for the Rhineland (this force was not completely withdrawn until 1930). The British Army was not withdrawn from Turkey until the Treaty of Lausanne (23 August 1923), and Britain also took responsibility under the new League of Nations mandates for parts of the old Ottoman Empire, including Palestine, Transjordan and Iraq. Serious revolts against British rule occurred throughout the Middle East, particularly in

'PLAN 1919'

In March 1918, as German forces advanced in dramatic fashion on the Western Front, Colonel J. F. C. Fuller of the Tank Corps observed the effects, recognizing that rear-area confusion and panic quickly led to collapse and retreat. Out of this experience emerged 'Plan 1919', which Fuller intended to carry out in that year if the war had continued. Choosing an enemy Corps frontage (about 90 miles), he planned to concentrate German attention by preparing a direct assault in the traditional way. Before this was launched, however, groups of fast-moving tanks would suddenly pierce the enemy flanks, advancing towards command centres in an attempt to take out the 'brain', severing its connection to the front-line 'muscle'. RAF bombers would simultaneously hit supply lines, helping to spread panic in the rear areas. When this panic was at its height, the bombers would shift to communications targets to 'blind' the enemy and the main assault forces would advance to destroy his front-line units. Pursuit would be carried out by mechanized infantry, artillery and supply elements, building up an unstoppable momentum. Although never put into effect, 'Plan 1919' became one of the key documents in the inter-war development of armoured doctrine, offering an alternative to costly and painful attritional war.

Palestine (*see box*, p. 123), in the 1920s and 1930s.

British troops had also been committed to Russia in 1917 in support of the 'White' Russians against Lenin's Bolsheviks. This commitment continued after the defeat of Germany, including sizeable contingents under General Rawlinson at Archangel and Murmansk, a mixed force of armoured cars and aircraft in the Ukraine, and 'Dunsterforce' under the flamboyant Brigadier Lionel Dunsterville (the original of Kipling's 'Stalky') at Baku. The last British units did not withdraw until 1919, marking the end of the only occasion that the Soviet Union actually fought a war against Britain, or for that matter the United States.

PEACETIME DUTIES

The creation of the Soviet Union and the Communist International only served to reinforce traditional British fears of a Russian threat to India. Following the First World War, India remained the British Army's single greatest commitment, both to defend against this threat and to retain control of a country that increasingly resisted the British presence. In 1919 the notorious 'Amritsar Massacre', in which Indian troops under British command opened fire on an unarmed crowd, helped fuel a protracted campaign of civil unrest for Indian independence. In the same summer the Indian Army committed nearly 100,000 men to the brief Third Afghan War in order to re-establish British domination of Afghanistan, and throughout the next two decades the North-West Frontier remained the British Army's turbulent training ground. Despite progressive 'Indianization' of the 190,000-strong Indian Army by the commissioning of native Indian officers, India remained a considerable drain on British military resources.

With so much of Europe in turmoil, the British government (rightly or wrongly) also took extremely seriously the possibility of a British revolution, particularly on 'Red Clydeside' from 1917 onwards. There were police strikes in 1918 and 1919, and troops were needed for riot control, strike-breaking and 'military aid to the civil power' throughout Britain until 1921, as well as one final emergency in the General Strike of 1926. Thereafter, the basic political neutrality of the Army largely prevented its involvement in the extreme right-wing politics which swept many European armed forces in the 1930s. The most significant exception was Fuller, who became a

Auxiliaries of the Royal Irish Constabulary pay their respects to one of their number, killed by the IRA in 1920. Ex-officers of the British Army, many of the mourners are still wearing regimental collar badges.

prominent member of the British Union of Fascists after leaving the Army in 1933.

Having taken control of German colonies as well as League of Nations' mandates round the world, the British Empire stood by 1922 at its largest in history. There was, however, one immensely significant loss. In January 1919 a major guerrilla war against British rule finally broke out in Ireland, leading after two years to the partition of the country and the establishment of the Irish Free State by the Treaty of London of 6 December 1921. At its height, the war involved 80,000 British troops and 15,000 police (the latter including Auxiliaries and the notorious 'Black and Tans', recruited from ex-Army officers at the end of the Great War). Coming at a time of enormous war-weariness, this was an unexpected defeat for the British Army, and the only case this century in Europe of a successful revolutionary guerrilla campaign leading to an independent state. This bitter and highly politicized form of warfare, in which acts of terror were committed by both sides and public opinion counted for as much as military victory, would become increasingly common as the century wore on. Its experiences in Ireland from 1919 to 1921 also laid the foundations for the British Army's counter-insurgency methods of the future (*see* p. 166). Although five Irish infantry regiments were disbanded following the partition – the Royal Irish Regiment, Connaught Rangers, Leinster Regiment, Royal Munster Fusiliers and Royal Dublin Fusiliers – the Army was allowed to continue recruiting throughout Ireland after 1921. Unlike a century before, however, the Army of this period was predominantly English, with Scotland, Wales and Ireland under-represented in proportion to their populations.

DEFENCE POLICY AND THE ARMY

Following the First World War, the Committee of Imperial Defence (CID) was revived, and in 1923 the Chiefs of Staff Committee was formed under it to co-ordinate policy between the three armed services. Successive governments believed that the revival of British industry and overseas trade was the key to future stability and defences, so the Royal Navy resumed its role as the senior service. The new RAF also made a good case for its own continued independence: in the unlikely event of a renewed war in Europe (the only enemy envisaged in 1923 was France), RAF bombers striking at enemy cities would break the will of the civilian population without the need for costly land campaigns. Meanwhile, the RAF developed a policy of 'air control' to take over much of the imperial policing role in the Middle East from the Army. The need to maintain its independence led to considerable RAF opposition to experiments in close air support for the Army. As late as 1939, the RAF had only five Army Co-operation Squadrons (light aircraft intended for artillery spotting) and no doctrine of close air support or interdiction.

This did not matter very much to the Army, which was not required to fight on any scale between 1922 and 1939, and was thus able to concentrate on its imperial policing role. In theory, the Army could provide a second BEF of four divisions and a cavalry division for overseas service, supplemented by a Territorial Army (as the Territorial Force was renamed in 1921) of 13 divisions liable for overseas deployment in an emergency. In practice, both the Regular and Territorial Army remained understrength and undertrained, with more than a third of the Regular infantry committed to India. In 1922 the CID decided that the new BEF would not be required in

THE EXPERIMENTAL MECHANIZED FORCE

One of the most important military lessons to emerge from the Allied victory in 1918 was the need for all-arms co-operation on the battlefield, combining the strengths of armour, infantry, artillery and airpower to create an overwhelming force. J. F. C. Fuller, a major-general by the late 1920s, continued to advocate the use of the tank as the centre-piece of such a force and, in 1926, found himself in a unique position of influence when he was appointed Military Assistant to General Sir George Milne, the Chief of the Imperial General Staff. Together, they endorsed the concept of an Experimental Mechanized Force, advocated by Colonel George Lindsay, then serving as Inspector of the Royal Tank Corps. He recommended a series of experiments in which aircraft, armoured cars, fast tanks, motorized artillery, motorized mortars and motorized machine guns would act together on a mock battlefield, with an eye to using such a composition as a model for the future organization of the Army. Some criticisms were raised – it was pointed out, for example, that no infantry as such were included – but the decision was taken to carry out the experiments on Salisbury Plain, starting in the summer of 1927. Fuller was offered command, but imposed so many conditions that he was re-placed; nevertheless, when the exercises were conducted, they were widely seen as a success, being brought to a natural end in early 1928. Between then and 1931, further experiments concentrated on the role of all-armour formations, incorporating light-tank reconnaissance and the use of radios for co-ordinated command, but these were stopped by the combined effects of military traditionalism and the beginning of the Depression. Unfortunately for Britain, and most of the rest of Europe, the ideas were then developed by the Germans as integral parts of their *blitzkrieg* ('lightning war') tactics employed in 1939–40.

Europe, seeing it as fighting no more than a medium-sized colonial war somewhere in the Empire.

The Cardwell system of county infantry regiments was now 50 years old and so well established that there was no impetus to change it. Despite the opportunity offered by the end of the war, no major reorganization of the infantry took place. The same was not true of the cavalry, however, which lost nine of its regiments by a process of amalgamation with more senior units in 1922, producing new titles (known as 'vulgar fractions') such as the 13th/18th Royal Hussars and 17th/21st Lancers (*see Appendix for details*). In 1923 the Royal Marine Light Infantry and Royal Marine Artillery were merged to form the Royal Marines, while the Royal Field Artillery and Royal Garrison Artillery lost their independent titles to become simply parts of the Royal Regiment of Artillery. But most of the large and flexible organizations which had proved so valuable during the war were disbanded, including the Army Cyclist Corps and the Machine Gun Corps. The Tank Corps survived for an inimitably British reason, by securing royal patronage as the Royal Tank Corps of four battalions in 1922. Another wartime creation to survive, perhaps inevitably, was the Welsh Guards, formed in 1915.

The period of the Ten-Year Rule has become notorious in British Army history as the 'Colonel Blimp' era, exemplified by General Sir George Milne who, as Chief of the Imperial General Staff (CIGS) between 1926 and 1933, has been (perhaps unfairly) condemned as the biggest Army reactionary since the Duke of Cambridge (*see* p. 71). Much of the Army's behaviour in this period may be explained as an attempted return to a 'golden age' of society, regiment and Empire before the Great War ruined it all. Certainly, the Army kept horses for artillery and transport for a decade or more after their function in civilian society had been usurped by the motor vehicle, at least partly because of their value to officers for polo and hunting. But in its clinging to the past and neglect of possible future war the Army also reflected the strong British anti-militarism and disillusion of the 1920s, as well as the financial restraints imposed by a country struggling to revive its economy. These forces became even more powerful with the Depression in the 1930s, and throughout the inter-war period there was a solid British consensus not to repeat the mass army strategy of the First World War under any circumstances.

INTER-WAR REFORMS

Despite the climate of stagnation, some progress was made towards Army reform. The infantry lessons of the First World War were codified in the 1920s in training manuals and minor tactics which remained standard for another 50 years. The artillery also reorganized itself, with an emphasis on heavy firepower and the development of a new field gun, the 25-pounder. In particular, the British lead in tank warfare established by 1918 was developed still further, culminating in the Experimental Mechanized Force of 1927 (*see box, p. 122*). Years ahead of its time, it was disbanded partly because money was needed to motorize the rest of the Army, and partly because it had no conceivable use other than for European war. By 1933, when Germany was identified once more as the greatest threat to Britain, the Army had lost its lead in tank development and armoured warfare over other European countries, and never recovered it.

This is often represented as a case of reactionary senior officers ignoring cries in the wilderness from a few

---

THE ARAB REVOLT (1936–9)

When Britain assumed responsibility for Palestine under a League of Nations mandate in 1920, many indigenous Arabs expected independence, but they soon grew concerned about the permitted immigration of Jews. In both 1929 and 1933 anti-British riots had to be put down by military force, but the depth of Arab feeling was not appreciated, chiefly because responsibility for the security of Palestine had been handed over to the RAF, whose intelligence-gathering capabilities were poor. By 1935, when a total of 61,844 Jews entered Palestine, Arab resentment and fear of Jewish domination had reached fever pitch. In April 1936, Arab attacks on Jewish settlements, followed by a general strike, forced the British to respond.

They did so by hastily reinforcing the military garrison and granting the Army special emergency powers to reassert control. By September, when martial law was declared, the garrison had been further increased to two cavalry regiments and 22 infantry battalions, all under the command of Lieutenant-General Sir John Dill. Faced with such a display of force, the Arabs accepted the offer of a Royal Commission to look into their grievances, but when this reported in July 1937, recommending a partition of Palestine into Jewish and Arab regions, the trouble flared up again. Between then and February 1939, when a special conference was held in London, the British used a variety of methods to control the country. The Army concentrated on splitting the active Arab insurgents from their supporters by seizing villages and using them as patrol bases from which to dominate the surrounding countryside; movement was curtailed by means of identity cards, traffic check-points and night curfews; and Jews were recruited into Special Night Squads (trained by Captain Orde Wingate, the future leader of the Chindits, *see* p.156) to carry out attacks on Arab guerrilla camps. The London Conference eventually offered Arab independence, ending the revolt, although this in turn alienated the Jews. They began their own anti-British campaign in 1944, with the assassination of Lord Moyne.

voices of Army reform, but such a view is hardly fair. Unlike the Germans, the British in the 1930s motorized their Army in depth, and from the rear forwards, rather than by concentrating mechanization in a few spearhead units. The result by 1939 was that, although the British had no formed armoured divisions or doctrine of armoured warfare, they did possess the only army in the world with completely motorized infantry, artillery and first-line transport. The continuing influence of the 19th-century regimental system in slowing reform appeared once more in 1937, when instead of expanding the Royal Tank Corps the Army mechanized by converting its cavalry regiments to tanks, further handicapping the development of an armoured doctrine. A late attempt to correct this error came in spring 1939 with the creation of the Royal Armoured Corps as a loose umbrella organization for all British armour – the Royal Tank Corps being renamed the Royal Tank Regiment. Horsed cavalry, including the Household Cavalry (Life Guards and Royal Horse Guards) and some Yeomanry regiments, remained part of the Army until after the start of the Second World War.

Rearmament from 1937 onwards was still based largely on the 1922 concept of a BEF of five Regular divisions – out of six then in existence – to send overseas. The idea of one of these being a cavalry division was shelved, and by 1939 there were two armoured divisions forming in Britain and another one in Egypt. In March 1939, as the prospect of a British Army commitment to Europe in the event of war was finally accepted, a programme to double the Territorial Army to 26 divisions was announced. Finally in May 1939, for the first time in British history, peacetime conscription was introduced with the Compulsory Training Act. Although this, and the mobilization of British society, would eventually produce a mass army, the BEF of 1939 was in all respects a less effective force than that of 1914. One important difference was that men who had been captains and majors in 1918 were now major-generals, and a few would become field marshals. They never forgot the experience of 'château generalship' seen from the front line, and their treatment of their troops was markedly different from that of their First World War counterparts. But as it faced its first mechanized war, the surprising thing about the British Army of 1939, looking back to 1914 or even earlier, was how very little it had actually changed.

. . . .

CHAPTER SIX

THE SECOND WORLD WAR (1939–45)

. . . .

THE NEW CHALLENGE

ON 1 September 1939 German troops crossed the border into Poland. Two days later Britain and France declared war on Germany for the second time in 25 years, heralding a conflict that was to change the face of the world. The news was greeted in Britain with none of the jingoism of 1914; most people viewed the prospect of war with a mixture of apprehension and resignation, remembering the slaughter of the Great War and aware of the enormous sacrifices that would have to be made to defeat the might of Nazi Germany.

When the new conflict began, the British Army was in the throes of change. On 3 September 1939, the paper strength of the Regular Army stood at 258,800 soldiers, with another 546,200 on the Reserve or members of the Territorial Army (TA). A significant proportion of these men were barely trained, having been called up since May 1939 as 'militiamen' under the Compulsory Training Act. The plan was for them to receive six months' training in the Regular Army before returning to civilian life as members of an expanded TA, ready for mobilization should the need arise, but none had made the transition when war was declared. Instead, on 3 September the government introduced full-scale conscription for all males between the ages of 18 and 41 under the terms of a National Service Act. It was a move designed to prevent the chaos and wastefulness of 1914 by imposing central control from the start, but it did condemn the Army to a period of instability as the conscripts were absorbed, trained and made ready for war. As before, in 1793 and 1914, it was expected that existing units would be able to hold the enemy at bay until the new recruits had been prepared for battle. As before, this proved to be a dangerous policy, made worse in 1939 by the previous 20 years of parsimony and neglect.

But the problem went deeper than that, for the creation of a mass army (officially known as the 'Land Forces of Great Britain') in 1939 was infinitely more difficult than before. It was not just a case of recruiting large numbers of men, giving them rudimentary training and throwing them into battle, for warfare had changed out of all recognition since 1914. As the Germans were demonstrating in Poland, success in battle now depended on a complex co-ordination of new technology, using tanks, mobile artillery and mechanized infantry in conjunction with close-support aircraft, at least in the spearhead of any advance. J. F. C. Fuller would have recognized the pattern, but he had enjoyed no influence on British Army development since the late 1920s, and the Army in 1939 was woefully deficient in both doctrine and equipment, to say nothing of the soldiers capable of carrying out the new methods of warfare. Training would therefore have to be more specialized, leadership more flexible and equipment more sophisticated before the British could hope to fight effectively.

In addition, industry would need to be geared up to the production of modern weapons, something that would inevitably affect the Army as a proportion of available manpower would have to be diverted into the factories. Indeed, between September and December 1939 over 11,500 TA soldiers had to be recalled to civilian life to fill key industrial posts, while workers in certain sectors, notably mining and the dockyards, were exempt from conscription. Women could, and did, step in to fill some of the gaps, as they had done in 1914–18, but the need for trained industrial manpower was greater than it had been in the previous conflict. In such circumstances, the Army could not expect to be given unlimited access to the youth of the nation, especially as the RAF, with its dreams of strategic bombing, demanded a far greater share than before, while the strong folk-memory of the trenches actively deterred many conscripts from joining the infantry if any alternative existed. Balancing all these factors together, while ensuring that the Army was expanded to meet the new challenge, was one of the most difficult aspects of Britain's transition to war in 1939. However well it was done – and some commentators have suggested that the balance was never properly achieved, pointing to the dramatic shortage of infantry replacements in 1944, after five years of conscription – it was clearly going to take time to produce an effective fighting force.

THE 'PHONEY WAR'

This was reflected in the fairly modest war plans adopted in September 1939. When war was declared, the Regular Army was spread thinly to defend key parts of the Empire. The strategic significance of the Middle East, with its access to the Suez Canal and oil resources, was shown by the fact that the equivalent of six infantry divisions were stationed there, plus a mobile division in the process of being formed. In India, there was only one infantry division and an infantry brigade of British troops, while in Malaya two infantry brigades had been formed. Elsewhere, the normal peacetime 'penny-packets' of troops existed in various overseas garrisons. Reinforcements could be expected from the armies of India, Australia, New Zealand, Canada and South Africa, but the British Army as such was no stronger than it had been in 1914 and was still deployed primarily for colonial protection. European commitment was a low priority. Even though a British Expeditionary Force existed, the most that could be deployed to France in 1939 was four infantry divisions. They had the advantages of high professionalism and total mechanization, but compared to the forces available to the enemy, they were puny.

The plan was for the BEF to be committed, as in 1914, to the extreme left of the Allied line, covering any German move into the Low Countries. Deployment of the four divisions, comprising 36 Regular battalions of infantry plus supporting arms, went smoothly, chiefly because the enemy was occupied elsewhere, and was reported to be complete by 12 October 1939. By then, Poland had fallen to a combined Soviet-German attack, and the Allies were lucky that Hitler delayed any assault on the West. For the next seven months, British and French forces remained on the defensive in what became known as the 'Phoney War', holding positions along the borders with both Germany and the neutral Low Countries. The British took the opportunity to reinforce the BEF, sending a fifth Regular division to France in late 1939 and gradually feeding in TA divisions as they became available. By April 1940, five TA divisions – the 42nd, 44th, 48th, 50th and 51st (Highland) – had crossed the Channel, with elements of another three manning base areas in France, while great efforts were being made to form an armoured division to join them. In terms of numbers, this was impressive, but standards of training, especially in some of the TA units, were low and equipment levels were poor: some units had less than 50 per cent of their official scales of anti-tank and anti-aircraft weapons, and only about 30 per cent of their war-stocks of ammunition.

Allied commanders expected any German attack to be a re-run of the 1914 Schlieffen Plan, with the main thrust coming through the Low Countries to sweep round Paris from the west. The French Maginot Line of elaborately prepared defences along the German border would, it was argued, prevent any assault from that direction, leaving the main Allied armies free to respond in the north. 'Plan D' was adopted, whereby British and French forces would move forward into Belgium as soon as the enemy attack began, occupying positions along the River Dyle to stall the advance. In January 1940, a complete set of German operational orders confirming this scenario was secretly passed to the Allies after a Luftwaffe aircraft crashed in Belgium, the incident leading to a certain amount of complacency which did nothing to add urgency to Allied preparations. Field Marshal Lord Gort, commanding the BEF, waited for his orders to put Plan D into effect, secure in the belief that German intentions had been accurately predicted.

NORWEGIAN SIDESHOW

Such complacency was reflected in the fact that British planners were prepared, in early 1940, to contemplate campaigns outside France. The first of these envisaged sending troops to aid the Finns, under attack from the Soviet Union in the so-called 'Winter War'. Special ski-units were formed, principally from Guards battalions in Britain, and stores were stockpiled at ports in northern Scotland. In the event, the Finns capitulated before the deployment could begin, but the forces involved were soon earmarked for another operation, designed to seize Norwegian ports to prevent the shipment of iron ore to Germany. A TA division (the 49th) was made ready, together with 24th Guards Brigade, for commitment in early April.

This coincided exactly with German plans to invade Denmark and Norway, put into effect on 9 April. Denmark fell quickly, followed by most of southern Norway. British plans were hastily altered to concentrate on the northern ports of Trondheim and Narvik, the occupation of which would sever the iron-ore route. A direct attack on Trondheim was ruled out, but brigades were landed at Namsos to the north and Aandalsnes to the south in an attempt to take the port in a pincer movement. It failed, chiefly because co-ordination between the two assaults was impossible in mountainous terrain and deep snow. Between 17 April and 3 May three brigades, the 146th and 148th from 49th Division and the 15th from the Regular 5th Division, fought a series of rather one-sided battles against German troops who proved to be superior in almost every respect. Vital equipment had been left behind in Scotland, command co-ordination was poor and the soldiers, despite a willingness to fight, found it difficult to operate in conditions for which they had not been trained. The first troops to engage the Germans in the Second World War were in fact Territorials, and their experience was salutary: in an abortive attack on the town of Dombaas, south-east of Aandalsnes, for example, the 1/5th Leicesters and 1/8th Sherwood Foresters between them were reduced to nine officers and fewer than 300 men in only four days of fighting. On 3 May, the area around Trondheim was evacuated.

A similar story emerged in the far north, where 24th Guards Brigade had been ordered to land close to Narvik. They arrived in mid-April, too late to take advantage of a naval victory which forced the Germans temporarily to evacuate the port, landing at a variety of points some distance from the objective. Deep snow, which the War Office had assured the battalions would not be present, disrupted any attempt to mount an immediate assault, and the brigade was split up to occupy small villages as much as 200 miles away from Narvik. French, Norwegian and Polish troops arrived as reinforcements, taking the port on 28 May, but by then attention had been diverted to mainland Europe, where German forces were rampaging through the Low Countries and France. The last Allied units left Norway on 7 and 8 June, having achieved little except to realize their own deficiencies. As far as the British Army was concerned, it was apparent that a great deal needed to be done before it could meet the Germans on equal terms.

FRANCE AND THE LOW COUNTRIES

This truth was painfully reinforced elsewhere. On 10 May German forces attacked the Netherlands and Belgium, seizing air superiority by pre-emptive strikes on Allied air bases and using airborne troops to take objectives in advance of ground units. To begin with, the Allies congratulated themselves on the accuracy of their predictions and immediately moved forward into Belgium to occupy the Dyle Line. The BEF encountered no opposition as two corps advanced as planned; on 13 May light reconnaissance units clashed with the German spearhead in what appeared to be a repetition of 1914. In reality, nothing could have been further from the truth.

The BEF, with the Belgian Army and French Seventh Army to its left and the French First Army to its right, was facing General Fedor von Bock's Army Group B, a total of 28 divisions (three of them Panzer) under orders to advance into the Low Countries to fix the Allies firmly in that area. Further south, General Ritter von Leeb's Army Group C, comprising 17 infantry divisions, was directed towards the Maginot Line with the same objective in view. In the centre, however, was General Gerd von Rundstedt's Army Group A, containing seven Panzer and 38 infantry divisions. Its task, under the codename *Sichelschnitt* ('cut of the scythe'), was to advance through the Ardennes, a region of forested hills and restricted roads that was widely believed to be impassable to large armoured formations, before crossing the River Meuse and aiming for the Channel coast. Such a move would split the Allied armies in Belgium from their support units in France, leaving them to face assaults from both Army Group A and Army Group B. Caught in a trap, the Allies would have to evacuate by sea or surrender, leaving the whole of northern France, as well as the Low Countries, in enemy hands. After regrouping, the combined forces of Army Groups A and B would then swing south to take Paris.

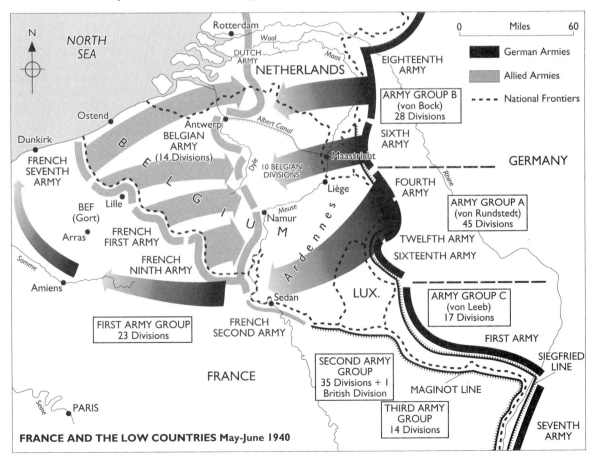

FRANCE AND THE LOW COUNTRIES May-June 1940

COUNTER-ATTACK AT ARRAS

On 20 May 1940, spearhead German units reached the Channel coast, severing the lines of communication between Anglo-French forces in Belgium and their support elements in northern France. Lord Gort, commander of the BEF, was ordered by London to mount a counter-attack, in conjunction with French units from the south, designed to restore the link. He had few forces unengaged, but directed parts of 5th and 50th Divisions, supported by 1st Army Tank Brigade (4th and 7th Battalions of the Royal Tank Regiment, comprising 58 Mark I and 16 Mark II tanks), to Arras, where they were to open a route through to the south. Intelligence was poor, co-operation between the armour and infantry virtually non-existent and the command chain weak: as the British troops assembled around Vimy early on 21 May, their commanders were unaware that they were about to be pitted against the forward units of General Erwin Rommel's 7th Panzer Division.

When the attack began at 3 p.m. on 21 May, some initial success was achieved, chiefly because the German columns were caught by surprise and dangerously over-extended. In the first two hours, elements of 4RTR managed to penetrate Rommel's defensive screen around Achicourt and Beaurains, but the advantage did not last long. Infantry support, provided by 6th and 8th Battalions Durham Light Infantry, could not keep up with the tanks, which in turn were quickly attacked by German artillery and Stuka dive-bombers. By the end of the day, the British counter-attack had stalled. In the absence of any corresponding French move from the south, Gort had no choice but to order a withdrawal.

But the operation should not be dismissed as a complete failure. Despite chronic problems that were to characterize British efforts for some time to come, the sudden appearance of enemy tanks on their flank put the Germans in a panic (calmed only by the presence of Rommel), disrupted the momentum of his advance and may have contributed to Hitler's insistence three days later that the Panzers should halt and regroup. It was the latter decision which enabled the bulk of the BEF to be withdrawn from Dunkirk.

It was an audacious plan, put into effect with speed and surprise. The early seizure of air superiority meant that the movement of Army Group A into the Ardennes was not monitored with any accuracy, and it was not until 13 May, when lead elements of General Heinz Guderian's Panzers crossed the Meuse, that the true nature of the assault began to be realized. By then, the Allied armies in Belgium had been engaged by Army Group B, losing their ability to respond to the threat to their rear. By 20 May the Panzers had reached the coast, spreading panic among rear-area troops and driving a firm wedge between them and the forward formations. Even without this, the Allies further north were hard-pressed. The Dutch had collapsed on 14 May and the inexorable advance of von Bock's troops had pushed the BEF, in conjunction with its Belgian and French allies, back almost to the positions occupied before the campaign had begun. Under continuous air bombardment, particularly from the notorious Junkers Ju-87 Stuka dive-bombers, British units were losing cohesion and, split from their support elements, were running desperately short of supplies. An extemporized counter-attack at Arras on 21 May, carried out by two battalions of infantry with the 1st Army Tank Brigade in support, caused the Germans to pause momentarily (see box), but this was a rare event. On 26 May, the British government, led since the 10th by Winston Churchill, ordered Gort to withdraw to the coast and await evacuation. The chances of saving much of the BEF were seen as slim, particularly as by that stage both Boulogne and Calais had been virtually lost.

Operation Dynamo – the evacuation from Dunkirk – has gone down in British history as a miracle, and in one sense it was: the fact that by 4 June a total of 224,717 British troops had been shipped home across beaches under almost continuous German attack was a remark-

able achievement. But in purely military terms, it was a disaster. In just three weeks of campaigning the BEF had been outmanoeuvred and utterly defeated, falling victim to a style of warfare, colloquially known as *blitzkrieg* ('lightning war'), which targeted the enemy 'brain' rather than his front-line 'muscle'. Confused, demoralized and exhausted, the BEF was destroyed by psychological as well as physical action; by early June it was in no condition to fight, having abandoned most of its heavy equipment and transport at Dunkirk. Many soldiers returned to Britain with little more than their rifles. Far from being the 'cheerful Tommies' portrayed in the newsreels, they were mentally drained and extremely angry, blaming their commanders for having let them down. It was going to take time and a great deal of careful leadership to rebuild the Army.

But Dunkirk was only part of the story, for over 140,000 British troops remained in France after 4 June, caught to the south of Army Group A's advance. Many of these were rear-area men, but they also included the whole of the 51st (Highland) Division, stationed on the Maginot Line when the German attack began. There were plans to use the division as the core of a new BEF, and elements of the recently formed 1st Armoured Division were shipped to Cherbourg as reinforcements while Operation Dynamo was in progress; some planners even talked about evacuating units from Dunkirk and transfer-

First-Hand Account:

THE EVACUATION FROM DUNKIRK

'. . . cold, hungry and miserable, I joined one of the long queues that were forming down the beach to the water's edge . . . Our attention was riveted upon a smudge on the horizon, which in due course was revealed as a destroyer heading straight toward our beach. It came to within a few hundred yards of the shore, turned broadside on and began to lower its boats . . .

'Slowly the boats headed for the shore, one to each column of waiting men; the sailors sounding the depth with an oar came in as close to the column heads as possible. The queue edged its way forward till the leaders, chest-deep in water were pulled aboard and ferried out to the ship. Unhurriedly and calmly the boats plied back and forth, carrying as many men as they could safely cram aboard, but never seeming to make any impression on the endless queue which edged forward continuously . . .'

Private Robert Holding, 4th Battalion Royal Sussex Regiment

From Robert Holding, *Since I Bore Arms*, privately printed, 1987

ring them directly south to join the tanks. Fortunately for the future of the Army, this did not happen on a large scale, although it did leave the Highland and 1st Armoured Divisions isolated. The latter, fielding 257 tanks but without artillery or motorized infantry, sustained heavy losses in fighting around Abbeville in the last few days of May and had to be withdrawn; the bulk of the Highland Division pulled back to St Valéry-en-Caux, where they were forced to surrender on 12 June. France collapsed 10 days later, leaving Britain to face the enemy alone.

If the Germans had carried out their threat to invade Britain in the summer of 1940, the Army would have been able to do little to stop them. The loss of *matériel* in France and the difficulties experienced in replacing it from an industrial base only just beginning to gear up to war meant that the troops available for home defence, including the newly raised Local Defence Volunteers (*see box*, p. 130), were ill-equipped. Human losses from recent campaigns were replaced quite quickly – between June and August 1940, 275,000 recruits joined the Army –

Lines of British troops wait patiently on the beaches at Dunkirk for evacuation to the ships off-shore, early June 1940. The vulnerability of the soldiers and their rescuers to air attack is apparent.

THE HOME GUARD

On 14 May 1940 the Secretary of State for War, Anthony Eden, broadcast an appeal for men between the ages of 17 and 65 who were not already serving in the armed forces to take up arms in defence of Great Britain. Over 400,000 men, many of them First World War veterans, enrolled in the Local Defence Volunteers during the next two weeks; by the end of July, when the name of the units was altered to Home Guard, just over a million had volunteered, spurred on by the threat of a German invasion.

Weapons were in short supply – many volunteers were issued with nothing more lethal than pikes – but priority was given to units on the south coast, where the invasion was likely to occur. As the German threat receded and equipment became available, Home Guard formations were trained to use machine guns, mortars and small artillery pieces; by the end of 1942 over 1.8 million men (but, officially, no women) were serving, carrying out regulation duties, such as guarding buildings and checking identity cards, which disguised their record of improvisation and specialized capabilities. Altogether, 1113 infantry battalions and hundreds of other units were formed, relieving the Regular Army of mundane domestic duties. But service of up to 48 hours a month, often in short night-time stints, placed great strain on the men, many of whom had normal day-time jobs. In February 1942 service in the Home Guard was made compulsory, destroying much of the early spirit of the force; two years later, with victory in sight, it was officially 'stood down', only to be re-raised in 1951. It finally disappeared in July 1957.

but the creation of fully integrated divisions, capable of fighting effectively on the modern battlefield, was sure to take time. The soldiers needed to spend months, even years, under training, and that training had to reflect the lessons of Norway and France. New commanders and junior leaders had to be found, confidence restored and victories won. Churchill's decision, taken in July 1940, to mobilize the full human and industrial potential of the state and to fight a 'total war' against the Fascist enemy, may have laid the foundations for future success, but there was a long way to go before it could be achieved. Put simply, the British Army had to be recreated from the ashes of the BEF.

NORTH AFRICA, SEPTEMBER 1940–JANUARY 1942

To make matters worse, the threat to British interests outside Europe increased significantly in the summer of 1940. On 10 June Italy declared war on Britain and France, hoping to take advantage of the imminent German victory to secure territorial concessions. In July, Italian forces from Ethiopia seized border posts in Kenya and Sudan; a month later they captured British Somaliland, displacing the small peacetime garrison with ease. In September a total of nearly 300,000 troops from Libya invaded western Egypt, advancing 60 miles in four days before constructing a line of fortified camps south of Sidi Barrani. With France by then defeated, making any British reinforcement through the Mediterranean extremely hazardous, the Italians appeared to have a free hand in Africa, their ultimate aim being to control the Suez Canal as well as British access to Middle Eastern oil and Far Eastern resources.

General Sir Archibald Wavell, Commander-in-Chief Middle East, had few forces available to him and a wide area to cover. His first priority had to be Egypt, where Major-General Richard O'Connor's Western Desert Force of 30,000 men, centred on the recently named 7th Armoured Division, was all that stood between the Italians and the Canal. In August, Churchill's Cabinet made the brave decision to send three tank regiments to Egypt, even though they were desperately needed at home, but this did little to correct the substantial imbalance of forces. It was therefore an enormous gamble when, in December 1940, Wavell authorized a 'raid' on the Italian camps, hoping to push the enemy back into Libya, for although the Italians had shown no initiative since September, the sheer size of their army was daunting.

Operation Compass began on 9 December and, against all the odds, was a major and much needed triumph. The attack on the camps caught the Italians by surprise and, as 7th Armoured Division cut off their line of retreat by taking Buq Buq, 38,300 Italians surrendered. In normal circumstances, this would probably have been the end of the operation, but both Wavell and O'Connor were generals who were prepared to exploit their success; indeed, the subsequent advance deep into Libya is often cited as the only example of 'British *blitzkrieg*' during the early war years. As the 6th Australian Division pursued the retreating Italians along the coast road, taking Bardia and then Tobruk in January 1941, 7th Armoured Division used the wide open spaces of the desert to conduct sweeping manoeuvres designed to cut the enemy off from his bases further west. By the beginning of February, the Italians had decided to abandon Cyrenaica (the eastern province of Libya) and were streaming back along the coast towards Sirte. O'Connor ordered the Australians to continue the pursuit, while his tanks cut across the 'bulge' of the Jebel Akhdar through Mechili to appear behind the retreating enemy. On 5 February, at Beda Fomm, the trap was sprung, leading to a spectacular Italian collapse. By

General Sir Archibald Wavell (right, in peaked cap),
C-in-C Middle East, and Major-General William Platt
(centre), commander of Imperial forces in East Africa,
inspect a British unit in Sudan, December 1940.

EAST AFRICA, 1940–1

The Italian declaration of war on the Allies in June 1940, followed by the collapse of France, left British positions in East Africa, guarding the southern approaches to the Red Sea, extremely vulnerable. British Somaliland was virtually surrounded, while substantial Italian forces in Eritrea, Ethiopia and Italian Somaliland stood poised to move into Sudan and Kenya. General Sir Archibald Wavell, British C-in-C Middle East, facing a simultaneous (and potentially far more serious) threat to Egypt, could do little to defend the area. In July Italian units seized Kassala in Sudan and Moyale in Kenya; in August the garrison in British Somaliland was overwhelmed and the survivors evacuated.

But the Red Sea was a vital part of the route to India and, once the Italian invasion of Egypt had been contained in late 1940, Wavell ordered a two-pronged campaign of recovery in East Africa. This comprised an advance from Sudan into Eritrea and another from Kenya into Somaliland, with the eventual intention of mounting a pincer attack from north and south into Ethiopia. Although conducted on a shoestring – Wavell later described it as 'an improvisation after the British fashion of war' – the campaign was a significant success. On 19 January 1941, 4th and 5th Indian Divisions, commanded by Lieutenant-General Sir William Platt, moved into Eritrea, aiming for Asmara. The Italians made a determined stand in the mountains around Keren, but by late March,

after heavy fighting, they were forced to retreat. Asmara was occupied on 1 April, by which time British and South African troops under Lieutenant-General Sir Alan Cunningham had marched out of Kenya to capture Mogadishu in Italian Somaliland before thrusting north into Ethiopia. Joined by forces from Aden, which had liberated British Somaliland in March, and by Ethiopian irregulars under Lieutenant-Colonel Orde Wingate, Cunningham's men entered Addis Ababa on 6 April, restoring Emperor Haile Selassie to his throne. They then moved north to link up with Platt's forces, fighting a tough mountain battle at Amba Alagi in May which led to an Italian collapse. Mopping-up operations continued until November 1941.

Personality Profile:

FIELD MARSHAL EARL WAVELL (1883–1950)

Commissioned from Sandhurst into the Black Watch in 1901, Archibald Wavell served in South Africa and India before attending Staff College in 1909. During the First World War he was badly wounded, losing his left eye, but this did not affect his future career.

In July 1939, having held a variety of peacetime posts, he was appointed Commander-in-Chief Middle East. The enormous problems he faced were exacerbated by the Italian declaration of war in June 1940. Short of resources, he was expected to defend an area that stretched from Egypt in the north to Kenya in the south, containing oilfields as well as vital communication routes between Britain and the Far East. His campaigns against the Italians in Libya and East Africa in 1941 were brilliant examples of improvisation, but he could not cope with the extension of his responsibilities to the Balkans, Syria, Iraq and Iran, nor with the appearance of German troops in North Africa. By July 1941, he had lost the confidence of Churchill, who insisted on his replacement by Auchinleck.

Wavell was appointed C-in-C India, just in time to face the Japanese attacks in the Far East. Made commander of ABDACOM (American, British, Dutch and Australian Command) with his headquarters in Java, he could not prevent the loss of Malaya, Singapore, the Philippines and Dutch East Indies, reverting to C-in-C India in February 1942. Promoted to field marshal in 1943, he became the penultimate Viceroy of India, handing over to Mountbatten in early 1947.

reinforce the Italians. Almost immediately, Rommel dispatched part of his force eastwards to engage the weakened British, reversing the route taken by Western Desert Force. By the end of April, German and Italian troops had advanced almost to the Egyptian frontier, capturing O'Connor in the process, and had laid siege to the important supply port of Tobruk. Simultaneously, German units invaded Yugoslavia and Greece, sweeping south through the Balkans with a speed reminiscent of the campaign in France. Few British troops were involved – Wavell had transferred Australian and New Zealand divisions from North Africa, reinforced by the British 1st Armoured Brigade – but this did not prevent the emergence of a familiar pattern of events. Between 24 April and 1 May nearly 51,000 British and Commonwealth troops were evacuated from ports in southern Greece, leaving behind over 7000 prisoners as well as quantities of valuable equipment. Nor was this the end of the saga, for a proportion of those saved were sent to Crete where, in late May, they fought a bitter and ultimately unsuccessful battle against invading German airborne troops. A further 12,000 made the sad journey into PoW camps.

Presented with such a catalogue of defeats, the British Army hit a new low in terms of morale. Its effectiveness, significantly enhanced under O'Connor, seemed to disintegrate as soon as the Germans were encountered, calling into question its ability to survive. Sound military reasons could be offered for its poor performance – in Libya it was overstretched, depending too much on a tenuous supply link that extended all the way back to the Nile Delta, while in Greece it had experienced grave problems of co-ordination with its allies – but they could not disguise the fact that deep problems existed. Command was often uninspired and confused, leading to a loss of confidence among the ordinary soldiers, and this was not helped by the obvious inferiority of equipment against that of the Germans. British tanks were poorly protected and frighteningly vulnerable to the German 88mm anti-aircraft gun firing in the anti-tank role; in the air, British fighters often fell victim to their German counterparts, leaving ground forces bereft of air cover. But of far more importance was a persistent lack of all-arms co-operation. Armoured units tended to fight their own battles with little regard for the needs or capabilities of the infantry; artillery, although invariably effective in terms of accuracy and killing power, was often not brought to bear because of poor communications or lack of mobility. This in turn led to a reluctance to take advantage of the terrain, particularly in the desert where Rommel, a past master in the art of mobile warfare, found it relatively easy to outmanoeuvre his enemy and destroy it piecemeal.

This was shown in attempts by Wavell to relieve Tobruk in May and June 1941. On both occasions his troops failed to make much headway in what were essentially frontal attacks against prepared German positions. Again, other reasons for failure could be cited – in this case forces had been withdrawn from the desert to

The crew of a 6-pounder anti-tank gun engages enemy armour during Operation Crusader, November 1941. The 6-pounder was of only limited value against German tanks and, as can be seen, the desert afforded little cover.

the end of the battle two days later, Western Desert Force could boast an advance of over 500 miles in less than two months, during which it had taken 130,000 prisoners for the loss of only 2000 casualties. As this coincided with news of further successes against the Italians in East Africa (*see box*, p. 131), the threat to the Middle East seemed to have been lifted.

Two factors prevented a full exploitation of victory. Just as O'Connor was poised to advance into Tripolitania, Churchill decided that it was more important to send aid to Greece, now under threat from the Germans as well as the Italians. On 12 February, Wavell was ordered to reduce his forces in Libya and to assume the defensive. On the same day, General Erwin Rommel arrived in Tripoli at the head of an *Afrika Korps* of German troops, sent to

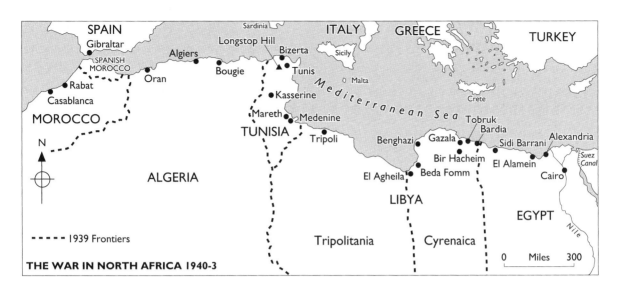

THE WAR IN NORTH AFRICA 1940-3

- - - - - 1939 Frontiers

SYRIA AND IRAQ, MAY–JULY 1941

In late March 1941, the Regent of Iraq was overthrown in a military coup led by the pro-Axis prime minister, Rashid Ali. A month later, Iraqi troops surrounded the British airbase at Habbaniya, to the west of Baghdad, and threatened to cut the oil pipeline from Kirkuk to Haifa. British reinforcements were flown into Habbaniya to join 1000 RAF personnel and 1200 locally raised levies, while part of the British 1st Cavalry Division, known as 'Habforce', prepared to enter Iraq from Palestine. In the event, the Iraqis melted away, allowing the

British to occupy Baghdad in early June.

Axis activities in the Vichy French colonies of Syria and Lebanon also threatened British security in the Middle East. On 8 June 1941, 20,000 British and Free French troops crossed the border from Palestine, advancing towards Damascus and Beirut. They were hoping that Vichy French defenders would put up only token resistance, but fierce fighting on the River Litani in Lebanon was followed by equally costly advances in the Damascus sector. On more than one occasion Allied

troops were forced to surrender to numerically superior enemy units. Airpower proved vital – by late June the Vichy French had been swept from the skies – but it was not until 14 July that an armistice was signed. The need to garrison Iraq, Syria and Lebanon, combined with a decision in August to commit British troops to occupy neutral Iran in conjunction with Soviet forces from the north – an operation designed to open up a supply route into southern Russia – meant that Middle East Command was stretched to breaking point.

occupy Syria, Lebanon and Iraq (*see box*) – but there could be little doubt that the British were outclassed. Wavell was removed as C-in-C Middle East and replaced by General Sir Claude Auchinleck, who set about restoring the morale of the recently constituted Eighth Army in North Africa, but he faced an uphill task among troops who were beginning to view Rommel as some sort of military 'superman'. At the same time, Auchinleck and the new commander of Eighth Army, Lieutenant-General Sir Alan Cunningham, came under enormous pressure from Churchill to lift the siege of Tobruk, seen as a symbol of Allied tenacity.

When the long-awaited offensive, Operation Crusader, took place in November and early December 1941, many of the familiar problems re-emerged. Cunningham's plan, involving an armoured advance to lure Rommel's Panzers into an encounter battle while infantry forces

marched to link up with the Tobruk garrison, merely reinforced the lack of all-arms co-operation and was less than inspired. In the event, the Eighth Army did succeed, relieving Tobruk on 10 December after extremely hard-fought battles around Sidi Rezegh and forcing Rommel to pull back into Libya, but the costs were high: 18,000 casualties in three weeks of fighting. It was, in General Sir Frank Messervy's words, 'an epic of British doggedness', a phrase which sums up the Army's approach to battle after two years of war. Unable to match the fluidity and flexibility of the *Afrika Korps*, the only way it could succeed was by engaging in attritional and costly engagements, sacrificing soldiers to cover its very real deficiencies. In this sense, it had learned nothing since the First World War.

But Crusader *was* a victory, achieved against an enemy who, until December 1941, had seemed invincible. The subsequent British advance retook the ground gained

THE LONG RANGE DESERT GROUP

On 23 June 1940 Major Ralph Bagnold of the Royal Corps of Signals received permission from GHQ Middle East to raise a small force of desert experts whose job it would be to move deep into southern Libya against the Italians. By September, using 30 cwt trucks scrounged from the American Chevrolet dealer in Cairo, Bagnold had organized three 'Patrols', each of 30 volunteers (most of them New Zealanders), and between then and the end of November they operated behind Italian lines, gathering vital information. Their success was such that, in December, extra Patrols were raised from the Guards, the Yeomanry and

the Rhodesians, and the force was formalized as the Long Range Desert Group (LRDG).

The Group's primary task was always reconnaissance. By watching enemy-held roads and counting the number of vehicles using them, they gained a fairly clear indication of any build-up for an attack. Reconnaissance entailed hundreds of miles of travel over the most inhospitable terrain, and each member of the LRDG had to be expert in navigation, desert driving and survival. But more offensive action was sometimes carried out: in January 1941, for example, Patrols raided Murzuq Oasis, more than 1500 miles from

Cairo, while in 1942 the LRDG teamed up with the equally unconventional Special Air Service (SAS) to attack enemy bases in Tobruk and Benghazi.

Once the war in North Africa was over, the LRDG became part of Raiding Forces Middle East, operating against Axis-held islands in the Aegean. Its New Zealand contingent was withdrawn after an abortive attack on the island of Levita in October 1943, and the remains of the Group, reinforced from the British Army, ended the war in Italy, scouting ahead of the main forces in the Po Valley. The LRDG was disbanded in 1945.

by O'Connor a year before and, by January 1942, Rommel had been pushed back as far as El Agheila. In the light of events elsewhere in the world, it was something to be savoured, a ray of hope in a sea of utter darkness.

DISASTER IN THE FAR EAST

By late 1941, British forces in the Far East – in Hong Kong, Malaya and Burma – were weak. Neglected in the inter-war period and left to occupy a backwater since the declaration of war against Germany, they were ill-equipped, poorly trained and badly deployed. Many of their better officers, thirsty for action in a war that seemed to be passing them by, had ensured a transfer to Europe or North Africa; the flow of new recruits had virtually dried up as units elsewhere took precedence, and the tradition of colonial invincibility had led to a dangerous complacency. The growing threat from Japan was largely ignored, not least by politicians back in Britain, who made no attempt to rectify the deficiencies of peacetime policies until it was far too late. When the Japanese opened their offensive in the Far East on 7 December 1941, aiming to seize resources denied to them by the Americans and Western colonial powers, the British Army was in no condition to fight effectively.

The first losses occurred in Hong Kong, attacked by overwhelming Japanese forces from mainland China on 8 December 1941. Local commanders had been requesting reinforcements for some time, but to little avail: two Canadian battalions had arrived in October, joining two Indian and two British battalions to form a garrison of about 11,000 men that was pitifully inadequate to the task of protecting the colony. In addition, pre-war policies of depending on the fleet to disrupt enemy movement in the Far East had been undermined by the need to devote naval forces to the war against Germany and Italy, leaving the region to be defended by land units only. In Hong Kong the garrison held out until Christmas Day, fighting well in a desperate situation but having to face the inevitability of defeat and captivity.

Similar problems beset the forces in Malaya, al-though there was less excuse for their swift collapse. When the Japanese Twenty-Fifth Army landed at three points on the Gulf of Thailand in the far north on 8 December, the British and Imperial forces defending the peninsula and the strategically vital island of Singapore seemed strong. A total of 31 infantry battalions with supporting arms – about 88,000 men – were available, a proportion of which were deployed in the north ready to respond to the Japanese assault. But a host of familiar problems emerged. Many of the battalions were badly trained, particularly in jungle warfare, equipment was in short supply and command co-ordination was poor, reflecting a peacetime complacency that pervaded the entire colony. Thus when the Japanese attacked using techniques not dissimilar to those of *blitzkrieg*, achieving air supremacy by destroying enemy aircraft on the ground and advancing swiftly across terrain that was widely regarded as impassable, British commanders dithered,

First-Hand Account:

THE FALL OF SINGAPORE

'The Japanese were entering the city. One of the biggest shocks I ever had in my life was my first sight of the troops who had defeated us. They were in an appalling way and slouched dispiritedly along in a completely dejected manner. In short, far from having a conquering air, they were at the end of their tether . . . I felt we had been cheated.

'I shouldered my haversack, left my weapons behind and set off into the city . . . I passed down the road and met some of the Norfolk Regiment to whom I attached myself temporarily. We all sat down on a large grassed area somewhere in the centre of the city, where very slowly I began to be joined by members of the battalion. At first a few stragglers and then in greater numbers. We sat there during most of the day and then we were ordered to march up to a place called Changi which was ostensibly an assembly point for all the Allied forces . . . And then the waiting began, day followed day, each one more demoralising than the last. It was obvious by now that the Japs intended to starve us as a matter of policy and there was no way in which we could resist . . .'

Private Harry Howarth, 9th Battalion, Royal Northumberland Fusiliers, 18th Infantry Division

From Harry Howarth, *Where Fate Leads*, Ross Anderson Publications, 1983

and lost the initiative. Once this happened, disaster followed disaster as demoralized and confused defenders fell back down the peninsula, unable to consolidate and convinced that the Japanese were invincible. The loss of the warships HMS *Prince of Wales* and *Repulse* to Japanese aircraft on 10 December did nothing to restore morale, but it was the speed of the Japanese ground advance, outflank-ing defended locations on the roads by using the sur-rounding jungle, that did the damage. On 10 January 1942 Kuala Lumpur fell; by the 28th the British com-mander, Lieutenant-General Arthur Percival, had no choice but to order his remaining troops to abandon southern Malaya and withdraw across the causeway to Singapore. More than 25,000 men were left behind, the vast majority as prisoners of war.

Percival was expected to hold Singapore for some time. The naval base on the island was well fortified, there were enough supplies to last for at least three months and, in early February, the 18th Division arrived as reinforce-ments, boosting the garrison to more than 100,000 men, a third of them British. By comparison, the Japanese were

Lieutenant-General Arthur Percival (right) leads a party of British officers to surrender Singapore to the Japanese, 15 February 1942. The loss of Singapore marked a low point of British efforts in the Second World War.

tired, their supply lines were stretched and they could muster only 30,000 assault troops. But their morale was high and the momentum of their advance made them virtually unstoppable. Even so, when they invaded Singapore on the night of 8/9 February, they were aided significantly by confusion and poor command on the British side. Garbled orders led to premature withdrawals from positions that could have been held, allowing the Japanese to capture four-fifths of the island and most of the stockpiled supplies by 12 February; three days later, Percival surrendered. It was a crushing blow to British prestige: in a campaign lasting 70 days they had lost two capital ships, about 200 aircraft and nearly 140,000 men, all but 10,000 as prisoners of war. The British, yet again, had been outclassed, outgeneralled and outfought.

The humiliation did not stop there, for while Percival was struggling to retain Malaya and Singapore, his counterpart in Burma, Lieutenant-General Thomas Hutton, was facing similar problems. Japanese troops crossed the border from Siam (Thailand) on 20 January 1942, encountering little resistance from Indian and Burmese units defending the approaches to Moulmein.

Although Hutton had nearly 50,000 troops at his disposal, they suffered the same problems as those elsewhere in the Far East – poor training, a history of neglect and dubious morale. In addition, the speed of the Japanese advance disrupted defensive plans, forcing Hutton's men to retreat from river line to river line without having the chance to consolidate.

Command cohesion collapsed – on 23 February, for example, a railway bridge over the River Sittang was demolished by British troops, trapping the bulk of 17th Indian Division on the east bank, facing the Japanese – and Hutton was replaced by Lieutenant-General Sir Harold Alexander when Rangoon came under direct threat on 1 March. There was little Alexander could do; by 8 March Rangoon had fallen, triggering a British retreat which did not end until the remnants of 'Burcorps' (Burma Corps) reached Assam in eastern India, more than 1000 miles away, in May. It was the longest retreat in the history of the British Army, conducted across extremely difficult terrain in intense heat, with soldiers succumbing to malaria and exhaustion as well as Japanese action. Over 13,000 troops were lost, adding to the toll of disaster, and those who survived were in no condition to fight on. The only consolation was that the Japanese were no better off, operating at the end of impossibly long supply lines. The war on the Indian border inevitably degenerated into a stalemate which would not be broken until British forces had been rebuilt. It would be a long hard process.

TURNING THE TIDE IN NORTH AFRICA

Logistics, the art of getting the right supplies in the right quantities to the right place at the right time, represented the difference between success and failure in many campaigns. The need for adequate port facilities in a campaign area was often crucial, as was the distance between those facilities and the front line, particularly if the terrain was difficult and road or river communications poor. This was seen in Burma, where the loss of Rangoon and the retreat to eastern India left British forces struggling to survive, and the same was true in North Africa, where the further away from Egypt the Eighth Army advanced, the more tenuous the supply link became. The efforts of logistic troops – offloading and storing supplies in reception ports, servicing and repairing equipment in the aftermath of battle and transporting *matériel* forward to fighting units – often went unnoticed, yet were vital to the achievement and exploitation of victory.

This was shown to good effect in the aftermath of Operation Crusader. Although Rommel's retreat to El Agheila was dramatic, implying decisive defeat, the British found it increasingly difficult to maintain their supply chain over a distance of nearly 300 miles of desert. Truck convoys, manned by the Royal Army Service Corps, had to use a single coast road, along which everything, from food and water to petrol and spare parts, had to be carried, at least until ports such as Tobruk and Benghazi had been reopened. At the same time, as Rommel pulled back towards Tripoli, his supply chain shortened and he was able to rebuild his forces quickly. Thus in January 1942 he paused only momentarily at El Agheila before mounting a counter-attack, pushing the overstretched Eighth Army back as far as Gazala, to the west of Tobruk. There the British occupied a series of strongpoints running south from the coastal village of Gazala, forcing Rommel (also subject to logistic problems because of naval and air attacks on convoys from Italy) to halt. Both sides took the opportunity to regroup before the next round of battle.

That came on 26 May, when Italian troops made a frontal assault on the Gazala Line defences. It turned out to be a feint. Further south, Rommel personally led his armoured units around the desert flank, aiming to come up behind the British defences and cut them off from their supply base in Egypt. Eighth Army, commanded by Lieutenant-General Neil Ritchie, who had replaced Cunningham during the latter stages of Crusader, should have been able to deal with the attack. Rommel had 560 tanks at his disposal, but Ritchie could field 850, a proportion of which were newly delivered Grants with 75mm main armament, while the British strongpoints (or 'boxes') were well protected by minefields and artillery. Indeed, in the early stages of the battle Rommel experienced grave difficulties, finding himself trapped with his back to the British mines, but after hard fighting he managed to break out, forcing Ritchie to retreat. Once again, the lack of inter-arm co-operation on the British side had enabled a numerically inferior force to prevail; on too many occasions the armour fought its own engagements, leaving the infantry isolated, while Rommel, with his customary aggression, concentrated his Panzers to restore momentum and spread confusion. On 14 June Ritchie disengaged and Eighth Army began streaming back towards the Egyptian border; a week later the inadequately protected port of Tobruk fell to German troops, yielding 32,000 prisoners, 5000 tons of supplies, half a million gallons of fuel and nearly 2000 serviceable vehicles. It also opened the gate to Egypt and the Suez Canal.

Gazala was Rommel's greatest victory; it was also Eighth Army's greatest defeat. Taken in conjunction with recent events in Malaya and Burma, it represented the nadir of British fortunes in the Second World War, made worse by the fact that once the retreat into Egypt began it was almost impossible to stop. Attempts by Eighth Army to halt the enemy at Mersa Matruh failed, upon which Auchinleck relieved Ritchie of his command and took over himself, organizing an extemporized defensive line even further back at El Alamein, less than 60 miles from Alexandria. The reasons for the disaster were difficult to analyse. Inferior numbers and equipment could clearly not be blamed – Ritchie had enjoyed significant advantages in both respects – and the capture of so many

THE BRUNEVAL RAID

Shortly after midnight on 27/28 February 1942 British airborne troops, drawn mainly from Major John Frost's C Company of the newly formed 2nd Parachute Battalion, landed close to the village of Bruneval on the northern coast of occupied France. Split into three groups, they moved swiftly towards German positions in an isolated villa overlooking the cliffs. Close to the villa was their objective – a German *Würzburg* radar set which it was intended to capture intact and return to England for analysis. In the event, the villa was virtually undefended and the paras, together with Flight-Sergeant Cox, an RAF radar expert, began to dismantle the *Würzburg*, photographing anything that could not be moved. Their actions attracted German fire from a wooded enclosure known as La Presbytère to their north, but by about 2.15 a.m. Frost's men had successfully withdrawn to the beach with their booty, which included two rather frightened German technicians. Half an hour later the paras, their prisoners and the *Würzburg* were picked up by the Navy and returned to Portsmouth, having lost three men killed, seven wounded and six inadvertently left behind.

Bruneval gave the Parachute Regiment its first battle honour and amply justified Winston Churchill's call for the raising of airborne forces in June 1940.

supplies at Tobruk implied that logistics was not a major problem.

In the end, it came down to the organization, command and fighting techniques of the troops in the front line: after two and a half years of conflict, the British Army had still not grasped how warfare had changed or how it might now be conducted. Commanders were unimaginative and easily overwhelmed by events, and different elements of the Army did not co-ordinate their actions. Indeed, there seemed to be almost a tradition that infantry and artillery were static units, leaving mobility to the tanks which, unsupported, fell victim to enemy all-arms teams. In addition, there was a strong tendency to prefer set-piece battles that ignored the opportunities offered by desert terrain. Individual units such as the Long Range Desert Group and Special Air Service may have been exceptions (*see box*, p. 134), but the bulk of the Army was hidebound. Rommel summed it up during Gazala when he witnessed the actions of 201st Guards Brigade, caught in the 'Knightsbridge' box: 'This brigade was almost a living embodiment of the virtues and faults of the British soldier – tremendous courage and tenacity combined with a rigid lack of mobility.' Later, in Tobruk, he greeted a group of captured British officers with the declaration 'Gentlemen, you have fought like lions and been led by donkeys'.

It was therefore a dispirited and angry Eighth Army which manned the El Alamein defences in July 1942, for although it enjoyed the advantage of extremely short supply lines and was able to replace its losses quickly, its soldiers could not understand why they kept being defeated, nor what they had to do to turn the tide. Many of them began to look backwards to the next line of defence, convinced that Alamein could not be held, and despite Auchinleck's undoubted leadership qualities, shown when he blunted Rommel's first assault on the Alamein Line, his army was still displaying its weaknesses. During the First Battle of Alamein in July, for example, the recently arrived 23rd Armoured Brigade, equipped with 104 brand-new Valentine tanks, charged into action with no attempt to co-ordinate their attack with infantry formations around them. In less than two hours they lost 97 tanks, having blundered into an 88mm anti-tank gun trap. It was a tragic reflection on the British Army's continued lack of fighting effectiveness.

But at least First Alamein gave the British time to pause and reassess. One of the results, after a visit by Churchill, was a radical shake-up of command. Auchinleck, despite his defensive success, did not enjoy the full confidence of his men, whose morale had been badly affected by the impact of Gazala and its aftermath. Sent to command forces in India, Auchinleck was replaced as C-in-C Middle East by Alexander and a new commander was appointed to Eighth Army. This was Lieutenant-General Bernard Montgomery, who arrived in early August. His actions, particularly those aimed at restoring the morale of his troops and ensuring victory through the build-up of overwhelming forces, helped to create a turning point in the desert campaign and, by association, in the history of the British Army during the Second World War. Before his arrival in Egypt, Eighth Army had suffered seemingly endless defeats; afterwards it enjoyed a string of victories that would take it across North Africa and deep into

Regimental Tradition:

THE RED DEVILS

Although it might be thought that the nickname of the Parachute Regiment – the 'Red Devils' – came from their adoption of the distinctive red beret, other origins have been suggested. One of these concerned the first operation carried out by 1st Parachute Brigade in North-West Africa in November 1942, as part of Operation Torch. According to men who were there, the paras landed in red sand which stuck to their uniforms. Emerging to face the enemy, they must have made a fearsome sight: covered in red sand and with the crotch straps of their jump-smocks hanging down, the description 'Red Devils' would seem to have been apt!

Europe. Whatever criticisms may be levelled at Montgomery – and there are many – there can be no denying that his promotion to high command transformed the situation.

Montgomery's first task was to restore the confidence of Eighth Army, which he realized was suffering from poor leadership, indiscipline and 'bellyaching'. He refused to discuss even the possibility of further retreat, replaced key commanders with men he trusted and toured front-line units to impose his personality on his troops, recognizing that, as 'civilians in uniform', they needed firm direction and a strong sense of purpose. At the same time, he opposed calls from Churchill for an immediate counter-attack, and insisted that he could not move until Eighth Army had been reinforced and prepared for battle. A defensive victory over Rommel at Alam Halfa (31 August–6 September), conducted according to plans laid down by Auchinleck before he left, gave Montgomery just the boost he needed: his soldiers began to believe that, under their new general, Rommel could be beaten.

But it would be naive to imagine that Montgomery achieved such a transformation on his own. Other factors were beginning to come into play, coinciding with his arrival in North Africa, that ensured improvements to the capabilities of Eighth Army. Churchill's interest in the Mediterranean, always apparent, was heightened by the entry of the United States into the war, for it was necessary to achieve purely British victories in that region before North-West Europe took precedence. President Franklin D. Roosevelt was keen to see the defeat of Germany, but was less likely to support a Mediterranean strategy which seemed designed to enhance Britain's imperial survival. Before the United States grew strong enough to dominate the alliance, therefore, the threat to the Suez Canal had to be lifted. Thus Churchill was quite prepared to send substantial reinforcements to Eighth Army. By October 1942, Montgomery could field seven British divisions – the 1st, 7th, 8th and 10th Armoured and 44th, 50th and (reconstituted) 51st Infantry – making Eighth Army for the first time a predominantly British force. Simultaneously, he received new US-manufactured equipment, including 300 Sherman tanks fitted with 75mm turret-mounted guns, as well as extra artillery and supplies. Rommel, by comparison, was existing at the end of an already tenuous supply chain that was further weakened by concerted Allied air attacks on Axis shipping in the Mediterranean.

Thus when Montgomery decided to attack at Alamein in late October, Eighth Army enjoyed considerable advantages, fielding 195,000 troops, 2300 artillery pieces and over 1000 tanks against an overstretched Italian-German force of 104,000 men, 1300 guns and about 500 serviceable tanks. Even so, the subsequent battle was not easy, lasting 12 days and costing 13,500 British and Imperial casualties (see p. 140). It ended with Rommel's retreat from Egypt in early November – an achievement that marked a true turning point in British fortunes during the war – but criticisms could still be made. The Second Battle of Alamein was a slogging match, won by a mixture of tenacity and numerical superiority; it lacked the fluidity of *blitzkrieg*, chiefly because Montgomery recognized the dangers of releasing his armour as a *corps de chasse*, and clearly suited the

British approach to war. The British Army, by late 1942, could fight effectively but unimaginatively, gaining victory by battering at the enemy's front-line 'muscle' rather than lancing through to destroy his 'brain'. This should not detract from the reality of Montgomery's achievement or the impressive fighting qualities of the soldiers at Alamein, but it was a costly way to wage war and one that could not be sustained without US aid in terms of both men and equipment. It is significant that Second Alamein was the last purely British offensive of the war against Germany; thereafter, the Americans played an increasingly dominant role.

This was shown by the fact that, only four days after Montgomery's victory, a combined Anglo-US force landed in French North Africa, threatening Rommel from the west. The Americans had been persuaded that such an attack would produce territorial gains for little real cost, while acting as a rehearsal of amphibious techniques that would be vital in the projected invasion of North-West

British Crusader II tanks, with American-built Shermans in the background, move up to the Alamein Line, October 1942. The lead tank has extra armour bolted on to the front glacis plate and nose.

THE SECOND BATTLE OF ALAMEIN

Personality Profile:

Field Marshal Viscount Montgomery of Alamein
(1887–1976)

Commissioned from Sandhurst into the Royal Warwickshire Regiment in 1908, Bernard Montgomery served on the Western Front throughout the First World War and spent the inter-war period climbing the ladder of promotion. In 1940 he commanded 3rd Infantry Division during the retreat to Dunkirk, after which he served as GOC South-Eastern Command in England, gaining a reputation as a harsh but effective trainer of men.

His opportunity for more decisive action came in August 1942, when he took over the demoralized Eighth Army in North Africa. Aware of the need for victory, he impressed himself on his troops by visiting and talking to them; at the same time, he stood firm against pressure from London and delayed his offensive at El Alamein until reinforcements had been delivered and the troops reorganized. The result was a major victory, although its rather 'set-piece' nature became a hallmark of many of Montgomery's future engagements.

He continued to command Eighth Army in the pursuit of Rommel into Tunisia and in the invasions of Sicily and southern

At 9.40 p.m. on 23 October 1942 nearly 900 British artillery pieces opened fire along the Alamein Line, mainly on a six-mile front in the northern sector. Under cover of the barrage – the largest mounted by the British since the First World War – Royal Engineers began to clear gaps in the German minefields, to be held open by the infantry of XXX Corps so that the armour of X Corps could pass through to engage Rommel's Panzers. At the same time, XIII Corps further south put in a diversionary attack designed to tie down 21st Panzer Division in that area. With the Alamein position secure between the coast and the Qattara Depression, the idea was to force Rommel to fight an attritional battle against a British force of overwhelming numbers.

The attack caught the Axis divisions by surprise – Rommel was on leave in Germany and did not arrive back in North Africa until the 25th – but creating gaps through the minefields proved more difficult than envisaged. During the night of 23/24 October, men of 51st (Highland) Division fought bravely to clear a way for 1st Armoured, while to their south the New Zealanders did the same for 10th Armoured, but by dawn there were grave doubts about the safety of the corridors. Montgomery, facing the fact that a breakthrough had not occurred, switched his main effort further north, where 9th Australian Division had made some progress, and ordered 1st Armoured, elements of which had penetrated Axis defences by the 25th, to forge ahead. But these assaults, too, soon bogged down in the face of German counter-attacks. Back in London, Churchill voiced doubts about Montgomery's generalship.

He need not have worried, for although the battle was proving more bitter than anticipated, Montgomery remained calm, regrouping his forces and concentrating them in a sector just south of the Australians. On 1/2 November, in an operation codenamed Supercharge, the New Zealanders, reinforced by two brigades of Highlanders and 23rd Armoured Brigade, put in the decisive blow, cracking the Axis defences apart. By the end of 2 November, Rommel had fewer than 35 tanks left intact and was in no position to continue the battle. Montgomery's forces were able to break out into more open terrain, although command reluctance and traffic chaos prevented an immediate pursuit. Over 30,000 Axis prisoners were in British hands and nearly all of Rommel's tanks, some out of fuel, were destroyed or captured. The cost to the British was high – 13,500 casualties and nearly 500 tanks – but there was no doubt that a major victory had been achieved.

Italy, before being recalled to Britain in December 1943 to take command of Anglo-US troops in the projected invasion of North-West Europe. As Land Force Commander until 1 September 1944, he supervised the D-Day landings and subsequent breakout from Normandy, before handing over to Eisenhower and assuming command of the Anglo-Canadian 21st Army Group, which he subsequently led through Holland, across the Rhine and deep into northern Germany. On 4 May 1945 he accepted the surrender of all German forces facing him; he then assumed command of the British sector of occupied Germany. He later served as Chief of the Imperial General Staff (1946–8) and as Chairman of NATO forces in Europe.

23 OCTOBER–2 NOVEMBER 1942

A British anti-tank gun crew prepare for action, Second Battle of Alamein, October 1942.

First-Hand Account

'On the afternoon of October 23, leaflets were distributed, giving Monty's eve-of-battle message. "Fight as long as you have breath in your body". It seemed unreal in the quiet afternoon . . .

'At 21.40 hours, the desert shook like an earthquake. For as far as we could see, the sky was ablaze from the guns. Such was the deafening noise that we could see enemy shells exploding on our positions, but could not hear them. Our gaunt stares said it all – we were scared stiff, but oddly enough, not frightened. In the hours that followed, the tension eased. Our barrage was having the desired effect, but the infantry and engineers had it rough . . .'

Gunner Henry Byrne, 154th (Leicestershire Yeomanry) Field Regiment, Royal Artillery

From *Images of War*, Issue 18,
Marshall Cavendish
Partworks Ltd, 1989

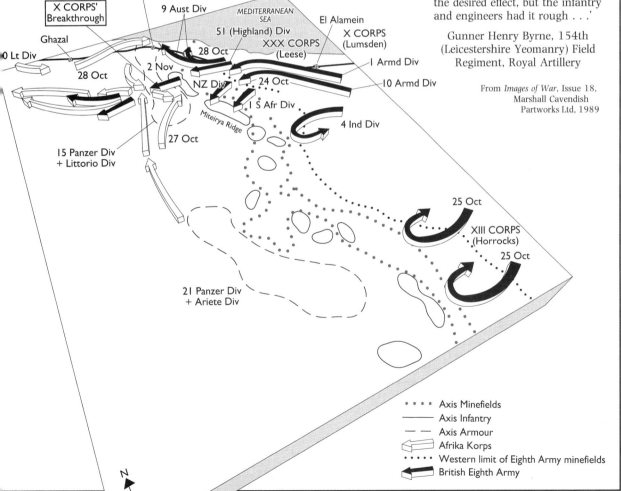

X CORPS' Breakthrough

Sidi Abd el Rahman

9 Aust Div

Ghazal

0 Lt Div

28 Oct

MEDITERRANEAN SEA

51 (Highland) Div

28 Oct

2 Nov

El Alamein

X CORPS (Lumsden)

XXX CORPS (Leese)

1 Armd Div

NZ Div

24 Oct

10 Armd Div

Miteirya Ridge

1 S Afr Div

4 Ind Div

27 Oct

15 Panzer Div + Littorio Div

21 Panzer Div + Ariete Div

25 Oct

XIII CORPS (Horrocks)

25 Oct

- • • • • Axis Minefields
- —— Axis Infantry
- – – Axis Armour
- ⇦ Afrika Korps
- • • • • Western limit of Eighth Army minefields
- ⬅ British Eighth Army

N

Europe. Three Task Forces were created for Operation Torch, two of which were American, landing around Casablanca in Morocco and Oran in Algeria, while the third, aiming for Algiers itself, was a combined Anglo-US undertaking. Early on 8 November 1942, men of the British 11th and 36th Infantry Brigades (the bulk of 78th Division) landed astride Algiers in conjunction with US forces, and had seized the city from Vichy-French defenders by the end of the day. Joined later by 6th Armoured and 46th Infantry Divisions, as well as 1st Guards Brigade and 25th Army Tank Brigade, they constituted the spearhead of the British First Army, commanded by Lieutenant-General Kenneth Anderson. Their task was to push rapidly eastwards to seize Tunis and Bizerta, 400 miles from the beachhead. At first, they achieved remarkable success: by 16 November, they had captured the ports of Bougie, Djidjelli, Philippeville and Bone (the latter using airborne forces) and entered Tunisia; by 2 December they were within 50 miles of their objectives. Meanwhile, Eighth Army had pursued Rommel as far as El Agheila, closing the trap.

As always, the Germans reacted swiftly. Aware that the whole of North Africa was under threat, Hitler ordered reinforcements (soon to be known as Fifth Panzer Army) to be rushed to Tunis. Their arrival, coupled to familiar problems of logistics experienced by British troops now far distant from their supply bases, was enough to slow Anderson down. An attempt by 6th Armoured Division to advance through the Medjerda Valley was stalled when infantry failed to take 'Longstop Hill' and, in deteriorating winter weather, the Allied Supreme Commander, Lieutenant-General Dwight D. Eisenhower, called a halt to the offensive. Heavy rain turned the ground to glutinous mud, condemning Allied soldiers to a campaign which was reminiscent of the Western Front in the First World War. To the newspapers back home, it was a 'lull'; to the men in the front line it was a nightmare of constant patrolling and artillery duels. Half the casualties of the entire Tunisian campaign were lost during the winter months.

Rommel linked up with Fifth Panzer Army in January 1943, abandoning Tripoli to Montgomery and preparing a defensive line at Mareth, just over the Tunisian border. Realizing that it would take time for Eighth Army to advance that far, he turned west towards Kasserine, inflicting a telling blow on the inexperienced US II Corps in February. British troops contributed to the defence of Thala, to the north-west of Kasserine, but Rommel could not afford to exploit his success. Instead, he moved south to face Eighth Army at Medenine where, on 6 March, he suffered a crippling defeat as his Panzers fell victim to a carefully laid anti-tank trap, organized by 51st (Highland) Division. Two weeks later, in what is regarded by many as Montgomery's finest desert engagement, the New Zealand Division, backed by 1st Armoured, outflanked the Mareth Line in a manoeuvre traditionally associated with Rommel. As the German and Italian forces withdrew, fighting rearguard actions in the Wadi Akarit, spearhead units of Eighth Army linked up with men of the US II Corps. On 23 April the 8th Battalion Argyll and Sutherland Highlanders took Longstop Hill in a renewed assault against murderous enemy fire. This helped to unlock the front in the north; the heights above the

Medjerda Gap were seized by Gurkhas of 4th Indian Division on 6 May and 24 hours later armoured cars of the 11th Hussars entered Tunis. On 12 May the last of the German forces in North Africa surrendered.

SICILY AND ITALY, JULY 1943–JUNE 1944

This was an impressive victory, particularly when the condition of Eighth Army only a year before was recalled, but it did raise the problem of where to go next. To the British, the strategy was straightforward – to move immediately into southern Europe via Sicily and Italy, securing the Mediterranean and, if possible, opening up the Balkans – but the same was not true of the Americans, still wary of their ally's post-war intentions. Roosevelt favoured an invasion of North-West Europe as the quickest route to victory over the Fascist powers, although he did recognize that this would be impossible before the spring of 1944. Rather than lose the momentum gained in North Africa, he was therefore prepared to support an invasion of Sicily, hoping to knock Italy out of the war, with the clear understanding that this would not lead to a major Mediterranean campaign. Churchill had to use all his arts of persuasion to ensure even this concession; as the war continued, Britain's subordinate position in the alliance grew more and more apparent.

THE WAR IN ITALY 1943-5

Operation Husky began at dawn on 10 July 1943 with seaborne landings by the US Seventh Army under Lieutenant-General George S. Patton and the British Eighth Army under Montgomery, across 26 beaches on the south-east coast of Sicily. Airborne landings, designed to seize airfields and bridges in advance of the ground forces, were disrupted by the weather – out of 144 British gliders committed to the invasion, nearly 70 were released too early and came down in the sea. The Allies were also surprised by German counter-attacks, but the operation was a success. Despite poor relations between Patton and Montgomery, triggered by a mutual desire to claim credit for the victory, the ordinary soldiers fought well. Eighth

Army, advancing north to Mount Etna and Messina, found the terrain difficult and was often stalled, but confidence was high. Improved leadership, greater tactical skill and a willingness to acknowledge the need for close inter-arm co-operation were all apparent as US and British troops linked up in Messina on 17 August, driving the enemy into southern Italy. Eighth Army suffered fewer than 10,000 casualties.

Infantry reinforcements wade ashore from a landing ship, Sicily, 10 July 1943. Disembarkation procedures seem little different from those at Gallipoli in 1915, although in this case enemy opposition is mercifully slight.

THE SALERNO 'MUTINY'

On 20 September 1943 over 1500 replacement troops, drawn from a transit camp in North Africa, were marched into a field close to the Salerno beachhead and ordered to join the hard-pressed 46th Infantry Division. Most obeyed, but a hard core of 192 refused. They were all highly experienced soldiers, wounded in Sicily, belonging to the 50th (Northumbrian) and 51st (Highland) Divisions, who believed that it was their right to return to their parent units; indeed, one of the divisional commanders had told them to insist on such a return. An officer repeated the order – 'Fall out on the road, pick up your kit, and move off to the 46th Division area' – but to no effect. Squads of military policemen disarmed the soldiers and marched them to a compound on the beach. They were then shipped back to North Africa where, in October, they were court-martialled for mutiny. Found guilty, the privates were each sentenced to seven years' penal servitude, the corporals to ten years and the sergeants to be shot. All sentences were then suspended as long as the soldiers agreed to serve in new units. They had no choice but to comply.

It was a grubby affair. The 'mutineers', loyal to their original divisions, were convinced that they were doing the right thing and never refused to fight, merely insisting that they did so in their parent units. Leadership was clearly poor – it would not have taken much to show a degree of understanding – although it must be remembered that 46th Division was in desperate need of men. The incident is perhaps best summed up as a negative by-product of the regimental system.

By then Benito Mussolini had been overthrown, raising the distinct possibility of an Italian collapse if Allied forces crossed to the mainland. Roosevelt was persuaded to support such a move, not least by the argument that a campaign in Italy would divert enemy forces from North-West Europe, although at the time few people could have foreseen just how difficult that campaign would be. On 3 September, the fourth anniversary of the outbreak of war, elements of Eighth Army crossed the Strait of Messina to land at Reggio, gaining a foothold without loss. Six days later, as news of an Italian surrender was announced, the British 1st Airborne Division landed by sea at Taranto and Brindisi, while the US Fifth Army under Lieutenant-General Mark Clark, half of which was British, went ashore at Salerno, south of Naples. Hoping to take advantage of the Italian collapse, the plan was for Clark to move north towards Rome while Montgomery linked up from the south.

It did not work. The Salerno landings (Operation Avalanche) were strongly opposed by German troops determined to prevent an Allied occupation of Italy, and for nine days the fighting in the beachhead was severe, with German Panzers mounting frontal attacks that were only stopped by salvoes from warships offshore. In the process, although the attacks tended to be concentrated against the less experienced Americans, the British X Corps suffered heavy casualties, requiring the despatch of reinforcements from North Africa (see box). Meanwhile, further south Montgomery had been delayed by German demolition teams and a shortage of engineering supplies. He did not link up with Clark until 20 September and it was not until 5 October that Naples was taken. By then Fifth Army alone had suffered 12,000 casualties, suggesting that any sustained campaign in Italy was going to be extremely costly. As the autumn rains began and the Germans pulled back skilfully to the first of a series of defensive lines to the south of Rome, the Allies found themselves sucked into a nightmare. The terrain of rapidly flowing rivers and precipitous mountains favoured the defender, necessitating a build-up of Allied forces considerably in excess of that envisaged when the campaign began. By 10 October over 200,000 men and 35,000 vehicles had poured ashore at Naples and Salerno.

The Allied advance – Fifth Army in the west and Eighth Army in the east – gradually bogged down. In mid-October, as Montgomery faced a series of defended river lines on the route to Ortona, British troops under Clark crossed the flooded Volturno. Their experiences were typical of operations throughout Italy at that time. The only approaches to the river were along raised causeways, interspersed with olive groves and small villages, each of which contained diehard defenders. Even when the Volturno was reached, it proved to be over 300 feet wide and, as the troops struggled against mud and mines, losing their tank support, they had to fight forward inch by painful inch to create a foothold. By November they were lucky if they were advancing more than a mile a day, even though the Germans had already decided to pull back to the Gustav Line, centred on the mountains around Monte Cassino at the head of the Liri Valley. To make matters worse, the build-up for the cross-Channel invasion was taking precedence: by the end of 1943 Fifth and Eighth Armies between them had lost seven divisions, withdrawn to Britain, and Montgomery had returned home to prepare for a new command in North-West Europe.

Between January and June 1944, the fighting in Italy was among the toughest of the war in any theatre, particularly around Cassino (see box, p. 145), which was not taken until May. By then, an attempt to bypass the Gustav Line by mounting an amphibious landing further north at Anzio (Operation Shingle) had failed to break the deadlock. When the US VI Corps, containing the British 1st Infantry Division, two Commando battalions and the 46th Royal Tank Regiment as well as American troops, landed on 22 January, hopes of an early breakthrough to the Alban Hills and the approaches to Rome were widespread, but uninspired command and German counter-attacks quickly contained the beachhead. British soldiers fought hard to advance towards Campoleone on the left, only to suffer horrendous casualties: the 2nd Battalion Sherwood Foresters was virtually wiped out, while battalions of the Scots and Irish Guards fared little

CASSINO

By early 1944 Allied forces in Italy were stalled along the Gustav Line, in the centre of which stood the historic Benedictine monastery of Monte Cassino, dominating the mountains in front of the Liri Valley and the road to Rome. A frontal assault in January made little progress, despite crossings of the Rivers Garigliano and Rapido to the south, and plans for a renewed offensive by New Zealanders in February were delayed while Allied bombers pounded the monastery to rubble. This proved to be counter-productive – the Germans merely used the ruins as defensive positions – and the attack soon bogged down in Cassino town amid some of the bitterest fighting of the Italian campaign.

After a pause to regroup, the Allies tried again on 11 May, launching a co-ordinated offensive along a 20-mile front from Cassino to the sea. Although British and American advances to the south were held, a Free French assault to the north managed to penetrate the mountains and cut enemy communications. On 18 May Polish troops finally took the shattered remains of the monastery.

better. Allied air and naval support was crucial, but it was not until the taking of Cassino that the Anzio forces could push forward. By then, over 10,000 British casualties had been suffered, with inevitable effects on the morale of the survivors.

This was exacerbated throughout Italy when the liberation of Rome on 4 June – the first European capital to fall to Allied troops – was overshadowed by the long-awaited invasion of North-West Europe two days later. An ill-considered remark by a British politician led the forces in Italy to be known as the 'D-Day Dodgers'. It was poor reward for their efforts, particularly as the breaching of the Gustav Line was followed by a 90-mile advance in 12 days to the north of Rome. Familiar problems of terrain and dogged German defence stalled the Allied armies in front of the Gothic Line, preventing a breakthrough to the Po Valley, but by then the Italian campaign had taken second place in people's minds to the fighting in Normandy.

Allied air and artillery attacks devastate the Italian town of Cassino, 15 March 1944. The destructive capability of weapons is graphically shown in this photograph.

OPERATION OVERLORD

Preparations for the Allied invasion of North-West Europe had started in earnest in early 1943, when Major-General Frederick Morgan was appointed COSSAC (Chief of Staff to the Supreme Allied Commander, even though the SAC had yet to be chosen). He faced the difficult tasks of deciding where the invasion would take place and of producing a preliminary plan. For this he required, first and foremost, accurate information about the enemy defences. Some of this could be provided by aerial reconnaissance, and some from Resistance agents in occupied Europe, but there was no substitute for that gained from trained men on the ground.

As early as June 1940 Churchill had called for the raising of 'specially trained troops of the hunter class who can develop a reign of terror down the enemy coast'. Such troops were later organized into 'Commandos', named after the Boer guerrilla units of the South African War (1899–1902). Drawn initially from the Army and then from the Royal Marines, these units quickly developed invaluable skills. Early raids, such as those against the Lofoten Islands and Vaagso in Norway in March and December 1941 respectively, concentrated on the destruction of important targets, but after the heavy losses suffered by Canadian troops at Dieppe (19 August 1942) – an operation in which the Commandos also took part – the emphasis shifted to the collection of information about the enemy. By 1944 small groups of canoeists known as Combined Operations Pilotage Parties (COPPs) were capable of landing secretly on the coast of occupied Europe to collect samples of sand for analysis (to see if it was firm enough to take the weight of a major amphibious assault) and to monitor German defensive positions.

This sort of detailed information helped Morgan to narrow his options. Bearing in mind that any assault had to be carried out within range of fighter aircraft in southern England, that the enormous logistic chain had to be kept as short as possible, and that German construction of the 'Atlantic Wall' of beach fortifications was proceeding apace, there were distinct limits to his choice

British Commandos pull back towards their landing craft after a successful raid on the German-held Lofoten Islands off northern Norway, March 1941. Fish-oil factories and shipping were destroyed, for no British losses.

D-DAY 'FUNNIES'

Faced with the problems of breaching German defences along the 'Atlantic Wall' during the invasion of North-West Europe, the British Army developed a series of specialized armoured vehicles, known collectively as 'Funnies'. Grouped together in the 79th Armoured Division, commanded by Major-General Sir Percy Hobart, they were designed to respond to specific problems. During the amphibious assault, for example, the infantry would need armoured support, so the Duplex Drive (DD) tank was invented: a collapsible wrap-around canvas screen gave the vehicle buoyancy, while propellers, driven by the tank engine, enabled it to swim at up to 4.3 knots. Once ashore, minefields would be cleared using a 'Flail' tank fitted with a large front roller from which chains would beat a path forward, exposing or exploding the mines; enemy blockhouses would be dealt with by Armoured Vehicles Royal Engineers (AVREs) armed with Petard mortars or by 'Crocodiles' fitted with flame-throwers. In addition, soft sand would be covered by carpet-laying 'Bobbins' and culverts or small streams spanned using self-propelled ramps. Despite heavy DD losses on 6 June 1944, the Funnies made a major impact on the D-Day landings in the Anglo-Canadian sector. In March 1945 they contributed to the Rhine crossings.

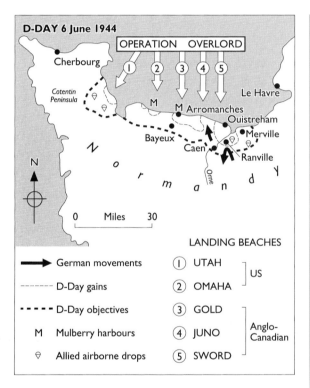

D-DAY 6 June 1944

OPERATION OVERLORD

Cherbourg

Cotentin Peninsula

Le Havre

M M Arromanches
Ouistreham
Bayeux
Caen Merville
Ranville

N o r m a n d y

Orne

N

0 Miles 30

LANDING BEACHES

→ German movements ① UTAH ⎤ US
------- D-Day gains ② OMAHA ⎦
- - - - D-Day objectives ③ GOLD ⎤
M Mulberry harbours ④ JUNO ⎥ Anglo-Canadian
⊖ Allied airborne drops ⑤ SWORD ⎦

of landing area. Norway, the Netherlands and the Bay of Biscay were all rejected as too far from British ports, and the Pas de Calais was seen as too dangerous because of German defences in the region. In the end, Morgan zeroed in on the coast of Normandy, between Le Havre and the Cotentin Peninsula, and advocated an initial assault by three divisions with airborne flank support. This was accepted officially in June 1943, although when Eisenhower was appointed SAC in December, with Montgomery as Land Force Commander for the assault phase, objections were made that this was too small a force to be decisive. Two more divisions were added.

The British Army contribution to 'D-Day' was the 3rd and 50th Infantry Divisions, with Commandos and the Canadian 2nd Division under command. Their task

First-Hand Account:

D-DAY

'. . . I could just see the shore line some 5000 yards away; it seemed a very long distance and in a DD tank, in that sea, it certainly was! . . . We battled on towards the shore through the rough sea. We were buffeted about unmercifully, plunging into the troughs of the waves and somehow wallowing up again to the crests. The wind, fortunately, was behind us, and this helped a little. The noise continued and by now the shells and rockets were passing over our heads, also, we were aware that we were under fire from the shore. The Germans had woken up to the fact that they were under attack and had brought their own guns into action. It was a struggle to keep the tank on course, but gradually the shore line became more distinct and before long we could see the line of houses which were our targets. Sea sickness was now forgotten. It took over an hour of hard work to reach the beach and it was a miracle that most of us did. As we approached, we felt the tracks meet the shelving sand of the shore, and slowly we began to rise out of the water . . . When the base of the screen was clear of the water, the struts were broken, the air released and the screen collapsed. We leapt into the tank and were ready for action.'

Corporal Patrick Hennessey, 13th/18th Royal Hussars, a DD tank commander on Sword beach, 6 June 1944

From Patrick Hennessey, *Young man in a tank*, privately printed, no date was to secure three beaches, codenamed Sword, Juno and Gold, along a 24-mile front between Ouistreham and Arromanches, the left flank of which, around Ranville, would be held by men of 6th Airborne Division dropped in advance. To their right, on Omaha and Utah beaches, US troops would go ashore at the same time, with the right flank of the landing area secured by the US 82nd and 101st Airborne Divisions. Once a foothold had been gained, troops and supplies would pour off the landing ships, the majority through special prefabricated harbours known as 'Mulberries', with the aim of creating such a rapid build-up that the Germans would be unable to react effectively. Overall, the Americans earmarked 72 divisions for the liberation of Europe. By comparison, the British could manage only 17, an indication of the extent to which they were dependent on the manpower resources of their ally; without the USA any plans for a cross-Channel invasion could not have been contemplated.

Even so, the 17 divisions represented a significant effort by the British Army. Of them, only four had seen action by 1944 – 7th Armoured, 50th and 51st Infantry and 1st Airborne, all withdrawn from the Mediterranean – leaving 13 to be 'blooded' in the invasion. These divisions constituted the 'new' British Army, created from the ashes of the BEF since 1940. They had been extensively trained, gaining confidence from exercises that progressed from battalion to multi-divisional levels over a period of nearly four years. Officers and NCOs had been specially selected and exhaustively prepared, lessons from North Africa and the Mediterranean absorbed, at least in theory, and new weapons developed. In addition, specialized units had been raised to deal with particular problems, including the provision of armour with the assault infantry. But the fact remained that these were inexperienced troops, raised in the main from conscripts called up since the beginning of the war, and although no-one doubted their ability to fight in the coming campaign, they were essentially 'civilians in uniform', requiring careful handling and husbanding. With commitments in the Mediterranean and Far East as well as in Europe, Britain was running out of manpower: by late July 1944, as the battle for Normandy raged, Montgomery had to be reminded that few replacements for casualties existed, particularly in the infantry. It inevitably affected the way that the campaign was fought and reinforced the subordinate position of the British in the Anglo-US alliance.

The invasion began early on 6 June 1944 ('D-Day'), when US and British airborne troops landed on the flanks of the projected beachhead area. At 12.16 a.m. three gliders, carrying men of D Company, 2nd Oxfordshire and Buckinghamshire Light Infantry, swept out of a stormy sky to seize a bridge at Bénouville across the Caen Canal, a likely route for German reinforcements. Although sudden gusts of wind dispersed many of the airborne units elsewhere, by 5 a.m. the village of Ranville had been taken and a potentially dangerous coastal battery at Merville destroyed. The latter overlooked Sword beach, on the extreme left of the Anglo-Canadian assault sector, across which men of the 3rd Infantry Division, supported by 1st Special Service Brigade and No. 41 Royal Marine Commando as well as Free French Commandos, began to land at 7.25 a.m. To their right, on Juno and Gold beaches, the

Canadian 2nd Infantry Division, with No. 48 Royal Marine Commando in support, and the British 50th Infantry Division, landed at much the same time, meeting heavy opposition around Le Hamel but seizing Ouistreham and Arromanches before the defenders could react effectively. By 1.30 p.m. Commandos under Lord Lovat, led by a piper, had linked up with the airborne forces at Bénouville and secured the left flank. Although the three beaches had yet to be joined up, sufficient depth had been gained to allow the build-up of supplies to begin. To the Anglo-Canadian right, US forces had seized footholds on Utah and Omaha beaches (the latter after heavy fighting), as well as some airborne objectives.

By nightfall, the Allies could congratulate themselves on a major military achievement. In less than ideal weather they had managed to put 150,000 troops ashore at a cost of only 2500 dead. In the Anglo-Canadian sector, over 80,000 men had been landed, along with 900 armoured fighting vehicles and 240 field guns, occupying areas of coast about 25 miles long and, on average, five miles deep. However, not all the planned objectives had been taken. At 4 p.m. on 6 June men of the Staffordshire Yeomanry and 2nd King's Shropshire Light Infantry, advancing out of Sword beach, were counter-attacked by elements of 21st Panzer Division and prevented from taking Caen, a vital road and rail communications centre. Realizing its importance, the Germans hurriedly reinforced the town.

The failure to take Caen on 6 June proved to be unfortunate, for although the Americans succeeded in cutting across the Cotentin Peninsula before taking Cherbourg on 29 June, Anglo-Canadian troops found the going hard, making little headway in difficult terrain against determined opposition. Men of 6th Airborne Division around Ranville, east of the River Orne, only just held on to their positions in the face of Panzer attacks, while to the west of Caen infantry units found themselves sucked into a nightmare of sunken lanes, thick hedges and small fields. Montgomery, as Land Force Commander, searched for a way through, only to find his forces blocked at every move. On 13 June, he sent the experienced (but tired) 7th Armoured Division in a right hook south of Caen, trying to outflank the town. Spearheaded by 4th County of London Yeomanry (Sharpshooters) and 1st Rifle Brigade, the attack was stalled at Villers-Bocage by a small group of Tiger tanks, led by SS Lieutenant Michael Wittmann, that destroyed 27 British tanks and killed or captured nearly 100 men.

Twelve days later, in a more elaborate offensive codenamed Epsom, 60,000 men and 600 tanks of VIII Corps (commanded by the same Lieutenant-General O'Connor who had led Operation Compass in North Africa in 1940-1, and had escaped from an Italian PoW camp in 1943) advanced into the Odon Valley to the south-west of Caen. In appalling weather, which severely limited air support and disrupted resupply, progress was slow, although on 28 June elements of 11th Armoured Division did manage to cross the River Odon and take Hill 112,

A Bren-gunner, supported by riflemen, lays down covering fire during operations in the bocage of Normandy, June 1944. Fighting through the hedgerows and small fields of Normandy proved difficult and costly.

south of Carpiquet. By then the commander of the British Second Army, Lieutenant-General Miles Dempsey, had received top-secret reports, gleaned from Ultra intercepts of German signals, warning him of the imminent arrival of II SS Panzer Corps. On the 30th he called the offensive off and withdrew across the Odon. VIII Corps had suffered nearly 4000 casualties and Caen was still in enemy hands.

There is considerable controversy about Montgomery's planning at this stage. According to his *Memoirs*, written soon after the war, he always intended to fight around Caen, drawing German reserves into attritional battles so that US forces to the west could break out of the Cotentin Peninsula against weak opposition. However, this was not apparent to British commanders on the ground, who thought that they were responsible for conducting their own breakout, following the earlier instructions from Montgomery 'to jab at the Germans from both flanks until their defences cracked'. Such differences of expectation led inevitably to command confusion, epitomized by events in mid-July when a fresh offensive, codenamed Goodwood, was mounted to the east of Caen. By then, after bitter fighting in Operation Charnwood, Canadian troops had seized part of the town and units of 43rd (Wessex) Division had renewed the assault on Hill 112, but German defences remained strong. To Montgomery, an attack south towards Falaise from a bridgehead east of the Orne around Ranville would ensure the commitment of enemy reserves; to Dempsey and O'Connor it heralded the long-awaited breakout into more open terrain. To complicate matters still further,

Churchill was putting pressure on Montgomery to avoid an attritional stalemate reminiscent of the Western Front in the First World War, the RAF was calling for the capture of airfields around Caen and the War Office was issuing dire warnings about the shortage of infantry replacements.

Goodwood showed how little had been learnt in nearly five years of war. Although the British now had the advantage of massive air support, the plan itself was poor, calling for the advance of three armoured divisions (Guards, 7th and 11th) out of a very restricted bridgehead to the east of the Orne against under-estimated German defences. Artillery support was theoretically strong, but many of the guns could not be brought across the river because of enormous traffic jams on the bridges, and the British Army had still not absorbed the crucial lesson of infantry-armour co-operation. The armoured divisions, 750 tanks strong, had only limited infantry support, most of which would be quickly absorbed in the stone-built villages that dotted the advance axis. In addition, each of these villages was defended by small enemy teams of determined fighters. British commanders were unsure of the purpose of the attack and unaware that their primary objective, the Bourguébus Ridge, four miles from their start-line, played host to nearly 180 artillery pieces, backed by Panzer reserves.

The outcome was inevitable: when the British tanks advanced on 18 July they lost their infantry units almost straightaway in the villages and proceeded to push forward unsupported. German 88mm anti-tank guns and self-contained pockets of Tiger tanks played havoc with the spearhead formations, which quickly advanced beyond the range of 25-pounder field guns stuck to the west of the Orne. Poor ground-to-air communication compounded the problem by denying close air support, while the need to feed the three armoured divisions into the battle piecemeal because of the restricted bridgehead precluded momentum. By the end of the day, amid deteriorating weather, nearly 200 tanks had been lost for little appreciable territorial gain. O'Connor halted the offensive two days later.

But Goodwood, despite its tactical shortcomings, did contribute to Montgomery's professed strategy, for while British armour was tying down the enemy in the east, US forces were preparing to attack in the west. On 25 July Lieutenant-General Omar N. Bradley's US First Army pushed south towards Avranches in Operation Cobra, breaking through into more open terrain by 1 August. By then, Patton's US Third Army had been deployed, exploiting the gaps now appearing in enemy defences to strike west into Brittany and south and east towards the Seine. Dempsey's Second Army contributed by attacking towards Vire and continuing the assault from Caen to Falaise. The fighting was hard – at Mont Pinçon, north-east of Vire, the 5th Battalion Wiltshire Regiment was virtually wiped out in less than two days – but when Patton diverted a corps towards Argentan on 12 August the German forces facing the Anglo-Canadians were threatened with encirclement. The so-called 'Falaise Pocket' was not closed until 20 August, although the enemy units within it were effectively destroyed, partly by ground assault but mainly by sustained air attack. Thus, despite the escape of nearly 40,000 German troops, over 60,000

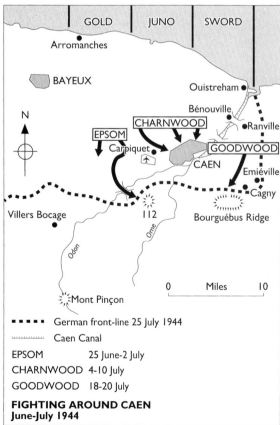

GOLD   JUNO   SWORD

Arromanches

BAYEUX

Ouistreham

Bénouville

N

CHARNWOOD   Ranville

EPSOM

Carpiquet

GOODWOOD

CAEN

Emiéville

Cagny

Villers Bocage   112   Bourguébus Ridge

Odon   Orne

0   Miles   10

Mont Pinçon

■ ■ ■ ■ German front-line 25 July 1944

〷〷〷 Caen Canal

EPSOM   25 June-2 July
CHARNWOOD   4-10 July
GOODWOOD   18-20 July

**FIGHTING AROUND CAEN
June-July 1944**

were captured or killed and almost all their equipment was destroyed. As Allied soldiers crossed the Seine to the north and south of Paris, little stood in their path. It was a crushing victory, in which the British contribution had been vital, but it had been achieved, as at Alamein, by a costly slogging match. Terrain, weather and tough enemy opposition all helped to create an Anglo-Canadian casualty list of 83,000 in Normandy between June and August 1944, but confused command, poor integration and inexperience also played their parts.

Nevertheless, important lessons had been learnt – not least the need for mechanized infantry to accompany the armour – and the subsequent advance of nearly 250 miles in less than two weeks, with British spearheads entering Brussels and Antwerp on 3 and 4 September respectively, was impressive. For once, the British seemed to have discovered the sort of mobility normally associated with the Germans, but it did not last. As the armour swept forward, it moved further and further away from its supply bases in Normandy. Although Montgomery, now a field marshal in charge of just the Anglo-Canadian 21st Army Group (he had transferred overall command of land forces to Eisenhower on the latter's arrival in France on 1 September), was marginally better off than his American counterparts further south, being able to capture a number of small Channel ports, his forward units soon began to run short of fuel and spare parts. In addition, the Germans were falling back towards their own frontier, where more organized defences existed, and the autumn was fast approaching. If the war was to be ended quickly, now was the time for a bold decisive stroke.

Montgomery's plan, codenamed Market Garden, was approved by Eisenhower on 10 September. Two US airborne divisions – the 82nd and 101st – were to drop behind enemy lines on 17 September to seize a number of key bridges in southern Holland, upon which ground units of 21st Army Group would advance to link up. This would create a corridor 60 miles long leading to the town of Arnhem, where the British 1st Airborne Division,

Parachutes and gliders litter the landing zone to the west of Arnhem, 17 September 1944, as more Dakota transport aircraft fly over. The 1st Airborne Division has been committed to its most famous engagement.

ARNHEM

On 17 September 1944 the lead elements of 1st Airborne Division landed by parachute and glider on heathland to the west of the Dutch town of Arnhem. Their task was to seize bridges and a ferry site over the Lower Rhine as the tip of an airborne spearhead stretching over 60 miles back to Allied lines in southern Holland. With US airborne troops securing bridges over intervening waterways and the British XXX Corps driving north to link up, Operation Market Garden would, it was planned, be completed within four days.

However, events were to turn out rather differently. Despite some American success, XXX Corps found it difficult to advance against hardening German opposition, leaving 1st Airborne isolated in Arnhem, where the presence of II SS Panzer Corps made any attacks by lightly armed airborne troops virtually impossible. In addition, a shortage of transport aircraft meant that 1st Airborne was not delivered as a complete division, requiring three separate lifts on succeeding days, while inadequate radios disrupted tactical communications on the ground and led to command confusion. Thus, although elements of Lieutenant-Colonel John Frost's 2nd Parachute Battalion, plus small

groups from other units, secured the main road bridge late on 17 September, they could not be reinforced; after an epic battle lasting four days, the survivors were forced to surrender. By then, the rest of the division, comprising five parachute and three gliderborne infantry battalions, had been pushed into a shrinking perimeter around the Hartenstein Hotel in the suburb of Oosterbeek, to the west of Arnhem. Under sustained pressure, they held on until the night of 25/26 September, when they were withdrawn across the Lower Rhine. The battle cost the division nearly 8000 casualties.

dropped at the same time as the Americans, would be holding bridges across the Lower Rhine. Once to the north of the river, 21st Army Group would attack towards Berlin, finishing the war by Christmas. In the event, despite a ground advance as far as the southern outskirts of Arnhem by 25 September, the British paras were forced to withdraw, having been asked to do too much (*see box*, p. 151). The campaign in North-West Europe ground to a halt, not just in Holland but all along the front line, which now extended from the Channel to the Swiss border. France may have been liberated – an event accelerated by the landing of US, Free French and some British forces in the south on 15 August (Operation Dragoon) – but there was still a lot of fighting to do.

Presented with the ultimate failure of Market Garden, Eisenhower decided to consolidate before advancing all his forces towards the Rhine in unison once the winter was over. Montgomery, convinced that a single thrust towards Berlin could still work if all supplies and most of the US forces were transferred to his command, continued to press his case, but to no avail. Instead, he was ordered to divert the bulk of 21st Army Group to clearing the Scheldt estuary so that Antwerp could be opened as a supply port, an operation that took until late November to complete using Canadian troops and Commandos. In December the Germans mounted a surprise attack against US forces in the Ardennes. Although British units as such were barely involved – Montgomery, given command of the northern sector of the 'bulge' which developed, moved XXX Corps down to guard the River Meuse, but it made little contact with the enemy – this delayed Allied preparations even more. It was not until February 1945 that Eisenhower felt confident enough to order his armies to close to the River Rhine, the last major obstacle in their path.

It had always been intended to concentrate attacks against the Rhine in the north, chiefly because of the proximity of the industrial region of the Ruhr. Thus the onus fell firmly on 21st Army Group. On 8 February a massive artillery barrage heralded Operation Veritable, designed to take the Canadian First Army, with the British XXX Corps under command, down a narrow corridor through the Reichswald to the west bank of the Rhine. At first, progress was reasonably good, but the operation soon degenerated into bitter fighting in rain-soaked forests and heavily defended villages. It did not end until 21 February, by which time the US Ninth Army, under Montgomery's command, had thrust north-east towards Düsseldorf, clearing the way for the assault river crossings. They had been planned for some time, involving all elements of 21st Army Group, although Montgomery was adamant that they should not begin until late March. The capture of an intact bridge across the Rhine further south at Remagen by US troops on 7 March did nothing to divert his attention.

Operation Plunder began at 9 p.m. on 23 March, when Commandos in special amphibious vehicles crossed the Rhine to establish a bridgehead to the west of Wesel. They were the spearhead of a remarkable assault, characterized for once by a complete integration of arms and services. RAF bombers had already pounded the German defences on the east bank and, as the 15th and 51st Scottish Divisions crossed at Xanten further north in

Buffalo amphibians manned by the Royal Tank Regiment, the bombers returned to complete their task. Later that night Royal Engineers constructed a number of bridges, under enemy fire, to allow armour and more infantry across, while the Royal Artillery provided close fire support to the assault troops. At 10 a.m. on the 24th, moreover, men of the British 6th and US 17th Airborne Divisions landed on high ground to the north-east of Wesel, quickly linking up with ground units. Although the fighting was hard, most notably in Rees, where the commander of the 51st (Highland) Division, Major-General Thomas Rennie, was killed, the Germans soon

Buffalo amphibious vehicles of 79th Armoured Division ferry troops across the River Ijssel in Holland, April 1945. Dealing with water obstacles demanded a degree of inter-arm co-operation that took time to perfect.

Field Marshal Montgomery (seated, right) reads the surrender document to Admirals von Friedeburg and Wagner, Lüneburg Heath, 4 May 1945. All German forces facing 21st Army Group were to lay down their arms.

collapsed, allowing Montgomery to concentrate 20 divisions and more than 1000 tanks for what he imagined would be the final thrust towards Berlin.

He was to be disappointed. On 28 March Eisenhower, presented with a series of crossings by US troops further south and aware of the political decisions already made concerning post-war spheres of influence in Europe, ordered 21st Army Group to concentrate on taking out the Ruhr while Bradley's 12th Army Group advanced deep into central Germany. By 1 April the Ruhr had been encircled and, despite British protests at Eisenhower's decision, 21st Army Group moved to clear northern Holland and the North German Plain instead of heading for the capital. By 17 April British units were on the outskirts of Bremen; after fighting to take the port, they moved on towards Hamburg and Lübeck. On 3 May German representatives appeared at Montgomery's Headquarters on Lüneburg Heath to discuss surrender terms. The documents, covering the forces facing 21st Army Group, were signed the next day, with complete surrender following on the 7th. It was the culmination of a remarkable campaign.

THE END IN ITALY

By then, the campaign in Italy had also been brought to a successful conclusion, although not without some difficulty. The winter of 1944–5 was particularly harsh and this, combined with exhaustion after the heavy fighting of the summer and autumn, undermined the effectiveness of Field Marshal Alexander's 15th Army Group. In addition, the Germans were occupying strong positions along the Gothic Line, stretching from Viareggio on the west coast, across the Apennines, to the River Senio in the east, and the Allied campaign in North-West Europe was taking precedence in terms of men and equipment. As early as December 1944, Alexander called off any further offensives until the spring, leaving his soldiers to spend a tough few months patrolling and preparing for the final push.

This began on 9 April 1945, when the British Eighth Army, commanded by Lieutenant-General Sir Richard McCreery, headed north-west across the Rivers Senio and Santerno towards Ferrara and the more open ground of the Po Valley. The Germans had flooded the area to the north of the Santerno, leaving only one dry route from Ravenna to Ferrara – the so-called Argenta Gap. In an attempt to minimize casualties, McCreery ordered Commandos to mount an amphibious assault across Lake Comacchio to tie down enemy reserves, while his main attack headed for Argenta. Despite considerable problems, caused in no small measure by the fact that the flooded areas had turned to mud in the early spring weather, the British managed to take Argenta on 17 April, by which time the US Fifth Army had attacked further west, aiming for Bologna. It was there that the two Allied armies linked up on 21 April, forcing the Germans to pull back across the River Po and, more importantly, to negotiate surrender terms. The relevant documents were signed at Alexander's headquarters on 29 April and the surrender came into effect on 2 May, five days before the main capitulation further north. By then, Eighth Army had liberated Venice and entered Trieste, ending a long and arduous campaign that had been cruelly overshadowed by events elsewhere. The 'D-Day Dodgers' had in fact achieved the virtually impossible – a successful invasion of Italy from the south – and had done so despite continued Anglo-US disagreements about the merits of a Mediterranean strategy. They could be justly proud of their victory.

THE WAR IN BURMA, 1943–5

Nor were they the only British troops to suffer from a combination of appalling terrain and strategic uncertainty, for while the men of Eighth Army were struggling in Italy, their compatriots in Fourteenth Army were slowly turning the tide in Burma. It was not an easy task.

By the beginning of 1943 the remnants of Burcorps, still recovering from the traumas of the recent retreat, were demoralized, ill-led and poorly supplied. Occupying positions in Manipur, eastern India, they were hundreds of mountainous miles from their logistic bases, their losses took time to replace and, for every man wounded in action, up to 120 had to be evacuated because of disease. It was no surprise, therefore, when 14th Indian Division, ordered to attack into Arakan on the north-west coast of Burma in late 1942, failed to make much headway, suffering over 5000 casualties by May 1943 for no territorial gain. The survivors, sick and exhausted, were more convinced than ever that the Japanese were superior jungle fighters.

Defeat in Arakan did have the effect of forcing change, however, and by autumn 1943 the situation had begun to improve. A new South-East Asia Command (SEAC) was formed, with Vice-Admiral Lord Louis Mountbatten in charge. More significantly, the forces in Burma were reorganized into Fourteenth Army under Lieutenant-General William Slim. The Indian Army, from

Personality Profile:

FIELD MARSHAL VISCOUNT SLIM OF BURMA (1891–1970)

'Bill' Slim, arguably the most impressive British general of the Second World War, joined the Army in 1914 as a temporary officer in the 9th Battalion Royal Warwickshire Regiment. By 1918, after service at Gallipoli and in Mesopotamia, he had managed to transfer to the Indian Army, receiving a permanent commission in the 6th Gurkha Rifles. During the inter-war period he attended Staff College at Quetta, served as an instructor at Camberley and, by 1939, was commanding 10th Indian Brigade, which he led in East Africa until wounded. After recovery, he commanded 10th Indian Division in Iraq and Syria before being transferred to Burma in March 1942.

It was in Burma that Slim's reputation was made. Promoted to lieutenant-general, he commanded Burma Corps during the ignominious retreat to India, then took over XV Indian Corps. In October 1943 he was appointed commander of the newly formed Fourteenth Army, which he meticulously prepared for action against the Japanese, concentrating on the morale and well-being of his troops. They repaid him by repulsing enemy attacks in Arakan and at Imphal/Kohima in early 1944, before assuming the offensive. Slim's conduct of the campaign to reconquer Burma, culminating in the liberation of Rangoon in May 1945, was masterful. In 1945 he was appointed C-in-C of Allied Land Forces in South-east Asia; three years later he became Chief of the Imperial General Staff and, in 1953, began a seven-year stint as Governor-General of Australia.

little without improvements to the morale of the 'Forgotten Army'. As Slim soon recognized, his men had to have their confidence restored, not just by pep-talks from their commanding general but, more importantly, by carefully planned operations which would achieve success and destroy the myth of Japanese invincibility. The First Chindit Operation, carried out deep behind enemy lines between February and April 1943 by forces under the command of Brigadier Orde Wingate, helped in this respect, but the losses had been prohibitively high (*see box*, p. 156). Something more elaborate and permanent was needed.

The plan that emerged in early 1944 was for another attack into Arakan, although this time it was properly organized and carried out in conjunction with a Chinese and Chindit operation further north at Myitkyina designed to split Japanese resources. At first, the Arakan advance went well – the lead units of 5th Indian Division took Maungdaw on 8/9 January 1944 – but the Japanese fought back, initially at Razabil and then at Sinzweya, where 7th Indian Division, reinforced by elements of the 5th, was besieged in what was known as the 'Admin Box'. Amid bitter fighting, characterized at one point by the massacre of British wounded by fanatical Japanese troops, the Box held out, resupplied by air in accordance with Slim's new policy of maintaining captured positions. On 24 February the siege was lifted, enabling British and Indian troops to advance as far as Buthidaung by 11

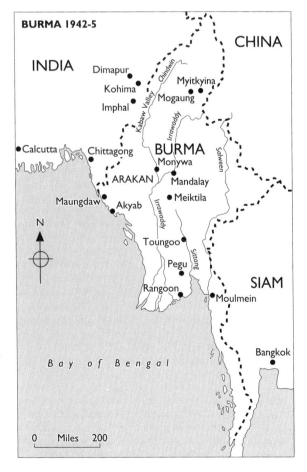

which nearly all reinforcements had to be drawn, was reformed with an emphasis on training for jungle warfare, and the practical problems of the region were addressed. New all-weather roads were constructed to link the supply ports at Chittagong and Calcutta to the forward positions in Manipur, the railway to Dimapur and Ledo was improved, and strict measures were taken, ranging from the issue of mepacrine tablets to the aerial spraying of swamps with DDT, to prevent the spread of diseases such as malaria and dysentery. But this would have counted for

General Sir William Slim as commander of Fourteenth Army, 1945. His campaign to defeat the Japanese in Burma was one of the most impressive fought by a British general in the Second World War.

THE CHINDITS

On 14 February 1943, nearly 3000 men of the 77th Indian Infantry Brigade, commanded by Brigadier Orde Wingate, crossed the River Chindwin in an operation designed to infiltrate Japanese defences and carry out sabotage attacks. Known as the Chindits from their adoption of a badge depicting the Chinthe, a mythical creature that protected Burmese pagodas, the brigade advanced in two groups towards the Irrawaddy, carrying most of their supplies by mule but expecting air-drops at pre-selected points. To begin with, the Chindits were successful, cutting the Mandalay-Myitkyina railway, destroying bridges and laying ambushes, but once Wingate decided to cross the Irrawaddy, the enemy began to close in. On 24 March, the brigade was ordered to return to India; although 2200 men made it back, many were unfit for further service. It seemed an expensive way to wage war.

But the propaganda value of such 'long-range penetration' was substantial, allowing Wingate to persuade his superiors to support a much more ambitious operation in 1944, designed to co-ordinate with a drive by Chinese and American forces towards Myitkyina. Wingate was promoted to major-general in command of 3rd Indian Division, an enhanced formation of 26 infantry battalions, some of which would be airlanded in gliders deep behind Japanese lines to set up 'strongholds'. Operation Thursday, more commonly called the Second Chindit Operation, began on 5 March 1944 with landings at 'Broadway' to the north-east of Indaw, from where attacks were made on the railway

at Mawlu. Other strongholds, known as 'White City', 'Aberdeen' and 'Blackpool', were subsequently established and, on 26 June, after a month of heavy fighting, the town of Mogaung was captured, enabling

Chinese troops to break out into the Hukawng Valley. By then, however, Wingate was dead and Chindit casualties were mounting. The survivors were flown back to India in early August.

March. By then, however, the emphasis had shifted firmly back to eastern India, where a major Japanese assault against Slim's main positions on the Imphal Plain had begun on 7/8 March. It was to prove a turning-point in the Burma campaign.

Operation *U-go*, the Japanese assault on eastern India, was dependent for success upon the capture of British supplies, particularly at Imphal, and on the severing of links between Slim's forward troops and their bases in Assam. Lieutenant-General Renya Mutaguchi, commanding the Japanese Fifteenth Army, crossed the River Chindwin with nearly 100,000 men on the night of 7/8 March to mount a three-pronged attack designed to take Imphal and, further north, to cut the rail link to Dimapur at Kohima. The 17th and 20th Indian Divisions fought hard to prevent the advance on Imphal, delaying the enemy and allowing Slim the time to air-lift reinforcements from Arakan. Even so, Imphal was cut off from its support bases on 5 April and had to depend on air resupply, organized as a deliberate policy by Slim in an attempt to block the Japanese advance while reserves were brought forward from India. They concentrated

Chindits conduct a river crossing on their move towards Mogaung, northern Burma, 1944. The Chindits did much to boost the morale of Fourteenth Army.

around the railhead at Dimapur, although their first priority turned out to be Kohima, which was besieged from 7 April. The fighting in Kohima was particularly fierce (*see box*), even after elements of the 2nd Infantry Division had relieved the garrison on 18 April. It took until 3 June for the siege to be lifted completely, by which time the situation at Imphal had also improved. Running desperately short of supplies, the Japanese began to pull back towards the Chindwin, having lost an estimated 65,000 men.

An opportunity now arose for a British advance, pursuing the enemy into Burma, but this was not as easy as it sounds. Monsoon weather had turned many of the jungle tracks to mud, British casualties had not been light (over 17,500 dead, wounded and missing since 8 March) and supplies had run down, requiring a substantial logistic effort across country devastated by the recent fighting before any of the forces could begin to move. Thus, although some British and Indian units harried the retreating Japanese in the Kabaw Valley, it was not until 19 November 1944 that Slim felt confident enough to approach the Chindwin. By 4 December he had three bridgeheads across the river, allowing him to send 19th Indian Division east towards Indaw (where they linked up with Chinese troops advancing south from Myitkyina) and other units south-east to Schwebo and the River Irrawaddy close to Mandalay.

The Irrawaddy was a major obstacle that the Japanese were sure to defend. Slim's response was to plan and carry out one of the most impressive operations of the Burma Campaign. He secretly shifted the emphasis of his attack further south towards Meiktila, threatening it with encirclement, but deceived the enemy into believing that Mandalay was the objective. In January and early February 1945, crossings to the north of Mandalay were heavily opposed, confirming Slim's analysis that the enemy was concentrated in that area; on 13 February his IV Corps crossed the Irrawaddy at Pakokku, nearly 100 miles downstream, against only light opposition. Spear-headed by 17th Indian Division, IV Corps rushed forward across the dusty central Burma plain to capture Meiktila on 3 March and, although the Japanese reacted by rushing reinforcements to the town, this merely weak-

THE SIEGE OF KOHIMA

When the Japanese arrived at Kohima on 5 April 1944, cutting it off from Dimapur to the north and Imphal to the south, it was defended by little more than a single British unit, the 4th Battalion Royal West Kent Regiment. For 15 days of savage hand-to-hand fighting, the garrison held out until relieved in epic fashion by the 1st Battalion Royal Berkshire Regiment, breaking through from Dimapur.

But the battle was by no means over. As the Royal Berks, joined by the rest of 6th Indian Brigade and, later, by 33rd Indian Brigade, held off renewed Japanese attacks in Kohima itself, other elements of 2nd Infantry Division advanced from north and south in a pincer movement designed to cut the enemy off. This involved fighting over extremely difficult terrain, made worse when, on 27 April, the monsoon broke, covering the area in sheeting rain and glutinous mud. Even so, some progress was made, gradually squeezing the Japanese into an area

around the Deputy Commissioner's bungalow and its tennis court, occupied by the enemy since 9 April. The fighting here was severe in the extreme, with British troops pinned down by withering fire from deeply constructed bunkers which could not be taken out using small arms alone. In the end, on 13 May, a single Lee-Grant tank was man-handled into position on the tennis court, forcing the Japanese to withdraw. By 3 June, the survivors were in full retreat.

ened their ability to defend further north. Mandalay fell on 21 March; eight days later the Japanese abandoned their positions around Meiktila and started to withdraw towards Rangoon. They had lost the most important battle of the campaign.

With the monsoon only about a month away and supply problems mounting, Slim now took an enormous gamble, ordering XXXIII Corps to continue down the Irrawaddy towards Prome while IV Corps advanced along the River Sittang further east, aiming for Rangoon. Progress was good, but IV Corps was soon overstretched, operating within a narrow strip nearly 300 miles long. On 2 May, therefore, 50th Indian Parachute Brigade was flown from Arakan, captured earlier in the year by XV Corps, to seize Elephant Point to the south of Rangoon, followed closely by 26th Indian Division, transported by sea. The Burmese capital fell on 3 May, solving Slim's supply problems at a stroke and rendering the Japanese positions in southern Burma untenable. It was to take until August for the last pockets of Japanese defenders along the southern Sittang to be rooted out, often in bitterly fought platoon actions, but the priority by then had moved to planning an invasion of Malaya (Operation Zipper). When the Japanese surrendered to the Allies on 2 September 1945, this proved to be unnecessary.

SUMMARY

The British Army could thus look back on almost exactly six years of total war, fought in just about every type of weather and terrain. For much of that time, it had been struggling to recover from the neglect and parsimony of the inter-war period – a common strand in its history –

and there was no doubt that mistakes had been made, even quite late in the conflict. Leadership had been poor, supplies of weapons and equipment inadequate and tactical expertise low, especially in the area of inter-arm co-operation on the battlefield. Indeed, it could be argued that, without the manpower and industrial capability of the United States to fall back on, the British war effort would probably have petered out sometime in 1943, with no chance of mounting campaigns in North-West Europe, let alone in the Mediterranean and Far East as well.

But this would be to ignore the very real lessons of the war. As time went on, the British Army did recover, training its citizen-soldiers to standards high enough to take on and defeat their enemies in open battle. Slim's victory in Burma, although perhaps peripheral to the Americans' campaign in the Pacific, did show what could be achieved, especially when the problems of morale, leadership and supply were addressed. Similarly, in both Italy and North-West Europe, the Army's contribution to overall victory was undeniable and its ability to absorb the lessons of its earlier defeats impressive. By 1945 it had regained its high record of professionalism and was capable of conducting sophisticated all-arms battles against even the most fanatical of its enemies. In the process, however, it had suffered 144,079 fatal casualties and was stretched to the limits. Although by June 1945 the Army could field 19 infantry and five armoured divisions, plus 40 independent brigades – a total of 2,920,000 men and women – it was nearing the end of its resources. By 1945 Britain was exhausted and virtually bankrupt, incapable of maintaining its commitment to three major campaigns. Like so many times before, the country had to face the prospect of peace in the knowledge that it had to give priority to economic recovery, sacrificing the main instrument of its victory – its large and painfully created Army – on the altar of financial savings. A familiar pattern looked set to re-emerge.

. . . .

CHAPTER SEVEN

THE MODERN ARMY
(1945–present)

·····························

THE AFTERMATH OF WAR

1945 marked a watershed in the history of the British Army. Gone were the days when the end of a European or global conflict could be greeted with a sigh of relief, heralding a swift return to 'peacetime soldiering' in the colonies, for the events of the previous six years had left Britain with increased commitments that could not be ignored. The Second World War was a 'total' war, fought for the complete destruction of the enemy. Once that was achieved, the victorious armies could not walk away from the countries they occupied; they had to stay for as long as it took to restore democratic government, public services and local administration. At the end of previous wars, the role of European commitment had usually been dropped or significantly downgraded, leaving a much reduced Army to cope with home defence and colonial policing only; in 1945 that option was just not available. British troops were needed in Germany, northern Italy and Austria if those areas were to stand any chance of returning to normality, committing the Army to European duty for at least the next few years.

But this did not mean that the other, more traditional duties declined in importance. In the Far East, colonies had to be reoccupied and pre-war trading patterns re-established. In the Middle East, bases had to be maintained if communication routes to India were to be kept open, while in India itself troops were needed to deal with growing unrest, fuelled by religious fervour and a desire for independence. Elsewhere, in the Caribbean, North and East Africa and the Mediterranean, forces were required to defend colonies, protectorates and captured territory. The Army in 1945 was being asked to do more than it had ever done before in a period of peace.

All this happened against a backcloth of chronic economic weakness, exacerbated by massive war debts. The newly elected Labour government of Clement Attlee, dedicated to recovery based on radical social reform, needed to find new resources, implying reductions to the size and cost of the armed forces. In addition, the government was aware of the demand from wartime conscripts for a swift demobilization. Indeed, by April 1947 the Army had been reduced from its wartime strength of 2,920,000 to 873,700, but this merely put increased pressure on the men who remained. It was a problem that was to become familiar as the peacetime period progressed – an ever-present gap between commitments and capabilities – but it was particularly acute in the years immediately after the Second World War. It was resolved in part by the government's recognition that, in a world now dominated by the United States and Soviet Union, Britain could not face all potential threats alone: as early as March 1948 the Brussels Treaty was signed with France and the Benelux countries, committing Britain for the first time in a period of peace to a military pact that demanded the permanent presence of troops in Europe.

That alone could not square the circle. The obvious answer was to maintain a large, relatively inexpensive Army, and that could only be achieved by a continuance of conscription. In May 1947 the first National Service Act came into force, introducing the unprecedented concept of compulsory military duty during peacetime. Initially, all 18-year-old males were to serve for 12 months, but this was amended in 1948 to extend the term to 18 months, followed by four years in the reserves. In 1950 a further amendment increased the period of full-time duty to two years, reducing that in the reserves to three and a half years. That was to remain the norm until 1960, when the last batch of National Servicemen were called up. By then, 1,132,872 had passed through the Army, giving it an annual intake of about 160,000 recruits; when they were added to the Regulars, who continued to serve, it produced an Army that could field up to 450,000 personnel at any one time. Their value was a matter of some controversy (see box, p. 160). To many Regulars, the National Servicemen were a nuisance, absorbing training time and scarce resources which should have been used to restore professionalism to the Army and re-equip it with more modern weapons; to many National Servicemen, the two years in the armed forces were a waste of time. But the fact remains that, without the conscripts, the Army would have been unable to cope with the demands placed

Rival Views:
NATIONAL SERVICE

'My service gave me self-confidence, taught me comradeship, understanding of my fellow men, discipline and an appreciation of my home and parents. I returned to Caernarvon a very responsible adult. I had come across quite a few hoodlums from the bigger cities, but the Army soon knocked them into shape and they left their National Service far better citizens than when they entered it.'

Lance-Corporal Griffith Roberts, Royal Corps of Signals

Quoted in Trevor Royle, *The Best Years Of Their Lives. The National Service Experience 1945–63*, Michael Joseph Ltd, 1986

'After four years at an art school I suddenly found myself in an establishment that was half adult boarding school, half lunatic asylum. The masters were the officers, the prefects were the NCOs and the rules were rampant and completely arbitrary.

'You had to polish the barrack-room bucket, knowing it would get dirty and have to be polished again the next day. You had to remove all the lettering from the lid of your boot polish tin and make it mirror-shine for inspections. (So you bought two tins: one for use, one for show). You had to fold your sheets and blankets every morning in certain ritualised ways. You had to greet other men with special salutes that involved twisting your neck, your wrist, your dignity. You had to move by numbers: turn, two, three, breathe in, pause, two, three, breathe out. You had to stop thinking "why" and do it. You had to unlearn being an individual and become a number and put that number on all your clothes and on your soul, if told to . . .'

Sergeant Mel Calman, Royal Army Educational Corps

From B.S. Johnson (ed), *All Bull: The National Servicemen*, Quartet Books Ltd, 1973

upon it in the late 1940s and 1950s. Even then, it was stretched almost to breaking point.

PROBLEMS OF EMPIRE

The first indication of overstretch occurred before National Service was officially introduced, at a time when Britain was still effectively on a war footing. As soon as the Japanese surrendered in August 1945, a political vacuum was created in South-East Asia as a number of occupied European colonies were left without proper government. British troops from Burma quickly moved in to reclaim Malaya, Singapore and Hong Kong, but neither the French nor the Dutch had forces immediately available to do the same in their colonial territories. Lord Mountbatten, as C-in-C South-East Asia, committed British units to both Indochina and the Dutch East Indies, ostensibly to disarm and repatriate the Japanese but in reality to prepare the way for colonial reassertion. It proved to be a tricky task.

Lead elements of Major-General Douglas Gracey's 20th Indian Division landed in Saigon on 8 September 1945, under orders to round up the Japanese in southern Indochina and await the arrival of French troops from Europe. The region was in chaos, for as soon as the Japanese announced their surrender in August, local nationalists tried to seize power, aiming to present the French with a *fait accompli* they would have to accept. In the north, Ho Chi Minh's Viet Minh, with American help, declared the independence of the Republic of Vietnam, but because the situation in the south was less clear-cut, Gracey faced a breakdown of accepted law and order and, on occasions, active resistance to the British presence. He responded firmly, issuing directives to prohibit demonstrations and the carrying of weapons, but until the rest of his division arrived in early October he had to restrict his activities to the area around Saigon and even rearm Japanese marines to bolster his forces. Although French units began to take over from the British in November, the last members of Gracey's division did not leave until February 1946, having been drawn into some bitter fighting. Altogether, 40 British and Indian soldiers were killed and over 100 injured in a campaign that seemed to bear little relevance to Britain's strategic needs.

The same was true in the Dutch East Indies. British forces landed at Batavia (Jakarta) on 29 September 1945, expecting a relatively straightforward restoration of Dutch authority, but they had reckoned without the growth of Indonesian nationalism under the Japanese. An Indonesian government was already in place, with control over most of Java, backed by military units intent on opposing any European return. In Batavia itself, law and order was imposed fairly quickly and British patrols sent inland, where many of them spent a frustrating year coping with bands of Indonesian guerrillas. Elsewhere, at Semarang on the north coast and Surabaya at the north-eastern tip of Java, the fighting was more conventional, but it took until January 1946 for the areas to be secured. By then, the British had been forced to commit a corps of three divisions and an armoured brigade, plus air and naval units, under the command of Lieutenant-General Sir Philip Christison, and had even moved into Sumatra. The

Dutch could not relieve them of their responsibilities until the autumn of 1946; by then the British casualty list was 60 dead and over 2000 injured.

Such experiences were not without advantage from a purely military point of view, for they prepared the Army for duties that were to become familiar throughout the British Empire. These began to manifest themselves in India in 1946, where the campaign for independence, simmering throughout the war years, gained fresh momentum, bringing to the fore inter-communal violence between Hindus and Muslims. In August 1946, six British battalions had to be deployed in Calcutta, taking five days (and nights) to restore order among rampaging mobs, and the violence spread rapidly to Bombay, Delhi and the Punjab. In June 1947 it was agreed that India should become two states – mainly-Hindu India and mainly-Muslim Pakistan – and on 18 July independence was confirmed for 15 August in a last-ditch attempt to curb the troubles. As soon as this was announced, British units were withdrawn to barracks and responsibility for law and order handed over to troops from the sub-continent, who dealt with the transition to independence amid continued fighting. On 26 February 1948 the 2nd Battalion Black Watch became the last British unit to leave Pakistan; two days later the 1st Battalion Somerset Light Infantry embarked on troopships at Bombay to end some two centuries of British military involvement in the region.

It was an emotional moment, but it implied something much more profound in terms of British policy. India was the hub of the Empire and its loss undermined an imperial trading system that had ensured Britain's wealth since the 19th century; indeed, it could be argued that many of Britain's colonies elsewhere in the world had been seized in order to protect trade routes to and from India or to cover the approaches to the sub-continent itself. Once India had been removed, the system inevitably fell apart, denying Britain the means to generate wealth at a time of chronic economic weakness and raising an obvious query about the value of maintaining the rest of the Empire, significant parts of which regarded Indian independence as a precedent. In addition, the loss of the Indian Army effectively halved Britain's military capability, leaving British regiments to carry out duties in the Far East and Arabia that had normally been the responsibility of their Indian counterparts. Bearing in mind the need to retain forces in Europe, now would have seemed a logical time for a major reassessment of British commitments elsewhere, based on a gradual withdrawal from the remains of Empire. Events in the Middle East and in Europe in the late 1940s suggested that this might be happening.

WITHDRAWAL FROM PALESTINE

The British presence in Palestine, guarding the eastern approaches to the Suez Canal, had been opposed by the indigenous Arab population in the 1930s (*see box*, p. 123), but by 1945 it was the Jews who were intent on forcing a British withdrawal. This was in response to British policies of restricting the flow of refugees from Europe and of opposing demands for the creation of a Jewish state. Trouble had begun as early as November 1944, when the British Minister Resident in the Middle East, Lord Moyne, was assassinated by Jewish gunmen in Cairo; by late 1945 it had escalated to large-scale riots in Jerusalem and Tel Aviv that necessitated the deployment of British troops in support of the civil police. They were drawn from the 1st Infantry and 6th Airborne Divisions, fresh from more conventional fighting in Italy and North-West Europe respectively, and they found their new duties frustrating, especially when faced with more violent actions by well-organized, ruthless groups such as the Irgun and Stern Gang. Tactics perfected in the 1930s were put into effect, with curfews imposed and key locations constantly guarded, but the Jewish groups proved more resilient than their Arab predecessors and, crucially, enjoyed a large measure of support from the Jewish population. Unable to gather accurate intelligence about their enemy, the British operated in a vacuum, reacting to events rather than controlling them.

On 22 July 1946, Irgun fighters blew up a wing of the King David Hotel in Jerusalem, killing more than 90 civilians and British military personnel. In response, the British mounted a major cordon-and-search operation that netted nearly 700 suspects, but this was a rare event and did not produce the breakthrough required. Instead, recognizing the intractable nature of the Palestine problem and the impossibility of committing large numbers of British troops to the area indefinitely, Britain gave notice to the United Nations that it intended to surrender the mandate given to it by the League of Nations in 1920, setting 15 May 1948 as the date of final withdrawal. The UN answer was to vote for a partition of Palestine into Arab and Jewish enclaves. This took some of the pressure off the British troops, joined in late 1947 by the 3rd Infantry Division, although their duties now shifted to keeping Arab and Jew apart in the run-up to partition. The last British unit left Palestine on schedule in May 1948, but the campaign could hardly be termed a victory. To many outsiders, it looked as if the British were dismantling their Empire, regarding the protection of the Suez Canal as less vital now that India had been granted independence. Even so, the campaign in Palestine had cost 338 British lives.

THE THREAT OF COMMUNISM

Meanwhile, in Europe a new threat had emerged. As early as 1945, British troops had clashed with Yugoslav partisans over the future status of the Adriatic port of Trieste, and this acted as a symbol of the growing menace of Communism. At the same time, British units were stationed in Greece to support the existing government in its fight against Communist guerrillas (a commitment handed over to the Americans in 1947), but it was in Germany that the threat caused most concern. It helped to trigger the Brussels Treaty in 1948, which tied Britain firmly to the defence of Western Europe through a military

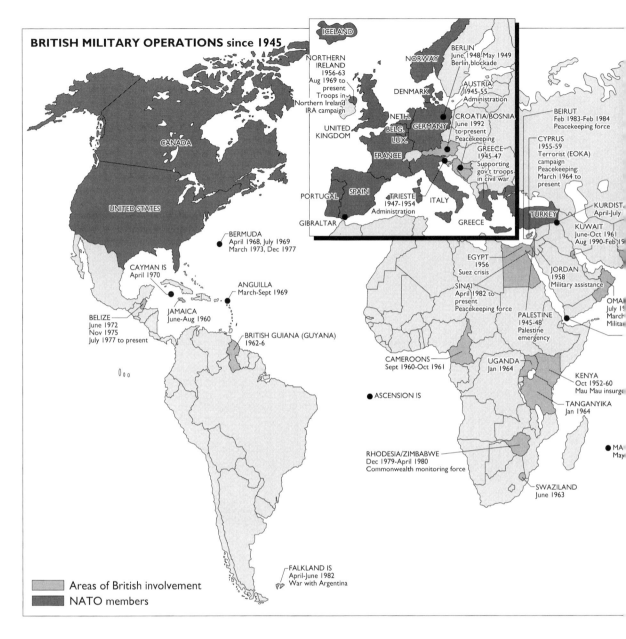

BRITISH MILITARY OPERATIONS since 1945

NORTHERN IRELAND 1956-63 Aug 1969 to present Troops in Northern Ireland IRA campaign

ICELAND

NORWAY

DENMARK

BERLIN June 1948-May 1949 Berlin blockade

AUSTRIA 1945-55 Administration

UNITED KINGDOM

NETH.
BELG.
LUX.
FRANCE

GERMANY

CROATIA/BOSNIA June 1992 to present Peacekeeping

BEIRUT Feb 1983-Feb 1984 Peacekeeping force

GREECE 1945-47 Supporting gov't troops in civil war

CYPRUS 1955-59 Terrorist (EOKA) campaign Peacekeeping: March 1964 to present

PORTUGAL

SPAIN

TRIESTE 1947-1954 Administration

ITALY

GREECE

KURDIST April-July

GIBRALTAR

TURKEY

KUWAIT June-Oct 1961 Aug 1990-Feb 19

CANADA

UNITED STATES

BERMUDA April 1968, July 1969 March 1973, Dec 1977

CAYMAN IS April 1970

ANGUILLA March-Sept 1969

BELIZE June 1972 Nov 1975 July 1977 to present

JAMAICA June-Aug 1960

BRITISH GUIANA (GUYANA) 1962-6

EGYPT 1956 Suez crisis

SINAI April 1982 to present Peacekeeping force

JORDAN 1958 Military assistance

OMA July 19 March Militar

PALESTINE 1945-48 Palestine emergency

CAMEROONS Sept 1960-Oct 1961

UGANDA Jan 1964

ASCENSION IS

KENYA Oct 1952-60 Mau Mau insurge

TANGANYIKA Jan 1964

MA May

RHODESIA/ZIMBABWE Dec 1979-April 1980 Commonwealth monitoring force

SWAZILAND June 1963

FALKLAND IS April-June 1982 War with Argentina

Areas of British involvement

NATO members

organization known as Uniforce, commanded by Field Marshal Lord Montgomery. The British contribution comprised the two divisions of British Army of the Rhine (BAOR) – 7th Armoured and 2nd Infantry – and it was from them that the forces needed to help deal with the Berlin Blockade of 1948-9 were drawn. Although that particular crisis was dealt with primarily by Allied air forces, Royal Engineers were used to build airstrips and men of the Royal Army Service Corps loaded and unloaded the supplies so desperately needed by the beleaguered citizens of Berlin.

Soviet actions in severing all road and rail links between the Western zones of Germany and Berlin led directly to the creation of the North Atlantic Treaty Organization (NATO) on 4 April 1949. Western powers, including the United States, were by now so alarmed by

perceived Soviet intentions that collective defence seemed the only answer, and although it would take time for a military structure to emerge – Uniforce was replaced by Supreme Headquarters Allied Powers in Europe (SHAPE) in September 1951 – the founder members of NATO were committed to providing some sort of response to Soviet aggression. In the case of Britain, this meant BAOR and a permanent presence in Germany, further reducing the opportunity to cut out European commitment as a response to military overstretch. Indeed, in 1954, when the French grew alarmed at the prospect of a rearmed West Germany, Britain did even more, promising to station four divisions and a tactical air force on the continent for as long as her allies deemed it necessary. That was to turn out to be a period of 36 years.

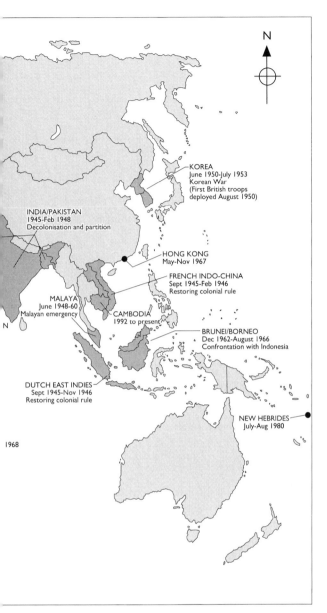

KOREA
June 1950-July 1953
Korean War
(First British troops
deployed August 1950)

INDIA/PAKISTAN
1945-Feb 1948
Decolonisation and partition

HONG KONG
May-Nov 1967

FRENCH INDO-CHINA
Sept 1945-Feb 1946
Restoring colonial rule

MALAYA
June 1948-60
Malayan emergency

CAMBODIA
1992 to present

BRUNEI/BORNEO
Dec 1962-August 1966
Confrontation with Indonesia

DUTCH EAST INDIES
Sept 1945-Nov 1946
Restoring colonial rule

NEW HEBRIDES
July-Aug 1980

1968

a move, was not slow to deploy its own contribution. On 28 August the 1st Battalion Middlesex Regiment and 1st Battalion Argyll and Sutherland Highlanders landed at Pusan, on the south-eastern tip of the peninsula, at a time when the Americans and South Koreans were under considerable pressure. Instead of being given an opportunity to acclimatize, the British troops were sent into battle on the River Naktong without delay.

A few weeks later, after MacArthur had outflanked the North Koreans at Inchon, the Allied forces broke out of the Pusan perimeter and, with the British on the left flank, advanced northwards against a tenacious but overstretched enemy. The fighting was by no means easy – in one particular incident, on Hill 282, the Argylls suffered 86 casualties, including their second-in-command, Major Kenny Muir, who was awarded a posthumous Victoria Cross for a bravely led counter-attack – but by the end of September the situation had stabilized enough to allow the British battalions to be pulled back for regrouping. Joined by the 3rd Battalion Royal Australian Regiment, they formed the 27th Commonwealth Brigade, and took part in the pursuit of the enemy into North Korea itself. By 30 October, they had captured Chongchen, close to the border with China, while US Marines further east,

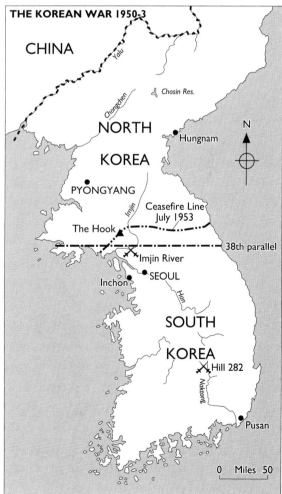

THE KOREAN WAR 1950-3

CHINA

Yalu

Chosin Res.

NORTH

Hungnam

KOREA

PYONGYANG

Imjin

Ceasefire Line
July 1953

The Hook

38th parallel

Imjin River

SEOUL

Inchon

Han

SOUTH

KOREA

Hill 282

Naktong

Pusan

0   Miles   50

WAR IN KOREA

But the response to Communism did not involve treaties alone, for in 1950 a much more overt threat to Western interests emerged in Korea. On 25 June North Korean forces, backed by the Soviets and the newly-Communist Chinese, crossed the 38th parallel into South Korea, a country under the patronage of the United States. As the invaders advanced rapidly southwards, US forces under General Douglas MacArthur were rushed to the region as part of a United Nations' response. Britain, as a permanent member of the UN Security Council that authorized such

THE BATTLE OF IMJIN RIVER

On 22 April 1951 combat patrols of the British 29th Brigade, probing the scrub-covered hills along the River Imjin in Korea, reported signs of an enemy build-up to the north. The brigade was deployed with three infantry battalions forward, occupying positions to protect the main road to Seoul. On the left was the 1st Battalion Gloucestershire Regiment, deployed around a dominant feature known as Castle Hill; in the centre was the 1st Battalion Royal Northumberland Fusiliers, astride the main road; on the right was a Belgian battalion, attached to the brigade, which was the only one stationed to the north of the river. In reserve were the 8th (King's Royal Irish) Hussars and the 1st Battalion Royal Ulster Rifles, with the 45th Field Regiment and 170 Mortar Battery Royal Artillery in support.

It soon became apparent that the Glosters were going to bear the brunt of the Chinese attack. Late on the 22nd a fighting patrol repulsed four separate enemy attempts to cross the Imjin before running out of ammunition and withdrawing to Castle Hill. This allowed the Chinese to cross the river in 'human waves' that threatened to overwhelm the Glosters; extremely heavy fighting went on until dawn on the 23rd.

By then, A Company had been badly hit and forced to relinquish Castle Hill – during counter-attacks later that morning, Lieutenant Philip Curtis was killed while destroying machine-gun nests with grenades – and the battle had extended into the areas occupied by the Northumberlands and Belgians, who were forced to give ground, leaving the Glosters isolated. Artillery and air strikes failed to stop the Chinese and by the end of the 23rd the Glosters' commanding officer, Lieutenant-Colonel James Carne, concentrated the remains of his battalion into a small perimeter around Hill 235 ('Gloster Hill') to the south-west of the original positions. Casualties had been so heavy that 'B' and 'C' Companies together amounted to no more than a platoon. The battalion, under constant pressure, held on until the morning of 25 April, when Carne, aware that relief columns had failed to break through, ordered the survivors to escape as best they could; most of them were killed or captured, although 39 officers and men of D Company did make it back to UN lines. In recognition of the bravery displayed, both Carne and Curtis were awarded Victoria Crosses and the battalion as a whole was honoured with a US Distinguished Unit Citation, denoted by a small blue retangle worn on the right sleeve.

with No. 41 Independent Commando Royal Marines under command, were moving towards the Chosin reservoir. The war seemed as good as over.

It was at this point that the Communist Chinese, concerned for the safety of their southern border, intervened with over 200,000 'volunteers', who attacked the Allied spearheads in 'human waves' with little regard for casualties. Men of the 27th Commonwealth Brigade held their ground on the River Chongchen, but when the Chinese infiltrated an entire army into the gap between them and the US Marines, retreat became inevitable. It did not stop until Allied forces reached Seoul, the capital of South Korea, just before Christmas, and was conducted in the depths of winter across rugged terrain. Meanwhile, in the east, US Marines had to fight through to Hungnam before being evacuated by sea, an operation in which No. 41 Commando acted as rearguard under constant attack. Their dogged courage acted as an inspiration to the Americans, many of whom were close to panic.

The Communists renewed their attack on New Year's Eve, pushing the Allies even further south. By then, 27th Commonwealth Brigade had been joined by the British 29th Brigade, comprising the 1st Battalions of the Royal Northumberland Fusiliers, Gloucestershire Regiment and Royal Ulster Rifles, with tanks of the 8th (King's Royal Irish) Hussars and guns of the 45th Field Regiment Royal Artillery in support. Together, the two brigades acted as rearguard, fighting off Chinese infiltrators along snow-covered roads until they reached the River Han, where a defensive line was established. An immediate counter-attack was ordered, backed by enormous artillery and air strikes, but it took more intimate infantry fighting to dislodge the enemy from a series of hill features, many of which fell to British units. By 8 March, the Chinese had suffered enough, enabling Seoul to be liberated, but this time there was no pursuit; as the winter weather cleared, the Allies dug in close to the 38th parallel.

This marked the end of the mobile phase of the Korean War, but the fighting continued in a series of set-piece operations as both sides tried to gain the advantage of terrain. In early spring 1951, the Allies advanced a few miles northwards to give them a deeper buffer in front of Seoul, and it was this move that placed 29th Brigade along a line from Choksong to the junction of the Rivers Imjin and Hanton. On 22 April the Chinese attacked, aiming to break through towards the South Korean capital, but were stopped by the 'Glorious Glosters' in an epic battle that virtually wiped out the battalion (*see box*). Five months later, by which time British units were part of a Commonwealth Division, Allied forces probed forward along the Imjin to set up new defensive positions. These were attacked by the Communists in November 1951, when the 1st Battalions of the King's Shropshire Light Infantry and King's Own Scottish Borderers were heavily engaged. The former suffered over 100 casualties amid hard fighting; the latter held off an attack by a Chinese force estimated to number more than 6000 men. But for the majority of British troops, the war was now one of stalemate in atrocious winter conditions, made worse by apparent progress in so-called 'peace talks' that invariably turned out to be meaningless.

Fresh British units were deployed on a rotational basis. Their experiences throughout 1952 and early 1953 consisted of defending hill features and conducting constant patrols. It was a costly process and one that put the pressure firmly on junior commanders; it was also one that was misunderstood at home, where public support for the war declined as progress was measured in yards rather than miles. But this did not mean that battles were things of the past. On 7/8 May 1953, for example, the 1st Battalions of the King's Regiment and the Duke of Wellington's Regiment came under sustained artillery and infantry attack on a ridge overlooking the Imjin, known as 'The Hook'. After a night of extremely heavy combat, the two battalions counted over 1000 enemy dead on the battlefield, having suffered 150 casualties themselves. The survivors were understandably bitter when their achievement received little press coverage, being overtaken by news of a breakthrough in the peace talks.

An armistice came into force on 25 July 1953, nearly three years after the first deployment of British troops. By then, a total of three armoured regiments and 16 infantry battalions, with full supporting arms, had served or were serving in Korea, reinforcing Britain's commitment to the UN but doing nothing to ease the problem of overstretch. It was one more commitment to add to the growing list, this time at a cost to the Army of 681 dead and nearly 2400 wounded. But the experience of conventional warfare, albeit in difficult terrain that put the onus on infantry fighting, was worthwhile, if only to emphasize the continuing flexibility and expertise of British forces. They were characteristics that were already being tested to the full elsewhere.

Royal Artillery gunners rest after a night spent firing their 25-pounder field gun in support of infantry in the hills of Korea, May 1951. The litter of shell-cases indicates the ferocity of battle.

First-Hand Account:

THE KOREAN WAR

'. . . as dark fell, I passed through the front trench of the front platoon, out of the last machine-gun post, and down through the gap in the wire to the track across the minefield that led to no-man's-land. From the front platoon three men were detailed off to show us the way through the wire and the mines. We were half-way through the minefield, down the slope where our own people could no longer see us, when the Chinese caught us.

'. . . As I led my patrol into the ambush their first flight of grenades cracked my right shin and slashed my scalp. Then they fired, the short groaning bursts of what we knew as burp guns, from ten yards off. My own first grenade went off between two of them, and they went over . . . I was on my knees, holding a second grenade in my right hand ready for throwing [when] I saw a man in a British steel helmet – one of my escorting party – aim and fire his Sten gun point blank at my chest. My left arm seemed caught in a hurricane of wind, a gust fluttered the arm away from my body, the man firing fell back, another man in a strange cap fell forward by me. My escort had shot a Chinese soldier who was standing behind me about to fire at my head . . .'

Lieutenant Nicholas Harman, 1st Battalion Royal Fusiliers, November 1952

From B.S. Johnson (ed), *All Bull: The National Servicemen,* Quartet Books Ltd, 1973

COUNTER-INSURGENCY CAMPAIGNING

The threat posed by Communism took many forms. Confrontation in Europe and open conventional war in Korea were two of them, but at the same time small groups of insurgents, intent on gaining political power in a state by a process of subversion, propaganda and military pressure, were also active, particularly in colonial areas where the desire for independence provided immediate appeal. In the late 1940s, the French faced this sort of campaign in Indochina, where the Viet Minh followed the teachings of the Chinese revolutionary Mao Zedong (Mao Tse-tung), who gained power himself in Beijing (Peking) by such means in October 1949. By then, the British had

experienced the beginnings of a similar campaign in Malaya, necessitating the commitment of quite considerable armed forces and the adoption of distinctive counter-insurgency (COIN) techniques.

A state of emergency was declared in Malaya in June 1948, after months of political and industrial unrest had culminated in the murder of British planters. At first, intelligence about the insurgents was poor – the Malayan Police were weak and the civil administration was still in the process of re-establishing itself in the aftermath of Japanese rule – but it quickly became obvious that the Malayan Communist Party (MCP), led by Chin Peng, was responsible for the trouble. The MCP had gained a degree of popular support, particularly among the Malay-Chinese, for its co-ordination of resistance during the Japanese occupation, and when its plans for a seizure of power in 1945 were thwarted by the British return, Chin Peng had ensured that its wartime organization (and its weapons dumps) remained. Using rural 'squatter camps' occupied by the Malay-Chinese as bases, his guerrillas, members of what became the Malayan Races' Liberation Army (MRLA), exploited their local knowledge to mount attacks on police stations, tin mines and rubber plantations before melting back into the jungle and mountain terrain that made up four-fifths of the country.

To begin with, the British reaction was one of emergency legislation, allowing the security forces to detain suspects without trial, impose curfews and curtail movement. When the Emergency began, the military garrison consisted of three British, six Gurkha and two Malay battalions, and they were quickly reinforced, initially by an extra battalion from Hong Kong and then, in October, by the whole of 2nd Guards Brigade from Britain. Their main job was to set up positions close to villages in the rural areas, from which patrols could be sent out to dominate the surrounding region. This worked well enough, but it was a frustrating business against guerrillas with intimate local knowledge, and military efforts were not always co-ordinated closely with police actions elsewhere. Thus, although Chin Peng was forced to split his units into smaller, less vulnerable groups, the level of violence did not really decline. The problem was being contained, but it was not being solved.

The key to success lay in co-ordinating the efforts of civil, political and military authorities so that everyone was working towards a common goal of defeating the insurgents in all aspects of their campaign. This was not immediately recognized, but a move in the right direction was made in 1950 when Lieutenant-General (retired) Sir Harold Briggs was appointed Director of Operations and ordered 'to plan, co-ordinate and direct the anti-bandit operations of the police and fighting forces'. Within days of his arrival in Malaya he came up with a plan based on four main aims – 'to dominate the populated areas and to build up a feeling of complete security, which would in time result in a steady and increasing flow of information coming from all sources; to break up the Communist organizations within the populated areas; to isolate the insurgents from their food and supply organizations in the populated areas; and to destroy the insurgents by forcing them to attack the security forces on the latter's own ground'.

To achieve these aims, Briggs persuaded the High

Personality Profile:
FIELD MARSHAL SIR GERALD TEMPLER (1898–1979)

Of Anglo-Irish stock, Gerald Templer was commissioned from Sandhurst into the Royal Irish Fusiliers in 1916, and saw service on the Western Front (1917–18). Although he attended Staff College at Camberley (1928–30), his peace-time promotion was slow; by 1939 he was still only a lieutenant-colonel. During the Second World War, however, his talents were recognized, and by September 1942, when he took over II Corps, he was the youngest lieutenant-general in the Army. Stepping down to major-general so that he could gain experience in the field, he commanded the 1st Infantry Division in Italy (1943–4) before being badly injured. Not fit enough for active command again during the war years, he became Director of Civil Affairs and Military Government in 21st Army Group (1945–6). In 1946 he was appointed Vice Chief of the Imperial General Staff, then Officer Commanding Eastern Command in UK. It was this background that made him such an ideal choice when he was appointed both High Commissioner and Director of Operations in Malaya (1952–4); this dual command, resolutely carried out by Templer, proved to be the turning point in the Malayan Emergency. Templer served as Chief of the Imperial General Staff (1955–9), taking the Army through a difficult period of change. In retirement he helped to found the National Army Museum.

But the Briggs Plan could not be expected to have an immediate impact. The policies took time to perfect and were not always supported by civil and military authorities more used to independence of action. This allowed the insurgents to continue their campaign, achieving dramatic success on 6 October 1951 when they assassinated Gurney in a roadside ambush. By then, Briggs had given notice that he wished to retire because of ill-health, allowing the British government in London to ensure the success of his policies by appointing one man to be both High Commissioner and Director of Operations. That man was General Sir Gerald Templer, a serving officer who arrived to take up his controversial post in January 1952. He had the authority to ensure that Briggs' ideas were fully implemented, insisting from the start that there was no distinction between the conduct of the Emergency and normal government. He also held out the promise of eventual independence once the insurgents had been defeated, and placed emphasis on what he termed 'the hearts and minds of the Malayan people'. By the time that he left Malaya in late 1954, a number of basic 'principles' of a COIN strategy had been imposed: a co-ordinated command structure had been set up; intelligence gathering had been reorganized and made more effective; and the idea of splitting the insurgent from his supporters, chiefly by offering the latter a vested interest in preserving the *status quo*, had been established.

The Army had roles to play in all aspects of this strategy. Military commanders were integral members of the co-ordination committees at every level, ensuring that any intelligence gained by Army patrols was fed into the system, and units were tasked with the delicate problem of supervising the movement of squatters into the New Villages – something that had to be done with tact and good humour if the ordinary people were not to be alienated by government actions. At the same time, of course, the policy of manning bases and mounting patrols was continued, both to protect vulnerable areas and to maintain the pressure on the guerrilla gangs. In the process, the Army gained invaluable local knowledge and experience of operating in jungle areas, training its men, a proportion of whom were conscripts, to a high level of effectiveness. Between May 1949 and February 1953, for example, the 1st Battalion Suffolk Regiment, operating chiefly in the forests of Selangor, accounted for 198 insurgents at a cost of 12 men killed and 24 wounded. This was achieved not only by endless patrolling (it was estimated that one 'kill' took 1800 hours of military operations), but also by expertise in the tedious and often frustrating business of ambush. The enemy was always capable of hitting back – in January 1952, the 1st Battalion Gordon Highlanders lost seven men to a Communist ambush – but as Templer's policies began to have an effect, this became less frequent. The key now was to pursue the isolated guerrillas into their jungle hideouts and root them out, thereby removing the threat once and for all.

This was effectively what happened between Templer's departure in 1954 and the end of the Emergency six years later. During that time, with a police force of 40,000 men (many of them recruited from the now defunct Palestine Police) and an Army strength, on average, of 24 battalions, backed by specialized units that

Commissioner, Sir Henry Gurney, to set up at federal, state and district levels a series of committees containing representatives of all civil and military agencies involved in the campaign, and used this structure to ensure the creation of joint Army–Police operations rooms. At the same time, the Police and Special Branch were reorganized with the specific duty of gathering intelligence that allowed the Army, with Police help, to move into the areas most affected by the insurgency. Finally, in an effort to split the active insurgents from their supporters among the people, the Malay-Chinese squatters were moved from their camps to purpose-built 'New Villages', where clean water, proper housing, education and medical care were on offer. By the end of 1951 over 400,000 squatters had been resettled in this way, accepting the advantages offered by the government in preference to the vague promises of a better life which came from the Communists. Indeed, many were so keen on their new way of life that they were prepared to form local Home Guard units to protect the villages.

THE SPECIAL AIR SERVICE

Formed in November 1941 by David Stirling, the Special Air Service (SAS) was one of a number of raiding groups used to good effect by the British in the Western Desert, Italy and North-West Europe during the Second World War. Disbanded once the war was over, the spirit of the SAS lived on in a Territorial Army unit, 21st SAS Regiment (Artists' Rifles) created in July 1947, comprising a number of men who had served under Stirling. In 1950, Lieutenant-Colonel 'Mad Mike' Calvert formed the Malayan Scouts for jungle operations in the Emergency, recruiting volunteers from Hong Kong (A Squadron), reservists from 21SAS (B Squadron) and men from Rhodesia (C Squadron); in 1952, with D Squadron and an HQ Squadron added, they became 22nd SAS Regiment (22SAS).

The regiment, less its Rhodesian contingent, has seen almost continuous service since that time, spe-cializing in counter-insurgency and counter-terrorism but also reasserting its wartime role of behind-the-lines reconnaissance and raiding. Its work in Malaya, operating deep in the guerrilla-controlled jungles, was a vital part of the military offensive against the Communists, and also included 'hearts and minds' work among the aborigines (*see* p. 167). Withdrawn from Malaya in 1958, two squadrons of 22SAS helped to put down a revolt in Oman by scaling a rugged mountain known as the Jebel Akhdar; in Borneo in the 1960s the regiment refined its techniques by operating among the tribesmen along the border, again concentrating on hearts and minds and intelligence gathering. Operations in Dhofar (1970–5), where 22SAS provided training teams and propaganda experts, and in Northern Ireland later in the decade, were not widely reported, but in May 1980 the regi-ment came firmly into the public eye when men of the Counter-Revolutionary Warfare (CRW) team stormed the Iranian Embassy in Princes Gate in London (*see box*, p. 182).

Two years later, it was SAS reconnaissance teams that provided the Task Force with much-needed information about Argentinian positions on the Falklands and in Argentina itself, even finding time to mount raids on enemy airfields in the best traditions of the regiment. Involvement in counter-terrorism has remained a priority, as the SAS shooting of three Provisional IRA members in Gibraltar in March 1988 showed, but 22SAS was used again for behind-the-lines work in the Gulf War in 1991. A small unit, recruited from among the rest of the Army rather than direct from civilian life, 22SAS is regarded by many as the most professional elite force in the world.

Field Marshal Sir John Harding (left) and General Sir Gerald Templer (right), September 1955, at the time of Harding's appointment as Governor of Cyprus. He was replaced as Chief of the Imperial General Staff by Templer.

Camels pass an SAS mortar pit at Mirbat, in the western Omani province of Dhofar, scene of the battle on 19 July 1972 in which an eight-man SAS team defeated nearly 200 rebels.

included a re-raised Special Air Service Regiment (*see box*, p. 168), it became increasingly possible to concentrate resources into selected areas, clearing them of guerrillas before moving on to neighbouring locations. Once an area had been cleared in this way, it was designated a 'White Area' and restrictions imposed on the local population were lifted, giving them an incentive to oppose any future infiltration by the insurgents. This coincided with political reforms and active preparations for independence, granted in August 1957. By 1960, over 1300 policemen and 500 soldiers had been killed in what was one of the longest campaigns in Army history, but there was no doubt that the insurgent threat had been turned back. It was a major achievement and one in which the Army had played an integral part.

While the Malayan Emergency was being fought to a successful conclusion, two other colonial campaigns were taking place, demanding further commitment of Army units. The first to materialize was in Kenya, where dissident members of the Kikuyu tribe, known as Mau Mau, expressed their dissatisfaction over land rights and continued British colonial rule by means of violent disorder. A state of emergency was declared by the Governor in October 1952 after the murder of a Kikuyu chieftain loyal to Britain, but as in Malaya four years earlier, it took time to organize an effective response to the insurgents. The Kenyan Police were numerically weak, and although reports had been available for some time suggesting a growth of tribal unrest, including the creation of groups bound together by oaths and ritualistic murder, these had not been co-ordinated or followed up. The military garrison (part of Middle East Command) comprised just three battalions of King's African Rifles, ill-prepared for operations.

The techniques that evolved to deal with the Mau Mau were a mixture of traditional colonial policing and modern COIN. No attempt was made to combine civil and military responsibilities on the Templer pattern – Kenya was thought to be too small to merit such a move – but the military command structure was reorganized to ensure a concentration of effort. An independent head-quarters was created in Kenya and, in June 1953, General Sir George Erskine was appointed C-in-C, with 'full powers of command over all Colonial, Auxiliary, Police and Security Forces', subordinate to the civil authority of the Governor. At the same time, the garrison was reinforced by three more battalions of King's African Rifles and three battalions of British infantry. Initially, they were distrib-uted in 'penny packets' on purely defensive operations, reflecting the paucity of good intelligence. Erskine's first and most important task was to create a much more efficient military-police intelligence organization, allow-ing the insurgents to be identified and then destroyed. Simultaneously, the civil authorities had to address the grievances of those Kikuyu who supported the Mau Mau, undermining the insurgents and contributing to their isolation.

It soon became obvious that the Mau Mau were a minority in the Kikuyu tribe, which was itself only one of a number of tribes in Kenya. Moreover, Mau Mau organization was crude, with no real command structure, and many of its 'supporters' were in fact intimidated rather than committed to any cause. This meant that

First-Hand Account:

THE MALAYAN EMERGENCY

'. . . I saw in front of me, some 20 yards ahead, the clear shape of a hut roof. A moment later we heard the clink of a metallic object . . . We moved ahead, slithering under and crawling round broken palm fronds and dead wood and vegetation, fearful of making the slightest noise. As we advanced the outline of the hut became clearer. I could see two men sitting inside . . . A little closer and I discerned, just below the hut, a third man crouched on his haunches, fully dressed and nursing a Mark V rifle. He was positioned to look back along the track towards the clearing and was, obviously, the sentry.

'. . . We crept further forward till we were within about 30 feet of the hut. Still they had not sensed our presence. Slowly I raised myself to my feet, put my carbine to my shoulder and took aim at the sentry. I opened fire and the others instantly followed. There was a deafening roar as the jungle echoed back the firing of our weapons. Two of the guerrillas slumped down lifeless immediately but the sentry, my target, was thrown forward by the impact of the shots and started to crawl into the undergrowth. We lunged forward to make sure there were no others and my leading scout crashed into the undergrowth and returned to report that the sentry was also dead . . .'

Lieutenant 'Arthur Hayward' MC, 1st Battalion Suffolk Regiment, 1950

From *War in Peace Partwork*, Issue No. 10, Orbis Publishing, 1983

substantial numbers of Kikuyu, once offered government protection and agrarian reform, were prepared to contrib-ute to the campaign, forming a local Home Guard which, as in Malaya, freed security forces for more offensive operations. These began in April 1954 with a cordon-and-search of Nairobi (Operation Anvil), which destroyed the Mau Mau structure in the capital and drove a wedge between the rural gangs and their urban-based support-ers. Over 16,000 Mau Mau suspects were rounded up and the information they provided allowed military units to move out of Nairobi to concentrate their efforts against gangs around Mount Kenya and the Aberdares. These were designated 'Prohibited Areas' and within them the security forces were under no real constraint. With the help of 'counter-gangs' of surrendered Mau Mau, who agreed to fight their erstwhile colleagues in exchange for their own freedom, British units conducted patrols, sweeps and ambushes to root out the remaining insurgents. The job was virtually complete by 1956, but the Emergency remained in force for another four years as the last of the diehard Mau Mau were hunted down. By 1960, it was estimated that nearly 12,000 insurgents had been killed at a cost to the security forces of just over 600 dead. The pattern of response may not have been exactly the same as in Malaya, but the results were similar.

The third of the COIN campaigns in the 1950s took place in the colony of Cyprus, where the majority Greek-Cypriot population demanded *Enosis*, or union with Greece, once the British had withdrawn. As they had no intention of pulling out – in 1954 the British government announced that, because of its strategic position in the eastern Mediterranean, Cyprus could not expect to be granted independence – the Greek-Cypriots recruited a right-wing, Cypriot-born colonel of the Greek Army, George Grivas, to lead a guerrilla campaign. He formed EOKA (the National Organization of Cypriot Fighters) which, although small – it consisted of no more than 300 activists – enjoyed virtually unlimited support from the Greek-Cypriot population. In 1955 EOKA organized riots and civil disturbances, aiming to wear the British down; when these developed into guerrilla and terrorist attacks, the Governor declared a state of emergency on 26 November 1955.

The Governor involved was in fact a serving soldier, Field Marshal Sir John Harding. He had been appointed as both Governor and Director of Operations in September 1955 in a conscious effort to duplicate the success enjoyed by Templer in Malaya. It did not work in Cyprus, for although Harding immediately set up a joint command and control structure involving the civil, military and police authorities, geared specifically to the gathering and collation of intelligence, the intense commitment of the Greek-Cypriots to *Enosis* created a barrier that was never breached. Information about Grivas and his guerrilla groups was virtually impossible to gain, particularly when EOKA deliberately targeted Greek-Cypriot members of the police force, intimidating them into inaction. This left the British dependent on Turkish-Cypriot policemen, but they were drawn from no more than 18 per cent of the population and were bitterly resented by the rest. Any military operations were therefore mounted 'blind', with predictable results. In June 1956, for example, a major cordon-and-search of the Troodos Mountains (Operation Pepperpot) failed to round up more than a handful of EOKA activists. By then, 14 British battalions were involved, organized into the 50th, 51st, 16th Parachute and 3rd Commando Brigades – a total of nearly 17,000 men – but in the absence of reliable information, there was little they could do. Grivas, realizing his advantage, shifted part of his campaign to the urban areas, hitting British servicemen and their families in an effort to terrorize. A withdrawal of British units to take part in the invasion of Port Said in October–November 1956 (*see below*) did nothing to ease the pressure.

Harding retired in November 1957, making way for a civilian Governor, Sir Hugh Foot, who was under orders from London to find a diplomatic solution to the crisis, using military force as a last resort. By 1959, the Greek-Cypriots had been persuaded to accept a compromise: Cyprus would become an independent state, with the British retaining 'Sovereign Base Areas' on the island. Neither side could be said to have 'won', but the campaign did show the limitations of British COIN policies, and emphasized the overriding need for accurate intelligence if insurgents were to be defeated. The Cyprus Emergency cost the British Army over 100 dead.

THE SUEZ CRISIS

As if simultaneous commitments to Malaya, Kenya and Cyprus were not enough, in 1956 the Army was also involved in a conventional operation in Egypt. The crisis had been building for some time. As early as March 1947 British troops had been withdrawn from Cairo and Alexandria into the Canal Zone, but this merely triggered armed opposition from Egyptians intent on forcing the British out altogether. Between October 1951 and January 1952, British units lost 40 men dead in clashes with paramilitary police auxiliaries known as the Bulak Nizam. Although the operation was a military success, it helped to polarize Egyptian opinion, leading in part to the overthrow of King Farouk in July 1952. The new Egyptian government, led initially by Major-General Mohammed Neguib and then, from April 1954, by Colonel Gamal Abdul Nasser, was vociferously anti-British, mounting a political campaign which forced the British to accept that bases in Egypt were no longer viable. On 19 October 1954 an agreement was signed whereby the Canal Zone was to be evacuated within 20 months and left under civilian control with rather vague promises about its use in future crises. The last British unit, the 2nd Battalion Grenadier Guards, was pulled out on 24 March 1956.

Within weeks, the Army was being prepared for a return to Egypt, this time as part of an Anglo-French expeditionary force designed to take control of the Suez Canal. On 26 July 1956 Nasser announced the nationalization of the Suez Canal Company, a joint British and French commercial concern that gained its profit from tolls paid by ships using the waterway. He needed the money to help finance the Aswan Dam irrigation project, which neither the Americans nor the Europeans had been prepared to back once it had become known that the Egyptians had negotiated an arms deal with Czechoslovakia. On 27 July Britain began to prepare a military force, accepting the offer of two French divisions from Algeria three days later. On 2 August a Royal Proclamation called up 20,000 reservists. It was intended to create an expeditionary force of 80,000 men (50,000 of whom would be British), 100 warships and 300 aircraft, all under the command of General Sir Charles Keightley, with Lieutenant-General Sir Hugh Stockwell as Land Force Commander, that would invade Egypt and reassert Anglo-French rights over the Canal.

The planning did not go smoothly. Britain's strategic reserve – 16th Parachute and 3rd Commando Brigades – was already committed to Cyprus and had to be withdrawn for regrouping and retraining; landing craft had to be taken out of mothballs and the techniques of amphibious warfare relearnt; and when it was decided in September to add armour to the invasion force, the Centurions of 1st and 6th Royal Tank Regiment had to be

transported to their embarkation ports in southern England by the removals firm Pickfords because of a shortage of Army tank transporters. In addition, co-operation with the French proved less than easy, leading to revisions to the plan that served to delay the preparations. Eventually, after it had been decided to restrict operations to an attack on Port Said, preparatory to a drive straight down the Canal towards Port Suez, the French insisted on Israeli involvement in Sinai to divert Egyptian attention and give the Allies an excuse to invade under the auspices of the UN. Once the Israeli attack began, the British and French, acting as permanent members of the Security Council,

would call for a ceasefire and a withdrawal of all forces away from the Canal to protect its status as an international waterway. The Egyptians would be highly unlikely to comply, allowing the attack on Port Said to begin.

From a purely military perspective, Operation Musketeer (Revised) worked remarkably well. The Israelis invaded Sinai on 29 October 1956, upon which the ultimatum was delivered. When Nasser refused to comply, Allied air attacks neutralized his air force and opened the way to a parachute assault on the outskirts of Port Said. At 5.15 a.m. on 5 November the 3rd Battalion Parachute Regiment landed on Gamil airfield, securing it despite

A Centurion of 6RTR imposes the British presence in Port Said, November 1956. The invasion of Egypt was a military success but a political nightmare, proving that the days of independent imperial policing were over.

A Centurion of 6RTR imposes the British presence in Port Said, November 1956. The invasion of Egypt was a military success but a political nightmare, proving that the days of independent imperial policing were over.

A ceasefire came into effect at midnight on 6/7 November, by which time the British had suffered 22 dead and 97 wounded. But this did not mean that the objectives had been achieved. Despite military success, the whole affair had been brought to a premature end by American pressure on Britain to cease operations because of the danger of escalation to superpower confrontation. It was a humiliating lesson in the realities of post-1945 international politics, making it apparent that Britain would have to accept that it was no longer in the same league as the USA and USSR and that its involvement in large parts of the world would have to be subject to the support of the Americans. At the same time, it was obvious from the problems experienced in 1956 over the creation of an expeditionary force that the British Army, despite conscription, was chronically overstretched. The fact that a significant number of reservists had reacted to their call-up by scrawling 'Bollocks!' over the papers acted as proof of just how unpopular National Service had become. It was clearly time for change.

THE SANDYS WHITE PAPER

This came on 4 April 1957 when the Conservative Minister of Defence, Duncan Sandys, introduced a White Paper entitled *Defence: Outline of Future Policy*. Its central feature was the decision to phase out National Service by 1962, thereby reducing the size of the armed forces as a whole from 690,000 to 375,000 personnel. The Army, having always taken more conscripts than the other two services, would suffer the most: its strength would decline from 373,000 in 1957 to 165,000 five years later, triggering a number of organizational changes. For a start, the Territorial Army, no longer receiving National Servicemen satisfying their reserve commitment, would be cut from 300,000 to 123,000 men, but the real impact was felt, as always, by the Regulars. The Sandys White Paper set in train substantial reductions to the number of regiments: the Royal Armoured Corps lost seven by means of amalgamation (*see Appendix*), the Royal Artillery lost 20 and the Royal Engineers lost four. The infantry was completely reorganized into 14 brigades; all of these – except the Fusilier, Light Infantry and Green Jackets Brigades – were to be regionally constituted and all were to comprise three or four battalions only. This meant a reduction overall from 77 battalions to 60, achieved by a series of amalgamations (*see Appendix*). In 1959, the Army was allowed to increase its projected numbers to 180,000, but this did not affect the planned changes, many of which were by then already being carried out.

Sandys could only afford to cut the armed forces in this way by recognizing that commitments had also to be reduced. He attempted to do so by substituting technology for manpower, placing more emphasis on nuclear

some Egyptian opposition, while French paratroopers took Port Fuad to the east. At 4.30 a.m. on the 6th, the seaborne invasion began, with Nos 40 and 42 Commando Royal Marines, backed by 14 Centurions of C Squadron 6RTR, coming ashore by landing craft; just over an hour later they were joined by No. 45 Commando RM, which deployed into battle by helicopter – the first time such a tactic had been used. By the end of the day, the 2nd Battalion Parachute Regiment and another squadron of tanks had also been landed, and British forces were moving rapidly down the Canal. There was little Egyptian opposition.

weapons in the defence of Europe and reducing the size of colonial garrisons, especially east of Suez, on the assumption that in the event of a crisis they could be reinforced quickly by air. This allowed the size of BAOR to be cut to 55,000 men in 1959, but elsewhere the policy had its dangers. The White Paper came at a time of substantial commitment, not just to the defence of remaining overseas possessions but also to active operations in Malaya, Kenya and Cyprus. In addition, it assumed that enough men (and women) would be willing to join the Regular Army, the attraction of which had been undermined by the years of National Service. Some advantages could be gained – part of the money hitherto spent on training conscripts could be diverted to introducing new equipment such as the Chieftain tank and Self-Loading Rifle (SLR), and the reintroduction of volunteer service offered an opportunity to restore high levels of professionalism – but the fact remains that by 1962, when the last of the National Servicemen should have left the Army, 9200 of them had to be kept on for an extra six months to cover a shortfall in Regular recruitment.

The Army was kept busy during this time of transition, for although the campaigns in Malaya, Kenya and Cyprus were all officially over by 1960, the period between the Sandys White Paper and the end of National Service was one of diverse commitments. In July 1957 a troop of the 15th/19th King's Hussars and a company of the Cameronians were sent to Oman, in the south-eastern corner of the Arabian peninsula, to help the Sultan against rebellious tribesmen. The operation did not end until January 1959, when two squadrons of the 22nd Special Air Service Regiment (22SAS) assaulted the main rebel stronghold on the Jebel Akhdar. Meanwhile, in July 1958 16th Parachute Brigade was flown into Amman, the capital of Jordan, to protect King Hussein, remaining there until October. A similar operation was mounted in June 1961, when No. 42 Commando RM and the whole of 24th Infantry Brigade were deployed to the newly independent state of Kuwait in an effort to deter an Iraqi attack. They remained until October, having achieved their aim. Elsewhere, British troops were sent to Jamaica to put down Rastafarian unrest (June–August 1960) and to the Trust Territory of The Cameroons to supervise a referendum on the future of the constitution (September 1960–October 1961). To top it all, the garrison in Northern Ireland faced a renewed campaign by the Irish Republican Army (IRA) that lasted from 1956 until 1963.

BRUNEI AND BORNEO

None of these commitments involved heavy fighting, which was probably just as well given the organizational changes to the Army then taking place, but the lull did not last. Despite British claims that they would gradually withdraw from residual imperial responsibilities – claims reinforced by Prime Minister Harold Macmillan's 'Wind of Change' speech in 1960, which recognized the inevitability of colonial self-determination – there was a necessity to ensure that political stability was retained. This was especially true in South-East Asia, where the remaining colonies of Singapore, Sarawak, Brunei and North Borneo (Sabah) were close to independence. The Prime Minister of Malaya wanted to incorporate these areas into a Malaysian Federation, a proposal supported by Britain and the majority of the indigenous population. At the same time, however, the President of Indonesia, Ahmed Sukarno, saw them as integral parts of a greater Indonesia, and was prepared to do all he could to thwart the Malayan plan.

The first sign of trouble occurred on 8 December 1962, when pro-Sukarno rebels in Brunei tried to capture the Sultan. Initially, they enjoyed some success, seizing control of key towns and holding a number of Europeans hostage. But the Sultan was not taken, and he immediately called on the British for aid. Their response was remarkably swift; by the evening of 8 December two companies of the 1st Battalion 2nd Goorkha Rifles had been airlifted into Brunei from Singapore, and when they were joined over the next few days by other units, the revolt was easily put down. By 20 December, over 40 rebels had been killed and nearly 2000 captured for a loss of only seven members of the Security Forces. Mopping-up operations took until May 1963.

By then, the crisis over the future of British Borneo had escalated, for Sukarno had decided to take more direct action. Faced with the imminence of the creation of the Malaysian Federation (it came into effect on 16 September 1963), he authorized cross-border incursions by local 'volunteers' in April, hoping that this would be enough to intimidate the population. The British response was to commit five battalions of British and Gurkha troops, under the command of Major-General Walter Walker, to defend the border areas. It was an immense undertaking, for the border extended for nearly 1000 miles over mountainous, jungle-covered terrain and was peopled by tribes that had little understanding of the politics involved. Walker therefore treated the problem as one of counter-insurgency rather than conventional warfare, introducing techniques he had learnt in Malaya during the Emergency. These included a unified command structure, an emphasis on intelligence gathering and collation and, most importantly, a policy of 'hearts and minds' designed to persuade local tribesmen to support the British. Policemen and soldiers, the latter drawn chiefly from 22SAS, supervised medical and agricultural projects, building up a rapport with the people that paid dividends in terms of information. Once that was received, helicopters were used to ensure a swift military response from bases set up along the jungle frontier. By late 1963, the Indonesian 'volunteers' were no longer a threat.

Sukarno responded by committing Indonesian regular troops to the conflict, transforming it into a *Konfrontasi* ('Confrontation') which necessitated the deployment of additional British forces. When Walker handed over to his successor in March 1965, there were 13 battalions of infantry available, backed by artillery, engineers and helicopters, plus the equivalent of a battalion of SAS and over 1500 locally recruited Border Scouts. Included in the total were troops from Malaysia, Australia and New Zealand. Together, they manned forward bases on the border and even mounted clandestine cross-border 'Claret' operations into Indonesian Borneo to pre-empt any

attack. By late 1965, the Indonesians had lost control of the frontier region, and although Sukarno tried to maintain the pressure by sending forces to attack Singapore, it was obvious that his strategy had failed. In March 1966 he was overthrown by General Suharto, who began to explore the possibility of peace with Malaysia. A treaty was signed on 11 August 1966, by which time Britain and her allies had suffered less than 100 dead. It was the first campaign fought by the new all-volunteer Army and was an impressive achievement, based on flexibility and professionalism rather than brute force. It was an approach that was to become familiar.

A Wessex helicopter of the Royal Navy picks up a British patrol from an extemporized landing-pad deep in the Borneo jungle, 1965. Without helicopters, operations in such hostile terrain would have been impossible.

RADFAN AND ADEN

But the Army could not rest on its laurels. While the Borneo Confrontation was taking place, another crisis arose, this time in the Federation of South Arabia, recently created from the colony of Aden and the plethora of small sheikdoms and sultanates formerly known as Aden Protectorates. The British plan was to prepare the Federation for independence in 1968, although it had been made clear that naval and military facilities would be retained in Aden itself. This alienated Arab nationalists who, backed by President Nasser of Egypt, called for the ejection of the British, by force if necessary. In June 1963 a National Liberation Front (NLF) was formed in neighbouring Yemen – a country taken over by pro-Nasser republicans in late 1962 – dedicated to saving South Arabia from the evils of colonialism.

The NLF campaign began on 10 December 1963, when a grenade was thrown at Federation ministers at Aden airport. A state of emergency was declared immediately, although for nearly a year thereafter the violence shifted away from the urban centre to the rural hinterland of Radfan, a mountainous area close to the border with Yemen. By late 1963 the local Quteibi tribesmen, resentful of Federation interference, were preventing lawful movement and firing on government positions, forcing the

CHAMPION LINES AND CRATER

On 20 June 1967, elements of the South Arabian Army and South Arabian Police, demoralized by the imminence of British withdrawal from Aden, mutinied in camps known as Lake Lines and Champion Lines. Eight British soldiers, belonging to 60 Squadron Royal Corps of Transport, were killed when their truck was fired on by the mutineers. Although order was restored relatively quickly – C Company, 1st Battalion King's Own Royal Border Regiment, supported by a troop of the Queen's Dragoon Guards, retook Champion Lines, while the mutiny in Lake Lines soon petered out – the sound of firing led to strong rumours that members of the British Army had systematically slaughtered their former comrades-in-arms.

The trouble spread to the Crater district, where a patrol from 'Y' Company of the 1st Battalion Royal Northumberland Fusiliers came under fire from a police barracks. The patrol withdrew, but a breakdown in communications led the company commander, Major John Moncur, to enter Crater with another patrol to investigate. He had with him Major David Malcolm and two men of the 1st Battalion Argyll and Sutherland Highlanders, who were due to relieve the Northumberlands in a few days' time. Moncur's patrol was caught in an ambush and virtually wiped out – only one wounded Fusilier survived as a prisoner of the rebels. The original 'Y' Company patrol returned to look for Moncur, but was never seen alive again. To make matters worse, a Sioux helicopter had also been shot down, injuring all occupants. By nightfall, the Army had been forced to pull out of Crater, leaving it in the hands of a jubilant mob, who proceeded to mutilate the bodies of the British dead and to engage in internecine warfare. Over the next few days, forces were stationed around Crater to contain the trouble, but political orders prevented any offensive action, much to the anger of many of the soldiers involved. It was not until 3 July that the garrison commander, Major-General Philip Tower, authorized the retaking of Crater by the Argylls, a process quickly completed that night.

PEACEKEEPING IN CYPRUS

The agreement that led to the independence of Cyprus in 1960 lasted just over three years. By December 1963 relations between the majority Greek-Cypriot and minority Turkish-Cypriot population had deteriorated to the point of armed clashes, particularly in the capital Nicosia; forces from Britain, Greece and Turkey (guarantors of the original agreement) were moved in to keep the peace. A 'Green Line' was established to keep the two factions apart, and the problem was referred to the United Nations.

In March 1964 it was agreed to commit the United Nations Force in Cyprus (UNFICYP) to replace existing peacekeepers. Contingents were drawn from Austria, Canada, Denmark, Finland, Ireland, Sweden and – surprisingly, given recent events – Britain, which contributed an infantry battalion, an armoured car squadron, a helicopter flight and support services from the Sovereign Base Areas. They were probably included because of their intimate local knowledge. UNFICYP's task was to monitor the boundaries between Greek and Turkish populations, patrolling to impose a presence and, if trouble occurred, mediating to defuse the situation. The troops were only allowed to fire their weapons in self-defence, making it a duty which required great patience and control. All the time, political moves were being made behind the scenes to try to find a lasting solution to the problem.

These seemed to be making progress until, in July 1974, Greek-Cypriot extremists, backed by the military junta in Athens, staged a coup in Nicosia, overthrowing Archbishop Makarios and demanding immediate *Enosis* (union with Greece). This triggered a Turkish invasion which quickly overran 40 per cent of the island: the UN forces could do nothing to prevent it but did use their weapons to protect the international airport in the capital. Since then, as Cyprus has become in effect two separate states, the UN role has changed to one of policing the border between them. Fewer troops are needed, and after 1974 the British contingent was reduced. It comprised, in 1993, about 800 personnel drawn from units in the Sovereign Base Areas.

Federal Regular Army (FRA) to act. In January 1964 three FRA battalions, with British air support, moved into Radfan and reimposed order. Their success was short-lived, for as soon as they withdrew the trouble began again, with the added concern of increased infiltration by NLF guerrillas from Yemen. On 29 April, therefore, a second punitive expedition was mounted, this time including No. 45 Commando RM, most of the 3rd Battalion Parachute Regiment, the 1st Battalion of the East Anglian Brigade and elements of 22SAS. Together with two FRA battalions, they advanced swiftly over extremely difficult terrain, assaulting a series of hill features and dominating the tribal areas. By 26 May they had captured the main rebel stronghold in the Wadi Dhubsan, after which dissident activity died down, allowing the British troops to be pulled out.

This was just as well, for less than six months later terrorist activity began again in Aden Town, where

THE DHOFAR WAR, 1970–5

By July 1970 Dhofar, the western province of Oman in the Arabian peninsula, was almost entirely in the hands of Communist-backed rebels belonging to the Popular Front for the Liberation of the Occupied Arabian Gulf (PFLOAG). The Sultan of Oman, Said bin Taimur, had failed to recognize the danger and had done little to gain support from among the indigenous people of Dhofar. The province, dominated by a range of mountains known as the Jebel, was ideal guerrilla country in which the Sultan's Armed Forces (SAF), led by British officers on contract or seconded from British units, found it difficult to operate. On 23 July the Sultan's son, Qaboos bin Said, seized power in a palace coup in an effort to save his inheritance.

He immediately introduced policies that owed much to British methods of counter-insurgency (COIN). New government agencies were set up and a 'Development Plan' announced, designed to modernize Oman and persuade the ordi-

nary people that the Sultan was worth supporting. The SAF was expanded and given the specific task of 'preparing Dhofar for civil development' by defeating PFLOAG, and elements of 22SAS were sent from Britain to gather intelligence. The latter proved to be the key, for once it became apparent that the Communists were opposed to Islam and the tribal system, it was possible to portray the Sultan as the natural protector of both, gaining popular support and isolating the active insurgents on the Jebel. In addition, the SAS trained and led groups of surrendered rebels, known as *firqat*, which proved particularly useful because of their knowledge of terrain, while the SAF, aided by their British officers and backed by artillery, aircraft and helicopters, gradually gained the initiative.

The aim was to project forces permanently onto the Jebel to protect Civil Action Teams (CATs) that would provide wells, schools and medical facilities to tempt the people to settle in government-control-

led locations. SAF units and *firqat* began their offensive in late 1971 on the eastern Jebel, as far as possible from PFLOAG supply sources in the People's Democratic Republic of Yemen (PDRY), setting up a CAT and patrolling into the surrounding countryside. Opposition was occasionally strong – on 19 July 1972 an eight-man SAS Training Team under Captain Mike Kealy won an epic battle at Mirbat against nearly 200 PFLOAG fighters – but by 1973 the eastern zone had been effectively cleared. Moving west, the SAF (with British and Jordanian engineer support) constructed a series of 'lines', designed to interdict rebel supplies and divide the Jebel into controllable areas that would then be patrolled. In late 1975, a final offensive cleared the region up to the PDRY border, allowing the Sultan to begin long-term modernization. The fact that there have been no major incidents since that time implies that it was a successful COIN campaign, based on well-tried British techniques.

members of the NLF, using the Sheikh Othman, Maalla and Crater areas as safe bases, targeted British servicemen and their families. At first, the attacks had little impact – in 1964 and 1965, only eight British servicemen were killed – and the Army was able to contain the problem using well-tried techniques such as cordon-and-search operations and patrolling, but the situation worsened significantly after February 1966. In that month the British government announced that, contrary to previous policy, no military or naval presence would be maintained after independence. Not only did this give an immediate boost to the rebels, but what little information about their activities that had been available dried up as people who had been pro-Federation saw the writing clearly on the wall. The rebels became more active, hoping to gain power in the aftermath of an inevitable British withdrawal, and the Army was caught in the middle of an internecine struggle between the NLF and its rival, the Front for the Liberation of Occupied South Yemen (FLOSY). Casualties rose as British units tried to maintain law and order; in 1967 44 British servicemen were killed, half of them in a series of incidents on 20 June (*see box*, p. 176). Morale was lifted on 3/4 July, when Lieutenant-Colonel Colin Mitchell led the 1st Battalion Argyll and Sutherland Highlanders into Crater, but the euphoria was short-lived. On 29 November 1967, the British left Aden for good, allowing the rival factions to fight for power on their own. The British departure led, after a short civil war, to the

creation of the Marxist-dominated People's Democratic Republic of Yemen (PDRY).

This was not the result that had been sought, but it was an inevitable by-product of British political confusion over defence policy. Within three months of the withdrawal, the government announced that British forces would be withdrawn entirely from major bases in the Far East and Persian Gulf by the end of 1971, leaving only a token presence east of Suez, in Hong Kong and Brunei. Further reductions to the size and composition of the Army followed, with most of the Brigades (many of which had now opted to become 'big regiments', comprising a number of battalions) being reduced to three battalions each. These changes led to more amalgamations and the demise of two historic units, the Cameronians and York and Lancaster Regiment (*see Appendix*).

According to Denis Healey's White Paper of January 1968, the emphasis was now firmly on the NATO role, with residual commitments elsewhere gradually disappearing. This may have resolved some of the problems of overstretch, but it did little for Army morale. 1968 was the only year since the end of the Second World War in which British forces were not on active service somewhere in the world, and as a result the Army began to fade from the public eye, particularly as its last campaign, in Aden, had hardly been a success. Some foreign commitments remained – since 1964 British troops had been involved in UN peacekeeping duties in Cyprus (*see box*, p. 176) – but the Army seemed set to become little more than a garrison force in West Germany. By 1970 the Army comprised 15 regiments of cavalry, four regiments of RTR, 21 regiments of artillery, seven battalions of Foot Guards and 41 battalions of infantry. Two of the latter, the Royal Hampshire Regiment and Argyll and Sutherland Highlanders, were down to company strength, and although they were saved when the Conservatives came to power later in the year, at under 180,000 men and women, the Army was the smallest it had been for some time.

NORTHERN IRELAND

But by then a new and potentially draining commitment had emerged in Northern Ireland, where British troops had been deployed on the streets of Belfast and Londonderry in August 1969, initially to keep Protestant and Catholic rioters apart. The troops were drawn from the normal peacetime garrison in the province – an armoured car regiment and two infantry battalions, organized into the 39th Infantry Brigade – but with the failure of the Royal Ulster Constabulary (RUC) to maintain law and order in the face of almost continuous riots, six more infantry battalions had to be added. They spent the first few months of the 'Troubles' conducting what were essentially peacekeeping duties, but as the IRA and Protestant extremists began to exploit the situation for their own political ends, the nature of the threat changed. By the middle of 1970, paramilitary gunmen from both sides of the sectarian divide were active on the streets, causing the government to increase Army commitment to 15 battalions and to raise an entirely new unit, the Ulster Defence Regiment (UDR).

To begin with, the campaign in Northern Ireland did not run smoothly. Seemingly endless street riots, exploited by a hooligan element as well as the paramilitary groups, stretched the Army to the full and showed that, despite a long history of similar situations, training standards had not been maintained. Stories abound of Army units committed to the streets in 1969 and 1970 following techniques based on the experience of the Cyprus Emergency, using tactics no more aggressive than issuing orders for the rioters to disperse or face unspecified retaliatory action.

But the problems ran deeper than the question of what was the right degree of force to use, for many of the lessons so laboriously learnt in previous counter-insurgency campaigns were either forgotten or proved impossible to effect. Until the imposition of Direct Rule from London on 24 March 1972, the Army was deployed in support of a Protestant (Unionist) government in Northern Ireland at Stormont. Many Unionists refused to treat the problem as anything more than a Catholic revolt against the established order, something that was patently not the case when Protestant paramilitary groups such as the Ulster Volunteer Force (UVF) and, from 1971, the Ulster Defence Association (UDA) were just as violent as the IRA. This lack of political direction was further reflected in the unsatisfactory command and control

system that operated in the province during the first few years of the Troubles. By 1970–1, four battalions were usually stationed in Londonderry (8th Infantry Brigade), six in Belfast (39th Infantry Brigade) and three battalions, plus the majority of the UDR, in Lurgan (3rd Infantry Brigade) with responsibility for the border areas. As such, the deployment did not coincide with that of the RUC, leading to poor co-ordination of intelligence and operational procedures. Indeed, Army-RUC relations were so bad that the Army refused to accept co-location of headquarters and intelligence services, even though the value of such an approach had been proved time after time since 1945. The RUC, demoralized by the events of 1969, was distrusted by the Army, who accused it of being sectarian in its attitudes; by the same token, the RUC distrusted the Army, resenting what it saw as ignorance among units that served normally for no longer than four months in the province.

In such circumstances, it was hardly surprising that success against the terrorists was difficult to achieve, and that it took time for the Army to find its feet. Political and military mistakes were made. In August 1971, for example, when the government ordered the internment of suspected IRA members and sympathizers, the Army's role was widely interpreted as sectarian. Alienated Catholic communities created 'No-Go Areas' in both Londonderry and Belfast. On 30 January 1972, in an incident in Londonderry known as 'Bloody Sunday', paratroopers shot dead 13 civilians in the course of a demonstration – a response that appeared to some observers to be an over-reaction, implying lack of control. The introduction of Direct Rule, with responsibility for the government of Northern Ireland transferred to Westminster, which appointed a Secretary of State as its political representative in the province, led to improved co-ordination of civil-military matters, while the destruction of the 'No-Go Areas' in Operation Motorman on 31 July 1972 (*see box*, p. 180) helped to reassert government authority, but it was obvious that the Army was involved in a long campaign.

Even so, it would be wrong to dismiss Army achievements in Northern Ireland. The shift from peace-keeping to counter-insurgency was successfully made and, by the end of internment in December 1975, the IRA had been badly hit. Constant military pressure through patrolling and observation, coupled to a steady improvement in information gathering and intelligence collation, meant that both the Official and Provisional IRA, formed when the organization split in late 1969, had lost cohesion as well as credibility among a significant propor-

British troops, armed with Self-Loading Rifles (SLRs) and wearing vizor-equipped helmets, face a crowd of protesters in a Londonderry street, early 1970s.

OPERATION MOTORMAN

At 4 a.m. on 31 July 1972, British forces moved into the 'No-Go Areas' established by Republicans in Belfast and Londonderry in the aftermath of internment the previous year. It was a delicate operation, fraught with the danger of heavy civilian casualties if the Provisional IRA decided to stand and fight. Thus, although the intention to carry out the operation was broadcast to give the gunmen time to pull out, precise timings were kept secret and the deployment of troops disguised. The aim was to go in hard and clear the barricades as quickly as possible, establishing an armed presence before the local population woke up.

Operation Motorman was a complete success. By 31 July over 21,000 troops had been concentrated in Northern Ireland, large numbers of which threw cordons around the No-Go Areas; these were gradually tightened as H-Hour approached. In Londonderry, Royal Engineer Centurion bulldozers (deployed by landing craft up the Foyle estuary) advanced into Rossville and onto the Creggan Estate, supported by infantry from four separate battalions. A gunman and a petrol-bomber were shot dead, but by 7 a.m. the areas were secure. In Belfast, the operation was far more elaborate, involving 11 battalions which moved into Ligoniel, Ballymurphy

and Whiterock, Andersonstown, the Ardoyne, New Lodge, City Centre and Markets, Beechmount and Falls Road. Not all were No-Go Areas, but the heavy Army presence prevented any outbreak of trouble; indeed, in some cases, local people helped the Royal Engineers to dismantle the barricades. Some arrests were made, but no gunmen or bombers were engaged. Smaller operations were carried out in Lurgan, Armagh, Newry and Coalisland. By the end of the day, the security forces, having suffered no casualties, had reasserted their right to go anywhere in the province, an essential move in the imposition of law and order.

Regimental Tradition:

THE LANCASHIRE FUSILIERS' PRIMROSE HACKLE

In 1968 the Lancashire Fusiliers became the 4th Battalion Royal Regiment of Fusiliers; as such, they continued to wear in their berets a distinctive primrose hackle, awarded to commemorate bravery at Spion Kop in 1901. However, in 1969 the battalion was disbanded and it looked as if the hackle would disappear. Instead, the Lancashire Fusiliers' allied regiment in Canada, the Lorne Scots (Peel, Dufferin and Halton) Regiment of Ontario, adopted the distinction themselves. According to a recent Lorne Scots' commanding officer, 'the regiment's point of view is that we hold the primrose hackle "in trust" for the Lancashire Fusiliers as it is their Battle Honour. Upon the LF being reformed we will return the hackle, having fulfilled our obligation to our Allied Regiment'.

Quote from *Badge Backings and Special Embellishments of the British Army*, The Ulster Defence Regiment Benevolent Fund, 1990

British government's attempt at a political initiative through 'power-sharing' failed in the face of a Protestant Workers' Strike in May 1974, merely prolonged the campaign and gave the Provisional IRA a chance to recover.

Since 1975, the nature of both the threat and the Army's role in the response to it has changed. In the aftermath of its failure in the early 1970s, the Provisional IRA was reorganized into a much tighter structure of 'cells' that proved extremely difficult for the security forces to penetrate. It also shifted some of the emphasis of its attacks to the rural areas of Northern Ireland, particularly the 'bandit country' of South Armagh, and to the British mainland. At the same time, reflecting the reality of long-term involvement, the Army settled into a pattern of commitment and became much more dependent on locally raised forces such as the UDR and a reformed RUC. The policy of 'Ulsterization' ensured that such forces took at least an equal part in the campaign, although in certain 'hard' areas, such as West Belfast and South Armagh, the Army was still needed as the first line of protection. This meant that Army units, whether on two-year tours as part of the 'permanent' garrison or on four-month Emergency Tours, bore the brunt of any terrorist pressure but did not need to cover every aspect of the campaign. For most soldiers, a tour often consisted of endless hours of patrolling and information gathering, interspersed with the occasional confrontation with a sniper or the results of a bomb attack. This did not mean that major incidents no longer occurred – on 27 August 1979, for example, 18 soldiers of the Queen's Own Highlanders and the 2nd Battalion Parachute Regiment were killed in an IRA ambush at Warrenpoint in County Down – but for many of those involved, Northern Ireland became just one more tour of duty.

Much has been learnt from the campaign. It has now, in 1993, been going on without respite for 24 years (the longest continuous campaign in Army history) and

tion of the Catholic community. But the Army could never solve the problems of Northern Ireland, it could only create a situation of relative calm (what one politician called 'an acceptable level of violence') within which political solutions could be discussed. The fact that the

British troops on exercise in Germany, preparing for possible war against the Warsaw Pact, mid-1960s. The vehicle on the left is a Saladin armoured car; that on the right a Saracen armoured personnel carrier.

the toll has risen inexorably to well over 600 Army dead, as against some 2500 civilian and paramilitary fatalities. In the process, however, the Army has recognized many of its earlier shortcomings and made improvements accordingly. Faced with the cellular structure of the Provisional IRA and its off-shoot the Irish National Liberation Army (INLA), it has placed far more emphasis on low-level intelligence, using its own specialist forces to confront the threat and liaising more closely with the RUC. As early as 1976, 22SAS was deployed to South Armagh to deal with terrorist activity along the border. Since that time the regiment has been involved in a number of incidents against 'active service' Republican units, most notably at Loughgall on 8 May 1987, when eight gunmen were killed in an ambush, and in Gibraltar on 6 March 1988, when three members of the Provisional IRA were shot dead while planning a bomb attack. Both cases provoked some media controversy over the legitimacy of the shootings. In addition, elements of the Army have gained unrivalled expertise in specialized aspects of countering terrorism, the most notable of which is bomb disposal, carried out by the Explosives Ordnance Disposal (EOD) teams of the Royal Army Ordnance Corps (now The

Royal Logistic Corps). Nearly every unit in the British Army has now seen service in Northern Ireland – some of them time after time – and it is a commitment that will continue until a political solution is found. The levels of violence have declined, but as long as the threat to law and order exists, the Army will have to remain, displaying the fortitude and basic self-control that have sustained it for nearly a quarter of a century. Similar characteristics have been, and still are, needed on the mainland, where the threat of more general terrorism has led to increased Army commitment, ranging from the guarding of airports to the spectacular SAS storming of the Iranian Embassy in London on 5 May 1980 (*see box*, p. 182).

THE TREND TOWARDS EUROPE

But these have not been the only duties carried out by the Army since 1969. In the early 1970s, a British Army Training Team (BATT) drawn from 22SAS, plus a number of officers seconded from British units, advised and actively helped the Sultan of Oman to put down a Communist-led insurgency in Dhofar (*see box*, p. 177), during which many of the techniques of counter-insurgency were refined and reinforced. Elsewhere, British

THE IRANIAN EMBASSY SIEGE

At 11.30 a.m. on Wednesday, 30 April 1980, six terrorists, dedicated to gaining autonomy for the predominantly Arab province of Khuzestan in Iran, seized the Iranian Embassy in Princes Gate on the southern edge of Hyde Park, taking 26 people hostage. They threatened to blow up the Embassy unless the Iranian authorities released 91 Arab prisoners by midday on Thursday, 1 May. Alerted by a secret alarm signal, the Metropolitan Police rapidly sealed off the building and called in Army bomb disposal experts as well as 22SAS.

Police negotiators managed to persuade the terrorists to extend their deadline and to release three of the hostages, but the British government refused to allow any concessions to be made. By the sixth day of the siege, Bank Holiday Monday, 5 May, the terrorists were growing increasingly frustrated, threatening to kill a hostage every 30 minutes unless they got what they wanted. Shots were heard from inside the Embassy and at 6.50 p.m. a body was thrown into the street. The government ordered the SAS to storm the building and release the surviving hostages.

At 7.23 p.m., in the full glare of television cameras, SAS troopers, dressed in black and wearing balaclavas and gas-masks, entered the Embassy from all sides. Two of them forced their way through the front first-floor window, while eight more abseiled down from the roof and crashed through the windows at the rear. A third group simply smashed through the wall from an adjoining building. The Embassy

was by now on fire, but the SAS men knew exactly where to go, having bugged the building and worked out where the hostages were being held. As they moved from room to room, they identified and shot five of the terrorists, although not before the latter had opened fire on a group of hostages, killing one and wounding a further two. The sixth terrorist was captured and all the

An SAS trooper, dressed in black and wearing a respirator, on a first-floor balcony of the Iranian Embassy in London, 5 May 1980. The storming of the Embassy was seen on television world-wide.

remaining hostages were freed unharmed. Even with the loss of one of the hostages, it was an outstandingly successful operation.

troops continued to contribute to UN peacekeeping in Cyprus, facing a particularly difficult time during the Turkish invasion of the island in July 1974. Guatemalan pressure on the colony of British Honduras (soon to be renamed Belize) led to the deployment of extra troops in June 1972. The latter action was repeated in November 1975 and July 1977, on each occasion deterring attack but leading to the creation of a garrison that stood in 1993 at 1500 personnel (soon to be reduced).

Such residual responsibilities may have been relatively small, but when they were added to commitments in Northern Ireland and NATO, the latter requiring

constant updating of equipment if the threat from the Warsaw Pact (formed in 1955) was to be met, they acted as one more call on an already overstretched defence budget. In March 1975 the Labour Secretary of State for Defence, Roy Mason, announced that £4.7 billion was to be cut from defence over the next five years. He took as his start-point the principle that Britain's top priority should now be the defence of Europe. All British forces were to be withdrawn from Malaysia/Singapore, the Indian Ocean and Malta by 1979, Hong Kong was to be made the responsibility of a self-contained Gurkha Field Force, and the status of other overseas commitments reviewed. As far as the Army was concerned, this was a fairly painless exercise. Although I (Br) Corps in Germany was reconstituted from three armoured divisions into four and units in Britain were reorganized into Field Forces, each a mix of Regular and TA units – all designed to enhance operational flexibility – the Mason Review confirmed a trend that had been apparent since 1945. The days of Empire were over and Britain had recognized at last that it was a European power with only regional capabilities.

But the remnants of Empire could not be abandoned overnight. Between December 1979 and April 1980, for example, 1100 British troops were deployed to Rhodesia as part of a Commonwealth Monitoring Force (CMF), supervising the disarmament of Popular Front guerrillas preparatory to multi-racial elections and independence as Zimbabwe. Three months later, 200 Royal Marine Commandos joined French paratroopers to restore order on the Pacific island of Espiritu Santo, part of the Anglo-French condominium of the New Hebrides, in the run-up to its independence as Vanuatu. None of this was enough to alter the new emphasis on European defence, but the fact that British forces were still having to satisfy overseas commitments meant that the financial pressure had not been eased. Another Defence Review was introduced on 25 June 1981 by Conservative Secretary of State John Nott in an effort to cut costs while paying for a replace-

ment nuclear deterrent. European priority was confirmed, but manpower and residual global capabilities were reduced. As in 1975, the Army was not deeply affected. I (Br) Corps was reorganized yet again, this time being altered from four back to three armoured divisions, but no regimental amalgamations were required to satisfy the call for a manpower reduction of 7000. Instead, the weight of the Nott Review fell on the Navy, one result of which was a decision to withdraw the ice-patrol ship HMS *Endurance* from the South Atlantic. To the Argentinians, desperate to realize their claim to the Falkland Islands, this was a clear sign that the British had lost all interest in the region.

THE FALKLANDS CONFLICT

Argentinian forces invaded the Falklands early on 2 April 1982, quickly overwhelming the 79-man Royal Marine garrison in Port Stanley. Twenty-four hours later they seized the dependency of South Georgia, defended by a further 23 Marines from *Endurance*. The intention was to present Britain with a *fait accompli* that the Conservative government under Margaret Thatcher would be forced to accept, but as news of the surrenders was released, the humiliation was enough to ensure a strong political and popular demand for retaliation.

This took a number of forms, all designed to put pressure on the Argentinians to withdraw. On 3 April the

A Chieftain Main Battle Tank on exercise, displaying its relatively low silhouette and 120mm main armament. The Chieftain began to be replaced in British armoured units by the updated Challenger in the late 1980s.

UN Security Council adopted Resolution 502, demanding the withdrawal of all forces from the disputed area, and six days later the European Community agreed to join Britain in imposing trade sanctions on Argentina. The United States, caught between two allies and initially intent on taking an 'even-handed' approach to the crisis, was persuaded to back Britain by the end of the month. Of far more significance, however, was the decision, taken as early as 2 April, to despatch a special Task Force to the South Atlantic to liberate the islands by force (Operation Corporate) should all other policies fail. A military contingent, comprising an enhanced 3rd Commando Brigade under Brigadier Julian Thompson, was added. Its normal units – Nos 40, 42 and 45 Commando Royal Marines, plus supporting arms – were reinforced by the 2nd and 3rd Battalions of the Parachute Regiment (2PARA and 3PARA) from 5th Infantry Brigade. Together with light tanks from the Blues and Royals, artillery and engineers, as well as elements of the SAS and its Royal Marine equivalent, the Special Boat Squadron (SBS), they boarded a variety of transports in early April, destined for the mid-Atlantic island of Ascension. At this stage, the decision to use force had not been taken.

Once that decision was reached, the first target was South Georgia, liberated by a force of 75 Royal Marines, SAS and SBS without casualty on 25/26 April. But this was only a preliminary to the fight for the Falklands themselves, garrisoned by an estimated 10,000 Argentinian troops. As the Task Force struggled to gain a degree of naval and air supremacy around the islands, preparations for an amphibious landing began. A direct assault on Port Stanley was ruled out when SAS and SBS covert intelligence teams, active on the Falklands from 1 May, reported that it was heavily defended, and the decision was taken to go ashore instead at San Carlos, a small settlement on the north-western coast of East Falkland about 50 miles from the capital. Major-General Jeremy Moore, recently appointed Land Force Commander, gave the go-ahead even though a reconstituted 5th Infantry Brigade, comprising 2nd Battalion Scots Guards, 1st Battalion Welsh Guards and 1st Battalion 7th Gurkha Rifles, with supporting arms, did not leave UK as reinforcements until 12 May. The 5000 men of Thompson's

Personality Profile:

MAJOR-GENERAL SIR JEREMY MOORE (1928–)

John Jeremy Moore was commissioned into the Royal Marines in 1947. Posted to No. 40 Commando, he served in Malaya during the Emergency, winning the first of his Military Crosses; after more peaceful duties in Malta and the Canal Zone, he saw further action in Cyprus, this time as adjutant of No. 45 Commando, before being posted to the Royal Military Academy Sandhurst as an instructor. In 1962 he won a second Military Cross in Brunei, and went on to serve in Borneo, with No. 42 Commando, a unit to which he was appointed commanding officer in 1971 and which he commanded in Northern Ireland, notably during Operation Motorman in July 1972 (*see box*, p. 180). Five years later, after commanding the Royal Marines Depot Regiment at Lympstone and the Royal Marines School of Music, he was promoted to brigadier in command of 3rd Commando Brigade. In August 1979 he became Major-General Royal Marines Commando Forces, from which post he was chosen in 1982 to command the land forces in the liberation of the Falklands, for which he was knighted. His appreciation of the need for close liaison between ground, naval and air units, together with his determination to see the campaign through despite setbacks and logistic problems, were keys to British victory. He retired in 1983.

brigade would have to carry out the initial assault on their own.

The landings began early on 21 May against minimal opposition, and by the end of the day the whole of 3rd Commando Brigade was safely ashore for the loss of only two helicopters and three men. Rapier surface-to-air missiles of the Royal Artillery were quickly deployed to protect the beachhead from air attack, but the Argentinian pilots preferred to concentrate against shipping in San Carlos Water, inflicting considerable damage on the Task Force. This increased the pressure on Thompson to effect a breakout, which he finally ordered on 27 May. Soldiers of 2PARA moved south to attack an Argentinian garrison at Darwin and Goose Green (*see* p. 186), while No. 45 Commando and 3PARA marched across the northern part of East Falkland towards Port Stanley, covering 32 miles of exceptionally difficult terrain in deteriorating weather conditions. On 31 May 3PARA pushed on to take Estancia House and high ground to the north-east, while elements of the SAS and No. 42 Commando were helicoptered forward to take Mount Kent, only 12 miles from Port Stanley. The rest of No. 42 Commando occupied Mount

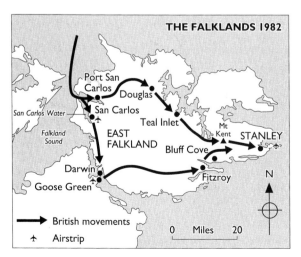

THE FALKLANDS 1982

Port San Carlos
Douglas
San Carlos Water
San Carlos
Teal Inlet
Falkland Sound
EAST FALKLAND
Mt Kent
STANLEY
Bluff Cove
Darwin
Fitzroy
Goose Green
N

→ British movements
✦ Airstrip

0   Miles   20

Challenger on 5 June, with No. 45 Commando dug in to the west of Mount Kent. The Argentinians, already demoralized by the battle at Goose Green, made no move to counter the British advance.

Meanwhile, 5th Infantry Brigade had come ashore at San Carlos on 1 June. Moore ordered its three battalions, with 2PARA temporarily attached, to open up a southern route through Fitzroy and Bluff Cove, completing the ring around the Argentinian garrison. Men of 2PARA, relieved at Goose Green by 1/7th Gurkhas, spearheaded the advance, reaching Fitzroy on 4 June, but the two Guards battalions had to be moved round by sea. Although the Scots Guards were landed at Bluff Cove on 5/6 June, bad weather disrupted the deployment of the Welsh Guards, elements of which were transferred to the landing ship *Sir Galahad*. On 8 June, as they waited to be offloaded at Fitzroy, Argentinian jets suddenly attacked, hitting both *Sir Galahad* and its sister-ship *Sir Tristram*: 51 British servicemen, including 33 members of the Welsh Guards, were killed.

Despite this tragedy, plans for the final assault on Port Stanley were rapidly finalized, with the initial aim of

Royal Marine Commandos begin the final march into Port Stanley at the end of the Falklands conflict, 14 June 1982. The bleakness of the terrain and lack of natural cover may be readily appreciated.

securing a series of rock features to the west of the town. On the night of 11/12 June No. 42 Commando took Mount Harriet, approaching to within 100 yards of the summit before the Argentinian defenders reacted, while No. 45 Commando seized Two Sisters after fierce fighting against well-protected machine-gun positions. Further north, 3PARA faced a tougher challenge when they assaulted Mount Longdon, only taking their objective after 10 hours of bitter fighting, most of it at section level in complete darkness. When dawn broke on 12 June, five Marines and 23 paratroopers were dead, including Sergeant Ian McKay of 3PARA, awarded a posthumous Victoria Cross for taking out a machine-gun nest on Mount Longdon, but the first line of the enemy defences had been breached.

The original idea had been for 5th Infantry Brigade to follow through immediately, but a shortage of helicop-

THE BATTLE OF GOOSE GREEN

The 2nd Battalion Parachute Regiment (2PARA), commanded by Lieutenant-Colonel 'H' Jones, moved from the beachhead at San Carlos towards its objectives on a narrow isthmus at Darwin and Goose Green on 27 May 1982. Its task was to defeat the Argentinian garrison and so protect the flank of the main British advance on Port Stanley across the northern part of East Falkland, while at the same time opening up the possibility of a southern thrust towards Fitzroy and Bluff Cove. The battalion comprised about 450 men, divided into four companies with their own mortar, anti-tank and machine-gun support; three 105mm guns of 29 Commando Regiment Royal Artillery and the Reconnaissance Troop from 59 Independent Commando Squadron Royal Engineers were also available, together with naval gunfire from the frigate HMS *Arrow*.

The attack began at 2.35 a.m. on 28 May. A Company moved down the east coast of the isthmus as far as Darwin Hill, while B Company fought through enemy positions on the west coast towards Boca House. While it was dark, progress was steady, but by dawn the paras, short of ammunition and denied air support because of overcast skies, temporarily lost the initiative, particularly around

First-Hand Account

'The surrender was arranged on a sports field outside Goose Green, close to the hidden position of D Company who had closed up on the settlement. It was a straightforward affair requiring the defenders to lay down their arms, which I allowed them to do with a degree of honour, to avoid rubbing their noses in defeat. There was nothing to gain from such a humiliation. About 150 of them assembled in a hollow square and after singing their national anthem, the commander, an

Lieutenant-Colonel 'H' Jones, C.O. of the 2nd Battalion, Parachute Regiment at Goose Green, 28 May 1982. His death in action galvanized the battalion, breaking the deadlock of the battle. Jones received a posthumous VC.

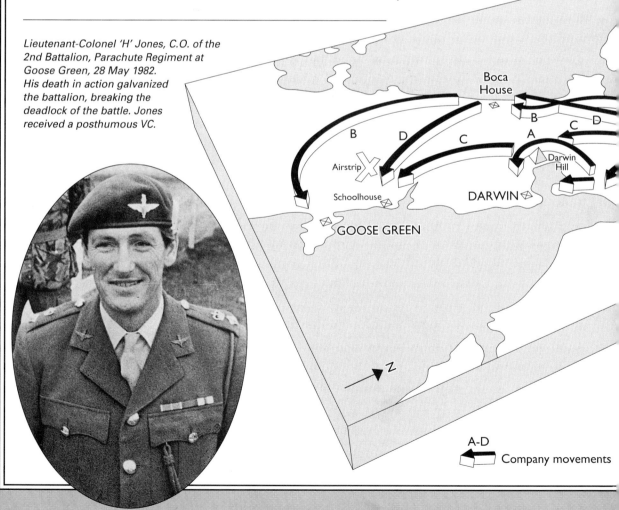

A-D
Company movements

28–9 MAY 1982

airman, saluted me and handed over his pistol. We were very concerned that we could not see any Argentine army personnel in the mass of defeated airmen. Some minutes later everything became clear as we watched some 1,000 soldiers marching up in files to surrender in the same way. It was an incredible sight.

We held our breath hoping they wouldn't change their minds. It was a very significant situation. Here, the Argentines had all the resources to defend the settlement for a long time, but they lacked the bottle. This lack of

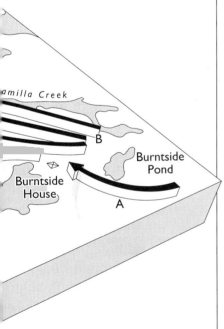

will, evident throughout the whole Argentine ground defence, lost them the Malvinas . . .'

Major Chris Keeble, acting commanding officer of 2PARA, describing events of 29 May 1982

From Max Arthur, *Above All, Courage*, Sidgwick and Jackson, 1985

Royal Marines man a machine-gun post on East Falkland, late May 1982. The weapon is a 7.62mm L7A2 General Purpose Machine Gun (GPMG), used in the sustained-fire role, principally at section level.

Darwin Hill, where A Company, joined by C Company and Colonel Jones' tactical headquarters, were pinned down by Argentinian machine-gun fire. As casualties began to mount, Jones rushed forward against an enemy position, only to be shot down by a sniper. His bravery (for which he was awarded a posthumous Victoria Cross) seemed to galvanize the paras, who forced their way forward to take Darwin Hill and Darwin settlement.

Meanwhile, on the west coast, B Company was still stalled in front of Boca House. Jones' successor, Major Chris Keeble, ordered D Company to move along the shoreline to outflank the Argentinians, after which they swung east towards Goose Green. During the afternoon, C and D Companies linked up and seized Schoolhouse, to the north of Goose Green, while B Company conducted a wide sweep to the south. By nightfall 2PARA had the Argentinian garrison penned in, although the cost had been high: 17 paras killed and 35 wounded.

Early on 29 May Keeble offered surrender terms which, to his great relief, were accepted. Altogether, more than 1200 enemy troops laid down their arms, emphasizing the scale of 2PARA's victory. It was the beginning of the end for the Argentinian invaders.

ters delayed their attack for 24 hours. Late on 13 June the Scots Guards moved against Tumbledown, to the east of Two Sisters, only to find it defended by Argentinian marines who laid down heavy defensive fire. It took six hours of hard fighting before the summit was secured by men of the Left Flank Company; by dawn the battalion had suffered nine dead and 43 wounded. By then, 2PARA (the only unit to fight two battles in the Falklands) had assaulted Wireless Ridge in the north, avoiding heavy casualties by advancing with full artillery and light tank support. Even so, it cost a further three men dead and 11 wounded. To their south, 1/7th Gurkhas took Mount William, while the Welsh Guards and elements of No. 40 Commando secured Sapper Hill, but the Argentinians had clearly suffered enough. On 14 June white flags began to appear and, as British forces moved into Port Stanley, the Argentinians signed a surrender document. It was the end of a brilliant campaign, for although it cost the British a total of 255 servicemen dead and 777 wounded, the crisis had been resolved and the Falklands restored in less than three months. As an example of combined operations, involving all three services, it could hardly be bettered.

OPTIONS FOR CHANGE

Nevertheless, the Falklands conflict acted as a reminder that Britain still had residual responsibilities outside Europe. This was reinforced by the fact that, once the fighting was over, a permanent garrison had to be maintained on the islands to deter any future Argentinian attack. With similar garrisons in Belize, Cyprus, Gibraltar and Hong Kong, plus a number of small training teams in a variety of Commonwealth countries, any hope of concentrating entirely on a NATO role in the 1980s was unrealistic, particularly when it was obvious that the commitment of troops to Northern Ireland was not going to be temporary. In addition, Britain was expected to contribute to periodic peacekeeping duties, not just under the banner of the UN in Cyprus, but also in concert with Western allies in both the Multinational Force and Observers (MFO) in Sinai and, between February 1983 and February 1984, in the Multinational Force (MNF) in Lebanon (see box). Although the size of the Army stabilized at about 160,000 men and women (plus over 7000 Royal Marines) in the mid-1980s, it was apparent that the gap between capabilities and commitments was still there.

This situation began to change quite unexpectedly at the end of the decade, when the Cold War confrontation between East and West was suddenly broken by the collapse of Communism, initially in Eastern European states belonging to the Warsaw Pact and then in the Soviet Union itself. In such circumstances, the British commitment to NATO, although not altered in principle, could be reduced, satisfying political and popular calls for financial savings on defence – the so-called 'Peace Dividend'. On 25 July 1990 the Conservative Secretary of State for Defence, Tom King, announced 'Options for Change', designed to reflect the realities of the new world order and project the armed forces into the 1990s. All three services were to be cut, but it was the Army that was to bear the brunt, chiefly because of its existing emphasis on the NATO role. Ground forces in Europe were to be reduced from 55,000 to 23,500 and regiments withdrawn to UK, leading to yet more amalgamations. The Royal Armoured Corps was to be reduced from 20 regiments to 12 and the infantry from 55 to 38 battalions

THE MNF IN LEBANON, 1983–4

Between 21 August and 10 September 1982, the United States, France and Italy deployed forces to Beirut to supervise the withdrawal of Palestinian and Syrian troops caught in the city by the Israeli invasion of Lebanon. Their task complete, they pulled out, only to be redeployed on 20 September as a Multinational Force (MNF) in the aftermath of the Israeli push into West Beirut and the massacre by Christian Lebanese forces of Palestinian civilians in camps at Sabra and Chatila. US Marines took up defensive positions around the international airport, with Italian forces to their north and a French contingent in West Beirut; their role was officially to ensure 'the restoration of the sovereignty of the Lebanese gov-

ernment', but this seems to have been interpreted differently by the contingents. The US and French forces gradually assumed a more offensive strategy, eventually using air and artillery strikes against Druze positions in the Shouf Mountains, while the Italians were more concerned with humanitarian aid to people within their particular zone. A small British contingent of about 100 men joined the MNF in February 1983 and adopted the Italian approach.

The soldiers involved – drawn initially from the Queen's Dragoon Guards and, after nine months, from the 16th/5th Queen's Royal Lancers, backed throughout by headquarters personnel chiefly from the Royal Signals – were deployed to an area along the 'Green Line' which separated Christian and Muslim communities in Beirut. Reflecting the experience of Northern Ireland, they mounted constant patrols in Ferret scout cars and concentrated on making contact with the local people, avoiding confrontation. As such, the British proved to be both popular and effective, but by February 1984, as the situation degenerated into a civil war that threatened to involve the MNF, the contingents were withdrawn. The operation as a whole was only a limited success, although it was one more example of the flexibility demanded of, and provided by, the modern British Army. It was also an example of low-intensity conflict at the intervention level.

(altered in 1993 to 40, *see Appendix*), with commensurate cuts to other elements such as the Royal Artillery, Royal Engineers and support units. The three armoured divisions in Europe were to be reduced to a single armoured division in Germany and an infantry division in UK, both contributing to a multinational Allied Command Europe (ACE) Rapid Reaction Corps (ARRC) under British command. By 1995, when the changes were to be complete, the Army would comprise no more than 119,000 men and women – the smallest it had been since the 1830s.

THE GULF WAR

Within two weeks of Tom King's announcement, however, a new international crisis arose. On 2 August 1990, Iraqi troops invaded Kuwait, at the head of the Persian Gulf, threatening not just the stability of the region but also Western access to cheap oil. Led by the United States, a substantial number of powers co-operated in condemning the invasion, isolating Iraq both diplomatically and economically through the UN and sending armed forces to defend Saudi Arabia, which was under threat as the next logical target of Iraqi aggression. Britain, as a permanent member of the Security Council and a close

ally of the United States, was in the forefront of the response, although in the early stages of the crisis the commitment of forces (Operation Granby) was restricted primarily to air and naval units. The Army was only minimally involved, contributing three companies of signallers and engineers by early September.

This situation changed as the Americans put pressure on their NATO allies to contribute more ground troops, and on 14 September it was announced that Britain had decided to send the 7th Armoured Brigade, commanded by Brigadier Patrick Cordingley, from Germany to the Gulf. The brigade, comprising two armoured regiments (the Royal Scots Dragoon Guards and Queen's Royal Irish Hussars) equipped with Challenger tanks, an armoured infantry battalion (1st Battalion Staffordshire Regiment) equipped with Warrior mechanized combat vehicles, and full supporting arms, was well suited to the task, having recently returned from training in Canada. Despite the inevitable chaos of preparing for and conducting a major, unexpected move from Europe to the Middle East, the first ships carrying heavy equipment left Germany on 28 September; a month later 80 per cent of the brigade had arrived in Saudi Arabia. By then, British Forces Middle East were under the command of Lieuten-

Members of the 1st Battalion, Staffordshire Regiment, photographed after an exercise in Saudi Arabia, 6 January 1991. As the mechanized infantry of 7th Armoured Brigade, they were soon to be in action against the Iraqis.

ant-General Sir Peter de la Billière, formerly of the SAS, and the decision had been taken to deploy 7th Armoured Brigade alongside the US 1st Marine Expeditionary Force on the Saudi coast. An HQ Force Maintenance Area, dubbed 'Blackadder Camp' because of its initially rudimentary nature by British soldiers familiar with the television comedy series, was established at Al Jubayl, increasing the number of troops involved to nearly 13,000.

It was not enough, particularly as it was becoming increasingly apparent that the Iraqis had no intention of withdrawing from Kuwait unless forced by military action. On 22 November the British contingent was increased, with the announcement that the 4th Armoured Brigade, commanded by Brigadier Christopher Hammerbeck, would also be deployed. The brigade, comprising one armoured regiment (14th/20th King's Hussars) and two armoured infantry battalions (the 1st Battalion Royal Scots and 3rd Battalion Royal Regiment of Fusiliers), with supporting arms, had not trained together and had to be considerably reinforced by contingents from other units, but by early January 1991 the bulk of it had arrived in theatre. The two brigades were

Personality Profile:
GENERAL SIR PETER DE LA BILLIÈRE (1934–)

Peter de la Billière joined the King's Shropshire Light Infantry in 1952 before being commissioned into the Durham Light Infantry, in the 1st Battalion of which he served in Japan, Korea, the Canal Zone and Jordan. In 1956, he transferred to the Special Air Service, in which he remained for most of his subsequent career, fighting in Malaya during the Emergency and winning a Military Cross for his part in the daring assault on the Jebel Akhdar in Oman in early 1959. A second Military Cross resulted from his command of A Squadron 22SAS in Radfan and Borneo (1964–6), and he won a Distinguished Service Order after commanding 22SAS in Oman during the Dhofar campaign. After leading a British Army Training Team in the Sudan (1977–9), he assumed command of the Special Air Service Group, supervising its involvement in the storming of the Iranian Embassy in London (1980) and the Falklands conflict (1982). He was knighted in 1988 and given command of South-East District, based at Aldershot. In 1990 he was appointed commander of British Forces Middle East in Saudi Arabia, liaising closely with the Americans during the liberation of Kuwait. He retired in 1992 as a full general.

First-Hand Account:
THE GULF WAR, 1991

'Visibility remained poor throughout the day [26 February] changing quickly from almost clear down to less than 400m. The swirling sand proved to be almost impenetrable to our thermal imaging sights and made everybody's lives far more difficult . . . From 1800hrs to midday all four squadrons were involved in direct fire engagements on three fronts. C Squadron managed to stop an enemy attempt to reinforce from the north by knocking out his two lead tanks with guided weapons at a range of just over 3,000m. B Squadron . . . were in the thick of it directing artillery and taking on tanks and APCs [armoured personnel carriers] as they emerged with both guided weapons and the 30mm cannon . . . On the south flank A Squadron should have had a rather quieter time but they met the vehicles trying to get away from 7 Armoured Brigade's attack. A fine troop shoot by Lt Horton's troop stopped an advancing T62 after it had been hit over 30 times with 30mm APDS [armour-piercing discarding sabot] and HE [high explosive] rounds. A Striker [anti-tank vehicle], which had acquired two prisoners, engaged a tank and scored a glancing blow on the side of the turret. Some prisoners, standing behind the Striker, were engulfed in smoke and flame as the missile launched but, notwithstanding their smouldering trouser legs, were quick to advise the crew to aim further left with the next missile! . . .'

From *The Scarlet and Green. 16th/5th The Queen's Royal Lancers in the Gulf 1991*, Tri-Service Magazines, 1991

organized into 1st (Br) Armoured Division, commanded by Major-General Rupert Smith, and were fully operational by 1 February. The division was supported by a host of logistic units and an elaborate medical infrastructure, the latter of which included a number of recalled reservists and the whole of 205th (Scottish) General Hospital (Volunteers). It was the largest deployment of British troops (about 33,000 men and women) since the Second World War.

The coalition campaign to liberate Kuwait had already begun at midnight on 16/17 January, with air and cruise-missile strikes against targets deep in Iraq as well as into Kuwait itself. By then, plans for a ground offensive (codenamed Desert Storm) were well advanced, based on an elaborate deception operation that would involve the movement of most of the coalition armoured formations to the west of the Kuwait-Saudi border. The coalition commander, US General Norman Schwarzkopf, was aware that the Iraqis were deployed to defend Kuwait against a direct attack from the south; this would occur, fixing the enemy in place, but would coincide with a wide left-flanking assault (Desert Sabre) designed to swing round behind the Iraqi defences, cutting them off from and destroying their armoured support further north. 1st (Br) Armoured Division, transferred from the coast to become part of the US VII Corps, was to spearhead the inner wing of the outflanking move, breaching Iraqi defences to the west of the Wadi al-Batin (a dry water-course) before turning sharp right into Kuwait to act as the 'anvil' against which the enemy armour would be smashed.

Major-General Smith decided to fight his part of the

Lance Corporal Suzannah Gray, attached to the Intelligence Corps in Saudi Arabia during the Gulf conflict, symbolizes a new Army policy of female integration. She is armed with an SA-80 automatic rifle.

campaign by committing his brigade groups sequentially while using his substantial artillery support (which included the 39th Heavy Regiment Royal Artillery, equipped with the devastating new Multiple Launch Rocket System) to engage targets in depth. Operation Desert Storm began on Sunday 24 February, although 7th Armoured Brigade did not cross the line of departure until the following day, exploiting a breach in the Iraqi defences created by the US 1st Mechanized Infantry Division. The 4th Armoured Brigade, on the right of the 7th, followed a few hours later, and by the end of the day initial objectives had been secured against scattered resistance. Some of the fighting was hard, but many of the Iraqis were clearly demoralized by the earlier air attacks and the unexpected nature of the coalition plan; indeed, on 26 February one of the problems facing the British was what to do with so many prisoners of war, 7th Armoured Brigade alone having taken over 1500. By late afternoon on the 26th it was apparent that the enemy was pulling back. This allowed the British to exploit eastwards to cut the road from Kuwait City to Basra, preventing the escape of Iraqi forces. 7th Armoured Brigade, with artillery support, led the way, reaching the road just before a ceasefire came into effect at 8 a.m. on 28 February. The British had advanced 180 miles in 66 hours, destroyed the equivalent of three Iraqi armoured divisions and taken over 7000 prisoners, all for the exceptionally low cost of 10 men killed. It was a truly remarkable achievement.

THE FUTURE

This would be the ideal note upon which to end a history of the British Army, illustrating as it does so many of the characteristics that have contributed to its reputation over the last 300 years – flexibility, improvisation, good command and impressive fighting skills. In addition, it shows that many of the shortcomings so prevalent in earlier campaigns – a lack of inter-arm and inter-service co-operation, a disdain for logistics and an inability to fit easily into a coalition partnership – have been recognized and avoided, enabling units to conduct a fast-moving and deeply penetrating battle using the very latest technology. Finally, it epitomizes the reality of British capabilities in the 1990s: the days of global power are over, and although soldiers can expect to be committed to trouble-spots anywhere in the world, as shown by the deployment of 3rd Commando Brigade to Kurdistan in northern Iraq in 1991 and the 1st Battalion Cheshire Regiment, with supporting arms, to Bosnia in 1992 (*see box*), they are only likely to do so as part of an allied or UN force. As such, their record of action since 1945 will always be a major asset.

But the fact remains that the Army is small and, as a result, overstretched. The success of Operation Granby did not lead to a suspension of Options for Change – by 1993 many of the amalgamations involved had already taken place – and there was widespread speculation that 40 infantry battalions (the revised number agreed in 1993) were insufficient to satisfy existing commitments, let alone any new ones that might arise. With troops in Northern Ireland, Germany, Belize, Cyprus, the Falklands, Gibraltar and, until 1997, Hong Kong, to say nothing of the need to maintain a ready reserve in the United Kingdom itself, the process of reduction may have gone too far. It is a criticism that has been raised during almost every period of peace since the formation of the standing army and it remains to be seen if it is justified on this occasion.

BOSNIA, 1992–3

The collapse of Communism in Yugoslavia produced a number of ethnic conflicts as the constituent republics fought for territorial and political control. Initially, clashes between Serbs and Croats posed the greatest threat to security, but in January 1992 a ceasefire was brokered by the UN, which committed a Protection Force (UNPROFOR 1) to monitor events. In June, Britain deployed 800 personnel of 24 Airmobile Field Ambulance as part of UNPROFOR 1 in what was codenamed Operation Celia.

But this did not prevent continued violence, particularly in Bosnia-Herzegovina, where a civil war between Serbs and Muslims had been raging for months. In August 1992 the UN Security Council passed a resolution authorizing 'all pos-sible means' to be used to protect UN aid convoys in the region. Another UN force was put together (UNPROFOR 2), to which Britain agreed to contribute a 2400-man infantry group. It was to be based at Vitez, in the centre of Bosnia-Herzegovina, from where it would supervise the delivery of food and other essentials to villages cut off by the Serbs. Known as Operation Grapple, the British commitment comprised the whole of 1st Battalion Cheshire Regiment, reinforced by 100 men of the 2nd Battalion Royal Irish Regiment (all equipped with Warrior mechanized combat vehicles), plus a squadron of the 9th/12th Royal Lancers (equipped with Scimitar armoured reconnaissance vehicles). Their task was to mark out routes and escort the convoys, while elements of 35 Regiment Royal Engineers defused mines and repaired the roads, and other support units kept the contingent going. Arriving in mid-November, the British came under the operational command of General Philippe Morillon, the French commander of UNPROFOR 2, and immediately began their humanitarian work. In May 1993 the Cheshires were replaced by 1st Battalion The Prince of Wales's Own Regiment of Yorkshire, supported by Scimitars of the Light Dragoons.

THE BRITISH ARMY – CHRONOLOGY, 1661–1993

....

1661	14 February	Creation of the 'standing army'
1689	28 March	First Mutiny Act passed
1702–13	War of the Spanish Succession	
1704	*13 August*	*Battle of Blenheim*
1706	*23 May*	*Battle of Ramillies*
1708	*11 July*	*Battle of Oudenarde*
1709	*11 September*	*Battle of Malplaquet*
1740–8	War of the Austrian Succession	
1743	*27 June*	*Battle of Dettingen*
1745	*11 May*	*Battle of Fontenoy*
1741	Royal Military Academy Woolwich opened	
1746	16 April	Jacobites defeated at Culloden
1755	9 July	Braddock's defeat on the Monongehela
1756–63	Seven Years War	
1757	*22 June*	*Battle of Plassey*
1759	*1 August*	*Battle of Minden*
	12/13 September	*Capture of Quebec; death of Wolfe*
1775–83	War of American Independence	
1775	*17 June*	*Battle of Bunker Hill*
1777	*17 October*	*British surrender at Saratoga*
1781	*19 October*	*British surrender at Yorktown*
1779–83	Siege of Gibraltar	
1793–1802	War against Revolutionary France	
1793–5	*Duke of York's Campaign in Flanders and Holland*	
1793	*19 December*	*Evacuation of Toulon*
1793–7	*Campaigns in the West Indies*	
1795	*10 February*	*Duke of York appointed C-in-C*
1798	*21 June*	*Battle of Vinegar Hill*
1799	*4 May*	*Seringapatam taken*
	Aug–Oct	*The Helder Expedition*
1801	*21 March*	*Battle of Alexandria*
1803–9	War against Napoleonic France	
1803	*23 September*	*Battle of Assaye*
1803–4	*Light infantry training at Shorncliffe Camp*	
1806	*4 July*	*Battle of Maida*
1807	*5 July*	*British defeat at Buenos Aires*
1808	*August*	*British victories at Rolica and Vimeiro*

1809	*16 January*	*Battle of Corunna; death of Moore*
	Jul–Dec	*Walcheren Expedition*
1809–14	The Peninsular Campaign	
1809	*27/28 July*	*Battle of Talavera*
1810	*27 September*	*Battle of Busaco*
1811	*11 May*	*Battle of Fuentes d'Onoro*
	16 May	*Battle of Albuera*
1812	*19 January*	*Ciudad Rodrigo taken*
	6 April	*Badajoz taken*
	22 July	*Battle of Salamanca*
1813	*21 June*	*Battle of Vitoria*
1814	*27 February*	*Battle of Orthez*
	10 April	*Battle of Toulouse*
1812	Royal Military College opened at Sandhurst	
1812–15	War in America	
1815	18 June	Battle of Waterloo
1845–6	First Sikh War	
1845	*21/22 December*	*Battle of Ferozeshah*
1846	*29 January*	*Battle of Aliwal*
	10 February	*Battle of Sobraon*
1848–9	Second Sikh War	
1849	*13 January*	*Battle of Chillianwala*
1853–6	The Crimean War	
1854	*20 September*	*Battle of The Alma*
	25 October	*Battle of Balaklava; Charge of the Light Brigade*
	5 November	*Battle of Inkerman*
1855	*8 September*	*Fall of Sevastopol*
1857–8	The Indian Mutiny	
1857	*10 May*	*Mutiny of Indian troops at Meerut*
	20 September	*Relief of Delhi*
1858	Staff College opened at Camberley	
1871–81	The Cardwell Reforms	
1879	The Zulu War	
	22 January	*Battle of Isandhlwana*
	22/23 January	*Rorke's Drift*
	4 July	*Battle of Ulundi*

1880–1	First Boer War	
	26 February	Battle of Majuba Hill
1882	Occupation of Egypt	
1885	26 January	Death of Gordon at Khartoum
1898	2 September	Battle of Omdurman
1899–1902	Second Boer War	
1899	10–15 December	'Black Week'; British defeats at Colenso, Magersfontein and Stormberg
1900	23/24 January	Battle of Spion Kop
	1 March	Ladysmith relieved
	17 May	Mafeking relieved
1904	The Esher Reforms	
1908	The Haldane Reforms	
1914	March/April	The Curragh 'Incident'
1914–18	The First World War	
1914	4 August	War declared on Germany
	23 August	Battle of Mons
	5–9 September	Battle of the Marne
	20 Oct–22 Nov	First Battle of Ypres
	21 November	Landing at Basra (Mesopotamia)
1915	10 March	Battle of Neuve Chapelle
	22 Apl–24 May	Second Battle of Ypres
	25 April	Landings at Gallipoli
	25 September	Battle of Loos
	8 December	Siege of Kut-el-Amara (to 29 April 1916)
1916	9 January	Evacuation of Gallipoli
	January	Conscription first introduced
	1 July	First Day of the Somme
	15 September	Battle of Flers-Courcelette (first use of tanks)
	13 November	Battle of the Somme ends
1917	9 April	Battle of Arras/Vimy Ridge
	7 June	Messines Ridge taken
	31 Jul–4 Nov	Third Battle of Ypres (Passchendaele)
	9 September	Mutiny at Étaples
	20 November	Battle of Cambrai
	9 December	Jerusalem captured
1918	21 March	Ludendorff Offensive begins
	8 August	Battle of Amiens
	19 September	Megiddo Offensive begins (Palestine)
	1 October	Damascus captured
	11 November	Armistice
1919–21	Campaign in Ireland	
1927–8	Experimental Mechanized Force tested	
1936–9	Arab Revolt in Palestine	
1939	March	Conscription reintroduced
1939–45	The Second World War	
1939	3 September	War declared on Germany
	12 October	BEF deployed to France
1940	9 April–8 Jun	Campaign in Norway
	10 May–22 Jun	Defeat in France and the Low Countries
	26 May–4 Jun	Evacuation of BEF from Dunkirk
	10 June	Italy declares war
	4 July	Italians invade Somaliland
	13 September	Italians invade Egypt
	9 December	British attack in Egypt (Op. Compass)
1941	19 Jan–18 May	British take Somaliland, Ethiopia and Eritrea

	7 February	Battle of Beda Fomm (Compass ends)
	6 Apr–31 May	Defeat in Greece and Crete
	April–July	Campaigns in Iraq, Lebanon and Syria
	18 November	Operation Crusader begins in N. Africa
	8 December	Japanese attack Hong Kong and Malaya
	25 December	Hong Kong falls
1942	15 February	Singapore surrenders
	27/28 Feb	Bruneval Raid (first use of paratroopers)
	8 March	Rangoon falls to Japanese
	26 May	Rommel's attack at Gazala
	21 June	Tobruk surrenders
	1–27 July	First Battle of Alamein
	13 August	Montgomery takes over Eighth Army
	30 Aug–2 Sep	Battle of Alam Halfa
	23 Oct–2 Nov	Second Battle of Alamein
	8 November	Allied landings in N.W. Africa (Op. Torch)
	17 December	British advance into Arakan (Burma)
1943	8 Feb–24 Mar	First Chindit Operation
	6 March	Battle of Medenine
	7 May	Fall of Tunis
	10 July	Invasion of Sicily
	3 September	Invasion of Italy; Italy surrenders
	9 September	Landings at Salerno
1944	9 January	British attack in Arakan
	22 January	Landings at Anzio
	5 February	Second Chindit Operation begins
	5 Mar–26 Jun	Battles of Imphal/Kohima
	18 May	Capture of Monte Cassino
	4 June	Liberation of Rome
	6 June	D-Day Landings in Normandy
	18–20 July	Operation Goodwood in Normandy
	3 September	Liberation of Brussels
	17–25 Sept	Operation Market Garden/Battle of Arnhem
	4 December	British troops cross the River Chindwin
1945	8–21 February	British advance to the Rhine
	21 March	Liberation of Mandalay
	23/24 March	British crossing of the Rhine
	9 Apl–2 May	Final campaign in Italy
	3 May	Liberation of Rangoon
	4 May	German surrender, Lüneburg Heath
	2 September	Japanese surrender, Tokyo Bay
	Sept–Oct	British involvement in Indo-china
	29 September	British troops land in the Dutch East Indies (committed until late 1946)
1945–8	Campaign in Palestine	
1946–7	Withdrawal from India	
1947	March	National Service introduced
1948–60	Malayan Emergency	
1950–3	The Korean War	
1951	22/23 April	Battle of the Imjin River
1953	7/8 May	Battle of The Hook
1952–60	Mau Mau Revolt (Kenya)	

1955–9	Campaign against EOKA in Cyprus	
1956	4–6 November	The Suez Operation
1957	4 April	Sandys White Paper
1962	December	Revolt in Brunei
1963	13 May	Last National Serviceman discharged
1963–6	Borneo 'Confrontation'	
1964–7	Campaign in Radfan/Aden	
1969	August	Commitment of troops to Northern Ireland (still continuing 1993)

1970–5	Campaign in Dhofar (Oman)	
1980	5 May	SAS seizure of Iranian Embassy
1982	The Falklands Conflict	
	28/29 May	*Battle of Goose Green*
	11/12 June	*Battles of Mount Harriet, Two Sisters and Longdon*
	13/14 June	*Battles of Wireless Ridge and Tumbledown*
1990	25 July	Options for Change announced
1991	24–28 Feb	The '100 Hours War' to liberate Kuwait
1992	June	Commitment of troops to Croatia/Bosnia.

....

THE REGIMENTS OF THE BRITISH ARMY

....

THE REGIMENTAL LINE-UP: 1993

The Household Cavalry Regiment

The Household Cavalry Mounted Regiment

The Royal Armoured Corps
1st The Queen's Dragoon Guards
The Royal Scots Dragoon Guards (Carabiniers and Greys)
The Royal Dragoon Guards
The Queen's Royal Hussars (The Queen's Own and Royal Irish)
9th/12th Royal Lancers (Prince of Wales's)
The King's Royal Hussars
The Light Dragoons
The Queen's Royal Lancers
Royal Tank Regiment

Royal Regiment of Artillery

Corps of Royal Engineers

Royal Corps of Signals

The Guards Division
Grenadier Guards   (*2 battalions until Nov 1994*)
Coldstream Guards   (*2 battalions until Dec 1993*)
Scots Guards   (*2 battalions until Nov 1993*)
Irish Guards
Welsh Guards

The Scottish Division
The Royal Scots (The Royal Regiment)

The Royal Highland Fusiliers (Princess Margaret's Own Glasgow and Ayrshire Regiment)
The King's Own Scottish Borderers
The Black Watch (Royal Highland Regiment)
Queen's Own Highlanders (Seaforth and Camerons)*
The Gordon Highlanders*
The Argyll and Sutherland Highlanders (Princess Louise's)

* To be amalgamated in September 1994; new title to be announced

The Queen's Division
The Princess of Wales's Royal Regiment (Queen's and Royal Hampshires)   (*2 battalions*)
The Royal Regiment of Fusiliers   (*2 battalions*)
The Royal Anglian Regiment   (*2 battalions*)

The King's Division
The King's Own Royal Border Regiment
The King's Regiment
The Prince of Wales's Own Regiment of Yorkshire
The Green Howards (Alexandra, Princess of Wales's Own Yorkshire Regiment)
The Queen's Lancashire Regiment
The Duke of Wellington's Regiment (West Riding)

The Prince of Wales's Division
The Devonshire and Dorset Regiment
The 22nd (Cheshire) Regiment
The Royal Welch Fusiliers
The Royal Regiment of Wales (24th/41st Foot)
The Gloucestershire Regiment*

The Worcestershire and Sherwood Foresters Regiment
(29th/45th Foot)

The Staffordshire Regiment (The Prince of Wales's)

The Duke of Edinburgh's Royal Regiment (Berkshire and
Wiltshire*)

*To be amalgamated in April 1994 as The Royal Gloucestershire, Berkshire
and Wiltshire Regiment*

The Royal Irish Division

The Royal Irish Regiment (27th (Inniskilling), 83rd, 87th
and UDR)

(1 'General Service' and 7 ex-UDR battalions)

The Light Division

The Light Infantry	*(2 battalions)*
The Royal Green Jackets	*(2 battalions)*

Corps of Royal Marines *(3 Commando Regiments)*

The Parachute Regiment *(3 battalions)*

The Brigade of Gurkhas*

2nd King Edward VII's Own Goorkha Rifles
(The Sirmoor Rifles)

6th Queen Elizabeth's Own Gurkha Rifles

7th Duke of Edinburgh's Own Gurkha Rifles

10th Queen Mary's Own Gurkha Rifles

Queen's Gurkha Engineers

Queen's Gurkha Signals

Gurkha Transport Regiment

** 2nd and 6th GR to amalgamate to form The 1st Royal Gurkha Rifles; 7th
GR to be renamed The 2nd Royal Gurkha Rifles and 10th GR to be
renamed The 3rd Royal Gurkha Rifles, all by March 1995; 2nd and 3rd
Royal Gurkha Rifles to be amalgamated to form The 2nd Royal Gurkha
Rifles, by 1997. Support services to be cut in proportion.*

Special Air Service Regiment

Army Air Corps

Royal Army Chaplains' Department

The Royal Logistic Corps

Royal Army Medical Corps

Royal Electrical and Mechanical Engineers

The Adjutant General's Corps

Royal Army Veterinary Corps

Small Arms School Corps

Royal Army Dental Corps

Intelligence Corps

Army Physical Training Corps

Queen Alexandra's Royal Army Nursing Corps

Royal Military Academy Sandhurst

Royal Military School of Music

The Gibraltar Regiment.

THE HOUSEHOLD CAVALRY REGIMENT
THE HOUSEHOLD CAVALRY MOUNTED REGIMENT

Formed 19 October 1992 by the 'amalgamation' of The Life
Guards and The Blues and Royals. In reality, the former
regiments remain, although they are now treated as one unit
from which a tank regiment (The Household Cavalry Regiment)
and a ceremonial regiment (The Household Cavalry Mounted
Regiment) are provided.

THE LIFE GUARDS

Brief History: Originally two troops of Horse Guards and two
troops of Horse Grenadier Guards, raised from soldiers who had
supported the monarchy in the Civil War and placed on the
English establishment in January 1661. The Horse Grenadiers
were disbanded in June 1788 and personnel transferred to the
Horse Guards, which were redesignated 1st and 2nd Life Guards,
amalgamated in May 1922 to form The Life Guards.

Battle Honours include: Dettingen, Peninsula, Waterloo,
Egypt 1882, Tel-el-Kebir, South Africa 1899–1900, France and
Flanders 1914–18, El Alamein, Italy 1944, North-West Europe
1944–5.

Nicknames: The Cheesemongers, The Piccadilly Butchers,
The Tin Bellies, The Patent Safeties.

THE BLUES AND ROYALS (ROYAL HORSE GUARDS AND 1st DRAGOONS)

Formed 29 September 1969 by the amalgamation of the Royal
Horse Guards (The Blues) and The Royal Dragoons (1st Dragoons).
Two troops served in the Falklands Conflict 1982.

Royal Horse Guards (The Blues)

Brief History: Originally a Cromwellian unit, disbanded in 1660
but re-raised as The Royal Regiment of Horse or Oxford Blues in
January 1661, ranking as the 1st Horse until 1747. Redesignated
as Royal Regiment of Horse Guards (The Blues) in 1819, placed
on the same footing as the 1st and 2nd Life Guards in 1827.
Restyled in 1877 as Royal Horse Guards (The Blues).

Battle Honours include: Dettingen, Peninsula, Waterloo,
Egypt 1882, Tel-el-Kebir, South Africa 1899–1900, France and
Flanders 1914–18, El Alamein, Italy 1944, North-West Europe
1944–5.

Nicknames: The Blue Guards, The Blues.

The Royal Dragoons (1st Dragoons)

Brief History: Formed 21 October 1661 as the Tangiers Horse;
redesignated in 1683 as The King's Own Royal Regiment of
Dragoons and referred to after 1690 as the Royal Regiment of
Dragoons. Redesignated in 1751 as 1st (Royal) Regiment of
Dragoons; after further minor changes became The Royal
Dragoons (1st Dragoons) in 1961.

Battle Honours include: Dettingen, Peninsula, Waterloo,
Balaklava, Sevastopol, South Africa 1899–1902, France and
Flanders 1914–18, El Alamein, Italy 1943, North-West Europe
1944–5.

Nicknames: The Royals, The English Horse.

ROYAL ARMOURED CORPS

1st THE QUEEN'S DRAGOON GUARDS

Formed 1 January 1959 by the amalgamation of the 1st King's
Dragoon Guards and The Queen's Bays (2nd Dragoon Guards).

1st King's Dragoon Guards

Brief History: Raised in June 1685 as the Queen's Regiment of
Horse, later the 2nd Horse; redesignated in 1714 as The King's
Own Regiment of Horse. Converted in 1746 as The King's
Dragoon Guards; redesignated in 1751 as 1st (The King's)
Dragoon Guards and in 1921 as 1st King's Dragoon Guards.

Battle Honours include: Blenheim, Ramillies, Oudenarde,
Malplaquet, Dettingen, Waterloo, Sevastopol, Taku Forts, Pekin,
South Africa 1901–02, France and Flanders 1914–17, Beda

Fomm, North Africa 1941–3, Italy 1943–4.

Nicknames: The KDGs, The Trades Union.

The Queen's Bays (2nd Dragoon Guards)

Brief History: Raised in June 1685 as the Earl of Peterborough's Regiment of Horse, later the 3rd Horse; redesignated in 1715 as The Princess of Wales's Own Regiment of Horse and in 1727 as The Queen's Own Regiment of Horse. Converted in 1746 as The Queen's Dragoon Guards; redesignated in 1780 as 2nd Dragoon Guards (Queen's Bays) and in 1921 as The Queen's Bays (2nd Dragoon Guards).

Battle Honours include: Lucknow, South Africa 1901–2, France and Flanders 1914–18, Gazala, El Alamein, Rimini Line, Argenta Gap.

Nicknames: The Bays, The Rusty Buckles.

THE ROYAL SCOTS DRAGOON GUARDS (CARABINIERS AND GREYS)

Formed 2 July 1971 by the amalgamation of the 3rd Carabiniers (Prince of Wales's Dragoon Guards) and The Royal Scots Greys (2nd Dragoons). Served in the Gulf as part of 7th Armoured Brigade 1990–1.

3rd Carabiniers (Prince of Wales's Dragoon Guards)

Formed in 1922 by the amalgamation of the 3rd Dragoon Guards (Prince of Wales's) and 6th Dragoon Guards (Carabiniers) as the 3rd/6th Dragoon Guards; redesignated in 1928 as 3rd Carabiniers (Prince of Wales's Dragoon Guards).

3rd Dragoon Guards (Prince of Wales's)

Brief History: Raised July 1685 as the Earl of Plymouth's Regiment of Horse, later the 4th Horse; redesignated in 1746 as 3rd Regiment of Dragoon Guards and in 1765 as 3rd (The Prince of Wales's) Dragoon Guards. Title changed in 1921 to 3rd Dragoon Guards (Prince of Wales's).

Battle Honours include: Blenheim, Ramillies, Oudenarde, Malplaquet, Talavera, Albuera, Vitoria, Peninsula, Abyssinia, South Africa 1901–2, France and Flanders 1914–18.

Nickname: The Old Canaries.

6th Dragoon Guards (Carabiniers)

Brief History: Raised in July 1685 as The Queen Dowager's Regiment of Horse, redesignated in 1692 as The King's Regiment of Carabiniers, eventually the 7th Horse, re-ranked 3rd Horse in 1746. Converted in 1788 as 6th Regiment of Dragoon Guards, known as Carabiniers from 1826.

Battle Honours include: Blenheim, Ramillies, Oudenarde, Malplaquet, Sevastopol, Delhi, Afghanistan 1879–80, South Africa 1899–1902, France and Flanders 1914–18.

Nicknames: The Carbs, Tichborne's Own.

The Royal Scots Greys (2nd Dragoons)

Brief History: Raised in Scotland in 1678 as three independent troops, regimented in 1681 as Royal Regiment of Scots Dragoons or His Majesty's Regiment of Dragoons. Redesignated in 1751 as the 2nd (Royal North British) Regiment of Dragoons and in 1866 as 2nd (Royal North British) Dragoons (Royal Scots Greys). Redesignated in 1921 as The Royal Scots Greys (2nd Dragoons).

Battle Honours include: Blenheim, Ramillies, Oudenarde, Malplaquet, Dettingen, Waterloo, Balaklava, Sevastopol, South Africa 1899–1902, France and Flanders 1914–18, El Alamein, Salerno, Hill 112, Falaise.

Nicknames: Scotch Greys, Bubbly Jocks.

THE ROYAL DRAGOON GUARDS

Formed 31 July 1992 by the amalgamation of the 4th/7th Royal Dragoon Guards and the 5th Royal Inniskilling Dragoon Guards.

4th/7th Royal Dragoon Guards

Formed 22 October 1922 by the amalgamation of the 4th Royal Irish Dragoon Guards and the 7th Dragoon Guards (Princess Royal's). Served in North-West Europe 1944–5.

4th Royal Irish Dragoon Guards

Brief History: Raised in July 1685 as the Earl of Arran's (later Duke of Hamilton) Regiment of Cuirassiers, eventually 5th Horse. Redesignated in Ireland in 1746 as 1st Horse, also known as the Blue Horse; converted in 1788 as 4th (Royal Irish) Dragoon Guards, brackets later dropped from title.

Battle Honours include: Peninsula, Balaklava, Sevastopol, Egypt 1882, Tel-el-Kebir, France and Flanders 1914–18.

Nickname: The Blue Horse.

7th Dragoon Guards (Princess Royal's)

Brief History: Raised in 1688 as Lord Cavendish's (later Earl of Devonshire) Regiment of Horse, eventually 8th Horse. Redesignated in Ireland in 1746 as 4th Horse, also known as the Black Horse. Converted in 1788 as 7th (The Princess Royal's) Dragoon Guards; redesignated in 1921 as 7th Dragoon Guards (Princess Royal's).

Battle Honours include: Blenheim, Ramillies, Oudenarde, Malplaquet, Dettingen, South Africa 1846–7, Egypt 1882, Tel-el-Kebir, South Africa 1900–2, France and Flanders 1914–18.

Nicknames: The Black Horse, The Virgin Mary's Bodyguard, Strawboots.

5th Royal Inniskilling Dragoon Guards

Formed in April 1922 by the amalgamation of the 5th Dragoon Guards (Princess Charlotte of Wales's) and The Inniskillings (6th Dragoons) to form 5th/6th Dragoons. Redesignated as 5th Inniskilling Dragoon Guards in 1927, Royal added to the title in 1935. Served in North-West Europe 1944–5 and in Korea 1951–2. Known as The Skins.

5th Dragoon Guards (Princess Charlotte of Wales's)

Brief History: Raised in July 1685 as the Duke of Shrewsbury's Regiment of Horse, eventually 6th Horse. Redesignated in Ireland in 1746 as 2nd Horse, also known as the Green Horse. Converted in 1788 as 5th Regiment of Dragoon Guards, redesignated in 1823 as 5th (the Princess Charlotte of Wales's) Regiment of Dragoon Guards and in 1921 as 5th Dragoon Guards (Princess Charlotte of Wales's).

Battle Honours include: Blenheim, Ramillies, Oudenarde, Malplaquet, Salamanca, Vitoria, Toulouse, Peninsula, Balaklava, Sevastopol, South Africa 1899–1902, France and Flanders 1914–18.

Nickname: The Green Horse.

The Inniskillings (6th Dragoons)

Brief History: Raised in June 1689 as Sir Albert Cunningham's Regiment of Dragoons, ranked 6th Dragoons in 1691. Redesignated in 1751 as 6th (Inniskilling) Dragoons; title changed in 1921 to The Inniskillings (6th Dragoons).

Battle Honours include: Dettingen, Waterloo, Balaklava, Sevastopol, South Africa 1899–1902, France and Flanders 1914–18.

Nicknames: The Black Dragoons, The Skillingers.

THE QUEEN'S ROYAL HUSSARS (THE QUEEN'S OWN AND ROYAL IRISH)

Formed in August 1993 by the amalgamation of The Queen's Own Hussars and The Queen's Royal Irish Hussars.

The Queen's Own Hussars

Formed in November 1958 by the amalgamation of the 3rd The King's Own Hussars and the 7th Queen's Own Hussars.

3rd The King's Own Hussars

Brief History: Raised in August 1685 as the Duke of Somerset's

Regiment of Dragoons; redesignated in 1694 as The Queen Consort's Own Regiment of Dragoons, in 1714 as The King's Regiment of Dragoons and in 1751 as 3rd (King's Own) Regiment of Dragoons. Converted in 1818 as 3rd (The King's Own) Regiment of (Light) Dragoons; redesignated in 1861 as 3rd (The King's Own) Hussars and in 1921 as 3rd The King's Own Hussars.

Battle Honours include: Dettingen, Salamanca, Vitoria, Toulouse, Peninsula, Kabul 1842, Mudkee, Ferozeshah, Sobraon, Punjab, Chillianwala, Gujerat, South Africa 1902, France and Flanders 1914–18, Beda Fomm, El Alamein, Italy 1944.

Nicknames: Lord Adam Gordon's Life Guards, Bland's Dragoons.

7th Queen's Own Hussars

Brief History: Raised in August 1715 as The Princess of Wales's Own Regiment of Dragoons, redesignated in 1727 as The Queen's Own Regiment of Dragoons, numbered 7th in 1751. Retitled 7th (or Queen's Own) Regiment of (Light) Dragoons in 1788, redesignated in 1861 as 7th (The Queen's Own) Hussars and in 1921 as 7th Queen's Own Hussars.

Battle Honours include: Dettingen, Peninsula, Waterloo, Lucknow, South Africa 1901–2, Mesopotamia 1917–18, Beda Fomm, Burma 1942, Italy 1944–5.

Nicknames: The Lily White Seventh, Young Eyes, Old Straws.

The Queen's Royal Irish Hussars

Formed on 24 October 1958 by the amalgamation of the 4th Queen's Own Hussars and the 8th King's Royal Irish Hussars. Served in the Gulf 1990–1 as part of 7th Armoured Brigade.

4th Queen's Own Hussars

Brief History: Raised in July 1685 as The Princess Anne of Denmark Regiment of Dragoons; redesignated in 1751 as 4th Regiment of Dragoons, in 1788 as 4th (Queen's Own) Regiment of Dragoons and in 1818 as 4th (Queen's Own) Regiment of Light Dragoons. Redesignated in 1861 as 4th (The Queen's Own) Hussars and in 1921 as 4th Queen's Own Hussars.

Battle Honours include: Dettingen, Talavera, Albuera, Salamanca, Vitoria, Toulouse, Peninsula, Afghanistan, Ghuznee, Alma, Balaklava, Inkerman, Sevastopol, France and Flanders 1914–18, Greece 1941, El Alamein, Italy 1944–5.

Nickname: Paget's Irregular Horse.

8th King's Royal Irish Hussars

Brief History: Raised in February 1693 as Henry Cunningham's Regiment of Dragoons, later 8th Dragoons; redesignated in 1775 as 8th Regiment of Light Dragoons, in 1777 as 8th (The King's Royal Irish) Regiment of (Light) Dragoons, in 1861 as 8th (The King's Royal Irish) Hussars and in 1921 as 8th King's Royal Irish Hussars.

Battle Honours include: Laswari, Hindoostan, Alma, Balaklava, Sevastopol, Central India, Afghanistan 1879–80, South Africa 1900–2, France and Flanders 1914–18, Gazala, El Alamein, North-West Europe 1944–5, Imjin, Korea 1950–1.

Nickname: The Cross Belts.

9th/12th ROYAL LANCERS (PRINCE OF WALES'S)

Formed 11 September 1960 by the amalgamation of the 9th Queen's Royal Lancers and the 12th Royal Lancers (Prince of Wales's).

9th Queen's Royal Lancers

Brief History: Raised in July 1715 as Owen Wynne's Regiment of Dragoons, later 9th Dragoons. Redesignated in 1783 as 9th Regiment of (Light) Dragoons, in 1830 as 9th (or Queen's Royal) Lancers, in 1861 as 9th (The Queen's Royal) Lancers and in 1921 as 9th Queen's Royal Lancers.

Battle Honours include: Peninsula, Sobraon, Punjab, Chillianwala, Gujerat, Delhi, Lucknow, Charasiah, Kabul 1879,

Kandahar 1880, South Africa 1899–1902, France and Flanders 1914–18, El Alamein, Italy 1944–5.

Nickname: The Delhi Spearmen.

12th Royal Lancers (Prince of Wales's)

Brief History: Raised in July 1715 as Phineas Bowles's Regiment of Dragoons, later 12th Dragoons. Redesignated in 1768 as 12th (The Prince of Wales's) Regiment of (Light) Dragoons, in 1817 as 12th (The Prince of Wales's) Royal Regiment of (Light) Dragoons (Lancers), in 1861 as 12th (The Prince of Wales's) Royal Regiment of Lancers and in 1921 as 12th Royal Lancers (Prince of Wales's).

Battle Honours include: Egypt, Peninsula, Waterloo, South Africa 1851–2–3, Sevastopol, Central India, South Africa 1899–1902, France and Flanders 1914–18, Gazala, El Alamein, Italy 1944–5.

Nickname: The Supple Twelfth.

THE KING'S ROYAL HUSSARS

Formed on 4 December 1992 by the amalgamation of The Royal Hussars (Prince of Wales's Own) and the 14th/20th King's Hussars.

The Royal Hussars (Prince of Wales's Own)

Formed on 25 October 1969 by the amalgamation of the 10th Royal Hussars (Prince of Wales's Own) and the 11th Hussars (Prince Albert's Own).

10th Royal Hussars (Prince of Wales's Own)

Brief History: Raised in July 1715 as Humphrey Gore's Regiment of Dragoons, later 10th Dragoons; redesignated in 1783 as 10th (Prince of Wales's Own) Regiment of (Light) Dragoons, in 1861 as 10th (The Prince of Wales's Own) Royal Hussars and in 1921 as 10th Royal Hussars (Prince of Wales's Own).

Battle Honours include: Peninsula, Waterloo, Sevastopol, Ali Musjid, Afghanistan 1878–9, Egypt 1884, South Africa 1899–1902, France and Flanders 1914–18, Gazala, El Alamein, Italy 1944–5.

Nicknames: Baker's Light Bobs, Chainy Tenth.

11th Hussars (Prince Albert's Own)

Brief History: Raised in July 1715 as Philip Honeywood's Regiment of Dragoons, later 11th Dragoons; redesignated in 1783 as 11th Regiment of (Light) Dragoons, in 1840 as 11th (or Prince Albert's Own) Regiment of (Light) Dragoons (Hussars), in 1861 as 11th (or Prince Albert's Own) Hussars and in 1921 as 11th Hussars (Prince Albert's Own).

Battle Honours include: Egypt, Salamanca, Peninsula, Waterloo, Bhurtpore, Alma, Balaklava, Inkerman, Sevastopol, France and Flanders 1914–18, Beda Fomm, Sidi Rezegh, El Alamein, Italy 1943, North-West Europe 1944–5.

Nicknames: The Cherry Pickers, The Cheribums.

14th/20th King's Hussars

Formed 1 October 1922 by the amalgamation of the 14th King's Hussars and the 20th Hussars. Served in Italy during the Second World War and, as part of 4th Armoured Brigade, in the Gulf 1990–1. Known as The Hawks.

14th King's Hussars

Brief History: Raised in July 1715 as James Dormer's Regiment of Dragoons, later 14th Dragoons. Redesignated in 1776 as 14th Regiment of (Light) Dragoons, in 1798 as 14th (The Duchess of York's Own) Regiment of (Light) Dragoons, in 1830 as 14th (The King's) Regiment of (Light) Dragoons, in 1861 as 14th (The King's) Hussars and in 1921 as 14th King's Hussars.

Battle Honours include: Douro, Talavera, Fuentes d'Oñoro, Salamanca, Vitoria, Orthez, Peninsula, Punjab, Chillianwala, Gujerat, Persia, Central India, South Africa 1900–2, Mesopotamia 1915–18.

Nicknames: The Emperor's Chambermaids, The Ramnuggur Boys.

20th Hussars

Brief History: Raised in 1858 by the East India Company as 2nd Bengal European Light Cavalry, transferred to Crown control in 1860 and to the British Army as 20th Regiment of Hussars in 1862. Redesignated 20th Hussars in 1877.

Battle Honours include: Vimeiro, Peninsula [inherited from 20th Light Dragoons, 1792–1818], Suakin 1885, South Africa 1901–2, France and Flanders 1914–18.

Nickname: The Dumpies.

THE LIGHT DRAGOONS

Formed 1 December 1992 by the amalgamation of the 13th/18th Royal Hussars (Queen Mary's Own) and the 15th/19th The King's Royal Hussars.

13th/18th Royal Hussars (Queen Mary's Own)

Formed in April 1922 by the amalgamation of the 13th Hussars and the 18th Royal Hussars (Queen Mary's Own). Served in North-West Europe 1944–5.

13th Hussars

Brief History: Raised in July 1715 as Richard Munden's Regiment of Dragoons, later 13th Dragoons. Redesignated 1783 as 13th Regiment of (Light) Dragoons and in 1861 as 13th Hussars.

Battle Honours include: Albuera, Vitoria, Orthez, Toulouse, Peninsula, Waterloo, Alma, Balaklava, Inkerman, Sevastopol, South Africa 1899–1902, France and Flanders 1914–16, Mesopotamia 1916–18.

Nicknames: Evergreens, Geraniums.

18th Royal Hussars (Queen Mary's Own)

Brief History: Raised in February 1858 as 18th Regiment of (Light) Dragoons; redesignated in 1861 as 18th Hussars, in 1905 as 18th (Victoria Mary, Princess of Wales's Own) Hussars, in 1910 as 18th (Queen Mary's Own) Hussars and in 1921 as 18th Royal Hussars (Queen Mary's Own).

Battle Honours include: Peninsula, Waterloo [inherited from 18th Light Dragoons 1759–1821], South Africa 1899–1902, France and Flanders 1914–18.

Nickname: Drogheda Light Horse.

15th/19th The King's Royal Hussars

Formed 1 January 1922 by the amalgamation of the 15th The King's Hussars and the 19th Royal Hussars (Queen Alexandra's Own). Served in North-West Europe 1944–5.

15th The King's Hussars

Brief History: Raised in March 1759 as Eliott's Light Horse, officially the 15th (or Light) Regiment of Dragoons. Redesignated in 1769 as 15th (The King's) Regiment of (Light) Dragoons; subtitle 'Hussars' added in 1807; redesignated 15th (The King's) Hussars in 1861 and 15th The King's Hussars in 1921.

Battle Honours include: Emsdorf, Villiers-en-Couche, Egmont-op-Zee, Sahagun, Vitoria, Peninsula, Waterloo, Afghanistan 1878–80, France and Flanders 1914–18.

Nickname: The Fighting Fifteenth.

19th Royal Hussars (Queen Alexandra's Own)

Brief History: Raised in 1858 by the East India Company as the 1st Bengal European Light Cavalry, transferred to Crown control in 1860; became part of the British Army as 19th Hussars in 1862. Redesignated in 1902 as 19th (Alexandra, Princess of Wales's Own) Hussars, in 1908 as 19th (Queen Alexandra's Own Royal) Hussars and in 1921 as 19th Royal Hussars (Queen Alexandra's Own).

Battle Honours include: Mysore, Assaye, Niagara [inherited from 19th Light Dragoons 1781–1821], Egypt 1882–4, Tel-el-Kebir, Nile 1884–5, Abu Klea, South Africa 1899–1902, France and Flanders 1914–18.

Nickname: The Dumpies.

THE QUEEN'S ROYAL LANCERS

Formed on 25 June 1993 by the amalgamation of the 16th/5th The Queen's Royal Lancers and the 17th/21st Lancers.

16th/5th The Queen's Royal Lancers

Formed in April 1922 by the amalgamation of the 16th The Queen's Lancers and the 5th Royal Irish Lancers. Served in North Africa 1942–3, Italy 1944–5 and the Gulf 1990–1.

16th The Queen's Lancers

Brief History: Raised in August 1759 as Burgoyne's Light Horse, officially 16th Regiment of (Light) Dragoons; redesignated in 1769 as 16th (or The Queen's Own) Regiment of (Light) Dragoons, subtitle 'Lancers' added 1816. Redesignated in 1861 as 16th (or Queen's) Lancers, in 1905 as 16th (The Queen's) Lancers and in 1921 as 16th The Queen's Lancers.

Battle Honours include: Talavera, Fuentes d'Oñoro, Salamanca, Vitoria, Nive, Peninsula, Waterloo, Bhurtpore, Afghanistan, Ghuznee, Maharajpore, Aliwal, Sobraon, South Africa 1900–2, France and Flanders 1914–18.

Nickname: The Scarlet Lancers.

5th Royal Irish Lancers

Brief History: Raised in June 1689 as Owen Wynne's, or Ross's Regiment of Dragoons, later 5th Dragoons; redesignated in 1756 as 5th (or Royal Irish) Regiment of Dragoons but disbanded in April 1799. Reformed in February 1858 as 5th (or Royal Irish) Regiment of Dragoons; redesignated 5th (or Royal Irish) Lancers in 1861 and 5th Royal Irish Lancers in 1921.

Battle Honours include: Blenheim, Ramillies, Oudenarde, Malplaquet, Suakin 1885, South Africa 1899–1902, France and Flanders 1914–18.

Nicknames: The Daily Advertisers, Redbreasts.

17th/21st Lancers

Formed in June 1922 by the amalgamation of the 17th Lancers (Duke of Cambridge's Own) and 21st Lancers (Empress of India's). Served in North Africa 1942–3 and Italy 1944–5.

17th Lancers (Duke of Cambridge's Own)

Brief History: Raised in November 1759 as Hale's Light Horse; originally 18th Regiment of (Light) Dragoons but redesignated 17th in 1763; additional subtitle 'Lancers' in 1822. Redesignated 17th Regiment of Lancers in 1861, 17th (The Duke of Cambridge's Own) Lancers in 1876 and 17th Lancers (Duke of Cambridge's Own) in 1921.

Battle Honours include: Alma, Balaklava, Inkerman, Sevastopol, Central India, South Africa 1879, South Africa 1900–2, France and Flanders 1914–18.

Nicknames: Death or Glory Boys, Bingham's Dandies, Horse Marines.

21st Lancers (Empress of India's)

Brief History: Raised in 1858 by the East India Company as the 3rd Bengal European Light Cavalry, transferred to Crown control in 1859; became part of the British Army in 1862 as 21st Regiment of Hussars. Converted in 1897 as 21st Lancers; redesignated in 1898 as 21st (Empress of India's) Lancers and in 1921 as 21st Lancers (Empress of India's).

Battle Honours include: Omdurman, North-West Frontier India 1915–16.

ROYAL TANK REGIMENT

Brief History: Formed in February 1916 as the Tank Detachment, redesignated in March 1916 as the Armoured Car Section, Motor Machine Gun Service, Machine Gun Corps, in May 1916 as the Heavy Section (later Branch), Machine Gun Corps. Reorganized as the Tank Corps in July 1917, Royal added in October 1923. Became a wing of the Royal Armoured Corps in April 1939 as the Royal Tank Regiment; all battalions termed regiments from September 1945. Currently two regiments in existence: 1RTR (formed in July 1993 by the amalgamation of 1RTR and 4RTR) and 2RTR (formed in August 1992 by the amalgamation of 2RTR and 3RTR).

Battle Honours include: France and Flanders 1916–18, Greece 1941, Burma 1942, North Africa 1940–3, Italy 1943–5, North-West Europe 1944–5, Korea 1951–3.

Nickname: The Tankies.

ROYAL REGIMENT OF ARTILLERY

Brief History: Two companies of artillery formed at Woolwich in 1716, being merged with companies from Gibraltar and Minorca in 1722 to form the Royal Regiment of Artillery. Organized into 1st and 2nd Battalions, Royal Artillery in 1757, with other battalions (up to 14th) being raised between 1759 and 1855. The Royal Horse Artillery was raised in 1793. In 1859 the Royal Artillery battalions were broken up and batteries distributed to new brigades, designated Royal Field Artillery and Royal Garrison Artillery in 1899. RFA and RGA designations dropped in 1924. By 1995 there will be nine field and four air defence regiments in existence.

Battle Honours: Ubique ('Everywhere').
Nickname: The Gunners.

CORPS OF ROYAL ENGINEERS

Brief History: The first Corps of Engineers formed in 1717 and a Soldier Artificer Company added in Gibraltar in 1772. In 1787 Corps redesignated the Corps of Royal Engineers and a Corps of Royal Military Artificers created. In 1812 the Artificers redesignated Royal Sappers and Miners; in 1856 the two units amalgamated as the Corps of Royal Engineers. In April 1992 the Postal and Courier Services of the Royal Engineers became part of The Royal Logistic Corps (*see* p.212). By 1997 the Corps will comprise 10 regiments and three independent squadrons.

Battle Honours: Ubique ('Everywhere').
Nickname: The Sappers.

ROYAL CORPS OF SIGNALS

Brief History: Formed in 1920 from the Corps of Royal Engineers. By 1995 to consist of 10 regiments and to reorganize its electronic warfare units into a new regiment.

THE GUARDS DIVISION

GRENADIER GUARDS

Brief History: Raised in 1656 as Lord Wentworth's Regiment to protect the exiled Charles II. Placed on the English establishment in August 1660 and amalgamated in March 1665 with the King's Royal Regiment of Guards (a unit raised in November 1660 as John Russell's Regiment of Guards) to form the First Regiment of Foot Guards, comprising two battalions. Redesignated in July 1815 as 1st (or Grenadier) Regiment of Foot Guards and in 1877 as the Grenadier Guards. The 2nd Battalion, in continuous existence since March 1665, is to be placed in 'suspended animation' in November 1994. A 3rd Battalion existed from 1760 until 1961.

Battle Honours include: Blenheim, Ramillies, Oudenarde, Malplaquet, Dettingen, Lincelles, Corunna, Barossa, Peninsula, Waterloo, Alma, Inkerman, Sevastopol, Egypt 1882, Tel-el-Kebir, Suakin 1885, South Africa 1899–1902, France and

Flanders 1914–18, North Africa 1942–3, Salerno, Anzio, Gothic Line, North-West Europe 1944–5.

Nicknames: Sandbags, Coalheavers, Old Eyes.

COLDSTREAM GUARDS

Brief History: Raised in August 1650 for the Parliamentary Army as George Monck's (later the Duke of Albemarle) Regiment; redesignated in 1660 as The Duke of Albemarle's Regiment of Foot or The Lord General's Regiment and taken into the King's service in February 1661 as the Lord General's Regiment of Foot Guards. Redesignated in 1661 as the Coldstream Regiment of Foot Guards. Initially only one battalion, but a 2nd added in April 1711. The 2nd Battalion is to be placed in 'suspended animation' in December 1993.

Battle Honours include: Oudenarde, Malplaquet, Dettingen, Lincelles, Egypt, Talavera, Barossa, Peninsula, Waterloo, Alma, Inkerman, Sevastopol, Egypt 1882, Tel-el-Kebir, Suakin 1885, South Africa 1899–1902, France and Flanders 1914–18, North Africa 1940–3, Salerno, Italy 1943–5, North-West Europe 1944–5.

Nicknames: Nulli Secundus Club, Coldstreamers.

SCOTS GUARDS

Brief History: Raised in November 1660 as six independent companies and made into a regiment under George, Earl of Linlithgow in May 1661 as the Scots Regiment of Foot Guards (although some sources trace the unit back to 1639). Redesignated in 1713 as the 3rd Regiment of Foot Guards, in April 1831 as the Scots Fusilier Guards and in April 1877 as the Scots Guards. A 2nd Battalion was raised in 1689; it saw service most recently in the Falklands Conflict 1982, and is to be placed in 'suspended animation' in November 1993.

Battle Honours include: Dettingen, Lincelles, Egypt, Talavera, Barossa, Peninsula, Waterloo, Alma, Inkerman, Sevastopol, Egypt 1882, Tel-el-Kebir, Suakin 1885, South Africa 1899–1902, France and Flanders 1914–18, Gazala, North Africa 1941–3, Salerno, Anzio, Italy 1943–5, North-West Europe 1944–5, Tumbledown Mountain, Falkland Islands 1982.

Nickname: The Jocks.

IRISH GUARDS

Brief History: Formed in April 1900 in recognition of the services of Irish soldiers in the Second Boer War. Originally the intention was to raise two battalions, but in the event only one was formed.

Battle Honours include: France and Flanders 1914–18, North Africa 1943, Anzio, Italy 1943–4, North-West Europe 1944–5.

Nickname: The Micks.

WELSH GUARDS

Brief History: Raised in February 1915 to comprise one battalion only. Served most recently in the Falklands Conflict 1982.

Battle Honours include: France and Flanders 1915–18, North Africa 1943, Italy 1944–5, North-West Europe 1944–5, Falkland Islands 1982.

Nickname: None recorded, although known by the general Guards' nicknames of Tick-Tocks and Woodentops.

THE SCOTTISH DIVISION

THE ROYAL SCOTS (THE ROYAL REGIMENT)

Brief History: Raised in 1625 as independent Scottish companies in the service of the French King; accompanied Charles I to Scotland in 1633, then returned to France as the Régiment de

Hebron. Journeyed to England in 1662 but returned the same year to France. Joined the English establishment in 1670 and in 1684 redesignated His Majesty's Royal Regiment of Foot. Redesignated 1747 as 1st of Foot, in 1751 as 1st (Royal) Regiment of Foot, in 1812 as 1st Regiment of Foot (Royal Scots), in 1881 as The Royal Scots (Lothian Regiment) and in 1921 as The Royal Scots (The Royal Regiment). A 2nd Battalion existed from 1686 until 1949. The 1st Battalion saw service most recently in the Gulf Conflict 1990–1, as part of 4th Armoured Brigade, and was scheduled to be amalgamated with the King's Own Scottish Borderers in October 1994, but this was cancelled in early 1993.

Battle Honours include: Blenheim, Ramillies, Oudenarde, Malplaquet, Louisburg, St Lucia, Egmont-op-Zee, Egypt, Corunna, Busaco, Salamanca, Vitoria, San Sebastian, Nive, Peninsula, Niagara, Waterloo, Nagpore, Ava, Alma, Inkerman, Sevastopol, Taku Forts, Pekin, South Africa 1899–1902, France and Flanders 1914-18, Gallipoli 1915–16, Palestine 1917–18, Burma 1943–5, Kohima, Italy 1944–5, North-West Europe 1944–5.

Nickname: Pontius Pilot's Bodyguard (*see* p.19).

THE ROYAL HIGHLAND FUSILIERS (PRINCESS MARGARET'S OWN GLASGOW AND AYRSHIRE REGIMENT)

Formed 20 January 1959 by the amalgamation of The Royal Scots Fusiliers and The Highland Light Infantry (City of Glasgow Regiment).

The Royal Scots Fusiliers

Brief History: Raised in September 1678 as the Earl of Mar's Regiment of Foot and transferred to the English establishment in 1688 as the Scots Fuziliers. Redesignated in 1708 as the North British Fusiliers and in 1713 as the Royal North British Fusiliers; ranked as 21st Foot in 1747. Redesignated in 1751 as 21st Regiment of Foot (Royal North British Fusiliers), in 1877 as 21st Regiment of Foot (Royal Scots Fusiliers) and in 1881 as The Royal Scots Fusiliers. A 2nd Battalion existed between 1857 and 1948.

Battle Honours include: Blenheim, Ramillies, Oudenarde, Malplaquet, Dettingen, Bladensburg, Alma, Inkerman, Sevastopol, South Africa 1879, Burma 1885–7, South Africa 1899–1902, France and Flanders 1914–18, Palestine 1917–18, Sicily 1943, Anzio, Italy 1943–4, Burma 1944–5, North-West Europe 1944–5.

Nickname: Earl of Mar's Grey Breeks.

The Highland Light Infantry (City of Glasgow Regiment)

Brief History: Formed 1 July 1881. The 1st Battalion had been the 71st (Highland) Regiment of Foot (Light Infantry), first raised as the 73rd (Highland) Regiment of Foot or McLeod's Highlanders in December 1777 and renumbered 71st in 1786; the 2nd Battalion had been the 74th (Highlanders) Regiment of Foot, first raised in 1787.

Battle Honours include: Carnatic, Mysore, Seringapatam, Hindoostan, Assaye, Egypt, Rolica, Vimeiro, Corunna, Busaco, Fuentes d'Oñoro, Cuidad Rodrigo, Badajoz, Almarez, Salamanca, Vitoria, Pryenees, Nivelle, Nive, Orthez, Toulouse, Peninsula, Waterloo, South Africa 1851–2–3, Sevastopol, Central India, Egypt 1882, Tel-el-Kebir, South Africa 1899–1902, France and Flanders 1914–18, Gallipoli 1915–16, Palestine 1917–18, North Africa 1940-2, Sicily 1943, Greece 1944–5, North-West Europe 1944–5.

Nicknames: The Glesca Keelies (71st), The Assayes (74th), Pig and Whistle Light Infantry (HLI).

THE KING'S OWN SCOTTISH BORDERERS

Brief History: Raised in March 1689 as the Earl of Leven's or Edinburgh Regiment of Foot, ranked as 25th Foot in 1747. Redesignated in 1751 as 25th (Edinburgh) Regiment of Foot, in 1782 as 25th (Sussex) Regiment of Foot, in 1805 as 25th (the King's Own Borderers) Regiment of Foot, in 1870 as 25th (The York) Regiment of Foot (King's Own Borderers) and in 1887 as The King's Own Scottish Borderers. A 2nd Battalion existed between 1860 and 1948. The 1st Battalion was scheduled to amalgamate with The Royal Scots in October 1994 but this was cancelled in early 1993.

Battle Honours include: Minden, Egmont-op-Zee, Martinique, Egypt 1801, Afghanistan 1878–80, South Africa 1899–1902, France and Flanders 1914–18, Gallipoli 1915–16, Palestine 1917–18, Imphal, Irrawaddy, North-West Europe 1944–5, Korea 1951–2.

Nicknames: The KOBs, The Botherers, The Kosbees (the latter is not liked by the regiment).

THE BLACK WATCH (ROYAL HIGHLAND REGIMENT)

Brief History: Formed 1 July 1881 as The Black Watch (Royal Highlanders); redesignated in 1935 as The Black Watch (Royal Highland Regiment). 1st Battalion had been the 42nd (Royal Highland) Regiment of Foot, formed in October 1739 from a number of independent companies, some dating back to 1662; the 2nd Battalion had been the 73rd (Perthshire) Regiment of Foot, raised in 1786. 1st and 2nd Battalions amalgamated in 1948.

Battle Honours include: Mysore, Seringapatam, Egypt, Corunna, Fuentes d'Oñoro, Pyrenees, Nivelle, Nive, Orthez, Toulouse, Peninsula, Waterloo, South Africa 1846–7, 1851–2–3, Alma, Sevastopol, Lucknow, Ashantee, Egypt 1882, 1884, Tel-el-Kebir, Nile 1884–5, South Africa 1899–1902, France and Flanders 1914–18, Mesopotamia 1915–17, Megiddo, El Alamein, North Africa 1941–3, Sicily 1943, Italy 1944–5, North-West Europe 1944–5, The Hook 1952, Korea 1952–3.

Nickname: The Black Watch.

QUEEN'S OWN HIGHLANDERS (SEAFORTH AND CAMERONS)

Formed 7 February 1961 by the amalgamation of the Seaforth Highlanders (Ross-shire Buffs, The Duke of Albany's) and The Queen's Own Cameron Highlanders. To be amalgamated with The Gordon Highlanders in September 1994.

Seaforth Highlanders (Ross-shire Buffs, The Duke of Albany's)

Brief History: Formed 1 July 1881. The 1st Battalion had been the 72nd, or Duke of Albany's Own Highlanders, Regiment of Foot, raised in 1777–8 as 78th (Highland) Regiment of Foot and renumbered 72nd in 1786; the 2nd Battalion had been the 78th (Highlanders) Regiment of Foot (or The Ross-shire Buffs), raised in March 1793. The 1st and 2nd Battalions were amalgamated in 1948.

Battle Honours include: Carnatic, Mysore, Assaye, Hindoostan, Egypt, Maida, Java, South Africa 1835, Sevastopol, Persia, Lucknow, Central India, Kabul 1879, Kandahar 1880, Afghanistan 1878–80, Egypt 1882, Tel-el-Kebir, South Africa 1899-1902, France and Flanders 1914–18, Mesopotamia 1915–18, Megiddo, El Alamein, North Africa 1942–3, Sicily 1943, Italy 1943–4, Imphal, Burma 1942–4, North-West Europe 1944–5.

Nicknames: Regiment of the Macraes (72nd), King's Men (78th).

The Queen's Own Cameron Highlanders

Brief History: Raised in 1793–4 as 79th (Highland-Cameronian Volunteers) Regiment of Foot; redesignated in 1804 as 79th Regiment of Foot (Cameron Highlanders), in 1873 as 79th (The Queen's Own Cameron Highlanders) Regiment of Foot and in 1881 as The Queen's Own Cameron Highlanders. A 2nd Battalion existed from 1897 until 1948.

Battle Honours include: Egmont-op-Zee, Egypt, Fuentes

d'Oñoro, Salamanca, Pyrenees, Nivelle, Nive, Toulouse, Peninsula, Waterloo, Alma, Sevastopol, Lucknow, Egypt 1882, Tel-el-Kebir, Nile 1884–5, South Africa 1900–2, France and Flanders 1914–18, Macedonia 1915–18, El Alamein, North Africa 1940–3, Gothic Line, Kohima, Burma 1944–5, North-West Europe 1944–5.

Nickname: The Cia mar thas (Kamarhas).

THE GORDON HIGHLANDERS

Brief History: Formed 1 July 1881. The 1st Battalion had been the 75th (Stirlingshire) Regiment of Foot, raised in 1787; the 2nd Battalion had been the 92nd (Gordon Highlanders) Regiment of Foot, raised as the 100th (Gordon Highlanders) Regiment of Foot in 1794 and renumbered 92nd (Highland) Regiment of Foot in 1798. The 1st and 2nd Battalions amalgamated in 1948; the existing 1st Battalion is due to be amalgamated with the Queen's Own Highlanders (Seaforth and Camerons) in September 1994.

Battle Honours include: Mysore, Seringapatam, Egmont-op-Zee, Egypt, Corunna, Fuentes d'Oñoro, Almarez, Vitoria, Pyrenees, Nive, Orthez, Peninsula, Waterloo, South Africa 1835, Delhi, Lucknow, Kabul 1879, Kandahar 1880, Afghanistan 1878–80, Egypt 1882–4, Tel-el-Kebir, Nile 1884–5, South Africa 1899–1902, France and Flanders 1914–18, Italy 1917–18, El Alamein, Mareth, North Africa 1942–3, Anzio, Italy 1944–5, North-West Europe 1944–5.

Nickname: The Gordons.

THE ARGYLL AND SUTHERLAND HIGHLANDERS (PRINCESS LOUISE'S)

Brief History: Formed 1 July 1881 as Princess Louise's (Sutherland and Argyll Highlanders); redesignated in 1921 as The Argyll and Sutherland Highlanders (Princess Louise's). The 1st Battalion had been the 91st (Princess Louise's Argyllshire Highlanders) Regiment of Foot, raised in 1794 as the 98th (Argyllshire Highlanders) Regiment of Foot and renumbered 91st in 1796; the 2nd Battalion had been the 93rd (Sutherland Highlanders) Regiment of Foot, raised in 1799. The 1st and 2nd Battalions amalgamated in 1948.

Battle Honours include: Cape of Good Hope 1806, Rolica, Vimeiro, Corunna, Pyrenees, Nivelle, Nive, Orthez, Toulouse, Peninsula, Alma, Balaklava, Sevastopol, Lucknow, South Africa 1846–7, 1851–2–3, 1879, 1899–1902, France and Flanders 1914–16, Gallipoli 1915–16, Palestine 1917–18, El Alamein, North Africa 1940–3, Italy 1943–5, North-West Europe 1944–5, Pakchon, Korea 1950–1.

Nicknames: The Thin Red Line (93rd), The Argylls.

THE QUEEN'S DIVISION

THE PRINCESS OF WALES'S ROYAL REGIMENT (QUEEN'S AND ROYAL HAMPSHIRES)

Formed 9 September 1992 by the amalgamation of The Queen's Regiment and The Royal Hampshire Regiment. In the process, the three battalions of The Queen's Regiment and one battalion of the Royal Hampshire Regiment were reduced to two battalions overall.

The Queen's Regiment

Formed as a four-battalion regiment on 31 December 1966 by conversion of the Home Counties Brigade, formed in 1958. The 1st Battalion had been The Queen's Royal Surrey Regiment, an amalgamation effected in 1959 between The Queen's Royal Regiment (West Surrey) and The East Surrey Regiment; the 2nd Battalion had been The Queen's Own Buffs, The Royal Kent Regiment, an amalgamation effected in 1961 between The Buffs (Royal East Kent Regiment) and The Queen's Own Royal West

Kent Regiment; the 3rd Battalion had been The Royal Sussex Regiment; the 4th Battalion had been The Middlesex Regiment (Duke of Cambridge's Own). The 4th Battalion was absorbed into the other three battalions in 1971.

The Queen's Royal Regiment (West Surrey)

Brief History: Raised in September 1661 as the Earl of Peterborough's Regiment of Foot or Tangier Foot; redesignated in 1684 as the Queen Dowager's Regiment of Foot, in 1703 as The Queen's Royal Regiment of Foot, in 1715 as The Princess of Wales's Own Regiment of Foot and in 1727 as The Queen's Own Regiment of Foot. Ranked as 2nd Regiment of Foot in 1747; redesignated 2nd (The Queen's Royal) Regiment of Foot in 1751, as The Queen's (Royal West Surrey Regiment) in 1881 and as The Queen's Royal Regiment (West Surrey) in 1921. A 2nd Battalion existed between 1857 and 1948.

Battle Honours include: Egypt, Vimeiro, Corunna, Salamanca, Vitoria, Pyrenees, Nivelle, Toulouse, Peninsula, Afghanistan, Ghuznee, South Africa 1851–2–3, Taku Forts, Pekin, Burma 1885–7, South Africa 1899–1902, France and Flanders 1914–18, Gallipoli 1915, Mesopotamia 1915–18, Palestine 1917–18, El Alamein, North Africa 1940–3, Anzio, Italy 1943–5, Kohima, Burma 1943–5, North-West Europe 1944–5.

Nicknames: Kirke's Lambs, 1st Tangerines, Sleepy Queen's.

The East Surrey Regiment

Brief History: Formed 1 July 1881. The 1st Battalion had been the 31st (The Huntingdonshire) Regiment of Foot, raised in March 1702 as George Villier's Regiment of Marines; the 2nd Battalion had been the 70th (The Surrey) Regiment of Foot, raised in December 1756 as 2nd Battalion 31st Foot, designated 1758–82 and 1812–25 as 70th (Glasgow Lowland) Regiment of Foot. The 1st and 2nd Battalions were amalgamated in 1948.

Battle Honours include: Dettingen, Guadeloupe, Talavera, Albuera, Vitoria, Pyrenees, Nivelle, Nive, Orthez, Peninsula, Kabul 1842, Mudkee, Ferozeshah, Aliwal, Sobraon, Sevastopol, Taku Forts, New Zealand, Afghanistan 1878–9, Suakin 1885, South Africa 1899–1902, France and Flanders 1914–18, Mesopotamia 1917–18, North Africa 1942–3, Cassino, Italy 1943–5, Greece 1944–5.

Nicknames: The Young Buffs (31st), The Glasgow Greys (70th).

The Buffs (Royal East Kent Regiment)

Brief History: Formed in England as the Holland Regiment in 1665, tracing its origins to Thomas Morgan's Company, raised in 1572 for service in the Low Countries. Redesignated in 1689 as Prince George of Denmark's Regiment of Foot, but by 1708 known as The Buffs. Ranked as 3rd Regiment of Foot in 1747, redesignated 1782 as 3rd (The East Kent) Regiment of Foot (The Buffs), in 1881 as The Buffs (East Kent Regiment) and in 1935 as The Buffs (Royal East Kent Regiment). A 2nd Battalion existed from 1857 until 1949.

Battle Honours include: Blenheim, Ramillies, Oudenarde, Malplaquet, Dettingen, Douro, Talavera, Albuera, Vitoria, Pyrenees, Nivelle, Nive, Orthez, Toulouse, Peninsula, Sevastopol, Taku Forts, South Africa 1879, 1900–2, France and Flanders 1914–18, Baghdad, Mesopotamia 1915–18, North Africa 1941–3, Anzio, Italy 1943–5, Burma 1945.

Nicknames: Buff Howards, Old Buffs, Nutcrackers, The Resurrectionists.

The Queen's Own Royal West Kent Regiment

Brief History: Formed 1 July 1881. The 1st Battalion had been the 50th (the Queen's Own) Regiment of Foot, raised as the 52nd Regiment of Foot in 1755 and renumbered the 50th two years later; the 2nd Battalion had been the 97th (The Earl of Ulster's) Regiment of Foot, raised in 1824. The 1st and 2nd Battalions were amalgamated in 1948.

Battle Honours include: Egypt, Vimeiro, Corunna, Almarez, Vitoria, Pyrenees, Nive, Orthez, Peninsula, Mudkee, Ferozeshah, Aliwal, Sobraon, Alma, Inkerman, Sevastopol, Lucknow, New

Zealand, Egypt 1882, Nile 1884–5, South Africa 1900–2, France and Flanders 1914–18, Gallipoli 1915, Palestine 1917–18, El Alamein, North Africa 1942–3, Italy 1943–5, Defence of Kohima, Burma 1943–5.

Nicknames: The Blind Half-Hundred, The Dirty Half-Hundred, The Devil's Royals, The Gallant Fiftieth (50th); the Celestials (97th).

The Royal Sussex Regiment

Brief History: Formed 1 July 1881. The 1st Battalion had been the 35th (Royal Sussex) Regiment of Foot, raised in 1701 as the Earl of Donegal's Regiment of Foot or the Belfast Regiment; the 2nd Battalion had been the 107th Regiment of Foot (Bengal Infantry), raised by the East India Company in 1853 as the 3rd Bengal European Light Infantry and transferred to the British Army in 1862. The 1st and 2nd Battalions were amalgamated in 1948.

Battle Honours include: Louisburg, Quebec 1759, Maida, Egypt 1882, Nile 1884–5, Abu Klea, South Africa 1900–2, France and Flanders 1914–18, Gallipoli 1915, Palestine 1917–18, Afghanistan 1919, El Alamein, North Africa 1940–3, Italy 1944–5, Burma 1943–5.

Nickname: The Orange Lilies.

The Middlesex Regiment (Duke of Cambridge's Own)

Brief History: Formed 1 July 1881 as The Duke of Cambridge's Own (Middlesex Regiment), redesignated in 1921 as The Middlesex Regiment (Duke of Cambridge's Own). The 1st Battalion had been the 57th (The West Middlesex) Regiment of Foot, raised in 1755 as the 59th Regiment of Foot but renumbered 57th in 1757; the 2nd Battalion had been the 77th (The East Middlesex) Regiment of Foot (The Duke of Cambridge's Own), raised in 1787. The 1st and 2nd Battalions were amalgamated in 1948. 3rd and 4th Battalions existed from 1900 until 1922.

Battle Honours include: Mysore, Seringapatam, Albuera, Ciudad Rodrigo, Badajoz, Vitoria, Pyrenees, Nivelle, Nive, Peninsula, Alma, Inkerman, Sevastopol, New Zealand, South Africa 1879, 1900–2, France and Flanders 1914–18, Suvla, Mesopotamia 1917–18, Siberia 1918–19, El Alamein, North Africa 1942–3, Sicily 1943, Anzio, North-West Europe 1944–5, Naktong Bridgehead, Korea 1950–1.

Nicknames: Steelbacks, Diehards (57th); The Pot-Hooks (77th).

The Royal Hampshire Regiment

Brief History: Formed 1 July 1881 as The Hampshire Regiment, redesignated The Royal Hampshire Regiment in 1946. The 1st Battalion had been the 37th (North Hampshire) Regiment of Foot, raised in 1702 as Thomas Meredith's Regiment of Foot; the 2nd Battalion had been the 67th (South Hampshire) Regiment of Foot, raised in 1756 as 2nd Battalion 20th Foot but renumbered 67th in 1758. The 1st and 2nd Battalions were amalgamated in 1948.

Battle Honours include: Blenheim, Ramillies, Oudenarde, Malplaquet, Dettingen, Minden, Tournai, Barossa, Peninsula, Taku Forts, Pekin, Kabul 1879, Afghanistan 1878–80, Burma 1885–7, South Africa 1900–2, France and Flanders 1914–18, Helles, Suvla, Megiddo, Palestine 1917–18, Siberia 1918–19, North Africa 1940–3, Salerno, Cassino, Gothic Line, North-West Europe 1944–5.

Nickname: The Royal Tigers.

THE ROYAL REGIMENT OF FUSILIERS

A four-battalion regiment formed on 23 April 1968 by the conversion of the Fusilier Brigade, created in 1958. The 1st Battalion had been The Royal Northumberland Fusiliers; the 2nd Battalion had been The Royal Warwickshire Fusiliers; the 3rd Battalion had been The Royal Fusiliers (City of London Regiment); the 4th Battalion had been The Lancashire Fusiliers. The 4th Battalion was disbanded on 1 November 1969. The 3rd Battalion

served in the Gulf 1990–1 as part of 4th Armoured Brigade. On 1 August 1992 the Regiment was reduced to two battalions.

The Royal Northumberland Fusiliers

Brief History: Raised in 1674 at Bois-le-Duc for Dutch service as the Irish Regiment or Viscount Clare's; transferred to English service in 1688 and ranked in 1747 as 5th Regiment of Foot. Redesignated in 1782 as 5th (Northumberland) Regiment of Foot, in 1836 as 5th Regiment of Foot (Northumberland Fusiliers), in 1881 as The Northumberland Fusiliers and in 1935 as The Royal Northumberland Fusiliers. A 2nd Battalion existed from 1857 until 1948.

Battle Honours include: Wilhelmstahl, Rolica, Vimeiro, Corunna, Barossa, Ciudad Rodrigo, Badajoz, Salamanca, Vitoria, Nivelle, Orthez, Toulouse, Peninsula, Lucknow, Afghanistan 1878–80, South Africa 1899–1902, France and Flanders 1914–18, Suvla, Gallipoli 1915, North Africa 1940–3, Salerno, Cassino, North-West Europe 1944–5, Imjin, Korea 1950–1.

Nicknames: Shiners, Old Bold Fifth, The Fighting Fifth, Lord Wellington's Bodyguard.

The Royal Warwickshire Fusiliers

Brief History: Raised in 1673 at Bois-le-Duc for Dutch service as Sir Walter Vane's Regiment; transferred to English service in 1688 and from 1747 ranked as 6th Regiment of Foot. Redesignated in 1782 as 6th (1st Warwickshire) Regiment of Foot, in 1832 as 6th (Royal 1st Warwickshire) Regiment of Foot, in 1881 as The Royal Warwickshire Regiment and in 1963, upon transfer from the defunct Midland Brigade to the Fusilier Brigade, as The Royal Warwickshire Fusiliers. The 2nd Battalion was raised in 1857 and, in 1948, it survived to be redesignated as 1st Battalion when the latter was disbanded.

Battle Honours include: Rolica, Vimeiro, Corunna, Vitoria, Pyrenees, Nivelle, Orthez, Peninsula, Niagara, South Africa 1846–7, 1851–2–3, 1899–1902, France and Flanders 1914–18, Gallipoli 1915–16, Baghdad, Mesopotamia 1916–18, North-West Europe 1944–5, Burma 1945.

Nicknames: Guise's Geese, The Warwickshire Lads, The Saucy Sixth.

The Royal Fusiliers (City of London Regiment)

Brief History: Raised in June 1685 by Lord Dartmouth from two companies of Tower guards in London as the Ordnance Regiment or Royal Regiment of Fuziliers. Ranked in 1747 as 7th Regiment of Foot but known as the Royal English Fuziliers. In 1782 it was redesignated as 7th (Derbyshire) Regiment of Foot, although there is little evidence that this was used. In 1881 it was redesignated The Royal Fusiliers (City of London Regiment). A 2nd Battalion existed from 1857 until 1948.

Battle Honours include: Martinique, Talavera, Albuera, Badajoz, Salamanca, Vitoria, Pyrenees, Orthez, Toulouse, Peninsula, Alma, Inkerman, Sevastopol, Kandahar 1880, Afghanistan 1879–80, South Africa 1899–1902, France and Flanders 1914–18, Gallipoli 1915–16, Megiddo, Palestine 1918, Archangel 1919, North Africa 1940, 1943, Salerno, Anzio, Cassino, Gothic Line, Greece 1944–5, Korea 1952–3.

Nickname: The Elegant Extracts.

The Lancashire Fusiliers

Brief History: Raised in 1688 as Sir Richard Peyton's Regiment of Foot, ranked in 1747 as 20th Regiment of Foot. Redesignated in 1782 as 20th (The East Devonshire) Regiment of Foot and in 1881 as The Lancashire Fusiliers. A 2nd Battalion existed from 1858 until 1948.

Battle Honours include: Dettingen, Minden, Egmont-op-Zee, Egypt, Maida, Vimeiro, Corunna, Vitoria, Pyrenees, Orthez, Toulouse, Peninsula, Alma, Inkerman, Sevastopol, Lucknow, South Africa 1899–1902, France and Flanders 1914–18, Gallipoli 1915, Macedonia 1915–18, North Africa 1942–3, Sicily 1943, Italy 1943–5, Kohima, Chindits 1944, Burma 1943–4,

North-West Europe 1944.

    Nicknames: Two Tens, The Minden Boys, Kingsley's Stand.

THE ROYAL ANGLIAN REGIMENT

A four-battalion regiment formed on 1 September 1964 by the conversion of the East Anglian Brigade, created in 1958. The 1st Battalion had been the 1st East Anglian Regiment (Royal Norfolk and Suffolk), created in 1959 by the amalgamation of The Royal Norfolk Regiment and The Suffolk Regiment; the 2nd Battalion had been the 2nd East Anglian Regiment (Duchess of Gloucester's Own Royal Lincolnshire and Northamptonshire), created in 1960 by the amalgamation of The Royal Lincolnshire Regiment and The Northamptonshire Regiment; the 3rd Battalion had been the 3rd East Anglian Regiment (16th/44th Foot), created in 1958 by the amalgamation of The Bedfordshire and Hertfordshire Regiment and The Essex Regiment; the 4th Battalion had been The Royal Leicestershire Regiment, transferred from the defunct Midland Brigade in 1964. The 4th Battalion was absorbed into the other three in October 1970. The Regiment was reduced to two battalions in October 1992.

The Royal Norfolk Regiment

Brief History: Raised in 1685 as Henry Cornewall's Regiment of Foot, ranked from 1747 as 9th Regiment of Foot. Redesignated in 1782 as 9th (The East Norfolk) Regiment of Foot, in 1881 as The Norfolk Regiment and in 1936 as The Royal Norfolk Regiment. A 2nd Battalion existed from 1857 until 1948.

    Battle Honours include: Rolica, Vimeiro, Corunna, Busaco, Vitoria, San Sebastian, Nive, Peninsula, Kabul 1842, Mudkee, Ferozeshah, Sobraon, Sevastopol, Kabul 1879, Afghanistan 1879–80, South Africa 1900–2, France and Flanders 1914–18, Suvla, Gallipoli 1915, Megiddo, Palestine 1917–18, Singapore Island, Kohima, Burma 1944–5, North-West Europe 1944–5, Korea 1951–2.

    Nicknames: The Holy Boys, The Fighting Ninth.

The Suffolk Regiment

Brief History: Raised in 1685 as the Duke of Norfolk's Regiment of Foot, ranked from 1747 as 12th Regiment of Foot. Redesignated in 1782 as 12th (The East Suffolk) Regiment of Foot and in 1881 as The Suffolk Regiment. A 2nd Battalion existed from 1858 until 1948.

    Battle Honours include: Dettingen, Minden, Gibraltar, Seringapatam, India, South Africa 1851–2–3, New Zealand, Afghanistan 1878–80, South Africa 1899–1902, France and Flanders 1914–18, Suvla, Gallipoli 1915, Megiddo, Palestine 1917–18, Singapore Island, Imphal, Burma 1943–5, North-West Europe 1944–5.

    Nickname: The Old Dozen.

The Royal Lincolnshire Regiment

Brief History: Raised in 1685 as the Earl of Bath's Regiment of Foot, ranked from 1747 as 10th Regiment of Foot. Redesignated in 1782 as 10th (The North Lincolnshire) Regiment of Foot, in 1881 as The Lincolnshire Regiment and in 1946 as The Royal Lincolnshire Regiment. A 2nd Battalion existed from 1858 until 1948.

    Battle Honours include: Blenheim, Ramillies, Oudenarde, Malplaquet, Peninsula, Sobraon, Punjab, Mooltan, Gujerat, Lucknow, South Africa 1900–2, France and Flanders 1914–18, Suvla, Gallipoli 1915, North Africa 1943, Salerno, Gothic Line, Italy 1943–5, Burma 1943–5, North-West Europe 1944–5.

    Nicknames: The Springers, The Poachers.

The Northamptonshire Regiment

Brief History: Formed 1 July 1881. The 1st Battalion had been the 48th (the Northamptonshire) Regiment of Foot, raised in 1741 as James Cholmondeley's Regiment of Foot; the 2nd Battalion had been the 58th (the Rutlandshire) Regiment of Foot, raised in 1755 as the 60th Regiment of Foot and renumbered 58th in 1757. The 1st and 2nd Battalions were amalgamated in 1948.

    Battle Honours include: Louisburg, Quebec 1759, Gibraltar, Maida, Douro, Talavera, Albuera, Badajoz, Salamanca, Vitoria, Pyrenees, Nivelle, Orthez, Toulouse, Peninsula, Sevastopol, New Zealand, South Africa 1879, 1899–1902, France and Flanders 1914–18, Suvla, Gallipoli 1915, Palestine 1917–18, North Africa 1942–3, Sicily 1943, Anzio, Cassino, Italy 1943–5, Burma 1943–5, North-West Europe 1945.

    Nicknames: The Heroes of Talavera (48th), The Steelbacks.

The Bedfordshire and Hertfordshire Regiment

Brief History: Raised in 1688 as Archibald Douglas's Regiment of Foot, ranked from 1747 as 16th Regiment of Foot. Redesignated in 1782 as 16th (Buckinghamshire) Regiment of Foot, in 1809 as 16th (the Bedfordshire) Regiment of Foot, in 1881 as The Bedfordshire Regiment and in 1919 as The Bedfordshire and Hertfordshire Regiment. A 2nd Battalion existed from 1859 until 1948.

    Battle Honours include: Blenheim, Ramillies, Oudenarde, Malplaquet, South Africa 1900–2, France and Flanders 1914–18, Suvla, Gallipoli 1915, Megiddo, Palestine 1917–18, North Africa 1940, 1943, Cassino, Italy 1944–5, Chindits 1944, Burma 1944, Greece 1944–5.

    Nicknames: The Old Bucks, The Peacemakers.

The Essex Regiment

Brief History: Formed on 1 July 1881. The 1st Battalion had been the 44th (the East Essex) Regiment of Foot, raised in 1741 as James Long's Regiment of Foot; the 2nd Battalion had been the 56th (the West Essex) Regiment of Foot, raised in 1755 as the 58th Regiment of Foot and renumbered 56th in 1757. The 1st and 2nd Battalions were amalgamated in 1948.

    Battle Honours include: Gibraltar, Egypt, Moro, Badajoz, Salamanca, Peninsula, Bladensburg, Waterloo, Ava, Alma, Inkerman, Sevastopol, Taku Forts, Nile 1884–5, South Africa 1899–1902, France and Flanders 1914–18, Gallipoli 1915–16, Megiddo, Palestine 1917–18, El Alamein, North Africa 1941–3, Cassino, Italy 1943–4, Chindits 1944, Burma 1943–5, Greece 1944–5, North-West Europe 1944–5.

    Nicknames: Two Fours, The Little Fighting Fours (44th); The Pompadours, Saucy Pompeys (56th).

The Royal Leicestershire Regiment

Brief History: Raised in 1688 as Soloman Richard's Regiment of Foot, ranked from 1747 as 17th Regiment of Foot. Redesignated in 1782 as 17th (the Leicestershire) Regiment of Foot, in 1881 as The Leicestershire Regiment and in 1946 as The Royal Leicestershire Regiment. A 2nd Battalion existed from 1858 until 1948.

    Battle Honours include: Louisburg, Hindoostan, Afghanistan, Ghuznee, Khelat, Sevastopol, Ali Musjid, Afghanistan 1878–9, France and Flanders 1914–18, Megiddo, Palestine 1918, Mesopotamia 1915–18, North Africa 1940–1, 1943, Salerno, Italy 1943–5, Crete, Malaya 1941–2, Chindits 1944, North-West Europe 1944–5.

    Nicknames: Lily Whites, Bengal Tigers, The Tigers.

THE KING'S DIVISION

THE KING'S OWN ROYAL BORDER REGIMENT

Formed on 1 October 1959 by the amalgamation of The King's Own Royal Regiment (Lancaster) and The Border Regiment.

The King's Own Royal Regiment (Lancaster)

Brief History: Raised in 1680 as the 2nd Tangier or Earl of Plymouth's Regiment of Foot; redesignated in 1684 as The Duchess of York and Albany's Regiment of Foot, in 1685 as The

Queen's Regiment of Foot, in 1688 as The Queen Consort's Regiment of Foot, in 1702 as The Queen's Regiment of Foot and in 1715 as The King's Own Regiment of Foot. Redesignated in 1751 as 4th (The King's Own) Regiment of Foot, in 1867 as 4th (The King's Own Royal) Regiment of Foot, in 1881 as The King's Own (Royal Lancaster Regiment) and in 1921 as The King's Own Royal Regiment (Lancaster). A 2nd Battalion existed from 1857 until 1949.

Battle Honours include: Corunna, Badajoz, Salamanca, Vitoria, San Sebastian, Nive, Peninsula, Bladensburg, Waterloo, Alma, Inkerman, Sevastopol, Abyssinia, South Africa 1879, 1899–1902, France and Flanders 1914–18, Gallipoli 1915, Mesopotamia 1916, 1918, North Africa 1940–2, Malta 1941–2, Italy 1944–5, Chindits 1944, Burma 1944.

Nicknames: Barrell's Blues, The Lions.

The Border Regiment

Brief History: Formed on 1 July 1881. The 1st Battalion had been the 34th (the Cumberland) Regiment of Foot, raised in 1702 as Lord Lucas's Regiment of Foot; the 2nd Battalion had been the 55th (the Westmorland) Regiment of Foot, raised in 1755 as the 57th Regiment of Foot, renumbered as 55th in 1757. The 1st and 2nd Battalions were amalgamated in 1950.

Battle Honours include: Albuera, Arroyo dos Molinos, Vitoria, Pyrenees, Nivelle, Nive, Orthez, Peninsula, Alma, Inkerman, Sevastopol, Lucknow, China, South Africa 1899–1902, France and Flanders 1914–18, Gallipoli 1915–16, Italy 1917–18, Afghanistan 1919, Tobruk 1941, Landing in Sicily, Imphal, Meiktila, Chindits 1944, Burma 1943–5, Arnhem 1944.

Nickname: The Two Fives (55th).

THE KING'S REGIMENT

Formed on 1 September 1959 by the amalgamation of The King's Regiment (Liverpool) and The Manchester Regiment. Initially designated The King's Regiment (Manchester and Liverpool), but subtitle dropped in 1968.

The King's Regiment (Liverpool)

Brief History: Raised in 1685 as The Princess Anne of Denmark's Regiment of Foot; redesignated in 1702 as The Queen's Regiment of Foot and in 1716 as The King's Regiment of Foot, ranked from 1747 as 8th Regiment of Foot. Redesignated in 1751 as 8th (The King's) Regiment of Foot, in 1881 as The King's (Liverpool Regiment) and in 1921 as The King's Regiment (Liverpool). A 2nd Battalion existed from 1857 until 1948.

Battle Honours include: Blenheim, Ramillies, Oudenarde, Malplaquet, Dettingen, Martinique, Egypt, Niagara, Delhi, Lucknow, Afghanistan 1878–80, Burma 1885–7, South Africa 1899–1902, France and Flanders 1914–18, Archangel 1918–19, Afghanistan 1919, Cassino, Italy 1944–5, Chindits 1943, 1944, Burma 1943–4, North-West Europe 1944, The Hook 1953, Korea 1952–3.

Nickname: The King's Hanoverian White Horse.

The Manchester Regiment

Brief History: Formed on 1 July 1881. The 1st Battalion had been the 63rd (the West Suffolk) Regiment of Foot, raised in 1757 as 2nd Battalion 8th (The King's) Regiment of Foot, ranked as 63rd in 1758; the 2nd Battalion had been the 96th Regiment of Foot, raised in 1824. The 1st and 2nd Battalions were amalgamated in 1948.

Battle Honours include: Egmont-op-Zee, Martinique, Guadeloupe, Egypt, Peninsula, Alma, Inkerman, Sevastopol, New Zealand, Afghanistan 1879–80, Egypt 1882, South Africa 1899–1902, France and Flanders 1914–18, Gallipoli 1915, Italy 1917–18, Megiddo, Baghdad, Mesopotamia 1916–18, Malta 1940, Italy 1944, Singapore Island, Kohima, Burma 1944–5, North-West Europe 1944–5.

Nickname: Bloodsuckers (63rd).

THE PRINCE OF WALES'S OWN REGIMENT OF YORKSHIRE

Formed on 25 April 1958 by the amalgamation of The West Yorkshire Regiment (The Prince of Wales's Own) and The East Yorkshire Regiment (The Duke of York's Own). Served in Bosnia, 1993.

The West Yorkshire Regiment (The Prince of Wales's Own)

Brief History: Raised in 1685 as Sir Edward Hales's Regiment of Foot, ranked from 1747 as 14th Regiment of Foot. Redesignated in 1782 as 14th (Bedfordshire) Regiment of Foot, in 1809 as 14th (The Buckinghamshire) Regiment of Foot, in 1876 as 14th (Buckinghamshire – The Prince of Wales's Own) Regiment of Foot, in 1881 as The Prince of Wales's Own (West Yorkshire Regiment) and in 1921 as The West Yorkshire Regiment (Prince of Wales's Own). A 2nd Battalion existed from 1858 until 1948.

Battle Honours include: Tournai, Corunna, Java, Waterloo, Bhurtpore, India, Sevastopol, New Zealand, Afghanistan 1879–80, South Africa 1899–1902, France and Flanders 1914–18, Suvla, Gallipoli 1915, Italy 1917–18, Keren, North Africa 1940–2, Imphal, Meiktila, Burma 1942–5.

Nicknames: The Old and Bold, Calvert's Entire.

The East Yorkshire Regiment (The Duke of York's Own)

Brief History: Raised in 1685 as Sir William Clifton's Regiment of Foot, ranked from 1747 as 15th Regiment of Foot. Redesignated in 1782 as 15th (The Yorkshire East Riding) Regiment of Foot, in 1881 as The East Yorkshire Regiment and in 1935 as The East Yorkshire Regiment (The Duke of York's Own). A 2nd Battalion existed from 1858 until 1948.

Battle Honours include: Blenheim, Ramillies, Oudenarde, Malplaquet, Louisburg, Quebec 1759, Martinique, Guadeloupe, Afghanistan 1879–80, South Africa 1900–2, France and Flanders 1914–18, Suvla, Gallipoli 1915, Gazala, El Alamein, Mareth, North Africa 1942–3, Sicily 1943, Burma 1945, North-West Europe 1944–5.

Nicknames: Snappers, Poona Guards.

THE GREEN HOWARDS (ALEXANDRA, PRINCESS OF WALES'S OWN YORKSHIRE REGIMENT)

Brief History: Raised in 1688 as Francis Lutterell's Regiment of Foot, ranked from 1747 as 19th Regiment of Foot. Redesignated in 1782 as 19th (The 1st Yorkshire North Riding) Regiment of Foot, from 1785 as 19th (The 1st Yorkshire North Riding – Princess of Wales's Own) Regiment of Foot, in 1881 as The Princess of Wales's Own (Yorkshire Regiment), in 1902 as Alexandra, Princess of Wales's Own (Yorkshire Regiment) and in 1921 as The Green Howards (Alexandra, Princess of Wales's Own Yorkshire Regiment). A 2nd Battalion existed from 1858 until 1949 and from 1952 until 1956.

Battle Honours include: Malplaquet, Alma, Inkerman, Sevastopol, South Africa 1899–1902, France and Flanders 1914–18, Suvla, Gallipoli 1915, Italy 1917–18, Archangel 1918, Gazala, El Alamein, Mareth, North Africa 1942–3, Sicily 1943, Anzio, Italy 1943–4, Burma 1945, North-West Europe 1944–5.

Nickname: The Green Howards.

THE QUEEN'S LANCASHIRE REGIMENT

Formed on 25 March 1970 by the amalgamation of The Lancashire Regiment (Prince of Wales's Volunteers) – itself an amalgamation of The East Lancashire Regiment and The South Lancashire Regiment (The Prince of Wales's Volunteers), effected in 1958 – and The Loyal Regiment (North Lancashire). Known – self-mockingly – as the Queen's Last Resort.

The East Lancashire Regiment

Brief History: Formed on 1 July 1881 as The West Lancashire

Regiment but soon altered to The East Lancashire Regiment. The 1st Battalion had been the 30th (the Cambridgeshire) Regiment of Foot, raised in 1702 as Thomas Saunderson's Regiment of Marines; the 2nd Battalion had been the 59th (2nd Nottinghamshire) Regiment of Foot, raised in 1755 as the 61st Regiment of Foot and renumbered as 59th in 1757. The 1st and 2nd Battalions were amalgamated in 1948.

Battle Honours include: Cape of Good Hope 1806, Egypt, Corunna, Java, Badajoz, Salamanca, Vitoria, San Sebastian, Nive, Peninsula, Waterloo, Bhurtpore, Alma, Inkerman, Sevastopol, Canton, Ahmad Khel, Afghanistan 1878–80, South Africa 1900–2, France and Flanders 1914–18, Helles, Gallipoli 1915, Kut-el-Amara 1917, Mesopotamia 1916–17, Burma 1944–5, North-West Europe 1944–5.

Nicknames: The Three Tens, The Triple Xs (30th); Lily Whites (59th).

The South Lancashire Regiment (Prince of Wales's Volunteers)

Brief History: Formed 1 July 1881 as The Prince of Wales's Volunteers (South Lancashire Regiment), redesignated in 1938 as The South Lancashire Regiment (The Prince of Wales's Volunteers). The 1st Battalion had been the 40th (the 2nd Somersetshire) Regiment of Foot, raised in 1717 as Richard Philip's Regiment of Foot; the 2nd Battalion had been the 82nd Regiment of Foot (Prince of Wales's Volunteers), raised in 1793. The 1st and 2nd Battalions were amalgamated in 1948.

Battle Honours include: Louisburg, Egypt, Montevideo, Rolica, Vimeiro, Talavera, Badajoz, Salamanca, Vitoria, Pyrenees, Nivelle, Orthez, Toulouse, Peninsula, Niagara, Waterloo, Kandahar, Ghuznee, Kabul 1842, Maharajpore, Sevastopol, Lucknow, New Zealand, South Africa 1899–1902, France and Flanders 1914–18, Suvla, Gallipoli 1915, Baghdad, Mesopotamia 1916–18, Baluchistan 1918, Kohima, Burma 1943–5, North-West Europe 1944–5.

Nicknames: The Excellers, The Fighting Fortieth (40th).

The Loyal Regiment (North Lancashire)

Brief History: Formed on 1 July 1881 as The Loyal North Lancashire Regiment, redesignated in 1921 as The Loyal Regiment (North Lancashire). The 1st Battalion had been the 47th (the Lancashire) Regiment of Foot, raised in 1741 as John Mordaunt's Regiment of Foot, numbered 58th in 1747 and renumbered 47th in 1751; the 2nd Battalion had been the 81st Regiment of Foot, raised in 1793 and subtitled The Loyal Lincoln Volunteers. The 1st and 2nd Battalions were amalgamated in 1949.

Battle Honours include: Louisburg, Quebec 1759, Maida, Corunna, Tarifa, Vitoria, San Sebastian, Peninsula, Ava, Alma, Inkerman, Sevastopol, Ali Musjid, Afghanistan 1878–9, South Africa 1899–1902, France and Flanders 1914–18, Suvla, Gallipoli 1915, Palestine 1917–18, Baghdad, Mesopotamia 1916–18, North Africa 1943, Anzio, Italy 1944–5, Singapore Island.

Nicknames: The Cauliflowers, The Lancashire Lads, Wolfe's Own (47th); Loyal Lincoln Volunteers (81st).

THE DUKE OF WELLINGTON'S REGIMENT (WEST RIDING)

Brief History: Formed on 1 July 1881 as The Duke of Wellington's (West Riding Regiment), redesignated in 1921 as The Duke of Wellington's Regiment (West Riding). The 1st Battalion had been the 33rd (The Duke of Wellington's) Regiment of Foot, raised in 1702 as the Earl of Huntingdon's Regiment of Foot and designated 33rd (the 1st Yorkshire West Riding) Regiment of Foot from 1782 until the award of the new subtitle in 1853; the 2nd Battalion had been the 76th Regiment of Foot, raised in 1787. The 1st and 2nd Battalions were amalgamated in 1948.

Battle Honours include: Dettingen, Mysore, Seringapatam, Hindoostan, Delhi 1803, Laswari, Deig, Nive, Peninsula, Waterloo, Alma, Inkerman, Sevastopol, Abyssinia, South Africa 1900–2,

France and Flanders 1914–18, Suvla, Gallipoli 1915, Italy 1917–18, Afghanistan 1919, North Africa 1943, Anzio, Italy 1943–5, Chindits 1944, Burma 1942–4, North-West Europe 1944–5, The Hook 1953, Korea 1952–3.

Nicknames: The Havercake Lads (33rd); The Immortals, The Pigs, The Old Seven-and-Sixpennies (76th); The Duke of Boots' (DWR).

THE PRINCE OF WALES'S DIVISION

THE DEVONSHIRE AND DORSET REGIMENT

Formed on 17 May 1958 by the amalgamation of The Devonshire Regiment and The Dorset Regiment. Known at one time as The Armoured Farmers.

The Devonshire Regiment

Brief History: Raised in 1685 as the Duke of Beaufort's Regiment of Foot, ranked from 1747 as 11th Regiment of Foot. Redesignated in 1782 as 11th (The North Devonshire) Regiment of Foot and in 1881 as The Devonshire Regiment. A 2nd Battalion existed from 1858 until 1948.

Battle Honours include: Dettingen, Salamanca, Pyrenees, Nivelle, Nive, Orthez, Toulouse, Peninsula, Afghanistan 1879–80, South Africa 1899–1902, France and Flanders 1914–18, Mesopotamia 1916–18, Palestine 1917–18, Italy 1917–18, Malta 1940–2, Sicily 1943, Italy 1943, Imphal, Burma 1943–5, North-West Europe 1944–5.

Nickname: Bloody Eleventh.

The Dorset Regiment

Brief History: Formed on 1 July 1881 as The Dorsetshire Regiment; redesignated in 1951 as The Dorset Regiment. The 1st Battalion had been the 39th (the Dorsetshire) Regiment of Foot, raised in 1702 as Richard Coote's Regiment of Foot and known between 1782 and 1807 as the 39th (East Middlesex) Regiment of Foot; the 2nd Battalion had been the 54th (the West Norfolk) Regiment of Foot, raised in 1755 as the 56th Regiment of Foot and renumbered 54th in 1757. The 1st and 2nd Battalions were amalgamated in 1948.

Battle Honours include: Plassey, Gibraltar, Egypt, Marabout, Albuera, Vitoria, Pyrenees, Nivelle, Nive, Orthez, Peninsula, Ava, Maharajpore, Sevastopol, South Africa 1899–1902, France and Flanders 1914–18, Suvla, Gallipoli 1915, Mesopotamia 1914–18, Megiddo, Palestine 1917–18, Malta 1940–2, Sicily 1943, Italy 1943, Kohima, Mandalay, Burma 1944–5, Arnhem 1944, North-West Europe 1944–5.

Nicknames: Sankey's Horse, Green Linnets (39th); Flamers (54th).

THE 22nd (CHESHIRE) REGIMENT

Brief History: Raised in 1688 as the Duke of Norfolk's Regiment of Foot, ranked from 1747 as 22nd Regiment of Foot. Redesignated in 1782 as 22nd (Cheshire) Regiment of Foot and in 1881 as The Cheshire Regiment. Scheduled to be amalgamated with The Staffordshire Regiment (The Prince of Wales's) in August 1993 but the decision was reversed in early 1993. A 2nd Battalion existed from 1858 until 1948. The 1st Battalion served in Bosnia 1992–3.

Battle Honours include: Louisburg, Meeanee, Hyderabad, Scinde, South Africa 1900–02, France and Flanders 1914–18, Suvla, Gallipoli 1915, Kut-el-Amara 1917, Mesopotamia 1916–18, Gazala, El Alamein, Mareth, North Africa 1940–3, Sicily 1943, Salerno, Gothic Line, Italy 1943–5, Malta 1941–2, North-West Europe 1944–5.

Nicknames: Two-Twos, Red Knights.

THE ROYAL WELCH FUSILIERS

Brief History: Raised in 1689 as Lord Herbert's Regiment of Foot, redesignated in 1714 as the Prince of Wales's Own Royal Welsh Fuziliers and in 1723 as The Royal Regiment of Welsh Fusiliers. Ranked from 1747 as 23rd Regiment, designated from 1751 as 23rd Regiment of Foot (Royal Welsh Fusiliers). Redesignated in 1881 as The Royal Welsh Fusiliers and in 1921 as The Royal Welch Fusiliers. A 2nd Battalion existed from 1857 until 1848 and from 1952 until 1957.

Battle Honours include: Blenheim, Ramillies, Oudenarde, Malplaquet, Dettingen, Minden, Egypt, Corunna, Martinique, Albuera, Badajoz, Salamanca, Vitoria, Pyrenees, Nivelle, Orthez, Toulouse, Peninsula, Waterloo, Alma, Inkerman, Sevastopol, Lucknow, Ashantee, Burma 1885–7, South Africa 1899–1902, France and Flanders 1914–18, Gallipoli 1915–16, Baghdad, Mesopotamia 1916–18, Kohima, Burma 1943–5, North-West Europe 1944–5.

Nicknames: Nanny Goats, Royal Goats, The Royal Welch.

THE ROYAL REGIMENT OF WALES (24th/41st FOOT)

Formed on 11 June 1969 by the amalgamation of The South Wales Borderers and The Welch Regiment.

The South Wales Borderers

Brief History: Raised in 1689 as Sir Edward Dering's Regiment of Foot, ranked from 1747 as 24th Regiment of Foot. Redesignated in 1782 as 24th (the 2nd Warwickshire) Regiment of Foot and in 1881 as The South Wales Borderers. A 2nd Battalion existed from 1858 until 1948.

Battle Honours include: Blenheim, Ramillies, Oudenarde, Malplaquet, Cape of Good Hope 1806, Egypt, Talavera, Fuentes d'Oñoro, Salamanca, Vitoria, Pyrenees, Nivelle, Orthez, Peninsula, Punjab, Chillianwala, Gujerat, South Africa 1877–8–9, Burma 1885–7, South Africa 1900–2, France and Flanders 1914–18, Landing at Helles, Gallipoli 1915–16, Baghdad, Mesopotamia 1916–18, North Africa 1942, Burma 1944–5, North-West Europe 1944–5.

Nicknames: Howard's Greens, Bengal Tigers.

The Welch Regiment

Brief History: Formed on 1 July 1881 as The Welsh Regiment, redesignated in 1921 as The Welch Regiment. The 1st Battalion had been the 41st (the Welsh) Regiment of Foot, raised in 1719 as independent companies of invalids (old soldiers fit only for garrison duty) and regimented in 1787 as 41st Regiment of Foot, receiving the subtitle Welsh in 1831; the 2nd Battalion had been the 69th (the South Lincolnshire) Regiment of Foot, raised in 1756 as 2nd Battalion 14th Regiment of Foot and renumbered 69th in 1758. The 1st and 2nd Battalions were amalgamated in 1948.

Battle Honours include: St Vincent, Bourbon, Java, Detroit, Queenston, Miami, Niagara, Waterloo, India, Ava, Kandahar, Ghuznee, Kabul 1842, Alma, Inkerman, Sevastopol, South Africa 1899–1902, France and Flanders 1914–18, Suvla, Gallipoli 1915, Kut-el-Amara 1917, Mesopotamia 1916–18, North Africa 1940–2, Sicily 1943, Italy 1943–5, Canea, Burma 1944–5, North-West Europe 1944–5, Korea 1951–2.

Nicknames: Royal Invalids, Wardour's Regiment (41st); The Old Agamemnons, The Ups and Downs (69th).

THE GLOUCESTERSHIRE REGIMENT

Brief History: Formed on 1 July 1881. The 1st Battalion had been the 28th (the North Gloucestershire) Regiment of Foot, raised in 1694 as Sir John Gibson's Regiment of Foot; the 2nd Battalion had been the 61st (South Gloucestershire) Regiment of Foot, raised in 1756 as 2nd Battalion 3rd Regiment of Foot and renumbered as 61st in 1758. The 1st and 2nd Battalions were amalgamated in 1948. The existing 1st Battalion is scheduled to

amalgamate with The Duke of Edinburgh's Royal Regiment (Berkshire and Wiltshire) in April 1994 to form The Royal Gloucestershire, Berkshire and Wiltshire Regiment.

Battle Honours include: Ramillies, Louisburg, Quebec 1759, Egypt, Maida, Corunna, Talavera, Barossa, Albuera, Salamanca, Vitoria, Pyrenees, Nivelle, Nive, Orthez, Toulouse, Peninsula, Waterloo, Punjab, Chillianwala, Gujerat, Alma, Inkerman, Sevastopol, Delhi, South Africa 1899–1902, France and Flanders 1914–18, Sari Bair, Gallipoli 1915–16, Baghdad, Mesopotamia 1916–18, Burma 1942, 1944–5, North-West Europe 1944–5, Imjin, Korea 1950–1.

Nicknames: The Old Braggs, Slashers (28th); Whitewashers (61st).

THE WORCESTERSHIRE AND SHERWOOD FORESTERS REGIMENT (29th/45th FOOT)

Formed on 28 February 1970 by the amalgamation of The Worcestershire Regiment and The Sherwood Foresters (Nottinghamshire and Derbyshire Regiment).

The Worcestershire Regiment

Brief History: Formed on 1 July 1881. The 1st Battalion had been the 29th (the Worcestershire) Regiment of Foot, raised in 1694 as Thomas Farrington's Regiment of Foot; the 2nd Battalion had been the 36th (the Herefordshire) Regiment of Foot, raised in 1701 as Thomas Allnutt's Regiment of Foot. The 1st and 2nd Battalions were amalgamated in 1948.

Battle Honours include: Ramillies, Mysore, Hindoostan, Rolica, Vimeiro, Corunna, Talavera, Albuera, Salamanca, Pyrenees, Nivelle, Nive, Orthez, Toulouse, Peninsula, Ferozeshah, Sobraon, Punjab, Chillianwala, Gujerat, South Africa 1900–2, France and Flanders 1914–18, Gallipoli 1915–16, Baghdad, Mesopotamia 1916–18, Italy 1917–18, Keren, Gazala, North Africa 1941–2, Kohima, Mandalay, Burma 1944–5, North-West Europe 1944–5.

Nicknames: The Vein Openers, Old and Bold, The Star of the Line (29th); The Saucy Greens (36th).

The Sherwood Foresters (Nottinghamshire and Derbyshire Regiment)

Brief History: Formed on 1 July 1881 as The Sherwood Foresters (Derbyshire Regiment) and redesignated in 1902 as The Sherwood Foresters (Nottinghamshire and Derbyshire Regiment). The 1st Battalion had been the 45th (Nottinghamshire) (Sherwood Foresters) Regiment of Foot, raised in 1741 as Daniel Houghton's Regiment of Foot; the 2nd Battalion had been the 95th (Derbyshire) Regiment of Foot, raised in 1823. The 1st and 2nd Battalions were amalgamated in 1948, although a new 2nd Battalion existed from 1952 until 1955.

Battle Honours include: Louisburg, Rolica, Vimeiro, Talavera, Busaco, Fuentes d'Oñoro, Ciudad Rodrigo, Badajoz, Salamanca, Vitoria, Pyrenees, Nivelle, Orthez, Toulouse, Peninsula, Ava, South Africa 1846–7, Alma, Inkerman, Sevastopol, Central India, Abyssinia, Egypt 1882, South Africa 1899–1902, France and Flanders 1914–18, Suvla, Gallipoli 1915, Italy 1917–18, Gazala, El Alamein, North Africa 1942–3, Salerno, Anzio, Gothic Line, Italy 1943–5, Singapore Island.

Nicknames: The Old Stubborns, Sherwood Foresters, Nottingham Hosiers (45th).

THE STAFFORDSHIRE REGIMENT (THE PRINCE OF WALES'S)

Formed on 31 January 1959 by the amalgamation of The South Staffordshire Regiment and The North Staffordshire Regiment (The Prince of Wales's). Served in the Gulf 1990–1 as part of 7th Armoured Brigade. Was scheduled to be amalgamated with The 22nd (Cheshire) Regiment in August 1993 but the decision was reversed in early 1993.

The South Staffordshire Regiment

Brief History: Formed on 1 July 1881. The 1st Battalion had been the 38th (the 1st Staffordshire) Regiment of Foot, raised in 1705 as Luke Lillingston's Regiment of Foot; the 2nd Battalion had been the 80th (Staffordshire Volunteers) Regiment of Foot, raised in 1793. The 1st and 2nd Battalions were amalgamated in 1948.

Battle Honours include: Egypt, Montevideo, Rolica, Vimeiro, Corunna, Busaco, Badajoz, Salamanca, Vitoria, San Sebastian, Nive, Peninsula, Ava, Mudkee, Ferozeshah, Sobraon, Pegu, Alma, Inkerman, Sevastopol, Lucknow, Central India, South Africa 1878–9, Egypt 1882, Nile 1884–5, Kirbekan, South Africa 1900–2, France and Flanders 1914–18, Suvla, Gallipoli 1915, Italy 1917–18, North Africa 1940, Sicily 1943, Italy 1943, Chindits 1944, Burma 1944, Arnhem 1944, North-West Europe 1944.

Nicknames: Pump and Tortoise (38th); Staffordshire Knots, Staffordshire Volunteers (80th).

The North Staffordshire Regiment (The Prince of Wales's)

Brief History: Formed on 1 July 1881 as The Prince of Wales's (North Staffordshire Regiment), redesignated in 1921 as The North Staffordshire Regiment (The Prince of Wales's). The 1st Battalion had been the 64th (the 2nd Staffordshire) Regiment of Foot, raised in 1756 as 2nd Battalion 11th Regiment of Foot and renumbered as 64th in 1758; the 2nd Battalion had been the 98th (The Prince of Wales's) Regiment of Foot, raised in 1824. The 1st and 2nd Battalions were amalgamated in 1949.

Battle Honours include: St Lucia, Surinam, Punjab, Persia, Reshire, Bushire, Koosh-ab, Lucknow, China, South Africa 1900–2, France and Flanders 1914–18, Sari Bair, Gallipoli 1915–16, Kut-el-Amara 1917, Mesopotamia 1916–18, Afghanistan 1919, North Africa 1943, Anzio, Italy 1944–5, Burma 1943, North-West Europe 1944.

Nickname: The Prince of Wales's Own (98th).

THE DUKE OF EDINBURGH'S ROYAL REGIMENT (BERKSHIRE AND WILTSHIRE)

Formed on 9 June 1959 by the amalgamation of The Royal Berkshire Regiment (Princess Charlotte of Wales's) and The Wiltshire Regiment (Duke of Edinburgh's). Is scheduled to be amalgamated with The Gloucestershire Regiment in April 1994 to form The Royal Gloucestershire, Berkshire and Wiltshire Regiment.

The Royal Berkshire Regiment (Princess Charlotte of Wales's)

Brief History: Formed on 1 July 1881 as The Princess Charlotte of Wales's (Berkshire Regiment), redesignated in 1885 as The Princess Charlotte of Wales's (Royal Berkshire Regiment) and in 1921 as The Royal Berkshire Regiment (Princess Charlotte of Wales's). The 1st Battalion had been the 49th (Princess Charlotte of Wales's) (or the Hertfordshire) Regiment of Foot, raised in 1743 as Edward Trelawney's Regiment of Foot, sometimes called the Jamaica Volunteers and from 1747 until 1751 ranked as the 63rd Regiment of Foot; the 2nd Battalion had been the 66th Regiment of Foot, raised in 1756 as 2nd Battalion 19th Regiment of Foot and renumbered as 66th in 1758. The 1st and 2nd Battalions were amalgamated in 1949.

Battle Honours include: Egmont-op-Zee, Copenhagen, Douro, Talavera, Albuera, Vitoria, Pyrenees, Nivelle, Nive, Orthez, Peninsula, Queenston, Alma, Inkerman, Sevastopol, China, Kandahar 1880, Afghanistan 1879–80, Egypt 1882, Suakin 1885, Tofrek, South Africa 1899–1902, France and Flanders 1914–18, Italy 1917–18, Macedonia 1915–18, Sicily 1943, Anzio, Italy 1943–5, Kohima, Mandalay, Burma 1942–5, North-West Europe 1944–5.

Nicknames: Green Howards (66th); The Dragons (Royal Berks).

The Wiltshire Regiment (Duke of Edinburgh's)

Brief History: Formed 1 July 1881 as The Duke of Edinburgh's (Wiltshire Regiment), redesignated in 1921 as The Wiltshire Regiment (Duke of Edinburgh's). The 1st Battalion had been the 62nd (the Wiltshire) Regiment of Foot, raised in 1756 as 2nd Battalion 4th Foot and renumbered as 62nd in 1758; the 2nd Battalion had been the 99th (Lanarkshire) Regiment of Foot, raised in 1824. The 1st and 2nd Battalions were amalgamated in 1948.

Battle Honours include: Nive, Peninsula, Ferozeshah, Sobraon, Sevastopol, Pekin, New Zealand, South Africa 1900–2, France and Flanders 1914–18, Suvla, Gallipoli 1915–16, Megiddo, Palestine 1917–18, Baghdad, Mesopotamia 1916–18, Sicily 1943, Anzio, Italy 1943–4, Burma 1943–4, North-West Europe 1944–5.

Nickname: The Springers (62nd).

THE ROYAL IRISH DIVISION

THE ROYAL IRISH REGIMENT (27th (INNISKILLING), 83rd, 87th AND UDR)

Formed on 1 July 1992 by the amalgamation of The Royal Irish Rangers (27th (Inniskilling), 83rd and 87th) and The Ulster Defence Regiment. It currently comprises one 'General Service' battalion, created by the amalgamation of the two erstwhile battalions of The Royal Irish Rangers in August 1993, and seven 'Home Service' (ex-UDR) battalions for service in Northern Ireland only. They were organized into The Royal Irish Division in early 1993.

The Royal Irish Rangers (27th (Inniskilling), 83rd and 87th)

A three-battalion regiment formed on 1 July 1968 by conversion of the regiments of the North Irish Brigade, created in 1958. The 1st Battalion had been The Royal Inniskilling Fusiliers; the 2nd Battalion had been The Royal Ulster Rifles; the 3rd Battalion had been The Royal Irish Fusiliers (Princess Victoria's). The 3rd Battalion was absorbed into the other two in November 1968.

The Royal Inniskilling Fusiliers

Brief History: Formed on 1 July 1881. The 1st Battalion had been the 27th (Inniskilling) Regiment of Foot, raised in 1689 as Zachariah Tiffin's Regiment of Foot; the 2nd Battalion had been the 108th Regiment of Foot (Madras Infantry), raised by the East India Company in 1854 as the 3rd Madras European Infantry and transferred to the British Army in 1862. The 2nd Battalion was disbanded in 1922, re-raised in 1937, disbanded in 1948, re-raised in 1952 and disbanded in 1956.

Battle Honours include: St Lucia, Egypt, Maida, Badajoz, Salamanca, Vitoria, Pyrenees, Nivelle, Orthez, Toulouse, Peninsula, Waterloo, South Africa 1835, 1846–7, Central India, South Africa 1899–1902, France and Flanders 1914–18, Macedonia 1915–18, Landing at Helles, Gallipoli 1915–16, Palestine 1917–18, North Africa 1942–3, Sicily 1943, Cassino, Italy 1943–5, Burma 1942–3.

Nicknames: The Skins (27th); The Lumps (108th).

The Royal Ulster Rifles

Brief History: Formed on 1 July 1881 as The Royal Irish Rifles; redesignated in 1921 as The Royal Ulster Rifles. The 1st Battalion had been the 83rd (County of Dublin) Regiment of Foot, raised in 1793; the 2nd Battalion had been the 86th (Royal County Down) Regiment of Foot, raised in 1793–4 as the 86th (The Shropshire Volunteers) Regiment of Foot, redesignated as 86th (The Leinster) Regiment of Foot in 1806 and as Royal County Down in 1812. The 1st and 2nd Battalions were amalgamated in 1948.

Battle Honours include: India, Egypt, Cape of Good Hope 1806, Bourbon, Talavera, Busaco, Fuentes d'Oñoro, Ciudad

Rodrigo, Badajoz, Salamanca, Vitoria, Nivelle, Orthez, Toulouse, Peninsula, Central India, South Africa 1899–1902, France and Flanders 1914–18, Suvla, Gallipoli 1915, Jerusalem, Palestine 1917–18, North-West Europe 1944–5, Imjin, Korea 1950–1.

Nicknames: Fitch's Grenadiers (83rd); Shropshire Volunteers (86th).

The Royal Irish Fusiliers (Princess Victoria's)

Brief History: Formed on 1 July 1881 as The Princess Victoria's (Royal Irish Fusiliers), redesignated in 1921 as The Royal Irish Fusiliers (Princess Victoria's). The 1st Battalion had been the 87th (or Royal Irish Fusiliers) Regiment of Foot, raised in 1793 as 87th (The Prince of Wales's Irish) Regiment of Foot and redesignated in 1827 as 87th Regiment of Foot (or Prince of Wales's Own Irish Fusileers) before taking on its final title later the same year; the 2nd Battalion had been the 89th (The Princess Victoria's) Regiment of Foot, raised in 1793. The 1st and 2nd Battalions were amalgamated in 1922. A new 2nd Battalion was raised in 1938 and amalgamated with the 1st Battalion in 1948.

Battle Honours include: Egypt, Montevideo, Talavera, Barossa, Tarifa, Java, Vitoria, Nivelle, Orthez, Toulouse, Peninsula, Niagara, Ava, Sevastopol, Egypt 1882–4, Tel-el-Kebir, South Africa 1899–1902, France and Flanders 1914–18, Macedonia 1915–17, Suvla, Gallipoli 1915, Megiddo, Palestine 1917–18, Bou Arada, Centuripe, Termoli, Cassino, Argenta Gap, Leros.

Nicknames: The Old Fogs, The Faugh-a-Ballagh Boys, The Faughs, The Eagle Takers (87th); Blayney's Bloodhounds, The Rollickers (89th).

The Ulster Defence Regiment

Formed on 1 April 1970 as a locally recruited, part-time military defence force for service in Northern Ireland only. It was organized initially into seven battalions – 1UDR (Antrim), 2UDR (Armagh), 3UDR (Down), 4UDR (Fermanagh), 5UDR (Londonderry), 6UDR (Tyrone) and 7UDR (Belfast) – but the number increased in the early 1970s, with the raising of 8UDR (Dungannon), 9UDR (Antrim), 10UDR (Belfast) and 11UDR (Portadown). In June 1984 1UDR and 9UDR were amalgamated to form 1/9UDR, and in October 1984 7UDR and 10UDR were amalgamated to form 7/10UDR. By then, all battalions were containing increased numbers of full-time soldiers, and in July 1991 it was formally announced that the UDR would amalgamate with The Royal Irish Rangers to form The Royal Irish Regiment, contributing seven battalions to the new unit. In September 1991 2UDR and 11UDR were amalgamated to form 2/11UDR, and 4UDR and 6UDR were amalgamated to form 4/6UDR, preparatory to becoming battalions of The Royal Irish Regiment in July 1992.

THE LIGHT DIVISION

THE LIGHT INFANTRY

A four-battalion regiment, formed on 10 July 1968 by conversion of the regiments of the Light Infantry Brigade, created in 1958. The 1st Battalion had been The Somerset and Cornwall Light Infantry, formed in October 1959 by the amalgamation of The Somerset Light Infantry (Prince Albert's) and The Duke of Cornwall's Light Infantry; the 2nd Battalion had been The King's Own Yorkshire Light Infantry; the 3rd Battalion had been The King's Shropshire Light Infantry; the 4th Battalion had been The Durham Light Infantry. The 4th Battalion was disbanded in March 1969 and The Light Infantry was reduced from three battalions to two on 23 February 1993.

The Somerset Light Infantry (Prince Albert's)

Brief History: Raised in 1685 as the Earl of Huntingdon's Regiment of Foot, ranked from 1747 as 13th Regiment of Foot.

Redesignated in 1782 as 13th (1st Somersetshire) Regiment of Foot, in 1822 as 13th (1st Somersetshire) Regiment of Foot (Light Infantry), in 1842 as 13th (1st Somersetshire) (Prince Albert's Light Infantry) Regiment of Foot, in 1881 as Prince Albert's (Somersetshire Light Infantry), in 1912 as Prince Albert's (Somerset Light Infantry) and in 1921 as The Somerset Light Infantry (Prince Albert's). A 2nd Battalion existed from 1858 until 1948.

Battle Honours include: Dettingen, Martinique, Egypt, Ava, Afghanistan, Jellalabad, Ghuznee, Kabul 1842, Sevastopol, South Africa 1878–9, Burma 1885–7, South Africa 1899–1902, France and Flanders 1914–18, Megiddo, Palestine 1917–18, Mesopotamia 1916–18, Afghanistan 1919, Cassino, Italy 1944–5, Burma 1943–4, North-West Europe 1944–5.

Nicknames: The Jellalabad Heroes, The Illustrious Garrison, The Bleeders.

The Duke of Cornwall's Light Infantry

Brief History: Formed 1 July 1881. The 1st Battalion had been the 32nd (Cornwall Light Infantry) Regiment of Foot, raised in 1702 as Edward Fox's Regiment of Foot, redesignated 32nd (the Cornwall) Regiment of Foot in 1782 and given the subtitle Light Infantry in 1858; the 2nd Battalion had been the 46th (the South Devonshire) Regiment of Foot, raised in 1741 as James Price's Regiment of Foot, ranked as 57th Regiment of Foot in 1747 and renumbered as 46th in 1751. The 1st and 2nd Battalions were amalgamated in 1948 (some sources say 1950).

Battle Honours include: Dettingen, Dominica, Rolica, Vimeiro, Corunna, Salamanca, Pyrenees, Nivelle, Nive, Orthez, Peninsula, Waterloo, Punjab, Multan, Gujerat, Sevastopol, Lucknow, Egypt 1882, Tel-el-Kebir, Nile 1884–5, South Africa 1899–1902, France and Flanders 1914–18, Gaza, Megiddo, Palestine 1917–18, Gazala, North Africa 1942–3, Cassino, Italy 1944–5, North-West Europe 1944–5.

Nicknames: Red Feathers, The Lacedemonians (46th).

The King's Own Yorkshire Light Infantry

Brief History: Formed on 1 July 1881 as The King's Own Light Infantry (South Yorkshire Regiment), redesignated in 1887 as The King's Own Yorkshire Light Infantry. The 1st Battalion had been the 51st (the 2nd Yorkshire West Riding) or The King's Own Light Infantry Regiment, raised in 1755 as the 53rd Regiment of Foot and renumbered 51st in 1757, receiving the subtitle Light Infantry in 1809; the 2nd Battalion had been the 105th Regiment (Madras Light Infantry), raised by the East India Company in 1839 as the 2nd Madras European Light Infantry and transferred to the British Army in 1862. The 1st and 2nd Battalions were amalgamated in 1948.

Battle Honours include: Minden, Corunna, Fuentes d'Oñoro, Salamanca, Vitoria, Pyrenees, Nivelle, Orthez, Peninsula, Waterloo, Pegu, Ali Musjid, Afghanistan 1878–80, Burma 1885–7, South Africa 1899–1902, France and Flanders 1915–18, Macedonia 1915–17, Italy 1917–18, North Africa 1943, Sicily 1943, Salerno, Anzio, Italy 1943–5, Burma 1942, North-West Europe 1944–5.

Nicknames: The Koylis.

The King's Shropshire Light Infantry

Brief History: Formed on 1 July 1881 as The King's Light Infantry (Shropshire Regiment), redesignated in 1882 as The King's (Shropshire Light Infantry) and in 1921 as The King's Shropshire Light Infantry. The 1st Battalion had been the 53rd (the Shropshire) Regiment of Foot, raised in 1755 as the 55th Regiment of Foot and renumbered as 53rd in 1757; the 2nd Battalion had been the 85th, or The King's Regiment of Light Infantry (Bucks Volunteers), raised in 1793 and subtitled Light Infantry in 1808. The 1st and 2nd Battalions were amalgamated in 1948.

Battle Honours include: Nieuport, Tournai, St Lucia, Talavera, Fuentes d'Oñoro, Salamanca, Vitoria, Pyrenees, Nivelle, Nive,

Toulouse, Peninsula, Bladensburg, Aliwal, Sobraon, Punjab, Gujerat, Lucknow, Afghanistan 1879–80, Egypt 1882, Suakin 1885, South Africa 1899–1902, France and Flanders 1914–18, Jerusalem, Palestine 1917–18, North Africa 1943, Anzio, Italy 1943–5, North-West Europe 1944–5, Kowang-San, Korea 1951–2.

Nicknames: The Brickdusts, The Old Five and Threepennies (53rd); Elegant Extracts (85th).

The Durham Light Infantry

Brief History: Formed on 1 July 1881. The 1st Battalion had been the 68th (Durham) Regiment of Foot (Light Infantry), raised in 1756 as 2nd Battalion 23rd Regiment of Foot, renumbered as 68th in 1758 and given the subtitle Light Infantry in 1808; the 2nd Battalion had been the 106th Regiment of Foot (Bombay Light Infantry), raised by the East India Company in 1839 as the 2nd Bombay European Light Infantry and transferred to the British Army in 1862. The 1st and 2nd Battalions were amalgamated in 1948, although another 2nd Battalion existed from 1952 until 1955.

Battle Honours include: Salamanca, Vitoria, Pyrenees, Nivelle, Orthez, Peninsula, Alma, Inkerman, Sevastopol, Persia, Reshire, Bushire, Koosh-ab, New Zealand, South Africa 1899–1902, France and Flanders 1914–18, Italy 1917–18, Archangel 1918–19, Afghanistan 1919, Tobruk 1941, Gazala, El Alamein, Mareth, North Africa 1940–3, Primosole Bridge, Sicily 1943, Salerno, Italy 1943–5, Kohima, Burma 1943–5, North-West Europe 1944–5, Korea 1952–3.

Nicknames: The Old Faithfuls, The Faithful Durhams.

THE ROYAL GREEN JACKETS

A three-battalion regiment created on 1 January 1966 by conversion of the regiments of the Green Jackets Brigade, formed in 1958. The 1st Battalion had been The Oxfordshire and Buckinghamshire Light Infantry (made into a rifle regiment in 1963); the 2nd Battalion had been The King's Royal Rifle Corps; the 3rd Battalion had been The Rifle Brigade (Prince Consort's Own). The Regiment was reduced from three to two battalions on 25 July 1992. Known throughout the Army as The Black Mafia.

The Oxfordshire and Buckinghamshire Light Infantry

Brief History: Formed on 1 July 1881 as The Oxfordshire Light Infantry, redesignated in 1908 as The Oxfordshire and Buckinghamshire Light Infantry and in 1958 as 1st Green Jackets, 43rd and 52nd. The 1st Battalion had been the 43rd (the Monmouthshire) Regiment of Foot (Light Infantry), raised in 1741 as Thomas Fowke's Regiment of Foot and subtitled Light Infantry in 1803; the 2nd Battalion had been the 52nd (the Oxfordshire) Regiment of Foot (Light Infantry), raised in 1755 as the 54th Regiment of Foot, renumbered as 52nd in 1757 and given the subtitle Light Infantry in 1803. The 1st and 2nd Battalions were amalgamated in 1948.

Battle Honours include: Quebec 1759, Mysore, Hindoostan, Vimeiro, Corunna, Busaco, Fuentes d'Oñoro, Ciudad Rodrigo, Badajoz, Salamanca, Vitoria, Nivelle, Nive, Orthez, Toulouse, Peninsula, Waterloo, South Africa 1851–2–3, Delhi, New Zealand, South Africa 1900–2, France and Flanders 1914–18, Defence of Kut-el-Amara, Mesopotamia 1914–18, Italy 1917–18, Archangel 1919, North Africa 1943, Salerno, Anzio, Italy 1943–5, Burma 1943–5, Pegasus Bridge, North-West Europe 1944–5.

Nickname: The Light Bobs.

The King's Royal Rifle Corps

Brief History: Raised in 1755 in America as the 62nd (Royal American) Regiment of Foot, renumbered in 1757 as 60th. Redesignated in 1824 as 60th (The Duke of York's Rifle Corps and Light Infantry) Regiment of Foot, in 1830 as 60th (The King's Royal Rifle Corps) Regiment of Foot, in 1881 as The King's Royal Rifle Corps and in 1958 as 2nd Green Jackets, The King's Royal Rifle Corps. A 2nd Battalion existed from 1819 until 1948 and from 1950 until 1957, a 3rd Battalion from 1855 until 1923 and a 4th Battalion from 1857 until 1923.

Battle Honours include: Louisburg, Quebec 1759, Rolica, Vimeiro, Martinique, Talavera, Busaco, Fuentes d'Oñoro, Ciudad Rodrigo, Badajoz, Salamanca, Vitoria, Pyrenees, Nivelle, Nive, Orthez, Toulouse, Peninsula, Punjab, Multan, Gujerat, Delhi, Taku Forts, Pekin, South Africa 1851–2–3, 1879, Ahmad Khel, Kandahar 1880, Afghanistan 1878–80, Egypt 1882, 1884, Tel-el-Kebir, South Africa 1899–1902, France and Flanders 1914–18, Macedonia 1916–18, Italy 1917–18, Sidi Rezegh 1941, Gazala, El Alamein, North Africa 1940–3, Italy 1943–5, Greece 1941, 1944–5, Calais 1940, North-West Europe 1944–5.

Nickname: The Royal Americans.

The Rifle Brigade (Prince Consort's Own)

Brief History: Raised in 1800 as an experimental rifle corps, designated The Corps of Riflemen and known unofficially as Manningham's Sharpshooters. Redesignated in 1802 as 95th Regiment of Foot, in 1812 as 95th Regiment of Foot (Riflemen), in 1816 as The Rifle Brigade, in 1862 as The Prince Consort's Own Rifle Brigade, in 1881 as The Rifle Brigade (The Prince Consort's Own), in 1921 as The Rifle Brigade (Prince Consort's Own) and in 1958 as 3rd Green Jackets, The Rifle Brigade. A 2nd Battalion existed from 1805 until 1948 and from 1950 until 1957, a 3rd Battalion from 1855 until 1922 and a 4th Battalion from 1857 until 1922.

Battle Honours include: Copenhagen, Montevideo, Rolica, Vimeiro, Corunna, Busaco, Barossa, Fuentes d'Oñoro, Ciudad Rodrigo, Badajoz, Salamanca, Vitoria, Nivelle, Nive, Orthez, Toulouse, Peninsula, Waterloo, South Africa 1846–7, 1851–2–3, Alma, Inkerman, Sevastopol, Lucknow, Ashantee, Ali Musjid, Afghanistan 1878–9, Burma 1885–7, South Africa 1899–1902, France and Flanders 1914–18, Macedonia 1915–18, Beda Fomm, Sidi Rezegh 1941, Gazala, El Alamein, North Africa 1940–3, Cassino, Italy 1943–5, Calais 1940, North-West Europe 1944–5.

Nickname: The Sweeps.

CORPS OF ROYAL MARINES

Brief History: His Majesty's Marine Forces were formed in April 1755 at Portsmouth, Plymouth and Chatham, although various marine regiments had been raised before that date, some of them later converting to regiments of foot. By 1763 there were 70 marine companies in existence, styled in 1802 as Royal Marines. In 1862 the Royal Marines were divided into two corps, known after 1890 as Royal Marine Light Infantry and Royal Marine Artillery. They were amalgamated in 1923 to form the Corps of Royal Marines. Currently organized into 3rd Commando Brigade, the corps comprises No. 40 Commando, formed in February 1942, disbanded in 1946 and reformed in 1947 by the redesignation of No. 44 Commando; No. 42 Commando, formed in February 1940; No. 45 Commando, formed in May 1940 as 5th Royal Marine Battalion, converted to No. 45 Commando in August 1943; and the Commando Logistics Regiment Royal Marines, formed in January 1971. The brigade fought in the Falklands Conflict 1982 and was deployed to northern Iraq/Kurdistan in 1991.

Battle Honours: Gibraltar; the Globe cap-badge symbolizes the world-wide commitment of the Royal Marines and is a battle honour in its own right.

Nicknames: The Jollies, The Little Grenadiers.

THE PARACHUTE REGIMENT

Brief History: Formed on 22 June 1940 as The Parachute Corps, part of the Army Air Corps; redesignated on 1 August 1942 as The Parachute Regiment, Army Air Corps, but withdrawn from the AAC to become a regiment of the line in August 1949. In 1950 The Parachute Regiment became part of The Glider Pilot and Parachute Corps, but the corps was disbanded in 1957 and The Parachute Regiment reverted to its independent status. It comprises three regular battalions: the 1st was formed in early 1940 as No. 6 Independent Company (Commando) and soon expanded to become No. 2 Commando, reorganized in November 1940 as No. 11 Special Air Service Battalion, redesignated in September 1941 as 1st Parachute Battalion; the 2nd and 3rd were formed in September 1941 as 2nd Parachute Battalion and 3rd Parachute Battalion. All three were wiped out at Arnhem in September 1944 but re-formed; the 2nd and 3rd Battalions fought in the Falklands Conflict 1982 as part of 3rd Commando Brigade. A 1st (Guards) Parachute Battalion existed from 1946 until 1948, replaced by No. 1 (Guards) Independent Company from 1948 until 1975.

Battle Honours include: Bruneval, Normandy Landing, Breville, Arnhem 1944, Rhine, Southern France, Oudna, Tamera, Primosole Bridge, Athens, Goose Green, Mount Longdon, Wireless Ridge, Falkland Islands 1982.

Nicknames: The Red Devils, The Paras, The Maroon Machine.

THE BRIGADE OF GURKHAS

2nd KING EDWARD VII'S OWN GOORKHA RIFLES (THE SIRMOOR RIFLES)

Brief History: Raised in April 1815 as the Sirmoor Battalion, redesignated in 1823 as Sirmoor Battalion (8th Local Infantry), in 1858 as Sirmoor Rifle Regiment, in 1861 as 2nd Goorkha Regiment and in 1864 as 2nd Goorkha (The Sirmoor Rifle) Regiment. Redesignated in 1876 as 2nd (Prince of Wales' Own) Goorkha Regiment (The Sirmoor Rifles), in 1903 as 2nd Prince of Wales's Own Gurkha Rifles (The Sirmoor Rifles), in 1906 as 2nd King Edward's Own Gurkha Rifles (The Sirmoor Rifles) and in 1936 as 2nd King Edward VII's Own Gurkha Rifles (The Sirmoor Rifles). Transferred to the British Army on 1 January 1948 without change of title, although later there was a return to the old-style spelling Goorkha. A 2nd Battalion, raised in 1886, was amalgamated with the 1st Battalion on 14 September 1992, preparatory to amalgamation with the 6th Queen Elizabeth's Own Gurkha Rifles to form the 1st Battalion The Royal Gurkha Rifles by March 1995.

Battle Honours include: Bhurtpore, Aliwal, Sobraon, Delhi, Kabul 1879, Kandahar 1880, Afghanistan 1878–80, Tirah, France and Flanders 1914–15, Tigris 1916, Kut-el-Amara 1917, Persia 1918, Baluchistan 1918, Afghanistan 1919, El Alamein, North Africa 1942–3, Cassino, Gothic Line, Italy 1944–5, Singapore Island, Chindits 1943, Burma 1943–5.

6th QUEEN ELIZABETH'S OWN GURKHA RIFLES

Brief History: Raised in 1817 as the Cuttack Legion, redesignated in 1823 as Rungpoor Light Infantry, in 1827 as Assam Light Infantry (8th Local Infantry), in 1861 as 46th (1st Assam) Regiment of Bengal Native Infantry and, later in the same year, as 42nd Regiment of Bengal Native Infantry (Light Infantry). Redesignated in 1886 as 42nd Regiment, Goorkha (Light) Infantry, in 1891 as 42nd Gurkha (Rifle) Regiment of Bengal Infantry, in 1901 as 42nd Gurkha Rifles and in 1903 as 6th Gurkha Rifles. Transferred to the British Army on 1 January 1948, redesignated 6th Queen Elizabeth's Own Gurkha Rifles in

1959. A 2nd Battalion existed from 1904 until 1969. The 1st Battalion is to be amalgamated with the 2nd King Edward VII's Own Goorkha Rifles (The Sirmoor Rifles) to form 1st Battalion The Royal Gurkha Rifles by March 1995.

Battle Honours include: Burma 1885–7, Helles, Suvla, Sari Bair, Gallipoli 1915, Mesopotamia 1916–18, Persia 1918, Afghanistan 1919, Italy 1944–5, Mandalay, Chindits 1944, Burma 1944–5.

7th DUKE OF EDINBURGH'S OWN GURKHA RIFLES

Brief History: Raised in 1902 with the designation 8th Gurkha Rifles; redesignated in 1903 as 2nd Battalion 10th Gurkha Rifles, split in 1907 to form two battalions of the 7th Gurkha Rifles. Transferred to the British Army on 1 January 1948, redesignated as 7th Duke of Edinburgh's Own Gurkha Rifles in 1959. The 2nd Battalion existed from 1907 until 1970. The 1st Battalion served in the Falklands Conflict 1982 as part of 5th Infantry Brigade; it is to be renamed 2nd Battalion The Royal Gurkha Rifles by March 1995, preparatory to amalgamation with the 3rd Battalion The Royal Gurkha Rifles (ex-10th Princess Mary's Own Gurkha Rifles) to form a more permanent 2nd Battalion The Royal Gurkha Rifles by 1997.

Battle Honours include: Megiddo, Palestine 1918, Kut-el-Amara 1915, 1917, Ctesiphon, Baghdad, Mesopotamia 1915–18, Afghanistan 1919, North Africa 1942, Cassino, Italy 1944, Imphal, Meiktila, Burma 1942–5, Falkland Islands 1982.

10th PRINCESS MARY'S OWN GURKHA RIFLES

Brief History: Raised in 1887 as Kubo Valley Military Police Battalion, redesignated in 1890 as 1st Regiment of Burma Infantry, in 1892 as 10th Regiment (1st Burma Rifles) Madras Infantry, in 1895 as 10th Regiment (1st Burma Gurkha Rifles) Madras Infantry and in 1901 as 10th Gurkha Rifles. Transferred to the British Army on 1 January 1948, redesignated as 10th Princess Mary's Own Gurkha Rifles in 1949. A 2nd Battalion existed from 1908 until 1968. The 1st Battalion is to be renamed as 3rd Battalion The Royal Gurkha Rifles by March 1995, preparatory to amalgamation with the 2nd Battalion The Royal Gurkha Rifles (ex-7th Duke of Edinburgh's Own Gurkha Rifles) by 1997.

Battle Honours include: Helles, Suvla, Sari Bair, Gallipoli 1915, Mesopotamia 1916–18, Afghanistan 1919, Iraq 1941, Syria 1941, Italy 1944–5, Imphal, Mandalay, Meiktila, Burma 1942–5.

QUEEN'S GURKHA ENGINEERS

Formed in 1955 from 67 Gurkha Field Squadron Royal Engineers, raised in 1948. The title Queen's was added later. To be reduced in size by 1997 to match the smaller size of the Gurkha Brigade.

QUEEN'S GURKHA SIGNALS

Formed in 1955 from Gurkha squadrons of the Royal Signals, the first of which had been raised in 1949. The title Queen's was added later. To be reduced in size by 1997 to match the smaller size of the Gurkha Brigade.

GURKHA TRANSPORT REGIMENT

Formed in July 1965 by the redesignation of the Gurkha Army Service Corps, raised in July 1958. Elements served in the Gulf 1990–1 as 28th Ambulance Squadron Group, Gurkha Transport Regiment. To be reduced in size by 1997 to match the smaller size of the Gurkha Brigade.

Nickname (common to all Gurkhas): Johnny Gurkha.

SPECIAL AIR SERVICE REGIMENT

22nd SPECIAL AIR SERVICE REGIMENT

Brief History: Formed in 1952 in Malaya from the Malaya Scouts, raised in 1950. The Special Air Service was formed originally by David Stirling in November 1941, achieving the status of the Special Air Service Regiment, Army Air Corps in April 1944, but was disbanded in June 1946. Elements of 22SAS have served most recently in the Falklands Conflict 1982, the storming of the Iranian Embassy in Princes Gate in May 1980 and behind enemy lines in the Gulf 1990–1, as well as in the forefront of Britain's fight against terrorism.

Battle Honours include: Tobruk 1941, Benghazi Raid, North Africa 1941–3, Landing in Sicily, Termoli, Italy 1943–5, Greece 1944–5, Adriatic, North-West Europe 1944–5, Falkland Islands 1982.

Nicknames: Saturday Afternoon Soldiers, Sass.

ARMY AIR CORPS

Formed in February 1942 to comprise army air observation/ artillery spotting units, The Glider Pilot Regiment and The Parachute Regiment (*see* p.211). The Special Air Service Regiment (*see* above) was added in April 1944 but disbanded in June 1946. The Parachute Regiment withdrew from the Army Air Corps in August 1949 and the corps was disbanded in May 1950. It was re-raised as the Army Air Corps in September 1957. Currently organized into six regiments, but there is to be a reduction of one squadron and four independent flights by 1995, with a further reduction of one squadron by 1997. Elements of the Army Air Corps served in the Falklands Conflict 1982 and in the Gulf 1990–1.

The Glider Pilot Regiment

Brief History: First units formed in 1941, becoming part of the Army Air Corps in February 1942 under the title The Glider Pilot Regiment, Army Air Corps. Became part of The Glider Pilot and Parachute Corps in March 1950. Regiment disbanded in September 1957 but traditions and honours transferred to the new Army Air Corps, formed at the same date.

Battle Honours include: Normandy Landing, Pegasus Bridge, Merville Battery, Arnhem 1944, Rhine, Southern France, North-West Europe 1944–5, Landing in Sicily, Sicily 1943.

ROYAL ARMY CHAPLAINS' DEPARTMENT

Formed in 1796 as the Army Chaplains' Department, redesignated Royal Army Chaplains' Department in 1919.

Nicknames: Sky-Pilots, God-Botherers.

THE ROYAL LOGISTIC CORPS

Formed on 5 April 1993 by the amalgamation of the Royal Corps of Transport, the Royal Army Ordnance Corps, the Royal Pioneer Corps, the Army Catering Corps and the Royal Engineers (Postal and Courier Service). Already known within the Army as the Really Large Corps.

Royal Corps of Transport

Brief History: Formed in July 1965 by renaming the Royal Army Service Corps. The RASC had its origins in the Corps of Waggoners created in 1794, redesignated as the Royal Waggon Train in 1799 but disbanded in 1833. It was replaced by The Land Transport Corps, formed in 1855, redesignated as the Military Train in 1856, the Control Department and the Army Service Corps in 1870, the Commissariat and Transport Corps in 1881, the Army Service Corps in 1889 and the Royal Army Service Corps in 1918.

Nicknames: London Thieving Corps (Land Transport Corps); Murdering Thieves, Moke Train, Muck Train (Military Train); Ally Sloper's Cavalry (ASC); Truckies (RCT).

Royal Army Ordnance Corps

Brief History: The Military Store Staff Corps was formed in 1875 as an officer-only corps; in 1896 it was redesignated as the Army Ordnance Department. In 1877 an Ordnance Store Branch was created for other ranks, redesignated as the Ordnance Store Corps in 1881 and as the Army Ordnance Corps in 1896. The Army Ordnance Department and Army Ordnance Corps were amalgamated in 1918 to form the Royal Army Ordnance Corps.

Nicknames: My Sister Sells Cabbage (Military Store Staff Corps); Sugar Stick Brigade (Ordnance Store Corps); Rag and Oil Company (RAOC).

Royal Pioneer Corps

Brief History: Formed in 1939 as the Auxiliary Military Pioneer Corps, although a Labour Corps had existed during the First World War. Redesignated as Pioneer Corps in 1940 and as Royal Pioneer Corps in 1946. During the Second World War conscientious objectors who were willing to serve but not carry weapons were attached to the Pioneer Corps as the Non-Combatant Labour Corps or Non-Combatant Corps.

Nickname: Chunkies.

Army Catering Corps

Brief History: Formed in 1941 as a centralized catering corps to control the training, administration and distribution of catering personnel.

Nickname: Andy Capp's Commandos.

Royal Engineers (Postal and Courier Service)

Brief History: A Postal Section of the Royal Engineers was formed in March 1913 and continued as a separate branch until about 1930. It was revived as part of the Royal Engineers during the Second World War.

ROYAL ARMY MEDICAL CORPS

The Army Hospital Corps, composed of other ranks only, was created in 1857, changing its name to The Medical Staff Corps in 1884. In 1873 The Army Medical Department, consisting of officers only, was formed, changing its title to Army Medical Staff, also in 1884. In 1898 The Army Medical Staff and The Medical Staff Corps were amalgamated to form the Royal Army Medical Corps.

Nicknames: Linseed Lancers, Poultice Whollopers, Rob All My Comrades.

ROYAL ELECTRICAL AND MECHANICAL ENGINEERS

Formed in 1942 from personnel of the Royal Army Ordnance Corps to deal with the increasing complexity of weapons systems.

Nickname: Reemee.

THE ADJUTANT GENERAL'S CORPS

Formed on 6 April 1992 by the amalgamation of the Royal Military Police, Military Provost Staff Corps, Royal Army Pay Corps, Royal Army Educational Corps, Women's Royal Army Corps and Army Legal Corps. It is divided into a number of branches: The Adjutant General's Corps (Provost) incorporates the Royal Military Police and Military Provost Staff Corps; The Adjutant General's Corps (Services and Personnel Support) incorporates the Royal Army Pay Corps and elements of the Women's Royal Army Corps; The Adjutant General's Corps (Education and Training Support) incorporates the Royal Army Educational Corps and elements of the Women's Royal Army Corps; The Adjutant General's Corps (Army Legal Corps) incorporates the Army Legal Corps. Royal Army Ordnance Corps staff clerks joined the AG Corps in April 1993 when the RAOC became part of The Royal Logistic Corps. The AG Corps is known in the Army as the All Girls Corps.

Royal Military Police

Brief History: The Military Mounted Police were formed in 1877 and the Military Foot Police in 1885. In 1926 they were amalgamated to form the Corps of Military Police, redesignated the Royal Military Police in 1946.
> *Nickname*: Cherrynobs, Redcaps.

Military Provost Staff Corps

Brief History: Formed in 1901 as the Military Prison Staff Corps, redesignated as Military Provost Staff Corps in 1906.
> *Nickname*: The Screws.

Royal Army Pay Corps

Brief History: In 1870 a Pay Sub-Department of the Control Department was formed, comprising officers only; this was redesignated as the Army Pay Department in 1878, Army Accounts Department in 1905 and back to Army Pay Department in 1909. Meanwhile, in 1893 the Army Pay Corps had been formed, consisting of other ranks only. In 1920 the Army Pay Department and the Army Pay Corps were amalgamated to form the Royal Army Pay Corps.

Royal Army Educational Corps

Brief History: Formed in 1920 as the Army Educational Corps, redesignated as Royal Army Educational Corps in 1946.
> *Nickname*: Schoolies.

Women's Royal Army Corps

Brief History: Formed on 1 February 1949 as part of the Regular Army. Its immediate forerunner was the Auxiliary Territorial Service, formed in 1938, although a variety of women's units had existed during the First World War. In 1992, not all WRAC personnel transferred to the Adjutant General's Corps – a number were 'rebadged' as members of other units, notably the Royal Corps of Signals, Royal Corps of Transport (now Royal Logistic Corps) and Royal Electrical and Mechanical Engineers.
> *Nickname*: Racks.

Army Legal Corps

Brief History: Formed 1 November 1978 from the Army Legal Services Staff List, created in 1948 from the uniformed section of the Judge Advocate General's Office. The ALC is an officer-only corps comprising legally qualified advocates, barristers and solicitors.

ROYAL ARMY VETERINARY CORPS

In 1858 an officer-only Veterinary Medical Department was formed, changing its title to Army Veterinary Department in 1881. In 1903 the Army Veterinary Corps was created for other ranks. In 1906 the Army Veterinary Department and Army Veterinary Corps were amalgamated to form the Army Veterinary Corps, redesignated Royal Army Veterinary Corps in 1918.
> *Nicknames*: Horse Doctors, Vets.

SMALL ARMS SCHOOL CORPS

A School of Musketry was formed in 1854, redesignated as Small Arms School, Hythe in 1919. In 1923 it was amalgamated with the Machine Gun School, Netheravon as the Small Arms and Machine Gun School, redesignated as Small Arms School Corps in 1929.

ROYAL ARMY DENTAL CORPS

Formed in 1921 as the Army Dental Corps, redesignated in 1946 as the Royal Army Dental Corps.

INTELLIGENCE CORPS

Formed in 1940 to gather and disseminate intelligence to the army as a whole, also absorbing personnel involved in censor and field security duties.
> *Nickname*: Eye-Corps.

ARMY PHYSICAL TRAINING CORPS

The Army Gymnastic Staff was formed in 1860 and later renamed the Army Physical Training Staff. In September 1940 it was redesignated as Army Physical Training Corps.
> *Nickname*: P.T.I.s.

QUEEN ALEXANDRA'S ROYAL ARMY NURSING CORPS

The Army Nursing Service was formed in 1897, being redesignated as Queen Alexandra's Imperial Military Nursing Service in 1902 and as Queen Alexandra's Royal Army Nursing Corps on 1 February 1949.
> *Nickname*: Q.A.s.

ROYAL MILITARY ACADEMY SANDHURST

Formed in 1947 by the amalgamation of the Royal Military Academy (Woolwich), opened in 1741 for the training of artillery (and later engineer and signal) officers, and the Royal Military College (Sandhurst), opened at Great Marlow in 1802 for the training of cavalry and infantry officers and transferred to Sandhurst in 1812.
> *Nicknames*: The Shop (RMA Woolwich); the College (RMC Sandhurst); RMA.

ROYAL MILITARY SCHOOL OF MUSIC

A Military Music Class was opened at Kneller Hall in 1857, redesignated the Royal Military School of Music in 1887.

THE GIBRALTAR REGIMENT

Raised in 1939 as the Gibraltar Defence Force and redesignated as The Gibraltar Regiment in August 1958. Now part of the British Regular Army.

DISBANDED REGIMENTS

The Royal Irish Regiment

Brief History: Raised in 1684 in Ireland as the Earl of Granard's Regiment of Foot; redesignated in 1695 as the Royal Regiment of Ireland. Ranked from 1747 as 18th Regiment of Foot, redesignated in 1751 as 18th (or Royal Irish) Regiment of Foot and in 1881 as The Royal Irish Regiment. A 2nd Battalion was raised in 1857. Both battalions were disbanded in July 1922.

Battle Honours include: Blenheim, Ramillies, Oudenarde, Malplaquet, Pegu, Sevastopol, New Zealand, Afghanistan 1879–80, Egypt 1882, Tel-el-Kebir, Nile 1884–5, South Africa 1900–2, France and Flanders 1914–18, Suvla, Gallipoli 1915, Gaza, Palestine 1917–18.

Nickname: The Royal Irish.

The Cameronians (Scottish Rifles)

Brief History: Formed on 1 July 1881 as The Cameronians (Scotch Rifles), redesignated later the same year as The Cameronians (Scottish Rifles). The 1st Battalion had been the 26th (Cameronian) Regiment of Foot, raised in 1689 from the Cameronian Guard and known originally as the Earl of Angus's Regiment of Foot; the 2nd Battalion had been the 90th Regiment of Foot (Perthshire Volunteers) (Light Infantry), raised in 1794. The 1st and 2nd Battalions were amalgamated in 1948. The regiment was disbanded in May 1968.

Battle Honours include: Blenheim, Ramillies, Oudenarde, Malplaquet, Mandora, Egypt, Corunna, Martinique, Guadeloupe, Sevastopol, Lucknow, Abyssinia, South Africa 1846–7, 1877–8–9, 1899–1902, France and Flanders 1914–18, Macedonia 1915–18, Gallipoli 1915, Palestine 1917–18, Sicily 1943, Anzio, Italy 1943–4, Chindits 1944, Burma 1942, 1944, North-West Europe 1944–5.

Nicknames: Cameronians (26th); Sir Thomas Graham's Perthshire Grey Breeks (90th).

The York and Lancaster Regiment

Brief History: Formed on 1 July 1881. The 1st Battalion had been the 65th (the 2nd Yorkshire North Riding) Regiment of Foot, raised in 1756 as 2nd Battalion 12th Regiment of Foot and renumbered in 1758 as 65th; the 2nd Battalion had been the 84th (York and Lancaster) Regiment of Foot, raised in 1793. The 1st and 2nd Battalions were amalgamated in 1948, although another 2nd Battalion existed from 1952 until 1955. The regiment was disbanded in December 1968.

Battle Honours: Nive, Peninsula, Arabia, Lucknow, India, New Zealand, Egypt 1882, 1884, Tel-el-Kebir, South Africa 1899–1902, France and Flanders 1914–18, Macedonia 1915–18, Suvla, Gallipoli 1915, Piave, Italy 1917–18, Tobruk 1941, North Africa 1941, 1943, Sicily 1943, Salerno, Italy 1943–5, Crete, Chindits 1944, Burma 1943–5.

Nicknames: The Tigers, Cat and Cabbage.

The Connaught Rangers

Brief History: Formed on 1 July 1881. The 1st Battalion had been the 88th Regiment of Foot (Connaught Rangers), raised in Connaught in 1793; the 2nd Battalion had been the 94th Regiment of Foot, raised in 1823 but owing its origins to the so-called Scotch Brigade, a force of Scottish soldiers in Dutch service from 1568 until 1783, accepted onto the British establishment in 1794 and disbanded in 1818. Both battalions were disbanded in July 1922.

Battle Honours include: Seringapatam, Egypt, Talavera, Busaco, Fuentes d'Oñoro, Ciudad Rodrigo, Badajoz, Salamanca, Vitoria, Nivelle, Orthez, Toulouse, Peninsula, Alma, Inkerman, Sevastopol, Central India, South Africa 1877–8–9, 1899–1902, France and Flanders 1914–18, Suvla, Scimitar Hill, Gallipoli 1915, Megiddo, Palestine 1917–18, Kut-el-Amara 1917, Mesopotamia 1916–18.

Nicknames: The Devil's Own (88th); Garvies (94th).

The Prince of Wales's Leinster Regiment (Royal Canadians)

Brief History: Formed on 1 July 1881. The 1st Battalion had been the 100th (or Prince of Wales's Royal Canadian) Regiment of Foot, raised in Canada in 1858; the 2nd Battalion had been the 109th Regiment of Foot (Bombay Infantry), raised by the East India Company in 1859 as the 3rd Bombay Regiment, transferred to the British Army as the 109th in 1862. Both battalions were disbanded in July 1922.

Battle Honours include: Niagara, Central India, South Africa 1900–2, France and Flanders 1914–18, Macedonia 1915–17, Suvla, Gallipoli 1915, Jerusalem, Megiddo, Palestine 1917–18.

Nicknames: Royal Canadians (100th); the German Legion (109th).

The Royal Munster Fusiliers

Brief History: Formed on 1 July 1881. The 1st Battalion had been the 101st Regiment of Foot (Royal Bengal Fusiliers), raised by the East India Company in 1652 in Bengal as the Guard of Honour, redesignated in 1846 as the 1st Bengal (European) Fusiliers and transferred to the British Army in 1862 as the 101st; the 2nd Battalion had been the 104th Regiment of Foot (Bengal Fusiliers), raised by the East India Company in 1839 as the 2nd Bengal (European) Regiment, redesignated in 1850 as the 2nd Bengal (European) Fusiliers and transferred to the British Army in 1862 as the 104th. Both battalions were disbanded in July 1922.

Battle Honours include: Plassey, Buxar, Carnatic, Sholingur, Guzerat, Deig, Bhurtpore, Afghanistan, Ghuznee, Ferozeshuhur, Sobraon, Punjab, Chillianwala, Gujerat, Pegu, Delhi, Lucknow, Burma 1885–7, South Africa 1899–1902, France and Flanders 1914–18, Macedonia 1915–17, Landing at Helles, Landing at Suvla, Scimitar Hill, Gallipoli 1915–16, Jerusalem, Palestine 1917–18.

Nickname: The Dirty Shirts (101st).

The Royal Dublin Fusiliers

Brief History: Formed on 1 July 1881. The 1st Battalion had been the 102nd Regiment of Foot (Royal Madras Fusiliers), raised by the East India Company in 1641 as independent companies of the Madras Army, regimented as the European Regiment in 1746, redesignated in 1843 as the 1st Madras (European) Fusiliers and transferred to the British Army in 1862 as the 102nd; the 2nd Battalion had been the 103rd Regiment of Foot (Royal Bombay Fusiliers), raised by the East India Company in 1662 as independent companies to garrison Bombay, regimented as the Bombay Regiment in 1668, redesignated in 1844 as the 1st Bombay (European) Fusiliers and transferred to the British Army in 1862 as the 103rd. The two battalions were disbanded in July 1922.

Battle Honours include: Arcot, Plassey, Buxar, Condore, Wandewash, Sholingur, Nundy Droog, Amboyna, Ternate, Banda, Pondicherry, Carnatic, Mysore, Mahidpoor, Guzerat, Seringapatam, Kirkee, Beni Boo Ally, Aden, Punjab, Multan, Gujerat, Ava, Pegu, Lucknow, South Africa 1899–1902, France and Flanders 1914–18, Macedonia 1915–17, Landing at Helles, Suvla, Sari Bair, Gallipoli 1915–16, Palestine 1917–18.

Nicknames: The Lambs, Neill's Blue-Caps (102nd); The Old Toughs (103rd).

FURTHER READING

Barnett, Correlli, *Britain and Her Army 1509–1970. A Military, Political and Social Survey* (Allen Lane The Penguin Press, 1970)

Beckett, Ian F. W., and Simpson, Keith (eds), *A Nation in Arms. A Social Study of the British Army in the First World War* (Manchester University Press, 1985)

Burne, Lieutenant-Colonel Alfred H., *The Noble Duke of York* (Staples Press, 1949)

Carver, Field Marshal Lord, *The Seven Ages of the British Army. The Story of Britain's Army from 1625 to the 1980s* (Weidenfeld and Nicolson, 1984)

Chandler, David, *The Art of Warfare in the age of Marlborough* (Batsford, 1976)

(ed), *Great Battles of the British Army as Commemorated in the Sandhurst Companies* (Arms and Armour, 1991)

Childs, John, *The Army of Charles II* (Routledge and Kegan Paul, 1976)

The Army, James II and the Glorious Revolution (Manchester University Press, 1980)

The British Army of William III 1698–1702 (Manchester University Press, 1987)

Duffy, Michael, *Soldiers, Sugar and Seapower. The British Expeditions to the West Indies and the War against Revolutionary France* (Oxford University Press, 1987)

Ellis, John, *The Sharp End of War. The Fighting Man in World War II* (David and Charles, 1980)

Fortescue, Hon J. W., *A History of the British Army*, 13 Volumes (Macmillan, 1899–1930)

Firth, Sir Charles, *Cromwell's Army* (Methuen, 1902)

Fraser, General Sir David, *And We Shall Shock Them. The British Army in the Second World War* (Hodder and Stoughton, 1983)

Frederick, J. B. M., *Lineage Book of British Land Forces 1660–1978*, 2 volumes (Microform Academic Publishers, Wakefield, 1984)

Guy, Alan J., *Economy and Discipline. Officership and administration in the British army 1714–63* (Manchester University Press, 1985)

Hall, Christopher D., *British Strategy in the Napoleonic War 1803–15* (Manchester University Press, 1992)

Houlding, J. A., *Fit for Service: The Training of the British Army 1715–1795* (Oxford University Press, 1981)

Johnson, B. S. (ed), *All Bull: The National Servicemen* (Quartet Books, 1973)

Keegan, John, *The Face of Battle. A Study of Agincourt, Waterloo and the Somme* (Jonathan Cape, 1976)

Oman, Sir Charles, *Wellington's Army 1809–1814* (Edward Arnold, 1912)

Perry, F. W., *The Commonwealth Armies. Manpower and organisation in two world wars* (Manchester University Press, 1988)

Pimlott, John (ed), *British Military Operations 1945–1984* (Hamlyn/Bison, 1984)

Smurthwaite, David, *The Ordnance Survey Complete Guide to the Battlefields of Britain* (Webb and Bower, Exeter, 1984)

Strachan, Hew, *Wellington's Legacy. The Reform of the British Army 1830–54* (Manchester University Press, 1984)

Strawson, Major-General John, *Beggars in Red. The British Army 1789–1889* (Hutchinson, 1991)

Sweetman, John, *War and Administration. The Significance of the Crimean War for the British Army* (Scottish Academic Press, Edinburgh, 1984)

Weller, Jac, *Wellington in India* (Longmans, 1972)
Wellington in the Peninsula 1808–1814 (Nicholas Vane, 1962)
Wellington at Waterloo (Longmans, 1967)

Young, Brigadier Peter, *The British Army 1642–1970* (William Kimber, 1967)

(All publishers located in London unless otherwise specified)

INDEX

· ·